Anne Stanton

Sams **Teach Yourself**

Microsoft®
Dynamics
CRM 2011

in **24**
Hours

 800 East 96th Street, Indianapolis, Indiana, 46240 USA

Sams Teach Yourself Microsoft® Dynamics CRM 2011 in 24 Hours

Copyright © 2012 by Pearson Education, Inc.

ISBN-13: 978-0-672-33537-2
ISBN-10: 0-672-33537-9

The Library of Congress Cataloging-in-Publication data is on file.

Printed in the United States of America

First Printing January 2012

Trademarks

All terms mentioned in this book that are known to be trademarks or service marks have been appropriately capitalized. Sams Publishing cannot attest to the accuracy of this information. Use of a term in this book should not be regarded as affecting the validity of any trademark or service mark.

Warning and Disclaimer

Every effort has been made to make this book as complete and as accurate as possible, but no warranty or fitness is implied. The information provided is on an "as is" basis. The author and the publisher shall have neither liability nor responsibility to any person or entity with respect to any loss or damages arising from the information contained in this book.

Bulk Sales

Sams Publishing offers excellent discounts on this book when ordered in quantity for bulk purchases or special sales. For more information, please contact

U.S. Corporate and Government Sales
1-800-382-3419
corpsales@pearsontechgroup.com

For sales outside of the U.S., please contact

International Sales
international@pearson.com

Editor-in-Chief
Greg Wiegand

Executive Editor
Loretta Yates

Development Editor
Sharon Fields

Managing Editor
Kristy Hart

Project Editor
Betsy Harris

Copy Editor
Kitty Wilson

Indexer
Erika Millen

Proofreader
Kathy Ruiz

Technical Editor
John O'Donnell

Publishing Coordinator
Cindy Teeters

Book Designer
Gary Adair

Senior Compositor
Gloria Schurick

Contents at a Glance

Table of Contents

Part V: Reporting

Part VI: Extending the Application

About the Author

Anne Stanton started her career in the 1980s, as a programmer working with ancient languages such as Fortran 77, Basic, Turbo Pascal, and Cobol. She then built out her expertise as a master of software applications, consulting, marketing, sales, social media, and grassroots marketing and customer relations. Anne has spent 27 years working with technology and is still passionate about all that it can do to help businesses achieve efficiency and growth. Her most recent focus has been working with the Microsoft Dynamics xRM platform and Microsoft Dynamics CRM software. She was awarded the seventh Microsoft MVP for CRM and has a long-running blog (www.crmlady.com) and Twitter feed (crmlady) on the subject. She has worked with Microsoft Dynamics CRM as a customer, partner practice leader, consultant, and enterprise user since version 1.2, released in 2004.

Dedication

This book is dedicated to the people who love and have loved me and to the children I was lucky enough to raise into adults, of whom I could not be more proud.

It is also dedicated to the community of passionate people who, for no other reason than to help, continue to participate in the online forums, post incredibly helpful knowledge on various blogs, keep Twitter updated in real time, and share their personal lives on Facebook and other social media platforms. This includes peers, friends, and family members who have been there in one form or another through some crazy times.

Acknowledgments

My deepest thanks to the following contributing writers, who, through their writing and dedication, have helped me to finalize and release this book despite a number of personal delays and distractions over the past year: Robert Peledie (Hours 6 and 19), Scott Colson (Hour 18), Guy Riddle (Hour 5), Steve Noe (Hours 7 and 14), Glenn Sharp (Hour 10), Kyle O'Connor (Hours 23 and 24), John Gravely (Hour 9), and Pierre Hulsebus (Hours 20, 21, and 22).

And an extra thank you to the team of people at Pearson Education and the editors who told me like it was, helped bring the content to the next level, and were a great team to work with. They were extremely valuable to this book and to the Microsoft Dynamics CRM community as a whole.

We Want to Hear from You!

As the reader of this book, *you* are our most important critic and commentator. We value your opinion and want to know what we're doing right, what we could do better, what areas you'd like to see us publish in, and any other words of wisdom you're willing to pass our way.

You can e-mail or write me directly to let me know what you did or didn't like about this book—as well as what we can do to make our books stronger.

Please note that I cannot help you with technical problems related to the topic of this book, and that due to the high volume of mail I receive, I might not be able to reply to every message.

When you write, please be sure to include this book's title and author as well as your name and phone number or e-mail address. I will carefully review your comments and share them with the author and editors who worked on the book.

E-mail: consumer@samspublishing.com

Mail: Greg Wiegand
        Editor-in-Chief
        Sams Publishing
        800 East 96th Street
        Indianapolis, IN 46240 USA

Reader Services

Visit our website and register this book at informit.com/register for convenient access to any updates, downloads, and errata that might be available for this book.

Introduction

Microsoft Dynamics CRM is a customer relationship management application, a sales force automation application, a customer service application, a marketing tool, a platform and framework for software development, and an application that can be configured to meet a variety of relationship management needs. You might have seen the term *xRM* within the Microsoft Dynamics CRM world; this term represents all that is mentioned above that is not necessarily considered CRM. Needless to say, Microsoft Dynamics CRM is a product that has great depth and great versatility.

If you have picked up this book, you most likely have been thinking about learning more about Microsoft Dynamics CRM.

Who Should Read This Book

This book is aimed at users of Microsoft Dynamics CRM and Microsoft Dynamics CRM Online, Microsoft partners expanding into the Dynamics CRM space, and software developers and others interested in learning more about the product. This book gets you started, but it could not possibly describe everything you'll ever need to know about Microsoft Dynamics CRM!

If you are already working with Microsoft Dynamics CRM, this book can help expand your depth of understanding about the product and organize your experiences with the product. If you have never worked with Microsoft Dynamics CRM, you can look to this book as a solid base that gets you started and helps you grow, learn, and expand in the right directions as you learn more about the software and its many areas of potential.

Microsoft Dynamics CRM has changed dramatically since its first release in the early 2000s, and many of these changes have come about through Microsoft incorporating suggestions and ideas from a variety of sources.

Now that Microsoft Dynamics CRM has matured to version 2011 R5, the product is rich with functionality, backed by a powerful community, and built for an almost-unlimited list of business needs.

How This Book Is Organized

This book is divided into six parts that will get you up to speed quickly with Microsoft Dynamics CRM:

▶ Part I, "Introduction to the Business Use of Microsoft Dynamics CRM"

▶ Part II, "The Structure of Microsoft Dynamics CRM"

▶ Part III, "Getting Started Using the Software"

▶ Part IV, "The Support Department"

▶ Part V, "Reporting"

▶ Part VI, "Extending the Application"

Special Features

This book includes the following special features:

▶ **Lesson roadmaps**—At the beginning of each lesson, you will find a list of what you will learn in that hour. This list enables you to quickly see the type of information the lesson contains.

▶ **By the Way**—Throughout the book, you will see extra information presented in these sidebars.

▶ **Did You Know?**—Throughout the book, you'll see tips and insight on items of related interest that you might want to know about.

▶ **Watch Out!**—Throughout the book, where topics warrant warnings, you'll see sidebars titled "Watch Out!"

▶ **Tasks**—Numbered lists of steps to complete tasks help to organize the material.

▶ **Workshop**—In this section, you will find an example of CRM in use and a case study of a company that is using Microsoft Dynamics CRM to solve business needs related to the topic of the lesson.

▶ **Q&A**—At the end of each chapter is a Q&A section that explores some questions likely to be asked by users who are using the features and functions addressed during the lesson.

▶ **Quiz**—At the end of each chapter is a quiz (and answers) to help you evaluate what you have learned during the hour.

▶ **Exercises**—At the end of each lesson is a set of recommended exercises to help reinforce what you learned in the lesson.

What Is Microsoft Dynamics CRM?

What You'll Learn in This Hour:

- ▶ Overview of CRM and the CRM industry
- ▶ Department roles: different perspectives
- ▶ Business applications, functions, and fundamentals
- ▶ A closer look at business processes
- ▶ Capturing processes

This hour focuses on opening the mind to a potential new world: the world of customer relationship management (CRM). This world did not start with the invention of technology, nor does it end with a specific application. This world has long been researched, studied, documented, debated, and discussed. As you consider this world of CRM realize that the success of a specific CRM initiative or the failure of the same initiative often does not have much to do with the software or technology that you use. A successful CRM project also demands understanding of process, the potential for technology and a team of people. The goal of this hour is to build a foundation of understanding that will leave a few doors open as you get started on the road toward mastery of Microsoft Dynamics CRM 2011 and potentially many successful projects.

Overview of CRM and the CRM Industry

What does CRM really stand for? As an acronym, it expands to customer relationship management. As an industry concept, it is the ability for a company to capture key details about its customers and future customers as they relate to a need, desire, and set of preferences. The CRM philosophy is all about encouraging and supporting a business strategy that leverages this key information to support better communication and a more accurate offering to the right audience at the right time. CRM as a way of thinking has been around since the first business opened, long before technological innovations of the 1980s allowed this business approach to become an industry. CRM also enters almost everyone's personal life. Take for instance the mail that you receive. Have you received a catalog or promotional mailing lately? Tracking you as a potential customer involves CRM. Let's take a look at a little bit of CRM history.

In the beginning, the idea of automating marketing arose. The idea of segmenting customers and prospects into groups that could be electronically approached took hold, offering grand promises of revolutionary changes in business process. Those promises and hopes were quickly balanced with reality. Too much data without properly configured tools to sort, filter, and use that data wasted large amounts of time and money.

Now, more than 20 years after the term *CRM* was first used, it is a still-maturing industry, and the debates and growth predictions within the CRM industry continue.

A simple online search for "CRM" will open some doors. You can find industry-specific magazines, generic and product-specific white papers, articles, books, debates, blogs and wikis, and a long list of successes and failures defining the best approaches and the best tools at all company levels. In this hour, we peek into this broad world.

CRM Software Packages

Common CRM marketing messages include faster access to information and more personal efficiency, but this is often not enough. Technology continues to break down barriers and offer more. It can increase success and support efforts to maintain success in an increasingly fast-paced world. Microsoft Dynamics CRM offers key features such as integration to mapping data with an easily reachable map to the contact's office or capturing instant customer-specific information from the Internet and feeding it up in the customer summary. It can summarize social buzz and organize instant posts and complaints in real time. It can also manage the data needed to offer support or returns as well as the complex needs of marketing and senior management.

CRM today is increasingly adding to the functionality of already much-loved and well-used tools through enhancement and integration with other applications. Bringing existing habits and tools to the next level can speed and increase adoption while also creating loyal users. This is one reason why Microsoft Dynamics CRM functions through the e-mail client Microsoft Outlook and works closely with other

Microsoft applications, such as Microsoft Word, Microsoft Excel, and Microsoft Office SharePoint Service.

According to Gartner, Inc., the CRM market will enter a three-year shake-up starting in 2011, as a number of key trends continue to take hold. These include growth in sales techniques, changes in marketing automation, and expansion of options in customer service technologies, projects, and implementations. Given that technology continues to evolve, the choices within the world of CRM continue to expand. Consider social media, mobile access, and access to data from devices such as your sunglasses or watch. The next three years will continue the pattern of rapid growth of options to automate process and considerations for process refinement.

CRM Application Technology

The list of CRM line-of-business applications was extensive prior to Microsoft Dynamics CRM coming to market. Companies such as PeopleSoft, Siebel, SAP, and Oracle have products within this niche. In fact, CRM software is one of the oldest applications available and has been released in numerous flavors by many vendors over the years. When solving the CRM business need with CRM application technology, we are talking about a well-researched subject. When it comes to technology, CRM software sits next to e-mail as the heart and soul of many companies. It also crosses all departments, offices, and niches within a company, and it is both a corporate and a personally needed toolset. The product supports an individual in his efforts to organize his day and to-do list, and it aggregates data from many individuals for corporate analysis and decision making. It automates a process to enhance and support corporate standards, it promotes and supports team work, and it automates processes to support an individual's interest in efficiency. CRM software not only has to be successful for the corporation, it must also empower the individual and the team. Ultimately, CRM software, when implemented correctly, can actually change the business direction of a company.

CRM and the Individual

We each have our own style for getting things done and reminding ourselves of what we have to do. When we apply these unique styles to a work environment, where common technology must support all, the application used must be flexible enough for different styles and easy enough to modify and master that it meets many different needs. The technology must also offer commonality and promote, or even enforce, corporate standards. E-mail software is a classic example of an application that is both corporate and standardized and yet flexible and individually empowering. CRM software is very similar to e-mail software, and yet it has to support many more needs than an e-mail application. CRM software must keep track of not only who you talk to, but who they talk to. It must also keep track of when you last talked to them and what was said. Think about it.

If we consider applying this technology to an audience of salespeople, we also have unique audience-specific considerations. Many times, salespeople have become successful because of their own talent, habits, style, and connections. These factors are often unique and come from a salesperson's experiences, trainings, and focus. When rolling out CRM software, changes are inevitable, but asking any salesperson to change a successful style is often an uphill battle. Unlike other audiences, an additional element to the salesperson audience is that a salesperson's success usually contributes and pays a part of his salary. To get a high level of adoption in this market, the CRM application must offer something to salespeople that they want and something that meets a need that can not be met without the tool.

Common CRM marketing touts include faster access to information and more personal efficiency, but this is often not enough when talking to an established and successful salesperson. However, technology continues to break down barriers and offer more. It can increase success and support efforts to maintain success in an increasingly fast-paced world. Offering key features, such as integration to mapping data (GeoData) with an easily reachable map to the contact's office or capturing instant customer-specific information from the Internet and feeding it up in the customer summary, can be very powerful.

Another powerful option is increasing the functionality of already much loved and well-used tools through enhancement and integration with other applications. Taking existing habits and tools and bringing them to the next level can speed and increase adoption while also creating loyal users. This is one reason why Microsoft Dynamics CRM functions through the email client, Microsoft Outlook, and it works closely with other Microsoft applications, such as Microsoft Word, Microsoft Excel, and Microsoft Office SharePoint Service.

We have talked about the mindset of a successful salesperson, but what about a salesperson who is not doing so well? We can attribute this to any number of variables, but how would an offer of or improvement to CRM software be considered in this situation? When the pressure is on from management and the "rope is short," having powerful tools to get the job done quickly, smoothly, and efficiently can help. These tools, if already existing prior to a failure, can also be blamed for an individual's lack of success. As the heart and soul of a firm and of individual productivity, CRM software sits in a very volatile space.

How many people can you keep track of without using technology or a piece of paper? Perhaps you have a special gift and can keep track of hundreds of people.

But what about all the specific details? We all have our methods, which might include a small black book, a manila file on each client, or technology (such as a laptop or a mobile device), but the small details are often captured in more places than just memory. CRM software enables us to capture, organize, and store more information, and it makes it easier to retrieve and analyze that information.

CRM also helps automate processes, and when it comes to individuals' habits and tasks, automation can reduce redundancy. If someone is spending time doing the same tasks over and over again for different clients, CRM software can automate this mundane process and free her up to do more advanced and unique tasks, tasks that require more intelligence or careful thinking or the unique skills of a human. Consider the rather repetitive process of sending out a follow-up packet when a new prospect inquires about a company. Instead of the salesperson redoing the entire process over again, he can customize the letter to a specific inquirer and let the system automatically compile standard electronic material to include for new prospects. CRM software can also customize the material for this specific prospect based on other criteria, such as industry, location, interest, or any set of the a variety of variables.

CRM Software Collects Firm-Wide Data

In this information age, one of the biggest assets for a company is the data captured and retained and the intellectual capital that this represents. The idea of captured information when it comes to relationships is a controversial one, and yet much of a corporation's success in marketing and customer service is based on knowledge about the customer and the relationship the corporation has with the customer, as well as knowledge about the other relationships a customer has.

Twenty years ago, employer/employee loyalty was pervasive, but that has changed. What happens when someone leaves your firm? How does this relate to the use of a CRM application? Every person who works in a company retains a certain amount of knowledge about the firm, his or her specific job, and the people he or she works with (internal staff and customer contacts). This knowledge is often overlooked but sometimes critical to the success of a business. The combined knowledge of all staff is also the single most unique difference between two companies offering the same product or service; it is a real competitive differentiator. A CRM application can help to capture some of this knowledge. It also supports company efforts to standardize, document, and automate company-specific processes. After these processes have been captured, they are not forgotten when key staff leave.

As staff turnover becomes more common, the retention of this critical data becomes even more difficult. Customer information needs to be captured. The size, location, industry, products purchased, purchasing habits, and preferred service variables are all data oriented, but what about the relationship? A relationship is often between two people or a small group of people and another group of people. A customer has a point person who regularly calls and places orders. The person taking the order might be the same person, the same one or two people, or always someone new. In the first scenario, a relationship exists between the point person at the customer site and the point person taking the orders. After an order is placed, these two people might share more information (a laugh, a question about the weather on the other side of the country, or more personal information). If either one of these people leaves, the customer still gets service, but the service level changes. In the second scenario, we have one specific point person, but when he calls to place an order, he talks to two or three different people. In this scenario, the risk of reducing the connection to the customer is slightly lower.

Increasingly, companies are trying to reduce the risk of compromising customer service when key staff people leave or when contacts within the customer company change positions. CRM software can capture some of the details needed to reduce this risk. A customer service point person who adds a note indicating that her customer always calls on a Friday morning and that recently her daughter was married, helps the next customer service person to offer much more personal service.

The Business Advantage of CRM

Let's now consider a corporation's return on investment (ROI) from the adoption of a CRM solution. The primary ROI is enhanced customer service or a shorter sales cycle based on already captured knowledge. However, the adoption of CRM software creates multiple ROIs, depending on which audience is accessing or working with the product. The board of directors of a corporation might be interested in the financial returns or the long-term predictive analysis of the data captured within the core line-of-business CRM application. A manager might have a totally different need. A manager might, for example, use CRM software as a coaching tool, standardizing his much-loved and much-tested best practices into an automated toolset used by his direct reports. A manager might also use CRM software for compliance and for managing the human resources he or she is responsible for. The ROI for a manager does not necessarily have to be the same ROI as that of a chief financial officer or a customer support representative. In addition, the success or failure of a CRM application can be contradictive. One department may experience great success, while another experiences frustration and limitations and time-consuming extra data entry. No other application crosses so many different audiences in so many different ways. And no other application brings with it such great risk from failed adoption and such great benefits from true corporate understanding and mastery.

In Figure 1.1 we show how multidimensional the world of CRM can be and how many different areas of impact this section of software can apply to.

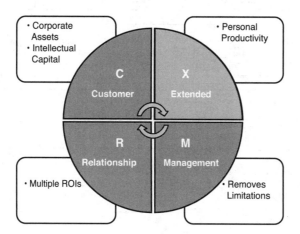

- Corporate Assets
- Intellectual Capital

C
Customer

- Personal Productivity

X
Extended

- Multiple ROIs

R
Relationship

M
Management

- Removes Limitations

FIGURE 1.1
CRM is multi-dimensional.

Successful CRM Projects

It is easy to focus only on purchasing a software package and the actual installation. However, a company needs to consider a whole project, including the level of involvement of people, the design of process, and the actual technology footprint to support the new solution. One of the key goals of Microsoft Dynamics CRM 2011 is to be a product that is extremely flexible and that can be reconfigured or changed as a company environment changes. These changes can include the people using the software, technology revolutions as the world of technology matures, and processes that a company either changes or refines. CRM is not just an application or a technology; it is a methodology, a culture, and a philosophy, and because of this wide-reaching paradigm, Microsoft Dynamics CRM 2011 requires executive decisions about configuration and use. In addition, management must understand what its options are when it comes to many of these decisions, so in addition to management decisions, a company also needs executive commitment to learn something new and to open their minds to additional options.

As earlier mentioned, there are a number of different considerations in each successful CRM projects. Let's take a look at each of these as diagrammed in Figure 1.2.

FIGURE 1.2
Elements of a
successful
CRM project.

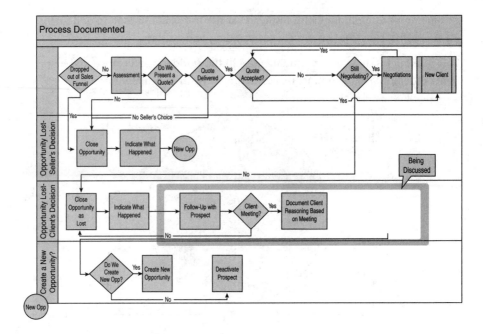

People

Every human is unique. Some have great skills dealing with people including social skills, management skills, and communication skills; some are passionate about software; others are incredible writers or excel at sports. Some are masters of any combination of skills. Human style and talent can impact the success of a project or application.

A core team may be critical to efficient adoption and change management; however, each person who will eventually be a user of the system is unique, and core teams rarely represent 100% of all unique user needs. When considering applying technology to the CRM space, consider the various levels of people who could be involved. There will be a variety of different individuals, and each individual has his or her own specific habits and technology in use.

There are a variety of different departments, and each department has different people and different needs and focuses, and there are a variety of different personalities. Some will make excellent champions, whereas others will be incredible users. You might find that the administrator role is best accomplished by a person who is a master of software, has a depth of understanding about the business, and is passionate about learning. The user champion might not need these skills. A user champion may need to have an outgoing personality, a likable demeanor, and an ability to put people at ease. This person would also need understanding and skill in the CRM software, as well as an understanding about how the new software impacts his or her world.

Management buy-in and involvement is the biggest single factor in the success of a CRM software implementation. Additionally the roles and responsibilities of each team member as they apply to a specific CRM project or as they apply to the long-term use of the CRM solution are also important. When considering roles think about information services, partners, and business users, and within each of these groups the roles of managing, developing, defining, and confirming that all is as expected as the project moves forward. We can't emphasize enough the need for communication and flexibility—communication so that all are on the same page and flexibility because technology growth and options never stop, and in many projects the business process is also a moving target.

Processes

If you are diving into the new world of Microsoft Dynamics CRM 2011, a helpful exercise is to document existing processes. These processes can be extremely small, or they can be large and complex. Process documentation can start at a very high level and then have supporting documents at a more detailed level, or it can be at a very detailed level from the start. Changing processes is not required for the success-ful adoption of this software, but at a minimum existing processes should be reviewed as part of a deployment of Microsoft Dynamics CRM 2011. In later sections we dive into explaining process diagramming in more depth, but let's take a quick look at an example.

When considering processes associated with specific tools, such as a CRM applica-tion, you can be sure that certain functions and features available can improve or change your process.

If your primary mode of transportation is a horse and buggy, for example, your process will have to include the care and feeding of the horse and the total number of hours a day that the horse could be used. You must also consider the conditioning of the leather components and the impact of weather on these components and the wear and tear of daily use. When you replace that horse and buggy with a car, the variables change so significantly that your processes change. You no longer have to consider the number of hours that you have available in any given day for trans-portation; after all, a car does not care whether it is used for 24 hours or for 1. However, you must continue to care about the wear and tear of daily use. Some processes do not change, but others do.

Another example is the introduction of the ATM. In prior days we used checks and a check register to withdraw cash. We often had an up-to-date running register of the money in our checking accounts. In today's world of the ATM we take out cash but do not necessarily write this withdrawal into a check register. We still need an accurate statement, but we might depend on the bank's electronic statement for this information.

When considering change in an existing firm, a person first outlines and documents existing processes and then chooses areas of inefficiency or poor workflow to improve and correct. Process modification generally requires change; change requires a broad spectrum of initiative.

Before we consider making changes before rolling out Dynamics CRM, we must also consider that within three to six months of Microsoft Dynamics CRM adoption, there will be options for additional change or process modification as the technology opens new doors.

Making initial decisions about process when first installing Dynamics CRM is important, but considering change after use is just as critical. Features don't change, but user knowledge and mastery of these features does. This knowledge motivates adoption of more functionality.

The key with process in the CRM space is continual learning by the teams involved and the leveraging of Microsoft Dynamics CRM's powerful flexibility when it comes to change and design.

As a last note on processes, always consider this: If your processes do not work, what happens when automation speeds up those processes?

Technology

Technology includes well-tested CRM software applications, the changes these applications will mean for your company, and the environment in which the new software will operate. New technology always involves new choices, which may push people into uncomfortable decision-making positions but may also present wonderful new opportunities.

Microsoft Dynamics CRM 2011 is both a foundation for development (often referred to as xRM, for *extended relationship management*) and a powerful line-of-business application focused on CRM features and functionality. The product is built on a solid foundation of proven and mature Microsoft technology and can be easily extended, configured, and modified into a unique fit for each business where it is deployed. The product is flexible, but it also comes with a number of standard features and functionalities that can be used without extra effort. Think of the product as having standard features, requested by almost all clients, and you can add unique features and functionalities specific for your company or project. Finally, never underestimate the requirement to learn the new technology well before implementing because by understanding what is available to you, you are given the chance to change your decisions and design. If you do not have this knowledge, then your decisions cannot be based on the power available within the system.

Department Roles: Different Perspectives

Depending on your responsibilities and focus, a CRM deployment can offer different benefits and challenges. Let's look at a few roles—not necessarily all roles within any given company.

Boards of Directors

If a board of directors (BOD) could choose one word when thinking of the company it oversees, that word might be *transparency*. Members of a BOD do not want surprises from either the press or from the chief officers on the management team. Hopefully the financials of a company are transparent. The G/L is available to the BOD, the financial statements are available to the BOD, but what is often missing is insight and perspective as to corporate culture and application of such to relationships with customers. In addition, board members often lack insight into the sales funnel, which offers a wide range of support from the extensive experience often found within a BOD. Board members have industry expertise and knowledge, but without something to compare this to from the company they oversee, their ability and contribution may be limited. Microsoft Dynamics CRM offers some of this insight from two perspectives. First, it is extremely good at capturing more data. Second, it is extremely good at offering this data in a user-friendly manner to people who do not necessarily use the application every day. Graphical reporting and dashboard analysis with a common Microsoft Office interface eliminates a number of barriers present in other vendor offerings.

Chief Executive Officers

Microsoft Dynamics CRM offers the chief executive officer (CEO) insight into the company and management variables via access to management teams, departmental decisions, and other "pure" data. It also provides analysis and integration points to other core applications running within a firm. A CEO who appropriately leverages CRM technology can more easily implement her vision with Microsoft Dynamics CRM. Microsoft Dynamics CRM software can help cutting-edge CEOs refine, change, and position a company and the processes within that company. CRM represents a pool of wisdom for the CEO.

Chief Financial Officers

Chief financial officers (CFOs) are tasked with reducing risk, lowering costs, and managing company financial investments. They also organize and classify corporate assets and work with managers to ensure efficiency. A CFO significantly benefits from the adoption of Microsoft Dynamics CRM. CFOs benefit from the additional available data, from the increased standardization of processes (which thus reduces risk and lowers costs), and from the analysis and predictive potential of this tool that captures the corporate asset known as data. They also benefit from the improvements and efficiencies in marketing that drive down the bottom line costs on sales.

Chief Information Officers and Chief Technology Officers

Microsoft Dynamics CRM results in key benefits for the chief information officer (CIO) and chief technology officer (CTO) because of the product's flexibility. The product's available framework and core building blocks are standard Microsoft tools. With these tools, technical staff can leverage the power of the platform without extensive extra training, and long-term support is available from multiple resources. Microsoft Dynamics CRM actually becomes a bridge between technology departments and the business. The software is a tool that technology departments can use to meet their own internal business needs (customer service or knowledge-base management, for instance), and it is a tool that can help meet corporate goals, such as automation of the sales process and prospect management.

Sales Managers

In meeting numbers, setting expectations, and reporting realistic goals to management and the BOD, the sales manager is well served with a tool that can capture his preferred and defined processes and the results and then communicate them to his superiors. If a sales manager has defined, refined, and implemented best-practice sales processes, these processes are defined, available, and transparent within the world of Dynamics CRM to the rest of the management team.

Microsoft Dynamics CRM can also help a sales manager to coach, mentor, and encourage team members to perform at a higher level through applicable experience applied to areas that Microsoft Dynamics CRM indicates need fine-tuning. Just as football coaches classify their players and then review their skills so that the appropriate weight training, running drills, and practices can be designed, so must a sales manager gain insight into who needs training, mentoring, and support.

With the right configuration Microsoft Dynamics CRM can capture skill sets, and it can also offer transparency into prospect interaction and completion of processes. Instead of a sales manager having to pull teeth to get numbers for analysis and management reporting, daily capturing of activities and status changes via Microsoft Dynamics CRM can show what is going on. This shift moves from a monthly reactive reporting model to an anytime proactive management paradigm.

Salespersons or Sales Executives

If we consider applying CRM technology to an audience of salespeople, we also have unique audience-specific considerations. In addition to having personal styles for task management and daily efficiencies, salespeople also have unique sales styles. In fact, extremely successful salespeople have often become successful because of their own talent, habits, experiences, training, and connections.

When rolling out CRM software, changes are inevitable, but asking any salesperson to change a successful style may be an uphill battle. Unlike other audiences, with the salesperson audience, an additional element is that a salesperson's success usually contributes and pays a part of his salary. To get a high level of adoption in this market, the CRM application must offer something to salespeople that they want and something that meets a need that cannot be met without the tool. Additionally sales management and executive management buy-in can make a critical difference.

A sales executive's resistance to sharing data is well founded. Sales executives either have a well-practiced and much-coveted technique that they do not want to share with their peers, or they are vulnerable to judgment and correction. Even in a team-oriented culture, style is individual, and success is important.

In addition, the features and functions available to a salesperson can be significant. The key is to give the salesperson a system with the features and functions and clean simplicity needed for the salesperson to do the job as he or she sees fit.

Customer Service Managers

A customer service manager strives to help her team meet a certain level of measurable statistics: total number of completed calls, number of cases successfully closed, customer success stories, and more. In addition, a customer service manager must quickly respond to any cases that escalate from any level within the team. The manager must receive alerts so that she can quickly resolve problems and have visibility into the tone and traffic coming across the wires. A customer service manager can use Microsoft Dynamics CRM 2011 to generate these much-loved statistics. Integration of Microsoft Dynamics CRM into social media applications, such as

Twitter, enables management to measure and track unregistered complaints and the organization of all activities associated with a tracked case.

Customer Service Representatives

Customer service representatives are often on the phone all day. They need to quickly capture the notes from a call, often while they are talking, so that they can transition to the next call. Customer service representatives often make promises during these calls, and they must follow up and remember these promises. Microsoft Dynamics CRM can easily remember promises and individual or team obligations. It can also automatically meet promises by having a workflow that kicks off on the closing of a case or an activity.

Marketing Managers

Marketing managers often have a specific budget or a set number of marketing dollars. They are also often focused on the ROI associated with the use of these marketing dollars. They do not have many tools available to them that can capture this black-and-white data in a world of a lot of gray, but Microsoft Dynamics CRM's marketing campaign feature not only captures ROI, it also helps organize all the planning tasks and campaign activities associated with the use of that investment. Marketing managers can also expand their use of Microsoft Dynamics CRM 2011 by working with one of the many independent software vendors that offer advanced marketing software for Microsoft Dynamics CRM 2011.

Marketing Professionals

Marketing professionals are often interested in slicing and dicing a wide variety of information. They need a tool that can encourage company staff members to collect as much data as possible on prospects, contacts, clients, opportunities, and campaigns as they happen. The marketing professional is interested in mailing to subsets of prospects and needs to have the details to create marketing lists of these subsets. Microsoft Dynamics CRM supports an almost unlimited number of details and the creation of marketing lists. A marketing professional might want to send out a mailing to all clients who have purchased a certain product in the past year or might want to set up a telemarketing campaign for all prospects with a certain Standard Industry Code (SIC).

As you work through the next 23 hours, keep in mind that the needs of marketing can be considered a whole new world of technology that complements the needs of sales professionals.

Business Applications, Functions, and Fundamentals

Fundamental changes need to take place in a company for CRM to be successful, and some companies have an advantage. They have made many of these changes. They have management that understands how technology and process impact each other, and they have synergy between business and technology expertise. They also have people who balance out the total formula. Most likely, they also have had at least one failed CRM attempt and are perhaps looking for more success, or maybe they are pushing the innovation envelope and understand some of the new paradigm shifts in communication. The companies without such advantages can also find success.

The world of CRM taps into the world of data flow within a company. A call comes in, and then what happens? A problem occurs. How does the company respond? What roles are affected? Who is responsible? What is happening with a prospect? What about a client? Who understands what is happening? Is this information stored so that others can have insight into the situation if that person is not available? What about the data on the available skills and knowledge that can be used to solve a problem or meet a request or accomplish a goal? Now think about contacts. How is a contact related to a specific company? How is that same contact related to other people? Does that contact have other relationships that would be beneficial to know about? What about a building? How is a building related to another building? Or how is a building related to a management company?

When we consider process as it relates to Microsoft Dynamics CRM, we are looking at the processes surrounding the flow of data within a company, the handling of that data, and the desired results of handling the data effectively to produce a desired end result.

A Closer Look at Business Processes

A business process is a series of activities or tasks that lead to a specific completed service or defined product. These activities can also be bundled into a specific step within the process, with the process being made up of a series of steps or stages.

A business process can be thought of as something that serves a particular goal for a particular prospect, customer, or customers. The automation of processes keeps promises and tasks from falling between the cracks and helps to organize and systemize particular business best practices. The automation of processes also supports the effort of a corporation to standardize processes within certain groups of users.

One of the first excitements when initially purchasing Microsoft Dynamics CRM is the power of using the software to automate processes. The risk with this approach is that, if there is no understanding of items that are automatically created, then the world gets very noisy. E-mails get automatically created, and activities get automatically generated, and a to-do list gets overwhelmed or an inbox gets full without comprehension of where these items are coming from. Ultimately, the goal is to make any given process more efficient and less complex. Automating can create more complexity, more noise, and more data in more places. When you automate based on a practiced and well-loved process, you gain more success. Needless to say, manually mastering a process at a variety of levels before automating is recommended.

When it comes to the concept of learning more about business process, there are many resources available. You can find books, articles, and magazines on business process by industry, by type of work, and by role (such as management processes, operational processes, and supporting processes). You can even find some good fiction, such as the 1948 book *Cheaper by the Dozen* by Frank Gilbreth, Jr., and Ernestine Gilbreth Carey.

By the Way

Process Reminder

One thing to keep in mind is that, if you can capture the processes that are in practice today, you can complement them, replace them, and fine-tune them as you roll out Microsoft Dynamics CRM.

One of the first tasks to do when learning to master Microsoft Dynamics CRM is to understand and learn your own processes and how these processes can either fit or change within your company as you adopt or increase your usage of Microsoft Dynamics CRM. It is extremely difficult to use a software package that supports a process without clarity and understanding of the process to begin with.

Capturing a process does not have to be difficult. In fact, it can be quite fun. Grab a white board or notepad and a set of appropriate markers. For those technically inclined (yes, you, Mr. Developer and Mrs. Infrastructure Specialist), open Microsoft Visio. You need to diagram both the high-level process and the lower-level details. You can even go so far as to think of some of the lower-level details as related subprocesses.

Now, you should put on the hat of a particular role—such as salesperson, administrator, financial officer, marketing expert, business engineer, software developer, or network administrator—and start drawing. Feel free to whip up a set of paper hats and make this a fun team exercise. If you are struggling with picking a role or thinking of all the roles that might be considered, check out this great Microsoft web page: www.microsoft.com/en-us/dynamics/about.aspx.

With a specific role hat on, what do you do in a given week? What about on a given day? What systems do you currently use? What decisions do you have to make? I know you know the details, but write them down and capture each decision and every step, using pictures. Pictures communicate a thousand words, so you might as well make it easy on yourself.

Remember that paper you had to write in seventh grade? The one where the teacher told you to document how you do something and then made someone else do it by only using the instructions on the paper? It was difficult to explain how to drink a glass of water, particularly when you forgot to include how to turn on the faucet, or perhaps you chose how to open your desk and forgot to include that the person had to first walk over to the desk to reach it. Documenting processes at work are not necessarily this difficult, but doing this exercise can be just as eye opening.

Pretend you are talking to someone who is going to fill in for you, or even to your 12-year-old son or perhaps your 20-year-old daughter who is considering careers. You can even think about telling your spouse, your mother, or a patient sibling. The concept is to really document the big picture and the specific details within that big picture.

Figures 1.3 and 1.4 show a few sample business processes diagrammed using different formats. Figure 1.3 uses flowchart boxes and outlines the handling of a list of leads received from a trade show.

Figure 1.4 uses a different format and shows a general process of a vendor bill arriving through the mail and being received by the receptionist at a specific company.

Figure 1.5 is more of a general, big-picture diagram of a process that shows a marketing department starting a process that flows through sales to order to delivery. It includes a small process surrounding manufacturing feeding inventory.

Another way to capture a process is by using a swim lane document. A *swim lane* is a horizontal or vertical format of a process flow diagram that offers a way of showing what or who is associated with a particular subprocess. Swim lane diagrams allow you to capture the big picture, and they also offer a smooth transition to capturing the related subprocesses.

As much as capturing processed is critical, it is also critical to realize that in office environments, processes changes. In today's world, many processes are continually being tweaked. Unlike in manufacturing, where certain items are built and the steps to build them rarely change, in the world of data, adaptability and riding the waves of change are keys to success.

FIGURE 1.3
Handling the
leads process.

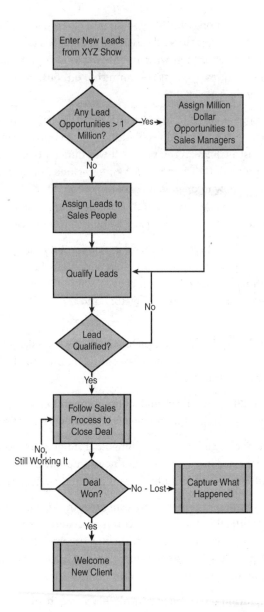

One of the benefits of Microsoft Dynamics CRM is that adding automated processes does not require a programmer or advanced programming skills. The ability to automate processes is achieved with the workflow functionality, which is part of the Microsoft Dynamics CRM application. Mastering the workflow feature allows a company to continually automate and change processes built into the technology as its world changes.

How Vendor Bills Are Handled

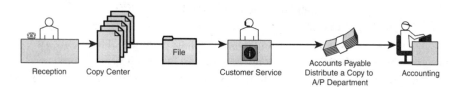

Reception   Copy Center

File

Customer Service

Accounts Payable
Distribute a Copy to
A/P Department

Accounting

Make Three Copies

Distribute a Copy to
Department Who Ordered Product

Pay Bill

G/L Analysis

FIGURE 1.4
A vendor bill
arrives.

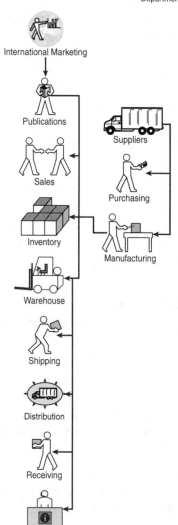

International Marketing

Publications

Suppliers

Sales

Purchasing

Inventory

Manufacturing

Warehouse

Shipping

Distribution

Receiving

Customer Service

FIGURE 1.5
General
overview
from sales
to delivery.

Capturing Processes

Microsoft Dynamics CRM helps automate processes in a few different ways. The first is that Microsoft Dynamics CRM captures, stores, and organizes data. The second is that, through the use of automation of workflow, Microsoft Dynamics CRM automates processes that would otherwise be done manually. In fact, beginners to workflow automation can take something as simple as a small business rule and apply it to something that happens in Microsoft Dynamics CRM.

Microsoft Dynamics CRM can generate an e-mail message when a new opportunity is closed with a status of win. This e-mail can also include a link that enables the sales manager to quickly click and see all the details of this win, or the e-mail can be set up to include the details of interest. The power of Microsoft Windows Workflow Foundation is part of Microsoft Dynamics CRM. Workflow can be scary and complicated—people even have advanced degrees in the concept—or it can be extremely simple. I encourage you to set up a few simple workflows as you are learning about them in Hour 16, "Workflows: Creating Simple Workflows," and then use them for a week or so to get familiar with how your processes and your entire team's processes are impacted.

Other examples of automating processes based on data entered into the system could include the following:

1. When a new opportunity is created, automatically generate all the activities associated with the first step of the sales process (if the first step is defined as a set of activities that need to be completed).

2. Further extend this to include the second, third, fourth, and final steps so when all the activities associated with the first step in the sales process are completed, Microsoft Dynamics CRM automatically updates the probability percentage of close on the opportunity and creates the second set of activities that need to be completed. This can continue until you close the deal.

You can also apply automation to services:

1. When a user creates a new service case in the system and that service case is of type "Fix Broken X," automatically create a set of activities that result in fixing the broken X and close the case.

2. When a user creates a new service case, automatically send an e-mail message to the client, indicating that a service technician is working on the case. For example, a common manual process, the assignment of leads, can be automated.

3. When a new lead is entered in the system, check the zip code, associate the territory, and assign the lead to the sales manager for that territory.

We know that workflow can take business rules and apply or automate processes based on those rules, but what about other process impacts from a CRM system? Let's look at some practical considerations.

Practical Considerations

Given that Microsoft Dynamics CRM captures, organizes, and manages data, a key consideration is to configure Microsoft Dynamics CRM so that it makes it extremely easy for users to enter data. You have the power to add new fields to Microsoft Dynamics CRM. You also have the power to remove data fields from the forms in Microsoft Dynamics CRM. And you have the power to organize how data fields are displayed within a structured offering in Microsoft Dynamics CRM.

Much can be learned from a popular search engine in use today. It offers you one box for data entry. The screen is not cluttered with distracting information that is perhaps not of interest. In addition, no training is needed to use this search engine, until you get into more advanced concepts. This key concept is of particular importance when people are starting to use Microsoft Dynamics CRM. The "keep it simple" concept is well married to mastery, usability, and adoptability.

Remember that Microsoft Dynamics CRM is a robust system but even in the first few hours of using it, much can make sense. Start slow, dive into a subset of your business processes, apply these to Microsoft Dynamics CRM, and then grow with the software or let the software grow on you. Your understanding of Microsoft Dynamics CRM will continue to increase, and this understanding will open doors for you. You might find that a process you captured and defined in the early weeks of use does not even apply anymore because of how you use Microsoft Dynamics CRM.

Another helpful habit is to visit the Microsoft Dynamics CRM Resource Center (http://rc.crm.dynamics.com/rc/regcont/en_us/onlinedefault.aspx) and read how others use the system or peek into a few of the Microsoft Dynamics CRM blogs or podcasts. You might find a helpful tip, a snippet of code, or a learning technique. Listed on my blog, The CRM Lady (www.crmlady.com), is a link list of many other Microsoft Dynamics CRM blogs that you might find interesting. (If you find a blog that is not listed, let me know.) Here are a few links that might be of interest:

- ▶ The Microsoft Dynamics CRM Team Blog: http://blogs.msdn.com/crm/

- ▶ The Microsoft Dynamics CRM Video Gallery: www.democrmonline.com

- ▶ The Microsoft Dynamics CRM Developer Center: http://msdn.microsoft.com/en-us/dynamics/crm/bb501031.aspx

Summary: Key Points to Remember

▶ The need for good CRM is not new, and CRM software is not a new technology.

▶ Microsoft Dynamics CRM is the heart and soul of many companies, and it is impacted by design decisions, business process decisions, country philosophy, corporate culture, style, and individual impact and adoption.

▶ Microsoft Dynamics CRM is extremely flexible and requires management decisions about configuration and use. Flexibility offers choice, and choice can increase complexity.

▶ There is a CRM industry packed with a wealth of magazines, white papers, and CRM successes above and beyond a specific CRM technology.

▶ If automation speeds up processes, what happens when the processes are incorrect? When thinking about CRM technology, remember to think about processes, even if changing processes is not required.

▶ Microsoft Dynamics CRM is built using standard Microsoft technologies, such as the Microsoft .NET Framework, Windows Workflow Foundation, and Microsoft SQL Server.

▶ The Microsoft Dynamics CRM Software Development Kit Software Developer Kit (SDK) is available for download and is regularly updated. You can find the SDK here: http://msdn.microsoft.com/en-us/library/bb928212.aspx.

▶ The Microsoft Dynamics CRM Help files are regularly updated and are available for download and customization.

Workshop

Q&A

Q. *How can I increase internal acceptance of our new Microsoft Dynamics CRM project?*

A. Management involvement and oversight is an important factor for company adoption of any CRM initiative.

Q. *What do you mean when you indicate that Microsoft Dynamics CRM can capture corporate assets?*

A. In today's information age, details on client and prospect interactions can be a valuable corporate asset, particularly when staff turnover is an issue and data is held within the head of a salesperson as opposed to a corporate system.

Q. *What benefit is there in reading some of the CRM industry magazines? I have my solution. What more do I need to know?*

A. CRM industry magazines have some great articles on topics such as getting management buy-in, improving business process with the help of technology, and listing ways to improve efficiency. These subjects are not technology specific, but they can be huge differentiators.

Q. *Our process is constantly changing. How can Microsoft Dynamics CRM keep up with all these changes?*

A. Microsoft Dynamics CRM offers users the power of workflow, which is a feature that CRM administrators can use to define, modify, and automate their own processes. A system administrator can also add or modify attributes/fields associated with specific entities, and a CRM architect can make changes to fine-tune the system as a company uses it. Additionally Microsoft frequently releases upgrades and regular maintenance updates.

Q. *What are some other places to find information on Microsoft Dynamics CRM?*

A. The Microsoft Dynamics CRM Team has a great blog at http://blogs.msdn.com/crm/, which includes links to many other resources.

Q. *We are putting together a team to document some of our company processes. Who would be the best members to include on the team?*

A. Good members for the team include management and staff members who have a long historical perspective of the existing business processes as well as someone who has fresh eyes and is learning about the business processes from a brand-new perspective. You might also want to include a mix of information technology, finance, management, and staff representatives.

Q. *What is an example of a process that may be good to automate?*

A. You might want to automate an alert when an opportunity is created that is outside the bounds of normal for the company or a reminder to follow up when a case is closed on an A-level client or a set of tasks that are created in association with completing a part of a sales process.

Quiz

1. What are two benefits to an individual staff member if a company rolls out Microsoft Dynamics CRM successfully?

2. What are the three components of a successful CRM project?

3. Why might a CxO (CEO, CFO, CIO, and so on) be interested in Microsoft Dynamics CRM?

4. Why is documenting processes so important to CRM adoption?

5. Why might salespeople be resistant to CRM software?

6. What process change occurs when Microsoft Dynamics CRM is installed and adopted?

7. What is an example of a process that can be automated?

8. Name four different roles, such as a salesperson, that could be users of Microsoft Dynamics CRM.

9. What is Microsoft Dynamics capable of doing when a piece of data is saved in the system?

Answers

1. Everything that is done today in Microsoft Outlook can be communicated to without having to retype anything into Excel, Word, or a summary e-mail.

2. The three components of a successful CRM project include people, processes, and technology.

3. A CxO interested in CRM is interested in the organization of data, efficiency, and a common environment that the entire organization is working within.

4. Microsoft Dynamics CRM offers so much choice that it is important to understand the processes you want to support with the Microsoft Dynamics CRM toolset.

5. Salespeople are often on the move, and capturing information within a technical tool does not lend itself to face-to-face conversations and travel time. Dynamics CRM overcomes some of this by being available in multiple formats including mobile and offline when Internet access is not available.

6. Many process changes can occur, but it is up to a Microsoft Dynamics CRM customer to decide what he or she wants to change through automation.

7. A process that can be automated is a sales process or the process of fixing a broken product.

8. A set of roles of users within the world of a CRM solution include a salesperson, administrator, financial officer, marketing expert, business engineer, software developer, or network administrator.

9. Microsoft Dynamics CRM's workflow functionality can automatically create an e-mail message or activity when a piece of data is saved.

Exercise

Using a flowchart or diagrams, document one of the business processes that is part of your working world. You can do this using Microsoft Office Visio, or you can leverage the power of paper and pen. If you have not done flowchart diagramming before, approach this exercise from the concept of pictures. Figures 1.6 and 1.7 provide examples.

FIGURE 1.6
A documented
business
process flow-
chart.

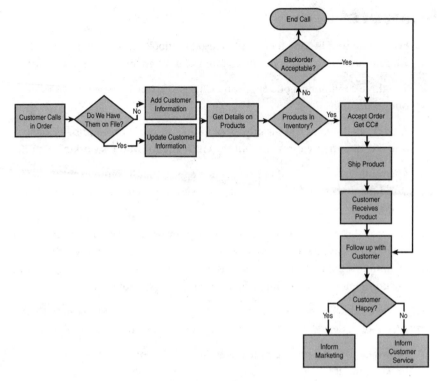

FIGURE 1.7
A documented
business
process with
pictures.

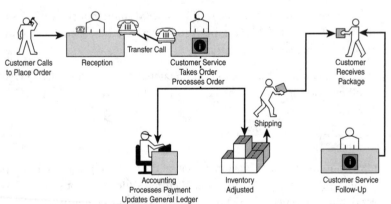

HOUR 2

The Basic Vocabulary of CRM Functionality

What You'll Learn in This Hour:

- ▶ Key building blocks
- ▶ Core entities
- ▶ Other selected entities
- ▶ Other important components
- ▶ Other components

In this hour, we explore the building blocks of Microsoft Dynamics CRM. The core entities, or building blocks, make up the Microsoft Dynamics CRM system. The building blocks include items such as an Account, Contact, Connections, and Opportunity entities. In addition, some building blocks—such as Case, Contract, Order, and Invoice entitites—might not be used by every company. This lesson provides insights into each of the building blocks.

Architectural Note

Be very careful not to design your system before you understand what has been built and what features are designed into the existing architecture. As extendable as Dynamics CRM is, it also comes with a ton of power already existing. Maximizing this power as opposed to fighting against it is highly recommended.

Watch Out!

Key Building Blocks

If we compare Microsoft Dynamics CRM to a brick house, the entities within Microsoft Dynamics CRM are the bricks, or building blocks. Each block can stand on its own and represents a specific thing (in this example, a brick). When put together, these bricks enable us to create a completely different structure—a tree, a house, tower, fireplace, or school. Microsoft Dynamics CRM is also built of "bricks," or "building blocks," and you can use a variety of these different blocks to create different structures. Microsoft Dynamics CRM is both a prebuilt and designed customer relationship management (CRM) application and an extendable xRM platform that can be designed and shaped into different applications. Let's look at a number of these specific building blocks, as outlined in Figure 2.1, starting with the Account entity.

FIGURE 2.1
Microsoft Dynamics CRM building blocks.

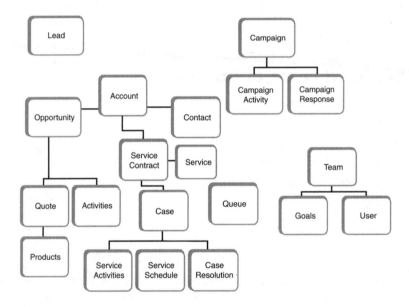

Core Entities

Core entities include all the tables within the Microsoft Dynamics CRM system that is shipped. These include items such as Account, Contact, and Connections. Each is discussed in the following sections.

The Account Entity

At first glance, an Account entity is a company or organization, but the automatic assumptions about an Account entity are not always correct. So, we will specifically look at the use of Account within the world of Microsoft Dynamics CRM. A first assumption is that an Account entity is an organization, a corporation, or a client. Although this may be correct, an Account entity is also much more. For instance, an Account entity can represent a vendor, a prospect, a contracting company, a location, a division headquarters, a legal firm that represents a client, a shared bank, one of the various locations of the bank, and more. In the world of Microsoft Dynamics CRM, Account is a key building block that has relationships to other core entities throughout the system, such as Contact, Case, and Opportunity.

The Account entity can also be defined to mean something unique for your business niche. Take, for instance, a company that manages the assets for one specific company. It does not need to track its only client, but it does need to track all the company's assets and the relationships of these assets to other assets. This company might decide to make the Account entity represent an asset. The company can easily change the name Account to Asset and configure the workflow and associated entities to match this unique business need. This change does not require the expensive skills of a programmer as you might want to assume. It is a configuration feature.

Your company might want to rename the Account entity to Corporation or Client. However, if you do this, you create a conflict with a need to have Account entity types such as Prospect, Vendor, or Supplier. You might also want to track a client's bank or the common accounting firms (Firm). Account is a wonderfully generic term that covers a variety of Account entities.

The Contact Entity

A Contact entity is slightly easier to explain than an Account entity. In most examples, a Contact entity represents a specific person and all the associated information that relates to that specific person. (Using the previous example, the Contact entity might be a specific person who is related to or manages an asset.) A Contact entity may also be represented as a specific individual thing (for instance, a specific plant that relates to a specific account location or family of plants).

Although Microsoft Dynamics CRM is a powerful CRM system, it is also a system that you can configure to track any kind of relationship. The Contact entities have a relationship to the Account entities out of the box and throughout the system. You can have an unlimited number of contacts associated with a given account, and for each Contact entity you can track a number of details. In most cases, you will see that contacts can be any number of different employees in a specific company. Later in this book, we examine what makes up a contact.

Connections

A Connection entity represents the connection between two other entities. Take for instance the connection between two different accounts, a customer and its supplier. Each of these are Account entities, but they have many fields that relate to their connection that can be tracked. For instance, the role one account plays (supplier) to the other (customer).

The Lead Entity

In the world of sales, a lead is an unqualified prospect who has the potential, with some qualification effort, to become a new client. The lead entity is flatter than an account with many contacts. A lead generally represents one contact that in the future might be expanded into a hierarchical tree of account, connections, and contacts. With Microsoft Dynamics CRM, a Lead entity can be a number of different things. If your company purchases a list of names of individuals that might be interested in your products, those names are considered unqualified contacts or leads in Microsoft Dynamics CRM. Once a lead is qualified by a salesperson screening them through a series of questions to determine interest, it can be converted to the hierarchical structure of account, contact, and/or opportunity, offering the ability to add more contacts and related building blocks (such as contract, quote, order, and case). In addition, all the history that has been done to qualify the lead is stored with the lead and related to the new account, contact, and/or opportunity.

Suppose you attend a trade show and obtain a list of all the attendees and you want to follow up with the attendees to see whether any might make future clients. In this case, a lead is a person you might (or might not) have met at the show. A lead is unqualified with regard to whether he or she truly is a potential new client for your company, but is categorized separately from existing clients. One of the most common misconceptions (and therefore frustrations) that can occur is when a company uses a lead as a qualified prospect.

The company may enter large amounts of data, notes, and activities about its leads, but when a lead is ready to have an associated opportunity, or more contacts, the system is not ready to serve that up until the lead is converted. You convert the lead, but all the captured history and activities do not get copied to the Account and Contact entity records. For instance, how would the system copy activities? Would they be copied to the account or the contact or both? If they were copied to both, wouldn't the redundancy be just as confusing? Microsoft Dynamics CRM retains the relationship between a lead and a new contact, but it only moves a certain amount of information to the new qualified account and contact. Once the lead is qualified, you can still access the original Lead record.

Again, a Lead entity is designed to capture a large list of unqualified Contact entities, and the brief history associated with the qualification process is filed with the Lead entity when it is converted and associated to its new Account, Contact, and Opportunity entities.

The Opportunity Entity

An Opportunity entity is sometimes a new concept for people learning about Microsoft Dynamics CRM. The first thing to remember is that an Opportunity entity is not a person or a company. An Opportunity entity is a potential sale and the process related to that sale; it relates to an Account entity, and it often contains the estimated dollar value, the estimated close date, the sales stage, and the probability percentage of closing. An Opportunity entity is used for forecasting and sales funnel analysis. Yes, an Opportunity entity is associated with an Account entity, but it is not defined as an account. For some companies, this works extremely well because they have many opportunities for any given account. For others, however, the concept is a bit more difficult because they only ever focus on one sale per account. Consider this: If you make a sale to a prospective account and that prospective account then becomes a client, you potentially have a new opportunity to resell, upsell, or even renew that relationship through a new opportunity.

Other Selected Entities

In addition to core entities there are other related entities which are further discussed in the sections below. These other entities are just as important, but are not necessarily considered part of the foundation of the system. Lastly there are smaller supporting entities that are not discussed in this chapter.

One *Core* Thought When Mastering the Ability to Think "Dynamics CRM"
Everything is an entity.

Did you Know?

The Activity Entity

An Activity entity is something that you are most likely familiar with. Although each Activity entity is really a set of different types of entities in Microsoft Dynamics CRM, including e-mail, fax, task, phone call, letter, and appointment, each type has unique qualities and can stand on its own. An Activity entity has eight different predefined types in Microsoft Dynamics CRM: phone call, task, e-mail, letter, service activity, appointment, reoccurring appointment, campaign activity, and campaign response. In Microsoft Dynamics CRM, you can also add other Activity types to the core list just outlined.

We will discuss activities as single entities as they work and act like one entity within the system, and from a usage perspective they are generally considered an "activity." For those more technically oriented, each activity type is actually its own entity, and the Activity entity is an activity pointer.

One of the key functionalities of an Activity entity is that it can be scheduled and pending; another way to think about an Activity entity is that it can be completed. Activities also have a special relationship to Microsoft Outlook, the e-mail application included within the Microsoft Office suite. For instance, a Microsoft Dynamics

CRM Activity entity with an activity type of task can optionally (based on user configuration) synchronize in real time with a Microsoft Outlook task. If you complete, check off, or close a task in Outlook, this task will also be shown as a completed Activity entity in Microsoft Dynamics CRM. If you take it one thought further, imagine someone who completes a task on his mobile device, which then flows through Microsoft Outlook, which synchronizes with the corporate Microsoft Dynamics CRM databases. This behind-the-scenes technique eliminates the need for anyone to send e-mail, asking whether a certain task has been completed.

The Case Entity

A Case entity is also referred to as a service ticket in some businesses, and when using Microsoft Dynamics CRM, it can be renamed. In most examples, a Case entity is affiliated with a customer service department that has incoming reported issues that need tracking, activities, notes, and resolutions. A Case entity can have an unlimited number of associated activities and can be related to a specific Account or Contact entity and an annual or monthly service contract. A Case entity can also accumulate a total number of hours or minutes invested in working the case, and this accumulation can offset a standard number of purchased hours defined in a service contract. A Case entity also has a Case Resolution entity associated with it when the case is closed through the Dynamics CRM Close Case function.

The Contract Entity

The Contract entity in Microsoft Dynamics CRM can be configured to track many different details. A Contract entity is associated with an Account entity and is an optional feature. The Contract entity functionality was designed in association with a Case entity. The concept is that an account might have purchased a certain number of service hours or service tickets, and the Contract entity captures the details of this agreement. The Contract entity also has an ongoing relationship with the total number of cases used or hours of service provided. A Contract entity not only captures the specific details of a contract but also the relationship of that contract to the services provided and tracked.

The Service Schedule Entity

Microsoft Dynamics CRM is not just about sales; it is also about serving existing clients. The software provides the ability to manage a complex service department, which includes functionality to support service scheduling. A service schedule specifically tracks who, what, when, and where a service will occur, with additional functionality related to managing service conflicts. This is different from a standard appointment activity, which is used for simple scheduling and therefore doesn't include tracking available sites and service personnel.

The Queue Entity

A queue is a data structure that organizes specific data in a "waiting to be processed" method. A queue does not contain its own building blocks; it contains other Dynamics CRM building blocks, such as cases or activities. Examples of a queue in Dynamics CRM include a configured queue to capture service cases and a queue to manage incoming activity requests that need to be processed by a specific department. Microsoft Dynamics CRM enables users to create different queues with associated tasks or business process. A queue is similar to a line of people waiting to be serviced, but the line is made up of something other than people (see Figure 2.2). A queue can also be managed by selecting items from the middle of the line so the older first in, first out methodology no longer applies.

FIGURE 2.2
A queue.

The Campaign Entity

A Campaign entity in Microsoft Dynamics CRM is a marketing feature that has many parts and comes in two versions. The first version, called a *quick campaign*, is designed for use by a salesperson. A quick campaign has an associated marketing list or subset of specific contacts. It is also usually used once to announce a month-end special or to send out one quick e-mail blast of information. A full campaign, the second version of a campaign, is more detailed, and it includes the ability to budget for a specific event, to compose or plan a long list of activities associated with a marketing event, and to capture results and costs when the marketing event is completed. Many CRM systems do not have campaign tracking and, therefore, you will find that the concept of tracking all the details of a campaign is new to most users. The full campaign is designed to be used by the marketing department as a tool to empower the department to organize and track the efforts surrounding a specific marketing event. A full Campaign entity includes campaign activities and campaign results as associated items.

The User Entity

A user is a staff person for a Microsoft Dynamics CRM organization who is assigned a CRM license and who is using Microsoft Dynamics CRM to capture specific information. A user has relationships to the Account entity (for example, she can be the owner of the account) and to specific activities and service-scheduling items. Microsoft Dynamics CRM leverages the user in much of its automatic system functionality. It is also assigned a Microsoft Dynamics CRM security role for other CRM functionality-specific security. For instance, a user may be assigned to the salesperson role, and the salesperson role may be limited to sales functionality only, preventing the user from creating service tickets or marketing campaigns.

Other Important Components

There are other critical components in Dynamics CRM. These include types of data such as an account that is marked as a prospect versus an account that is marked as a client.

What Is a Prospect?

A prospect is a potential client or customer who has usually been qualified through at least one conversation or a salesperson's researched effort. A Prospect entity is a type of Account entity and is generally created when a lead has been converted to an Account entity, a Contact entity, or optionally an Opportunity entity. One of the key concepts to grasp is that a Lead entity and a Prospect entity are different in terms of how the system thinks about them. They both represent a company and, most likely, a primary contact, but a Lead entity is often a name that might or might not be real, and a Prospect entity is a name with an associated company, a salesperson's understanding, other key data, and even an expressed specific interest in the salesperson's products or services behind it. In linear terms, you start with a Lead entity, you qualify the Lead, and then once qualified you convert and create a Prospect entity, and you sell the Prospect entity product or services (and thus creating a Customer entity).

The goal of every salesperson is to close deals by first qualifying leads to the point that they become a sales prospect. Of the numerous configurations of Microsoft Dynamics CRM that are deployed, you will find that not every sales process uses the concepts of Lead entities and Prospect entities in this manner; however, it helps to understand the concepts behind the design of the system. It has been noted that, at any given company, you might not want to have all your Lead entities configured as robust Prospect entities in the system. The Microsoft Dynamics CRM Lead and

Prospect entities allows for a pool of many leads that does not interfere with or muddy the waters for the core data in the system. This gives a company elbow room for importing large lists of Lead entities without showing numerous unqualified leads on sales funnel and prospect reports. Figure 2.3 shows how a lead might flow from Lead entity to Prospect entity to Customer entity.

Leads   Prospects   Customers

FIGURE 2.3
A lead moving from Lead to Prospect to Customer entities.

Adding Addresses

The Account entity in Microsoft Dynamics CRM has two addresses directly associated with it. However, Microsoft Dynamics CRM offers you the option of adding even more addresses. If you have ever ordered something online, you understand why customers might want an unlimited number of addresses that they can provide and associate with any given Account entity. For instance, you might want to have more than one shipping address, or you might find that a specific contact resides in two locations. Each Account entity within a system and each Contact in the system can have an unlimited number of associated addresses. Each has a primary address, but they each can also have more addresses.

What Are Connections and Relationships?

Relationships exist in many forms within Microsoft Dynamics CRM. One of them is the Relationship entity, which includes associated relationship roles. Relationship roles can be defined by the user through system configuration and might consist of items such as association member and association, banker and customer, or other relationships that differ from how a standard Contact entity as it relates to an account that contact might work for. Relationships can be tracked between two contacts in several ways: between Contact and Contact, between Account and Contact, or between Contact and Account. In addition, relationships can be represented between an Opportunity entity and a Contact entity and between an Opportunity entity and an Account entity. Figure 2.4 shows a list of relationships. When you set up a relationship, you choose the Account, Contact, or Opportunity entity and its role as it relates to a different Account, Contact, or Opportunity entity.

FIGURE 2.4
Relationships.

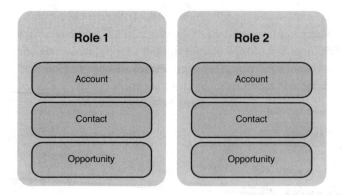

Other Components

Most of the items that we have just reviewed are classified as entities within the world of Dynamics CRM. Entities are the building blocks of Microsoft Dynamics CRM, and, from a structural design perspective, an entity is a set of Microsoft SQL database tables. Each entity has forms, views, charts, field, messages, and relationships. For instance, entities can have relationships to other entities from many different perspectives. An entity can have a parental relationship with another where there is a key connection between the two entities. Or entities can have other types of relationships, such as referential (they refer to each other). Or for any given entity, there may be many other related entities, such as the relationship between Account and Contact entities. For any given Account entity, you can have many Contact entities. The relationship can also go the other way. For instance, for any given Opportunity entity, you can only have one Account entity, but your choice of which Account entity is unlimited. If you consider all the different ways that entities can relate to other entities, you start to see the full picture of Microsoft Dynamics CRM being a foundation of any relationship management need. In this way, Microsoft Dynamics CRM is not only a CRM software application and a sales force automation application, it is also an "any relationship" (xRM) development platform, which is a term you will see and hear much more as you delve deeper into Microsoft Dynamics CRM.

Some of the other components in the world of Microsoft Dynamics CRM include Option Set, Client Extension, Web Resource, Process, Plugin Assembly, SDK Message Processing, Service Endpoint, Dashboard, Report, Connection Role, Article Template, Contract Template, E-mail Template, Mail Merge Template, Security Role, and Field Security Profile.

Summary

We explored the building blocks of Microsoft Dynamics CRM, but this is only the tip of the iceberg when it comes to understanding the complete set of building blocks available to you. Dive deep into getting your mind around a building block having key features and functionalities and each building block having a set of relationships to other entities within the Microsoft Dynamics CRM platform.

Workshop

A small alternative medicine clinic is using Microsoft Dynamics CRM to organize and run its practice. The clinic uses the CRM scheduling features to keep track of its patient appointments. Each staff member is set up as a CRM user, and each one can access Microsoft Dynamics CRM from his or her main office machine or from any other available machine in the clinic upon individual login. The clinic also schedules appointment follow-up telephone calls, and it leverages the mailing features of Dynamics CRM to send out regular appointment postcard reminders.

The clinic also uses a sophisticated medical billing line-of-business application. This application handles the insurance company management and billing compliance. The clinic has integrated Microsoft Dynamics CRM with its medical insurance billing software so that data can be shared.

During the winter, the clinic gets a high number of incoming telephone calls that require a return call from a doctor or specialist. One feature important to the clinic was the ability to manage the priority of the necessary follow-up calls using queues. The clinic uses Microsoft Dynamics CRM to schedule appointments, send out mailings, track the contact details of their patients, and manage the many relationships that it has with the pharmaceutical representatives.

Q&A

Q. *What if I do not want to use one of the entities described here? Can I ignore it in Microsoft Dynamics CRM?*

A. You can ignore an entity and not use it. You can also delete an entity, although that is not recommended because you might want to use it later.

Q. *I rely on the Tasks feature in Microsoft Outlook. How do these tasks associate with activities in Microsoft Dynamics CRM?*

A. An Outlook task synchronizes to a Microsoft Dynamics CRM activity of type Task. You can manage your activities/tasks from either Outlook tasks or Microsoft Dynamics CRM activities.

Q. *What are the disadvantages of renaming Account to Customer and using leads for all prospects?*

A. Although the system supports your ability to do this, you will significantly limit your ability to associate other powerful built-in functions to your Prospect entities, including Opportunity, Quote, Order, Invoice, Relationship, and other entities. In addition, you might want to use Account to track vendors, suppliers, and other companies.

Quiz

1. The building blocks of Microsoft Dynamics CRM are referred to as **entities**. Name some of these entities.

2. What is the Opportunity entity?

3. Do entities have relationships? If so, what are some of these relationships?

4. How does the term **entity** relate to the Microsoft SQL Server database foundation on which Microsoft Dynamics CRM is built?

Answers

1. The building blocks of Microsoft Dynamics CRM include Account, Contact, Activity, Opportunity.

2. The Opportunity entity is an entity that tracks the details of a potential sale, including estimated premium, estimated close date, and probability of closing.

3. Yes, entities have relationships. The relationship between Account and Contact is a good example.

4. An entity represents a Microsoft SQL Server table.

Exercise

Using paper or Microsoft Word, create a list of the entities that you consider to be the core building blocks for your firm. For this exercise, do not worry about the Microsoft Dynamic CRM names of the entities. Instead, focus on the specific entities as you define them. How do these entities map to the entities listed in this lesson? How would you define the Account entity? What are the advantages and disadvantages of this design? Will this design cause issues for your firm in two or three years? What would be some of those issues?

Using paper or Microsoft Visio or any of the family tree applications, create an example of how you would organize some of the entities within your firm and how they relate to other entities. Figure 2.5 shows an example of how to do this.

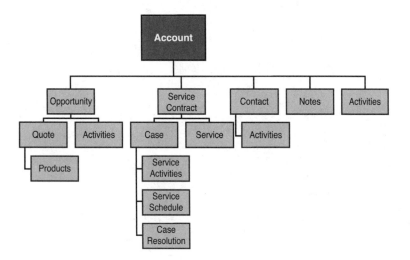

FIGURE 2.5
Some of the
Firm entities.

Microsoft Dynamics CRM 2011: What's New

What You'll Learn in This Hour:

▶ The new user interface, dashboards, and charts

▶ Entity architecture areas of change

▶ Small yet important enhancements to Dynamics CRM 2011

▶ Processes: workflow and dialogs

▶ Special new features for the Microsoft CRM developer

In this hour, we will explore some of what is new in Microsoft Dynamics CRM 2011, including the changes to support business process and the capturing and matching of business processes to the technology application. Understanding which features were released with which upgrade and what is new in Dynamics CRM 2011 vs. Dynamics CRM v4 allows a CRM administrator and partners to better determine which features they want to push to their maximum potential and which features might need a bit more watching and maturing. Microsoft Dynamics CRM 2011 has more than 500 new features, and we cover as many of them as possible throughout this book.

The New User Interface, Dashboards, and Charts

If you are familiar with Microsoft Dynamics CRM 4.0, the first thing you will notice when you access Microsoft Dynamics CRM 2011 is that the user interface (UI) has changed. The grumblings from the field about tabs and too many clicks created change from the extremely responsive development team. The appearance of the UI has flattened. In addition, user-definable charts and dashboards have been added.

Now although it has been flattened and looks a bit different, the concept of sections within a form still applies. It is not that different from the old version, just different enough to streamline data entry.

Now to get started we are going to look at the new Get Started pane that has been added to every display. This pane is optional but by default is turned on. Take a look at Figure 3.1.

FIGURE 3.1
The Get Started with Accounts pane.

Entity Views, Forms, and Displays

The new look and feel of the Account entity gives you a good idea of how things have changed for all entities in Dynamics CRM 2011. The top of the Accounts screen now has the Get Started pane, which we discussed previously and which is populated with user resources such as quick tips on how to import, use, modify, and manage your account information.

Another new visual enhancement is the consistent use of the Microsoft Office ribbon. You might love the ribbon or hate it, but it is the Microsoft Office standard, and Microsoft Dynamics CRM embraces it fully in the 2011 release. Figure 3.2 shows the Office ribbon as it appears with Dynamics CRM Workplace, Accounts selected.

Did you Know?

The Ribbon

The Ribbon can be configured and customized by someone who is familiar with Microsoft Office. If you don't like it, ask your partner or CRM administrator for help in configuring it to fit your needs. You will save some bellyaching.

FIGURE 3.2
The Office
ribbon.

Dashboards

Dashboards allow you to construct multiple sets of charts and grids that make the most sense for your business or for your individual requirements at work. Several dashboards are shipped out of the box, but the ability to pick and choose different charts to put into your dashboard is limited only by your imagination.

Charts

Charts now apply to every entity. Microsoft Dynamics CRM 4.0 has views associated with every entity, and a similar architecture has been applied to charts in Microsoft Dynamics CRM 2011. For each entity, you can establish a set of charts. Charts and views go hand in hand; you can take a view of data and show it graphically using a chart. Figure 3.3 shows the chart on the Activity entity called Activities by Type.

FIGURE 3.3
An Activities by
Type chart.

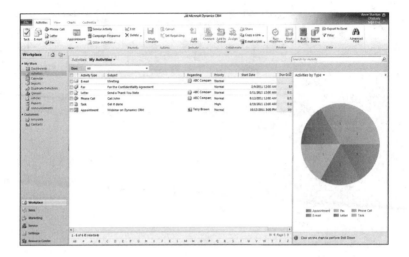

Department- or Group-Specific Forms

When getting started with Dynamics CRM, you might want to continue to stick with one form for each entity. However, you now have the option to configure your data entry forms based on different user security roles. This significantly reduces the amount of scripting used to hide fields that might exist in your Dynamics CRM 4.0 system. Figure 3.4 shows the forms that come with the product: main and mobile. You can add more forms if you like and then apply forms to different groups of users.

FIGURE 3.4
A List of forms
on the Account
entity.

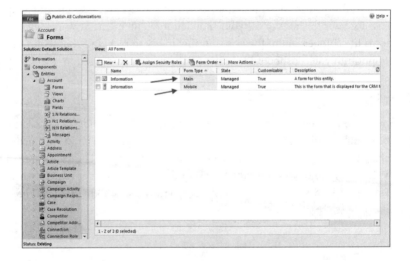

Entity Architecture Areas of Change

The architecture within Microsoft Dynamics CRM has a familiar quality and also significant changes. There are some specific new entities and entity sets that we talk about in the following text, and there is a significant shift in the developer's approach. This shift better aligns with how senior developers who are not working with Dynamics CRM write code.

Connections

The new Connections entity enables a user to track complex relationships between any two entities. It is a new feature that is designed to replace the relationships feature in Dynamics CRM v4 and is designed to add more depth and functionality. This functionality includes the relationships between contacts and companies as well as the relationship between other entities that might have overlapping properties. Connections are different than the Microsoft Dynamics CRM 4.0 relationship feature (which still exists for backward compatibility). The key difference between relationships and connections is that the connection functionality offers detailed tracking information on the actual relationship and it is considered more robust and flexible. Figure 3.5 shows the connections configuration.

FIGURE 3.5
Connections access from an account.

Goals and Goal Management

Goals and goal management are new features in Microsoft Dynamics CRM 2011 that support the user's ability to enter goals that can then be compared to a number of different entities. This comparison model can also change as business needs change without reprogramming or redesign. You can use goals for the more traditional sales goals, but they are also designed for goals that are not sales oriented. For instance you might have a service level agreement goal or a time management goal. Figure 3.6 offers a brief glimpse at goals.

FIGURE 3.6
Goals.

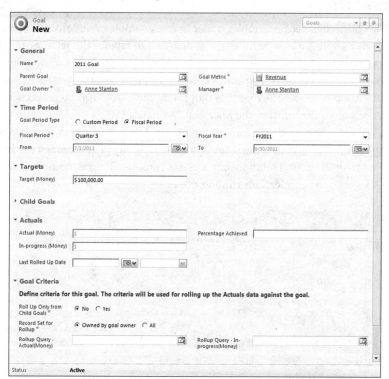

Changes within the Software Development Process and the SDK

The changes within Dynamics CRM v2011 are significant, so if you have been developing on the Microsoft Dynamics CRM v4 platform, it is critical that you take a long look at what is new. The new features include a new programming model using Windows Communication Foundation (WCF), extended use of Windows Workflow Foundation 4.0, and support for .NET Language-Integrated Query (LINQ).

I strongly recommend that you tap into some of the great free videos and webinars on the xRMVirtual User group found at www.xrmvirtual.com and some of the many developer-focused books on Dynamics CRM. The software development methodologies within Dynamics CRM v2011 are new, improved, more automated, and just plain cool. Additionally more technologies come into play such as Silverlight and SharePoint. A small list of these changes include better handling of transactions for rollbacks, changed support around child plugins, a need to master the ribbon editor, and new sitemap controls, and this is just the tip of the iceberg. Any senior developer reading this can now be very excited about the possibilities that they can accomplish with this platform and can just plain ignore any grumblings about CRM v4 as a potentially immature xRM platform.

Small yet Important Enhancements to Dynamics CRM 2011

If you're unaware of some of the small changes to Dynamics CRM 2011, they can be much wanted and yet missed, and so I highlight them as follows.

Bulk E-mail Messages and Attachments

In Microsoft Dynamics CRM 2011, it's now possible to include attachments when sending bulk e-mail messages. The system stores only one version of the attachment even when you send out many different e-mails with the same attachment to many different people. So the attachment design does not overwhelm your CRM database with multiple copies of the same material. Originally there was a core concept that firms should not blast out attachments as it is just not great e-mail best practices, but now the team allows the user to do this if they want to.

Negative Pricing

The negative pricing feature now allows for negative quantities, amounts, and negative prices. Negative pricing was not supported in earlier versions and as such integration to powerful ERP systems with unique accounting needs became more problematic. This issue has now been eliminated.

Enhanced Decimal Precision

Depending on the company, decimal precision needs can be very from one extreme to the next and can be very different. System Settings now supports setting decimal precision based on a variety of high level category choices, including Pricing Decimal Precision, Currency Precision, and Field Precision and then some low level fine tuning. The feature is a hour of training all on its own.

Opportunity Enhancements

The opportunity feature now supports the ability to create a quote, an order, or an invoice directly from the opportunity. You can also add write-in products to an opportunity. Figure 3.7 shows access to quotes, orders, and invoices from the Opportunities form. Now when you are working on an opportunity you can look at all the details, move the sales process forward, connect with your prompts via a sales dialog, and continue right through creating and printing the quote. You can also manage the quote if changes need to be made during the negotiation process.

FIGURE 3.7
Quote access
from a specific
opportunity
form.

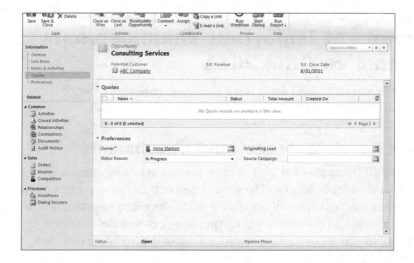

View Filters

The advanced find feature is handy and extremely powerful but can be a bit intimidating for some users. All that power when all you want to do is filter a view is unnecessary, so to help with this, CRM 2011 offers filters in the views. You can now create a personal or shared view (that is similar to advanced find) directly out of a filtered view. Now this concept can seem a bit ho-hum, but consider this: Dynamics CRM is built on top of a complex SQL Server database. Microsoft Dynamics CRM is designed with secure and controlled access to the underlying SQL Server database. The team provides an API layer, security services (permissions, roles, and so on), and some business logic. Needless to say, hacking at the CRM databases with a SQL

Server query is not supported nor does it always return the results expected. Dynamics CRM v2011 now has access to filtered views right from the user interface. A nice wow when you really think about it from a technical perspective.

Recurring Appointments

Recurring appointments are a special type of activity, and in Dynamics CRM v4 they were not supported nor available; luckily the recurring appointment activity type is now available as a new entity completely designed to support all those extra requirements such as the different types of reoccurrence. You can use this type of activity to track recurring appointments from Outlook in CRM and from CRM back to Outlook. Figure 3.8 shows the details on the new recurring appointment activity type.

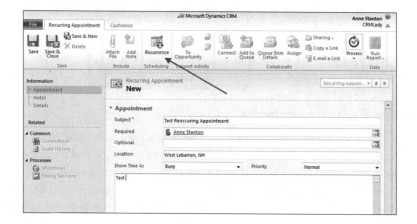

FIGURE 3.8
Recurring appointments.

Dynamic Marketing Lists

Marketing lists once configured in the Dynamics cRM v4 days were static until a user made changes. In Microsoft Dynamics CRM 2011, you can create a dynamic marketing list in which you define or specify a query. So, instead of requiring you to manually update an existing marketing list, Microsoft Dynamics CRM 2011 runs the query and updates it for you on the fly. Depending on the list type, the leads, accounts, or contacts that fulfill the query, criteria are automatically added as the members of the list whenever the list is used. Figure 3.9 shows this new setting.

FIGURE 3.9
The Dynamic
Marketing List
setting.

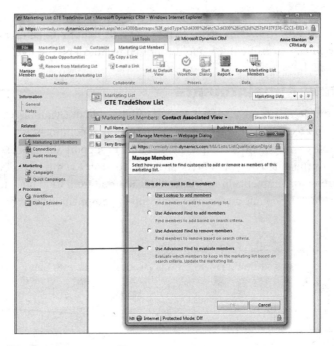

Queue Enhancements

Queues have been significantly enhanced in Microsoft Dynamics CRM 2011, as has the service module. The queues have moved from a set of simple first in, first out offerings to a feature-packed suite of numerous different choices as seen here. The service module has matured into a "follow the sun" model. If you have a 24x7 multiple team member support team, you can now easily hand cases between members in any 24 hour period of time.

The following are some of the enhancements to queues:

- You can secure queues through role privileges.

- You can add a default queue to users and teams.

- You can enable all entity types for queues.

- You can customize the Queue entity.

- Process workflows support queues and queue items.

- You can separate a queue item's working on assignment and record ownership.

Queues are discussed in more detail in Hour 18, "Contracts, Cases, and Capturing Time."

The following are some of the enhancements to the service module:

- You can check out a case as a "working on" team member.

▶ Queue integration to case management has a number of new features, as listed previously.

▶ You can now define a service process similarly to a sales process that is stepped and either manual or automated.

Processes: Workflow and Dialogs

Workflows continue to be a powerful feature in Microsoft Dynamics CRM 2011, and now they are supported by a complementary automation of process called dialogs. To understand dialogs, think about a call center and the scripts it might use when making calls. Such a script can be configured and automated in Dynamics CRM as a dialog. Administrators and users now have the ability to create workflows or dialogs to support the automation or documentation of the business processes used. Figures 3.10 and 3.11 show dialog setup and process access.

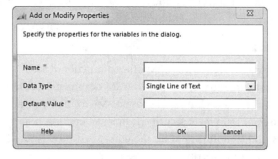

FIGURE 3.10
Dialog setup.

FIGURE 3.11
Access to defining a process.

Security: Team and Field

Team Ownership of Entities

In previous versions of Microsoft Dynamics CRM, each entity record is either owned by the organization or owned by a specific user. This ownership then supports one dimension of the security roles. For instance you can set read, write, and update capabilities to owner access only. In Microsoft Dynamics CRM 2011, the system now also supports team ownership. This feature is useful when you have a number of people working on a specific account as a team or on a specific project. Instead of worrying about who should own the records and then sharing those one at a time, you can create a team for the project or account and set the entity to have a team ownership module. Records are then owned by a specific team of people. This ensures that everyone who needs access is a member of that team and that each individual team member can see all the accounts or projects that they need to see.

Field-Level Security

Prior version of Microsoft Dynamics CRM offered functional security and form based security, but when it came to a specific field CRM administrators and partners had to tap into extending. This is no longer the case as Microsoft Dynamics cRM v2011 introduces level one of Field-level security. It has just enough power to solve some immediate needs and is maturing at an incredibly fast rate. Figure 3.12 shows the first step in utilizing team security.

Security Decisions

Security decisions about how you set up your Microsoft Dynamics CRM system should be done as part of your roll-out project architecture. Many different areas need to work together.

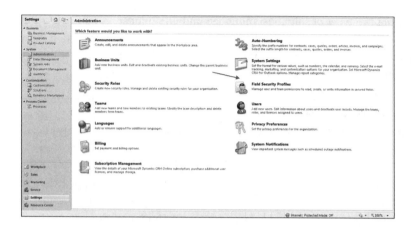

FIGURE 3.12
Field security
profiles access.

Special New Features for the Microsoft CRM Developer

When diving into a quick hour training on various areas of Microsoft Dynamics CRM as an application it is sometimes easy to forget that almost every Dynamics CRM rollout is configured to fit a specific business. This configuration can also lead to some intense extensions. As mentioned earlier in this chapter, Microsoft has embraced this xRM Platform concept and is adding more features and functionalities to support the senior software engineers and developers.

Solution Management

Microsoft Dynamics CRM 2011 has a new concept called solution management. Solution management enables you to bundle all your solution customizations into one managed or unmanaged package. You can also pick and choose what goes into a solution. For example, if you want to share customizations from one organization with another, you can do so via solutions. Solutions support the xRM process and are similar to software company release bundles. Solution management is ideal for companies and partners who want to produce solutions and sell them or reuse them as packaged solutions for other projects, or for partners who want to sell their solutions on the new Microsoft Dynamics CRM marketplace, and so on.

There are two types of solutions: managed and unmanaged. A managed solution can be edited only by specific users, and if it is exported and imported at another organization, users of the other organization will not be able to edit or modify the solution. Managed solutions are fully secured and cannot be edited.

A Tip on Managed Solutions

There are strengths and weaknesses in the managed solution offering. Make sure you understand both before you attempt to use them.

An unmanaged solution can be edited by any user who has an appropriate user role. Unmanaged solutions are usually fairly dynamic from a usage perspective and are a great feature for the multi-developer teams. Unmanaged solutions should be the developers default until mastery of both managed and unmanaged solutions is achieved.

Import and Export Data

The import and export of data from Microsoft Dynamics CRM has been expanded to significantly enhance what an end user or CRM administrator can do when it comes to getting data into the system or getting data out of the system in a variety of formats.

The first milestone for importing is that you can import from an XML format, which means you have much more flexibility for data migration. The .csv offering in previous versions still exists but has always been more limiting. In addition, Microsoft Dynamics CRM 2011 now offers you the option of exporting an Excel spreadsheet template with all your data fields in the order you want, which can then be populated and reimported. This helps standardize the data import process when you're collecting data from multiple sources and is a big win for users doing data organization and data cleansing. Yet, there is still more in Microsoft Dynamics CRM 2011: You can create new entities while importing. This saves a number of steps during the build process and offers even more power once the system is running. In addition to the whole entity you can dynamically create fields to map against source fields in source data files, such as Excel spreadsheets. Data import has taken many of the formerly preparation steps and moves them to real time interaction with the importing tools (see Figure 3.13).

FIGURE 3.13
Imported data
files.

SharePoint Integration

Microsoft Dynamics CRM 2011 now integrates with SharePoint out of the box, with
no development or custom code needed. Ben Hosk shares his enthusiasm for the
available information on the feature and some of the configuration. You can read
Ben's post here: http://crmbusiness.wordpress.com/2011/03/07/crm-2011-how-to-
setup-sharepoint-integration. Integration addresses a couple of key areas. The first is
the management of all that unstructured data that comes with business process:
managing and editing documents, sharing documents, and doing key word searches
against blobs of text. Additionally you get the ability to show CRM structured data
in SharePoint web pages or to take some of those great graphs and share them via
web parts. This marriage between SharePoint and Dynamics CRM existed as part of
the back channel culture in the Dynamics CRM v4 days, but now it is fully
embraced by Microsoft. The bridge between these two product groups is extremely
exciting, particularly when you start thinking about automating business processes.
See Figure 3.14 for a snapshot.

FIGURE 3.14
SharePoint con-
figuration.

Workshop

Q&A

Q. *Why has Microsoft created the solutions feature in Microsoft Dynamics CRM 2011?*

A. Solutions make it easy for users to share with other users or between different projects.

Q. *Was integration with SharePoint an option in Microsoft Dynamics CRM 4.0?*

A. Yes, but only with custom development.

Q. *Why does Microsoft Dynamics CRM 2011 have both workflows and dialogs?*

A. Dialogs are used to automate the more traditional scripts, such as what you might find in a call center. They prompt or remind the user about what to do next. Workflows are used to automate a process such as a sales process and more traditionally create pending activities that need to get done when other activities are completed.

Quiz

1. How many new features were introduced in Microsoft Dynamics CRM 2011?

2. What are two of the biggest changes in Dynamics CRM 2011?

3. Who can own records in Microsoft Dynamics CRM 2011?

4. Does field-level security exist in Microsoft Dynamics CRM 2011?

5. What new format is available for importing data in Microsoft Dynamics CRM 2011?

Answers

1. Microsoft Dynamics CRM 2011 has more than 500 new features.

2. Dialogs and solutions are two of the biggest changes in Dynamics CRM 2011.

3. Users and teams can own records in Microsoft Dynamics CRM 2011.

4. Yes, field-level security exists in Microsoft Dynamics CRM 2011.

5. XML and Excel Exported Templates are new formats available for importing data in Microsoft Dynamics CRM 2011.

Exercise

Each entity in Microsoft Dynamics CRM 2011 starts with a Getting Started pane. Open Microsoft Dynamics CRM 2011 and choose Explore and then choose About This Getting Started Pane. Read the information provided on why the Getting Started pane was created and click the purple Learn More button to confirm that you can access the additional information available from Microsoft.

HOUR 4

Infrastructure Choices

What You'll Learn in This Hour:

▶ Application placement: choices and implications

▶ Tenant architecture and its implications, including multitenant options

▶ Microsoft Dynamics CRM infrastructure components

▶ Asynchronous services and Microsoft Workflow Foundation

▶ Diving into development

▶ Integration options

▶ Big business versus small business

In this hour, we dive into the various options that surround the installation and implementation of the Microsoft Dynamics CRM software. There are many choices within the world of Microsoft Dynamics CRM, and consideration and careful thought about these choices can make a big difference in the success and adoption of this powerful application for companies. This hour also offers insight into where someone might want to focus more training and which roles within a company might be best suited to mastery of which pieces of the Microsoft Dynamics CRM environment.

Application Placement: Choices and Implications

Microsoft Dynamics CRM is all about choice, and choice offers more opportunity for learning. When it comes to where Microsoft Dynamics CRM is installed, it is important to understand what your options are and why.

On-Premises Microsoft Dynamics CRM

Companies have the choice to purchase the Microsoft Dynamics CRM software in an on-premises model. On-Premises Microsoft Dynamics CRM is installed locally in a company's server environment, and it allows for full internal control of all application files and associated data. The actual program files, the database where all the data is stored, the connection to the company's Microsoft Exchange e-mail environment, the web interface, and web page hosting, plug-ins, and any customizations are all stored, managed, and installed locally.

With an on-premises installation, it is highly recommended that an experienced (and ideally, a Microsoft Dynamics CRM infrastructure certified) team be available for the initial installation and ongoing responsibility for the maintenance of the infrastructure environment. Mastery of the infrastructure of Microsoft Dynamics CRM requires a unique set of skills, and this mastery is required for long-term error-free success. The necessary skills are best mastered by someone who has a background as a network architect, network engineer, or network administration. Experience in the following areas is also extremely helpful:

▶ Hosting web environments and mastery of Internet Information Services (IIS)

▶ Managing the sharing and integration of data between different applications and systems

▶ Analyzing and interpreting system logs and error messages

▶ Microsoft Server 2005 and 2008 and 2008 R2

▶ Performance tuning and management of Microsoft SQL Server databases

On-Premises Microsoft Dynamics CRM offers a business total control over the entire environment. Data is under the protection of the company; the software is under the internal change management and upgrade processes; and the ability to change, customize, and expand is not affected by external partner companies.

 By the Way

Dynamics CRM Architecture

For a diagram of the Microsoft Dynamics CRM architecture, see the Microsoft Dynamics CRM Developer Center, at http://msdn.microsoft.com/en-us/library/bb928229.aspx.

Microsoft Dynamics CRM Online

Unlike On-Premises Microsoft Dynamics CRM, Microsoft Dynamics CRM Online is hosted by Microsoft Corporation. Microsoft Dynamics CRM Online also offers a few additional add-in components, such as those for Internet lead capture and marketing campaign optimization. It also has a few limitations, such as the inability to upload custom Microsoft SQL Server Reporting Service reports and a set prebuilt report set.

Mastery of the infrastructure, having the right hardware, investing in Microsoft Dynamics CRM infrastructure specialists, and other infrastructure specifics are not required with Microsoft Dynamics CRM Online. You also have access to a much larger environment, with powerful hardware that can offer more scalability to small and midsize businesses.

In addition, with Microsoft Dynamics CRM Online, Microsoft takes on the responsibility of offering you long-term maintenance on the software and a level of uptime of 99.99%, with financial backing. The long-term responsibility includes items such as installing maintenance updates to keep your company current with the development cycles and team and offering upgrades full of new features on a yearly basis. This can be a significant time saver for many companies. For an article on the announced service-level agreements for Microsoft Dynamics CRM Online, see http://crm.dynamics.com/deployment/ondemand.aspx.

You might also have concerns about not having access to your data if it is all hosted, but Microsoft has also mastered that by offering their integration to Microsoft Office Outlook.

You can choose to install local software with Microsoft Dynamics CRM Online: the Microsoft Dynamics CRM Outlook Client. Yes, even with Microsoft Dynamics CRM Online, you can have integration with your local version of Microsoft Outlook e-mail. This is a no-cost option and not only offers you the ability to run Dynamics CRM from Outlook, but also gives you the power to go offline! You don't need to have access to the Internet to get access to your data.

What you can't have in the world of Microsoft Dynamics CRM Online are hosted custom code sets and extensions that need to be installed on the same server as the Microsoft Dynamics CRM software and custom Microsoft SQL Server Report service reports, which need to be installed on the Microsoft hosted SQL Server. This server environment is owned, managed, and operated under the Microsoft umbrella, and, therefore, it has to be standardized for many different company databases, which are referred to as "tenants" of Microsoft Dynamics CRM.

> **What Is a Tenant?**
>
> A *tenant* is generally related to one specific company's Microsoft Dynamics CRM data footprint. However, in large enterprise clients, you might find different independent projects and non-CRM projects using their own sets of databases (that is, their own CRM tenants).

Microsoft Dynamics CRM Partner Hosted

Microsoft Dynamics CRM Partner Hosted is similar to Microsoft Dynamics CRM Online, but it is hosted by an independent vendor. This external vendor can be a Microsoft Partner or one of the many hosting companies offering Microsoft Dynamics CRM. One of the benefits of working with a Microsoft Dynamics CRM Hosted partner is that you might have access to more third-party add-in products that are also hosted, such as integrated phone system software, the BlackBerry server with Microsoft Dynamics CRM BlackBerry mobile support, and much, much more. In addition, some third-party hosting partners have an offering for customers who want to host their own integrated custom code.

The Cloud and Microsoft Windows Azure

Many developers who are working with the xRM platform and extending Dynamics CRM are excited about a new combination of hosted and on premise in the world of Microsoft Dynamics CRM v2011. Microsoft Dynamics CRM supports integration with the "AppFabric Service Bus" feature of the Windows Azure platform. What this means is that by integrating with the AppFabric Service Bus, developers can register plug-ins with Microsoft Dynamics CRM that can pass run-time message data to one or more Windows Azure solutions in the cloud. For more information on the advanced development concept of integration with Azure, you can read the section in the SDK called Azure Extensions for Microsoft Dynamics CRM located at http://msdn.microsoft.com/en-us/library/gg309276.aspx.

Tenant Architecture and Its Implications, Including Multitenant Options

There are so many pieces and options to Microsoft Dynamics CRM. How do we put them all together? You can have a hosting company offering Dynamics CRM to many different companies, which lends itself to a multitenanted architecture, and you can have a medium-sized company with all the software and data locally installed. The relationship between the Microsoft Dynamics CRM infrastructure and the existing infrastructure and the almost unlimited choices of add-in options is extensive. Microsoft Dynamics CRM is a web application and so has hosted web access and it is a database application using the power of Microsoft SQL Server. In addition, how you host Microsoft Dynamics CRM changes what some of your options are, and this can be an eye-opener. For instance, the details that a hosting provider needs to know (or even a large enterprise that might host many xRM projects) differ significantly from the details that a small On-Premise network administrator needs to master.

Still, some items are core design, no matter where Microsoft Dynamics CRM lives. We will look at some of the pieces that make up the Microsoft Dynamics CRM infrastructure in the next sections.

Microsoft Dynamics CRM Infrastructure Components

When it comes to mastering the infrastructure components in an On-Premises environment, one of the best pieces of documentation is the Microsoft Dynamics CRM Implementation Guide. In this busy world it is easy to skip much of the documentation that comes with applications, but this guide is worth its weight in gold and is worth reading a few times!

If you choose to ignore the Microsoft Dynamics CRM implementation documentation, you do so at high risk and are pretty much guaranteed future headaches and heartaches.

Watch Out!

The implementation guide is available online in both download (www.microsoft.com/downloads/en/details.aspx?FamilyID=9886ab96-3571-420f-83ad-246899482fb4) and instant-read format (http://msdn.microsoft.com/en-us/library/gg269274.aspx).

Microsoft Dynamics CRM Application Software

The Microsoft Dynamics CRM program files are generally installed to a designated CRM server. The installation design and the architecture of the application take into consideration that independent software vendors (ISVs), Microsoft Dynamics partners, and Microsoft Dynamics CRM customers will extend, modify, customize, and configure the core application.

In addition, the architecture of the software platform takes into consideration that long-term ongoing updates and upgrades will be part of the solution and will be released from the Microsoft Dynamics CRM development team on a regular basis. Further considerations in design provide for the need of the hosting providers and the Microsoft CRM Online team, which have one set of shared CRM application software and yet many different instances of Microsoft Dynamics CRM databases (that is, many tenants).

Microsoft Dynamics CRM SQL Server Databases

Microsoft Dynamics CRM stores all its data in a Microsoft SQL Server database environment. You can find out more about Microsoft Dynamics SQL Server 2008 and earlier versions at www.microsoft.com/sqlserver/en/us/default.aspx.

Watch
Out!

A Caution for Those Familiar with Microsoft SQL Server
For those familiar with Microsoft SQL Server, there is one key fact to keep in mind when working with Microsoft Dynamics CRM and Microsoft SQL Server: Data within the world of Microsoft Dynamics CRM is designed to be secure. It has specific rules related to it that are driven by the security rules defined in Microsoft Dynamics CRM, the business unit configuration defined in Microsoft Dynamics CRM, and the user authentication set up through Windows Server. Given all these variables, it is a bad idea and highly unsupported to directly add data to the Microsoft Dynamics CRM SQL Server databases or change any of the data within the databases through any method other than using the Microsoft Dynamics CRM software and software extensions designed with knowledge of Microsoft Dynamics CRM. Making such changes is unsupported and can cause significant data corruption and application issues.

Microsoft Dynamics CRM uses a concept called *filtered views*. Data is served up by a filtered view to honor security roles. These filtered views can be used to display data in a number of different formats.

In terms of database versions, Microsoft Dynamics CRM 2011 supports the use of either Microsoft SQL Server 2005 or Microsoft SQL Server 2008 or above. Microsoft SQL Server 2008's upgrade path focused on business intelligence, graphical displays of data, and analysis; so, if these items are important to you, consider upgrading the core database engine.

Multitenant Support

Microsoft Dynamics CRM 2011 provides support for multiple tenants. Multitenant support allows hosting companies to efficiently offer Microsoft Dynamics CRM within the world of the large, shared, and secured data center. In addition, large companies that want to offer multiple instances of CRM can do so by using the multitenant feature. When using a tenant of a multitenant environment, there are a few considerations, particularly if you are adding your own custom additions:

▶ A few of the pieces of Microsoft Dynamics CRM 2011 continue to be shared and have not yet been upgraded to multitenant. For example, the core Microsoft Dynamics CRM Help files reside with the Microsoft Dynamics CRM application directory. You can customize Help, but the customizations will be seen by all users of the Microsoft Dynamics CRM software. Help is configured to allow you to add documentation to specific new custom entities, but on a wide search others might see this new documentation.

▶ Any changes to the core application files will impact everyone sharing these files. This is one reason you are not allowed to upload your own custom software to extend the application if you are a Microsoft Dynamics CRM Online customer.

▶ Allowing outside code on internal servers is risky at best.

Microsoft SQL Reporting Services

When you access the standard reports in Microsoft Dynamics CRM (from the Reports menu), you are accessing reports that were created in CRM using Microsoft SQL Reporting Services (SRS). Figure 4.1 shows a list of some standard Microsoft SRS reports.

Other reporting choices include the Microsoft Dynamics CRM Ad Hoc Report Wizard that is built into the software, fetch-based custom reports, report authoring extension for BIDS, and integration to Microsoft Office, including Excel, through security-enabled dynamic Excel spreadsheets and Word. For more on reporting, see Hour 20, "Utilizing the Power of Microsoft Excel with CRM Data," and Hour 21, "Reporting and Query Basics."

FIGURE 4.1
Reports from
Microsoft SRS.

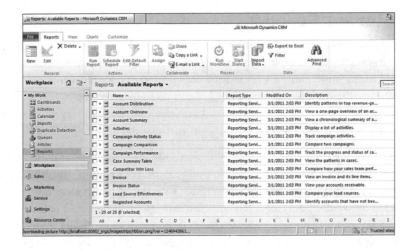

Microsoft Windows Server and Microsoft Dynamics CRM

On-Premises Microsoft Dynamics CRM requires Microsoft Windows Server and other components that have been mentioned in this hour.

If you are a CRM On-Premises customer, when you open Microsoft Dynamics CRM, the system does not ask you for a username and password. Why not? Microsoft Dynamics CRM already knows who you are, based on the fact that you were already authenticated to your company's environment via Active Directory when you logged in to your computer.

The CRM security model uses Windows-based authentication (Kerberos/NTLM) and internally driven authorization. It also offers further role-based layers of enhanced security, based on additional configuration options. In Hour 5, "Security," you dive into the details of the application security.

Microsoft Dynamics CRM E-mail Router Software

Microsoft Dynamics CRM offers an independent and yet integrated solution to sharing e-mail with Microsoft Exchange; this option is available for both On-Premises and Online environments. The Microsoft Dynamics CRM e-mail router can live independently and yet definitely has an interest in all the mail coming into Microsoft Exchange. You also have the option of not using the Microsoft Dynamics CRM e-mail router, choosing instead to configure Outlook to communicate directly. If you configure Outlook, you must configure each and every user and his or her instance of Outlook to track e-mail. Using the Microsoft Dynamics CRM e-mail router is more efficient. For a conceptual peek, look at Figure 4.2.

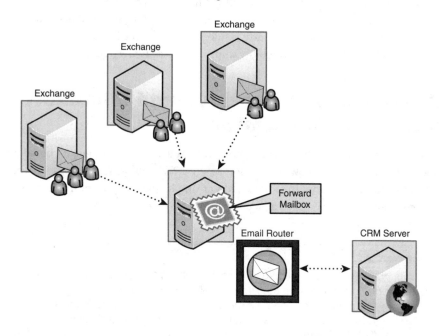

FIGURE 4.2
The e-mail router in a multiple-Exchange environment.

Microsoft Dynamics CRM Outlook Clients

There are two Microsoft Dynamics CRM Outlook clients. The first is the Microsoft Dynamics CRM Outlook client, which supports the ability to go offline and is designed for a laptop environment. This piece of software has continual drip synchronization between the Microsoft Dynamics CRM database and the local laptop Microsoft SQL database. This design allows a user to undock a laptop without specifically choosing Go Offline. This creates more overhead, so you do not want to install the Microsoft Dynamics CRM Outlook client for the laptop where it is not needed (such as on a desktop machine).

The second version of the Microsoft Dynamics CRM Outlook client is designed for a desktop machine or a Citrix or terminal server environment. This version of the software allows multiple users using the same machine to work with the Microsoft Dynamics CRM Outlook client, and it has less overhead because it does not need to communicate with a local copy of a Microsoft SQL database.

Microsoft Dynamics CRM Mobile Express

The Microsoft Dynamics CRM mobile client, called Mobile Express for Microsoft Dynamics CRM 2011, is included with all version of the software. If the Microsoft-released mobile client doesn't meet your needs, you can find powerful and extremely well-proven solutions from third-party vendors, such as Ten Digits (www.tendigits.com), CWR Mobility (www.cwrmobility.com), and Resco (www.resco.net).

Asynchronous Services and Microsoft Workflow Foundation

One of the key powers of Microsoft Dynamics CRM is the workflow engine based on Microsoft Windows Workflow Foundation (WWF). WWF allows for a number of different functionalities, from the automation of simple and complex business rules to the more advanced programming logic required for parallel processing.

> **Microsoft .NET 4.0**
>
> A major goal of the latest release of Microsoft .NET 4.0 is to make WWF a standard part of the programming toolkit for all .NET developers, from small businesses to enterprises. You can read more about this at http://msdn.microsoft.com/en-us/library/dd851337.aspx and at http://msdn.microsoft.com/en-us/magazine/ff714593.aspx.

Microsoft Dynamics CRM takes WWF one step beyond just being a tool for programmers. Microsoft Dynamics CRM makes WWF a user-enabled built-in function, empowering users who are not necessarily programmers to automate and organize. Microsoft Dynamics CRM also takes the power of WWF and automates more and more processes, using a concept called *dialogs*.

When it comes to the infrastructure and the moving parts of Microsoft WWF, one of the key building blocks of Microsoft Dynamics CRM is the asynchronous services. The asynchronous services execute long-running operations independent of the main Microsoft Dynamics CRM system process. They are often associated with Microsoft WWF and a component of things such as queue processing. They can also be hosted on a different server, thus taking the load off the main CRM server in enterprise architecture. The Microsoft Dynamics CRM Software Development Kit (SDK) is a great place to learn more about the asynchronous services used by Microsoft Dynamics CRM. The SDK is available for download, or you can access the asynchronous services section directly from http://msdn.microsoft.com/en-us/library/gg309408.aspx.

Diving into Development

We can't leave this hour without commenting on the potential for experienced developers to become masters of Microsoft Dynamics xRM development.

xRM

xRM stands for *relationship management software*, where the x might mean something other than a customer (as in CRM). Microsoft Dynamics CRM is an xRM development platform.

An example of an xRM solution includes configuring Microsoft Dynamics CRM to manage staffing and human resources or building an xRM solution to manage buildings, rental agreements, leases, and tenants.

Developers diving into the world of Microsoft Dynamics CRM have a number of areas of expertise to master, and here are just a few of them:

► Extending the core Microsoft Dynamics CRM code

► Using Microsoft WWF

► Using form- and field-based scripting and scripts

► Integrating with Silverlight

► Using Microsoft SharePoint also known as Windows SharePoint Server and Microsoft Office SharePoint Server (WSS/MOSS) for complementary unstructured data support

► Integrating with the world of finance and enterprise resource planning (ERP), using products such as Dynamics AX, Dynamics GP, Dynamics NAV, and Dynamics SL

► Charting, using dashboards, and using business intelligence tools and techniques

► Taking advantage of mobility, such as creating Windows Phone 7 or Windows Slate integrations

► Making changes to the Microsoft Dynamics CRM Outlook client

Integration Options

What about connecting with all the other applications we use? Microsoft Dynamics CRM is built for and often expects long-term integration. Just as salt goes with pepper, Microsoft Dynamics CRM goes with many other complementary applications, from other Microsoft departments, outside vendors, or Microsoft partners. Hour 22, "Integrating Microsoft Dynamics CRM 2011 into Other Applications," Hour 23, "Microsoft Dynamics CRM Tools and Utilities," and Hour 24, "Microsoft Dynamics CRM as a Development Framework," take an in-depth look at the world of integration.

Big Business Versus Small Business

When it comes to managing the hardware and infrastructure installation of Microsoft Dynamics CRM in small business, the balance is delicate. Microsoft Dynamics CRM integrates with many other applications, the operating system, and core functionality. If you layer this on top of a single server, the hardware needs to be beefy enough to handle the extra layer. There is good reason to outsource the hosting of Microsoft Dynamics CRM in the world of small business—not only because of hardware but because of the labor required to maintain this new layer of integration. Just as many small businesses do not host their own websites, hosting a web-based application for just a tiny little business might not be worth the investment.

In the world of big business, there may be many people and departments to juggle, and the interconnection between who is doing what and when is a key factor for getting things done. The functions of Microsoft Dynamics CRM within big business might be divided among different roles and departments, such as the marketing department using the marketing functions and features, the service department focused on service scheduling and cases, and the sales department using the sales features. This division of labor doesn't always mean the division of information. In big business, security layers become even more important, as does the security offering. Needs for role-based, feature, and function and division security are not uncommon.

Now that you have a better understanding of many of the choices surrounding Microsoft Dynamics CRM installation and use, let's dive into a workshop including a few questions for review.

Workshop

Chase Boats is a company that manages the funding and sponsorship of crews and tall ships entered into various worldwide races. Given that races are held all over the world, Chase Boats needed a CRM software package that could handle multiple currencies, localized dates and time, and the organization and management of potential sponsorship income. Chase Boats already had a good accounting system managed by its accounting firm, but it wanted a CRM product that could empower each staff member to be more organized, more collaborative, and more responsive to the sponsors and crews that they work with. Charlie Chase is the CEO of Chase Boats. He accesses his Microsoft Dynamics CRM software from all over the world; his company uses Microsoft Dynamics CRM Online. In addition, because Charlie might spend a month or two in different countries, he sets Microsoft Dynamics CRM to the country he is in and immediately gets localized settings.

Chase Boats also has employees who reside in different locations. When a big race is happening, Charlie works closely with the employees in numerous locations to coordinate logistics. Microsoft Dynamics CRM e-mail and activity tracking allow Charlie to quickly see all the conversations from around the world that are happening with any given sponsor or crew member.

Q&A

Q. *Our Microsoft Dynamics CRM software is having difficulties. It seems like we keep having issues. What might be the problem?*

A. Microsoft Dynamics CRM needs to be installed correctly by an experienced Microsoft Dynamics CRM administrator and managed by an experienced network administrator.

Q. *We are waffling between Microsoft Dynamics CRM Online and Microsoft Dynamics CRM On-Premises. Are there any other resources to help us decide?*

A. Talk with one or two Microsoft Dynamics CRM partners and the Microsoft Dynamics CRM Online Team. This choice can be determined based on key factors, such as whether you need to create complex extensions to the software or the resources that are available for you to manage the infrastructure. You might also consider talking with one of the many Microsoft Dynamics CRM users. Microsoft gives you the ability to move your data between systems in case you at some point decide to switch.

Q. *What are some of the best resources for our people to get more training?*

A. Some of the Microsoft Dynamics CRM boot camps are excellent. You can also build your own library of reading materials from a set of available books on Microsoft Dynamics CRM and from the material available on the Microsoft websites and at the bookstores.

Quiz

1. What is one reason a large corporation might want to use Microsoft Dynamics CRM Online rather than Microsoft Dynamics CRM On-Premises?

2. What is one benefit that Charlie Chase gets out of using Microsoft Dynamics CRM?

3. Name three other applications that Microsoft Dynamics CRM might work well with.

4. What can't you do in the world of Microsoft Dynamics CRM Online?

5. What does *multitenant* mean?

6. What are two areas that a developer new to Microsoft Dynamics CRM can choose to master?

Answers

1. Microsoft Dynamics CRM Online offers the application without requiring a skilled infrastructure specialists and hardware requirements needed for a robust On-Premises application.

2. Charlie Chase depends on the localization of dates and time, as well as the management and handling of multiple currencies associated with his products and services.

3. Microsoft Excel, Microsoft Office SharePoint Services, and Microsoft Word are three other applications that Microsoft Dynamics CRM works well with.

4. In the world of Microsoft Dynamics CRM Online, you can't import custom Microsoft SQL Server Reporting Service reports.

5. *Multitenant* means that you have the ability to have many different instances of Microsoft Dynamics CRM databases sharing the same set of core application program files.

6. Two of the areas that a developer new to Microsoft Dynamics CRM can master are the core Microsoft Dynamics CRM .NET code, Silverlight, and form- and field-based scripts.

Exercise

Download the Microsoft Dynamics CRM Implementation Guide and the Microsoft Dynamics CRM SDK. Spend some time familiarizing yourself with key areas of these two documents. You might not be a software developer or the person or team responsible for installing the software, but these two documents offer real insight in a number of areas.

HOUR 5

Security

What You'll Learn in This Hour:

- ▶ How it all comes together
- ▶ Business units
- ▶ Users
- ▶ Security roles
- ▶ Maintaining security roles
- ▶ Sharing records
- ▶ Teams
- ▶ Field security

The Microsoft Dynamics CRM security model is extremely comprehensive and has been designed to protect data integrity, provide an efficient mechanism for accessing data, and facilitate easy collaboration.

Microsoft's goals for the security model include the following:

- ▶ Provide users with access only to the information required to perform their job functions

- ▶ Categorize types of users to define roles and restrict access based on those roles

- ▶ Support data sharing for collaboration so that users can be explicitly granted access to data they do not own

Successfully implementing security in Microsoft Dynamics CRM requires an understanding of the four core elements that make up the security model:

- ▶ Business units
- ▶ Users
- ▶ Security roles
- ▶ Teams

Figure 5.1 shows where these four elements are located on the Administration interface, which is accessible from the Settings menu.

FIGURE 5.1
Where to access business units, users, security roles, and teams.

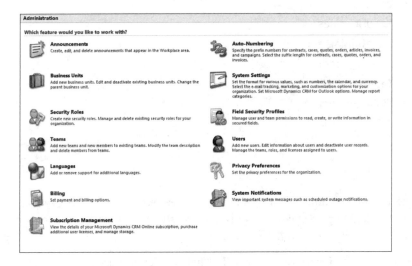

All people (users) who access your Microsoft Dynamics CRM system must be uniquely identified. The system must know where they sit in the organization structure (business unit) and what they are allowed to do (security role) once logged in.

By the Way

> **Can't Log In Without This**
>
> All three pieces of information must be defined for a person to log in to the system. If a user is unable to log in, check that he or she is enabled, has been assigned to a business unit, and has a security role.

Both users and security roles are stored in a business unit. Therefore, when you add a user to the system, you must define the business unit that user belongs to and the user's security role within that designated business unit. It is possible to have different/unique security roles within each business unit, but it is not a recommended practice. (We discuss this in more detail in the "Security Roles" section.)

Business units form the basis of your organization structure, and it is helpful to work from an organizational chart when setting these up. However, it is important to remember that a key reason you are building this hierarchical structure is to govern access to data. The structure you build in Microsoft Dynamics CRM might not directly match your physical organizational structure. You want to ensure that your users have access to all the information they require to perform their job function, but you also want to be able to limit access to any sensitive data.

Teams provide a mechanism to establish collective groups in CRM. Teams may also own records. (We discuss this in more detail in the "Teams" section.) Before we delve into the security model itself, it's important that you understand how data is referenced in Microsoft Dynamics CRM so that you can better understand how and where you might need to control access to it. There are two kinds of data records in Microsoft Dynamics CRM:

- ▶ **User/team owned**—User/team-owned records are typically records that relate to a customer (for example, a lead, an account, a contact, an opportunity, an order, an invoice, a case, a contract, activities). Typically, these types of records are managed by or actioned by users.

- ▶ **Organization owned**—Organization-owned records are typically records that are used for reference data and are associated with a business unit (for example, a product, services, queues, teams, resources). In other words, they are not directly related to or associated with any user.

By the Way

Exception to the Rule

Three special items in CRM can be created:

- ▶ Reports
- ▶ Mail merge templates
- ▶ E-mail templates

By default they are individually owned, but they may be promoted to the organization.

Individual security privileges govern whether users can create these items. A separate privilege also exists to determine whether a user can promote individual security privileges to the organization.

Every record in Microsoft Dynamics CRM is automatically marked with its respective "owner." When you access Microsoft Dynamics CRM and select any of the key customer-related record types (lead, account, contact, opportunity, and so on), by default you are provided with a list of "your" records. This is because the default view (My Active Contacts) filters and selects records owned only by you to help you focus on those you manage.

Figure 5.2 highlights how, by default, Microsoft Dynamics CRM filters records wherever possible to simplify finding and accessing the records that relate to a particular user.

FIGURE 5.2
Records filtered
by owner.

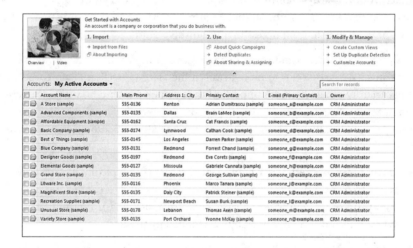

The owner of a record is displayed on the Administration tab of the record itself; although it is possible to change the owner of a record, the ability to do this is governed by a *security privilege* within the security role, which allows control over who can perform this kind of function.

Figure 5.3 shows where the owner identification is located for each record.

The concept of security privileges is key to the Microsoft Dynamics CRM security model.

FIGURE 5.3
A record owner displayed in the Administration section.

itself, which is made up of ction that can be performed

How It All Comes Together

W   ss unit, user, and security
ro

Yo   hese you add users. This
gi   ever, you have not
decided what users are permitted to do or what they can access because that information comes from the security role. Remember that security is primarily determined by the security role, not by which business unit a user is assigned to.

A security role is three dimensional, but we will first look at it in a two-dimensional way and build on what we learn.

Table 5.1 illustrates how a two-dimensional security role, as a matrix of actions against specific record types (entities), might look.

TABLE 5.1 If Security Roles Were Two Dimensional

	Create	Read	Write	Delete	Etc.
Account	Yes	Yes	Yes	No	
Contact	Yes	Yes	Yes	No	
Opportunity	Yes	Yes	Yes	No	
Case	No	Yes	No	No	
Activity	Yes	Yes	Yes	Yes	
Etc.					

If the security role were just two dimensional, you would not be able to define which set of records a user may perform this action (because there is no qualification). In Table 5.1, the action for Write Opportunity is Yes, which would give the ability to update any opportunity in the system. However, in reality, it is more likely that *only* the salesperson who is managing that opportunity would be allowed to update it. So you might want to restrict the Write privilege to only those records that the user owns. This is where the third dimension, or "qualifier," comes into play and completes the picture of the security role. The qualifier allows you to grant privileges to specific sets of records (for example, opportunities that the user owns).

Table 5.2 shows how the two-dimensional Yes/No actions have been replaced with qualifiers to give the three-dimensional aspect, exactly as they appear in Microsoft Dynamics CRM.

TABLE 5.2 Sample Microsoft Dynamics CRM Security Role Structure

	Create	Read	Write	Delete	Etc.
Account	■	■	■	○	
Contact	■	■	■	○	
Opportunity	■	■	◔	○	
Case	○	■	○	○	
Activity	■	■	◔	■	
Etc.					

Key:
Organization (systemwide)—(■)
User (own data only)—(◔)
None—(○)

Table 5.2 explicitly declares the appropriate action on a particular set of data records. For example, users can do the following:

▶ Read any account, contact, opportunity, case, or activity in the entire Microsoft Dynamics CRM system

Terminology

The action Write refers to the ability to update (change) a record.

▶ Update any account or contact in the entire Microsoft Dynamics CRM, but not a case, and only update opportunities and activities they own

Table 5.2 is for example purposes only and does not cover all the possible privileges. We cover the full extent of the security role later. However, these principles form the basis of the security role concepts.

Tailoring Security Roles to Match Job Roles

It is important to understand that certain actions can apply to some users who perform a specific job function but not to others within your organization. This is why Microsoft Dynamics CRM provides the capability to define many security roles so that you can tailor each role to apply to a particular job function/role within your organization.

Business Units

The top-level business unit is automatically created when your Microsoft Dynamics CRM system is provisioned and has the name of your organization. (This is the only one that does not have a parent.)

A business unit can be defined as a subsidiary, a division, an operating unit, a branch office, and so forth, depending on how your specific organization is structured.

There is nothing wrong with having a single business unit (the default) and every user in your organization sitting in that one business unit. Although not a rule, it is often the case that, for smaller organizations, it makes sense to have everyone in the same business unit because the lines of demarcation between job roles and responsibilities are often blurred and overlap (because people tend to wear many hats in smaller companies). In such a situation, you need to make sure that people have access to all the information they need to fulfill the roles they perform. If you initially place every user in the same business unit, you can at any time in the future add business units and move users as required.

Creating a business unit is a straightforward process. In Figure 5.4, you can see a list of existing business units, and from here, you can click the New button in the ribbon to create a new business unit (see Figure 5.5).

FIGURE 5.4
A list of existing business units.

FIGURE 5.5
Creating a new business unit.

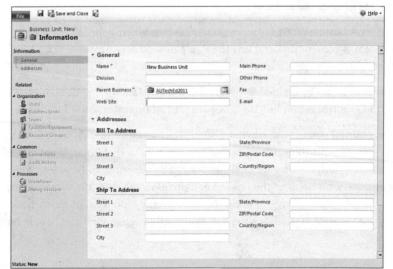

Reorganizing Your Business Unit Hierarchy

It is possible to reorganize your business unit hierarchy. (Any business unit, except the top-level parent, can be repointed to a different parent business unit.) There are two methods for doing this:

▶ From the list of all business units, highlight the one that needs to change. Click the More Actions button in the ribbon, select Change Parent Business, and select the new parent from the dialog box.

▶ From the list of all business units, double-click the required business unit to open the record. Click the Actions button in the ribbon, select Change Parent Business, and select the new parent from the dialog box.

Business Unit Naming and Renaming Cautions

Remember: If you want to delete a business unit, you *must* disable it first.

By the Way

Users

Users represent each and every person who will access a Microsoft Dynamics CRM system. For an On-Premises deployment, each user is uniquely identified by a network logon identifier and, in the case of Microsoft Dynamics CRM Online, by their Windows Live ID.

For Microsoft Dynamics CRM Online, there is only one license. For Microsoft Dynamics CRM On-Premises installations, there are both client and server licenses. For client licenses, there are three different scenarios for a user license, and this information is stored in the user record itself. The type of client access license (CAL) determines what users can do with Microsoft Dynamics CRM. Organizations usually have a limited number of each type of CAL. A CAL is licensable, and it is the responsibility of each organization to ensure that it has licensed sufficient numbers of CALs for its users. A CAL is required for each user, except those with only administrative access. When a user is created in Microsoft Dynamics CRM, you need to specific which type of CAL that user will be assigned:

▶ **Full**—The user will have full access to any part of Microsoft Dynamics CRM that he or she has the security roles and privileges to access.

▶ **Administrative**—The user will have read-only access to the Sales, Marketing, and Service areas and full access to the Settings area. This type does not consume a CAL.

▶ **Read-only**—The user will have read-only access to the Sales, Marketing, and Service areas that he or she has the security roles and privileges to access.

There is also an employee self-service CAL, which grants limited API access, designed for employee self-service in managing leads, cases, and so on via an internal portal application.

Every organization is different, and therefore it is strongly recommended that each organization consult with its licensing provider to determine the exact needs and requirements for Microsoft Dynamics CRM licensing for its situation.

> **CALs Can Either Be Assigned to Users or Devices**
>
> For On-Premises deployments, Microsoft allows a CAL to be assigned to a device rather than to a named user. This is useful for organizations that have a lot of part-time workers or shift workers (for example, call centers).

Depending on whether you are using Microsoft Dynamics CRM On-Premises or Microsoft Dynamics CRM Online, there are two slightly different procedures for creating users. In both cases, you need some minimum pieces of information before you can create the users:

▶ Network login and e-mail address (for CRM On-Premises) or Windows Live ID (for CRM Online)

▶ First and last name of user

▶ Business unit

Each user must be assigned to a business unit (which defaults to the top-level unit), and this is automatically set for CRM Online users. This can be changed at a later date, if required (as discussed later in this hour).

Creating CRM On-Premises Users

You can access users from the Microsoft Dynamics CRM Administration page. Figure 5.6 shows a list of existing users.

When you click the New button in the ribbon to create a new user, you are presented with two options (see Figure 5.7): You can either add a single user or multiple users.

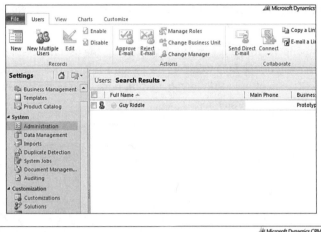

FIGURE 5.6
A list of exist-
ing users.

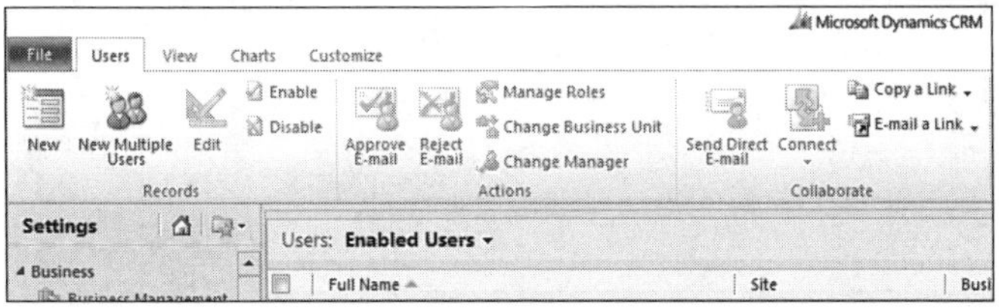

FIGURE 5.7
Options pre-
sented for cre-
ating users.

Option 1: Adding a Single User

You can click User to add a single user to the system. When you do, you are presented with the user interface shown in Figure 5.8.

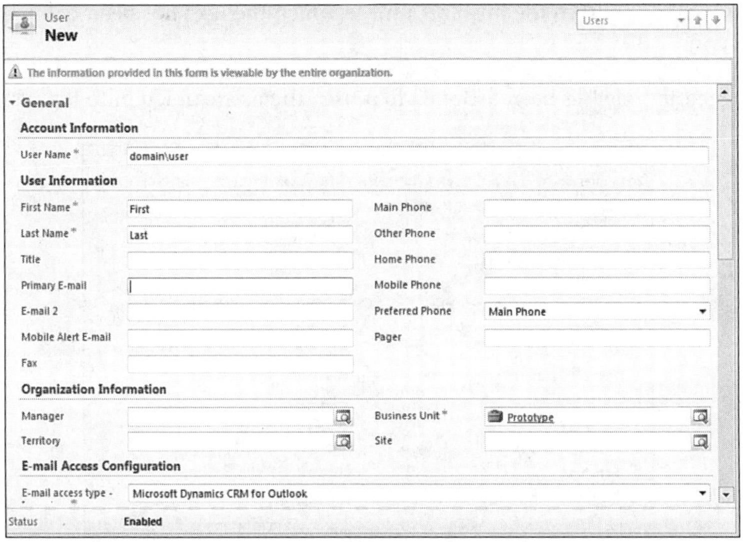

FIGURE 5.8
Adding a user.

Using this method, you must select the correct business unit; it will default to the top-level business unit in your hierarchy.

You must also append to the user a security role after the user has been created; otherwise, the user will not be able to access the system. To add a security role to the user, click the Roles button in the side navigation pane. The User's Roles interface will appear, as shown in Figure 5.9.

FIGURE 5.9
A user's
security roles.

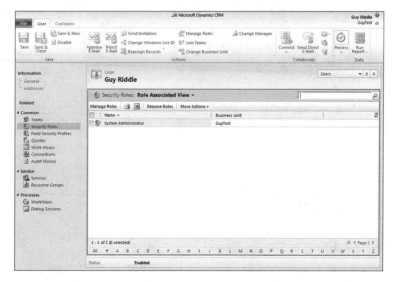

To add a security role, click Manage Roles in the toolbar. A dialog appears, in which you can select an appropriate security role for the user from the list of security roles available within the business unit to which the user has been assigned (see Figure 5.10).

After a security role has been assigned to a user, the user can log in to the system.

FIGURE 5.10
Available
security roles.

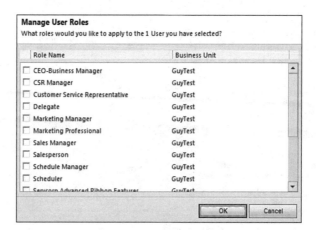

Option 2: Adding Multiple Users

You can click Multiple Users to create one or several users at one time. Note that when you choose this option to create new users, they will all be created with same values for business unit, security roles, and license type.

If you choose this method, you are taken through a wizard to define the new users, as shown in Figures 5.11 through 5.15.

FIGURE 5.11
Wizard step 1: Choosing a business unit.

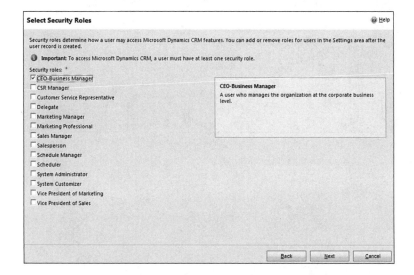

FIGURE 5.12
Wizard step 2: Choosing security roles.

FIGURE 5.13
Wizard step 3:
Selecting the
license type.

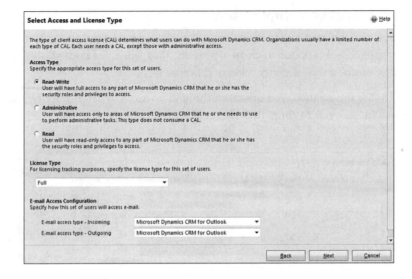

FIGURE 5.14
Wizard step 4:
Selecting users
from domains
or groups.

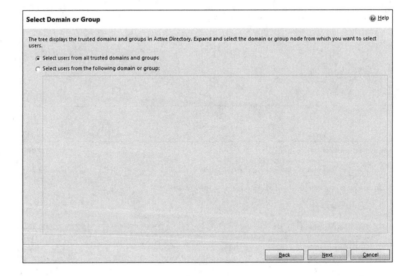

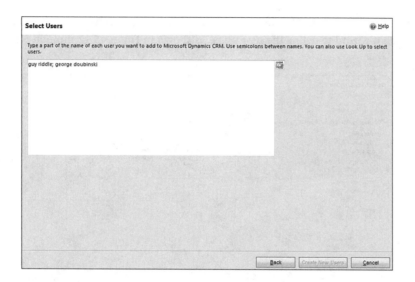

FIGURE 5.15
Wizard step 5:
Selecting users.

After all your users have been selected from your domains/groups, you can click the Create New Users button to have them all created as Microsoft Dynamics CRM users.

Creating Microsoft Dynamics CRM Online Users

You can access users from the Microsoft Dynamics CRM Administration page. Figure 5.16 shows a list of existing users.

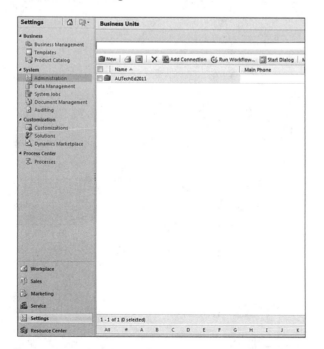

FIGURE 5.16
A list of existing users.

When you click the New button in the ribbon to create a new user, you are taken through a wizard to define the new users, as shown in Figures 5.17 through 5.19.

FIGURE 5.17
Wizard step 1:
Choosing security roles.

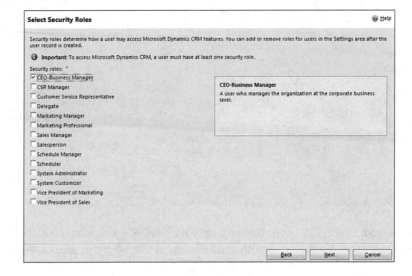

FIGURE 5.18
Wizard step 2:
Adding users.

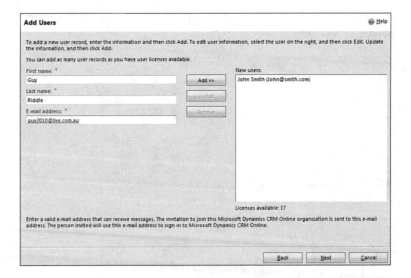

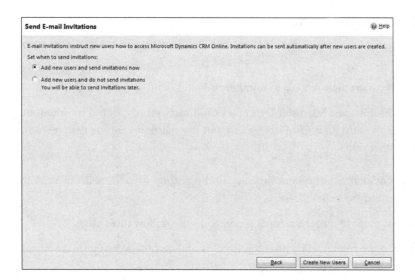

FIGURE 5.19
Wizard step 3:
Sending e-mail
invitations.

On the wizard page, you can enter the details of one or many users you want to add to the system. At the bottom of the screen, you will see the available number of licenses decrease as you add more users.

You can choose not to send invitations, but it is recommended that you do so in order that the user receives an e-mail with the correct URL to access your Microsoft Dynamics CRM system. If you choose not to send invitations now, you can send them later. This is done from the users list view (refer to Figure 5.16). You just select the users you want to send the invitation to, click the More Actions button in the ribbon, and then choose the Send Invitation option.

After you decide on your preferred option for sending e-mail invitations, you click the Create New Users button to have them all created as Microsoft Dynamics CRM users.

How to Change the Business Unit of a User

From the list of all users, you double-click the required user to open the record. Then you click the Change Business Unit button in the ribbon and then select the new parent from the dialog box.

Note that the same procedure applies if you have assigned the user a manager and want to change this assignment later.

By the Way

User Administration

When users leave your organization, you should carry out a few housekeeping functions:

▶ Reassign their records to another user.

▶ Disable their Microsoft Dynamics CRM user records. Doing so automatically frees up their CRM licenses so that these licenses can be assigned to other users.

In the navigation pane, click Settings. In the Settings area, click Business Unit Settings and then click Users.

To reassign all of a user's records to someone else, follow these steps:

1. On the ribbon, click Reassign Records and then click Assign to Another User or Team.

2. From the lookup dialog select User or Team from the drop-down list.

3. Click the Lookup icon, type a part of the other user's name, and click Find.

4. In the results list, double-click the user's name and then click OK.

To deactivate a record, follow these steps:

1. Find and open the user record for the departing person.

2. On the ribbon, click Disable and then click OK. The system allows you to disable a user who owns records. The user stays in the system but is deactivated.

By the Way

> **You Can Change the Information You Capture About Your Users**
>
> The Microsoft Dynamics CRM record type User is customizable. You can therefore extend the information that is captured about a user by using standard Microsoft Dynamics CRM customization techniques.
>
> However, remember that any user record is visible to all users in the system.

Security Roles

Security roles govern what a user can do after he or she is granted access to the system. Microsoft Dynamics CRM ships with 14 predefined security roles, together comprising more than 350 individual security privileges:

▶ Shipped Security Role

▶ CEO-Business Manager

▶ CSR Manager

▶ Customer Service Representative

▶ Delegate

▶ Marketing Manager

▶ Marketing Professional

▶ Sales Manager

▶ Salesperson

▶ Schedule Manager

▶ Scheduler

▶ System Administrator

▶ System Customizer

▶ Vice President of Marketing

▶ Vice President of Sales

Generally, the components of a security role fall into two categories:

▶ **Entity**—Relates to a record type of data/information captured and entered into the system (for example, account, contact, product, quote, case, activity) and typically maintained by our users

▶ **System features**—Specific functions that you can perform within the system (print, export to Excel, import data, mail merge, override quote pricing, and so on)

When it comes to understanding the security role, you have to understand how the privileges for them are defined. System features are simple: You can or you can't perform the privilege. On the other hand, with entity privileges, you have to qualify where the privilege may be performed. An entity privilege has three elements: entity (record type), action, and access level (qualifier).

Actions

You can perform eight actions on any given entity (record type). The security role must know all of these for every entity. Table 5.3 shows the actions that a user may perform against any given entity.

TABLE 5.3   List of Actions

Action	Description
Create	Creates a new record.
Read	Views or open an existing record.
Write	Saves changes to an existing record.
Delete	Deletes an existing record.
Append	Appends (attaches) this record to another record.
Append To	Appends (attaches) other records to this record. The Append and Append To privileges typically work in conjunction with each other. For example, if you want to add a note to an account, you must have the Append privilege on the note and the Attend To privilege on the account.
Assign	Assigns this record to another user.
Share	Shares this record with another user (or team).

Access Levels

Five access levels (qualifiers) define the set of records on which a user can perform the respective action. Table 5.4 shows the list of access levels to determine where a user could perform an action against any given entity.

TABLE 5.4   List of Access Levels

Access Level	Symbol	Description
Organization	■	Can perform this privilege on any record in the system
Parent/child	◕	Can perform this privilege on any records in the same business unit as the user and any records in any child business units sitting under the user's business unit
Business unit	◒	Can perform this privilege on any records in the same business unit as the user
User	◔	Can only perform this privilege on records owned by the user
None	○	No access to perform this privilege at all

Table 5.5 shows a list of sample privileges to highlight how the three elements come together to define a privilege.

TABLE 5.5   Privileges

Entity	Action	Access Level	Result
Account	Write	Organization	Can update any account record in the entire system
Contact	Write	User	Can only update contacts that are owned by the user
Opportunity	Read	Business unit	Can only read opportunities that are owned by the user and any that are in the same business unit
Activity	Delete	User	Can delete any activities that are owned by the user

TABLE 5.5 Privileges

Entity	Action	Access Level	Result
Contract	Read	None	Has no access to view any contracts at all (and therefore this option will disappear from any screen where it would normally appear for that user)*

As a user navigates through Microsoft Dynamics CRM, each user interface is dynamically rendered, based on the security privileges within their security role. This means that if a user does not have the privilege to perform a system function or access certain types of data records, those corresponding buttons on the user interfaces will disappear.

In the case of system features, privileges are based on the ability to perform the function; in the case of entities, it is based on the Read privilege. For example, if you set the Export to Excel privilege to None, the button will disappear from every user interface to which in normally applies. If you set the invoice entity Read privilege to None, the user will not see the Invoice button on any user interface in the system.

Changing the security for users is the process that is recommended for removing unwanted items from the user interface for each of your users and their security roles as required.

By the Way

> **Users Can Have More Than One Security Role**
>
> It is permissible for a user to be granted more than one security role. In this case, you might find that a conflict arises. If this happens, Microsoft Dynamics CRM always applies the least restrictive principle. For example, if you give a user Role A that denies a specific permission, but you also give him a second Role B that grants the permission, using the least restrictive principle, he will be granted permission.

Maintaining Security Roles

Although Microsoft Dynamics CRM provides 14 "out of the box" security roles, you do not have to use them. In fact, you can define your own security roles from scratch, or you can modify any of the shipped roles. Both of these capabilities are possible, but it is highly recommended that you at least start with a default role, clone it, and then modify that role. This is a much more reliable and recommended practice. Preserving the original roles (even if you don't use them) allows you to go back and reference them if ever you need to in the future. The best practice is to copy an existing role and then modify it to meet your exact requirements. That way you only have to make changes by exception.

Reviewing the Shipped Security Roles Before You Use Them

By default, every shipped security role (except System Customizer) permits the user to do the following

▶ Read almost every record in the entire system

▶ Delete any record that the users owns

Therefore, you should review all the security roles to ensure that they meet your requirements before using them.

You can edit any of the default security roles except the System Administrator role.

You can access security roles from the Microsoft Dynamics CRM Administration page. Figure 5.20 shows a list of existing security roles.

FIGURE 5.20
A list of existing security roles.

From the list of existing security roles, you can highlight which role you want to copy, click More Actions in the toolbar, and select the Copy Role option.

You can also provide a name for the new security role you are creating (see Figure 5.21).

FIGURE 5.21
Naming a new
security role.

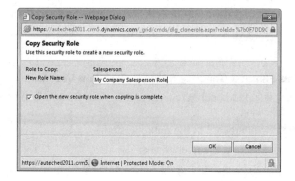

If you leave the Open the New Security Role When Copying Is Complete check box selected, the new role will automatically open for you after it is created (see Figure 5.22).

FIGURE 5.22
A security role.

Because more than 350 privileges make up a security role, there are too many to display on one screen. Therefore, the privileges have been grouped logically onto individual tabs. Figures 5.23 through 5.30 show the privileges for the default Salesperson security role.

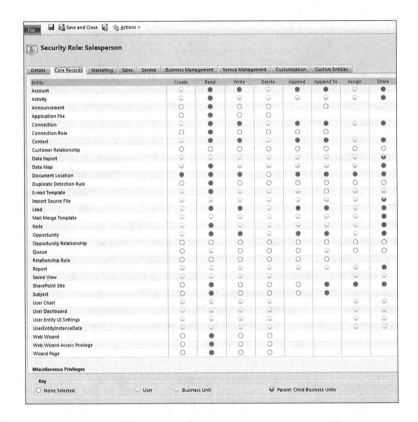

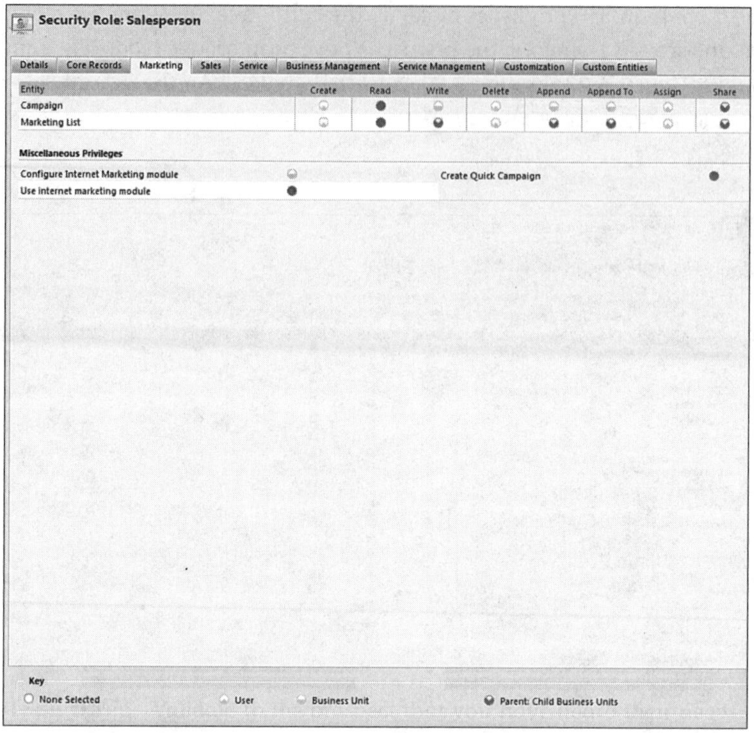

FIGURE 5.24
The Marketing
tab for the
Salesperson
role.

FIGURE 5.25
The Sales
tab for the
Salesperson
role.

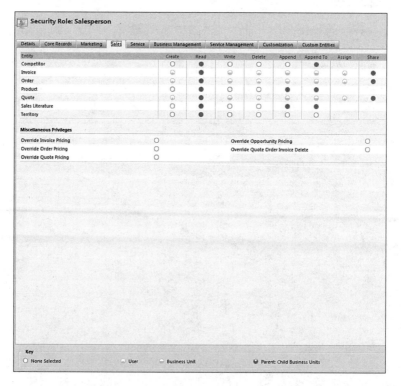

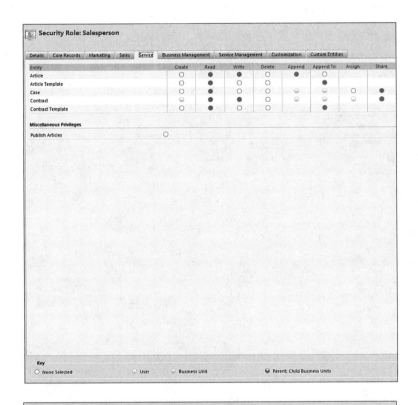

FIGURE 5.26
The Service tab for the Salesperson role.

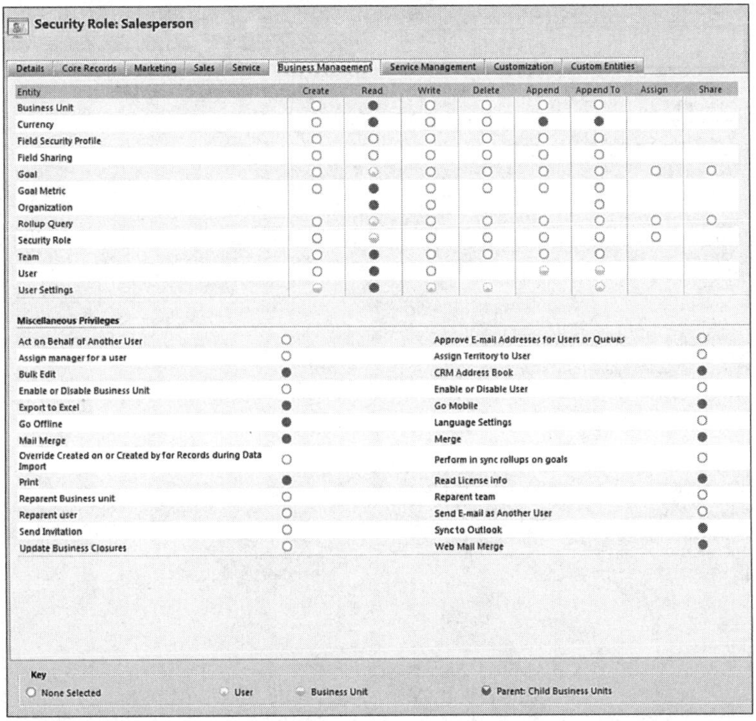

FIGURE 5.27
The Business Management tab for the Salesperson role.

FIGURE 5.28
The Service Management tab for the Salesperson role.

FIGURE 5.29
The Customization tab for the Salesperson role.

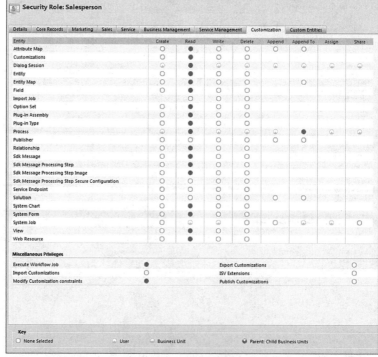

FIGURE 5.30
The Custom Entities tab for the Salesperson role.

Don't Forget Permissions for New Entities

If you add a custom entity to Microsoft Dynamics CRM, it will automatically be enrolled into every security role, and there will be a set of security privileges related to it. However, by default, every privilege will be set to None (no access). The exception is with the System Administrator role, which has the Organization privilege for every action. This allows you to explicitly define what privileges you require for each of your security roles.

By the Way

Sharing Records

You have learned that by using security roles, you can restrict user access to specific data records. However, sometimes a user might need access to a data record that isn't included (access-wise) in his or her security roles. To accommodate this need, you can collaborate through a Microsoft Dynamics CRM concept called *sharing*. Typically, any record in CRM that can be associated with a customer (lead, account, contact, opportunity, case, quote, and so on) can be shared.

> **Security Roles Cascade Down the Hierarchy**
>
> Security roles are created and associated with business units.
>
> Each time you create a new business unit within your hierarchy, it inherits all the security roles associated with the parent business units.
>
> Because in Microsoft Dynamics CRM children business units inherit security roles, you cannot vary the privileges of a security role to be different for each child business unit. Alternatively, you can create additional security roles for each business unit as required.

Security roles govern what you can do in Microsoft Dynamics CRM, and because sharing is an action, there is also a privilege associated with it. Therefore, to share a record with another user, you must have the ability to share that record type. This is so that you can control who can share records (and which types) in the system.

You might not need to be concerned about sharing in your organization. Because, by default, every shipped security role permits every user to "read" every record, you might find that the need for sharing (and explaining this feature to your users) is not necessary.

Sharing is an explicit process, initiated by users. You can share a record in Microsoft Dynamics CRM in two different ways. In both instances, a Sharing User interface will display. In it, the user must define who the record is to be shared with and what privileges are assigned to the user.

At first glance, it might appear that when you share a record with another user, you can grant security privileges that change the user's security role. This is not actually the case. The user's underlying security privileges will prevail. You are granting privileges to that specific record itself, but only if the user already has the privilege to perform the similar action to his or her own records.

For example, if you share a Contact record with another user and grant her the Delete privilege, that user will not be able to delete the record if her base security role has the Delete Contact privilege set to None.

Removing the share of a parent record removes the sharing properties of the records that it inherited from the parent. Therefore, all users who could previously read this record will no longer be able to read the child records either. It is possible that some child records might still be shared to a user if they were shared individually.

After a sharing request is initiated, a user interface opens (see Figure 5.31). Through this interface, a user can nominate whether to share records with a single user, several users, or a team.

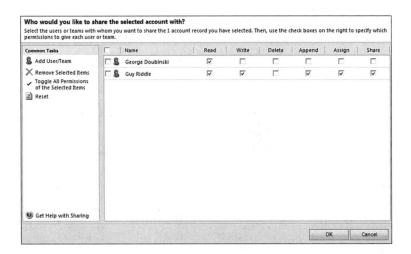

FIGURE 5.31
Setting the sharing options.

Either single or multiple records can be shared at a time.

As shown in Figure 5.32, with an individual record open, the user can click Share in the ribbon and then choose the Sharing options.

FIGURE 5.32
Sharing a single record.

Figure 5.33 shows that with a list view open, the user can select several records in the list, click Share in the ribbon, and choose the Sharing options.

FIGURE 5.33
Sharing multi-
ple records.

> **A Hidden Option**
>
> Share reassigned records with original user?
>
> A system setting determines whether records are shared back to the original owner when they are reassigned. What this means is that you give the record to another user but retain full rights to make changes to that record, *or* on reassign you give up all rights.
>
> If your CRM environment is locked down so that users can see only their own records, this might be a useful feature; otherwise, the user who created the record (or previously owned it) might lose access to it.

> **Owner Sees Everything**
>
> The "owner" of a parent record will always see every child-related record.
>
> If your security model is set up such that salespeople cannot see the opportunities of others, you need to be mindful of sharing. For example, say that John is the owner of an account, and he shares the account with Mary. Usually, if Mary adds an opportunity, John would not see it. However, if she adds the opportunity to the account that John owns, John will see that opportunity.

Teams

A team is a group of users (for example, National Accounts Team, Customer Service Team, Southern Branch). A team can be designated as the owner of a record and therefore may have a security role assigned to it. (If you do not assign a security role to a team, records will not be able to be assigned to that team for ownership.) By giving a team a security role, you can establish rules about what record types a team can own.

Teams can also facilitate sharing. When a user shares a record, it is an explicit action associated with a specified user. (For example, a user shares a record with a named coworker.) In some situations, users might have to share a record with several users, and this can be laborious for the users. A feature of sharing is that instead of sharing a record with a named user, you can elect to share the record with a team.

The key benefit of this approach is that if a new employee joins the organization, as soon as you add the new employee to the team, he or she is automatically shared with all the records that the team has been granted access to or owns. Similarly, if a user is taken out of a team, that user's right to access those shared records is removed.

A user can be a member of several teams.

CRM will automatically create a team for each business unit created. When new users are created, they are automatically enrolled as members of the team associated with the business unit to which they belong. For organizations that prefer records to be owned by elements of the business (for example, branch, office, division, subsidiary) rather than being owned by individuals, the core record structures are already in place to facilitate that through the business unit/team/user relationships.

Defining and maintaining teams is a straightforward process. Team definitions are accessed via the Administration interface from the Settings menu.

Figure 5.34 shows a list of existing teams. On this screen, you can click the New button in the ribbon to create a new team (see Figure 5.35).

FIGURE 5.34
A list of existing teams.

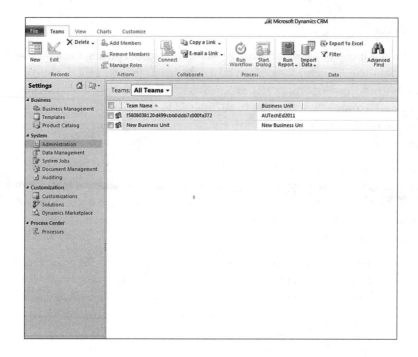

FIGURE 5.35
Creating a new team.

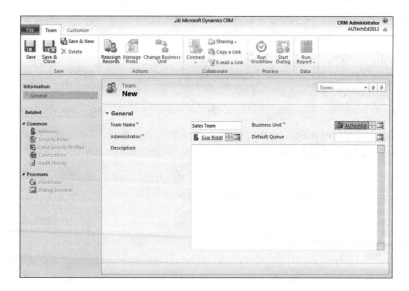

You can manage team members from the team record. You can add and remove users (see Figure 5.36).

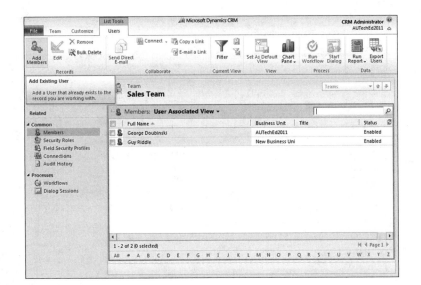

FIGURE 5.36
Managing team members.

Field Security

Through security roles, you can effectively control access to records. Sometimes this is not enough; some organizations also require the capability to lock, or protect, certain fields in a record. This can be implemented via field security.

Whenever a new field is created in CRM, you have the option to mark it as a field that requires additional security. When implemented, the field is displayed on a form with a key symbol next to it, to provide visual recognition that field security is applied to it and that some users may not be able to see the contents of the field. Where a field with security is designated and the user does not have access to the contents, CRM will automatically replace the real characters with black dots (see Figure 5.37).

At present, shipped fields in CRM cannot be marked with field security. So if you need a shipped field to have field security associated with it, you should elect not to use the Shipped field, remove it from the form, and add your own custom field in its place.

FIGURE 5.37
A field with a
security desig-
nation where
the user cannot
see the con-
tents of the
field.

To control who has access to fields with security, you have to create one or more field security profile(s). Within a profile you can include one or more individual fields that have security applied to them. For each field, you include in the profile what a user with that profile can do with that field. For example, if the field is empty, can users create? If it contains data, can they edit? Can they only read? This approach provides flexibility in management of the secure fields so that you can easily grant users the ability to do all, some, or none of these actions, as required.

From the Microsoft Dynamics CRM Administration page, you can access Field Security Profiles. Figure 5.38 shows a list of existing profiles.

From the list view you can click the New button in the ribbon to create a new field security profile (see Figure 5.39).

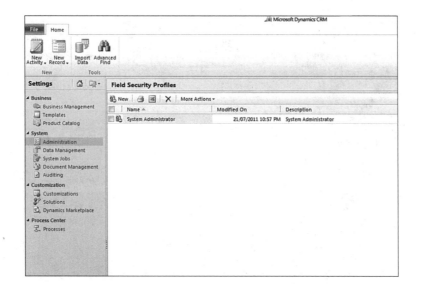

FIGURE 5.38
A list of existing profiles.

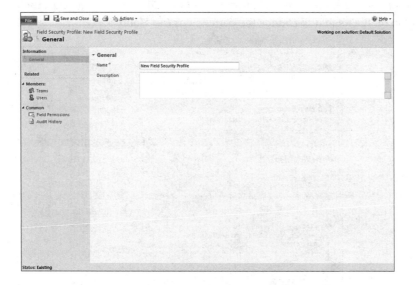

FIGURE 5.39
Creating a new profile.

After you have created the profile, select Field Permissions in the left navigation pane. By default, every field marked with Field Security will appear in the list (as shown in Figure 5.40), with the Read, Update, and Create permissions for each set to No.

FIGURE 5.40
Field permissions.

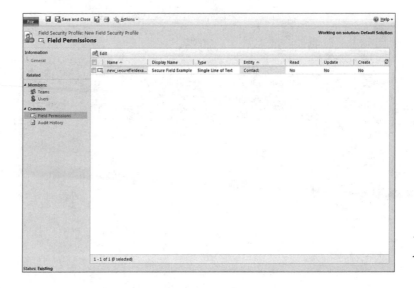

You can select each required field from the list of fields, and you can click the Edit button on the toolbar to change the permissions (see Figure 5.41).

FIGURE 5.41
Modifying field permissions.

Once the profile has been created and all required field permissions set, the field security profile can be assigned to users individually and/or teams—whichever is more practical from an administrative perspective. Each of the options to assign the field security profile is available in the left navigation pane of the profile itself.

Workshop

Q&A

Q. *Why can't I assign a record to a team?*

A. Before a team can be assigned a record, it *must* have a Security role.

Q. *One of my users has been promoted, and I now need give him more access through his security role. What do I need to do?*

A. Open the user's record, and in the left navigation pane, click Roles. In the toolbar, click Manage Roles and choose the appropriate security role for the user. Remember that a user might have more than one security role.

Q. *I moved a user to a different business unit, and now she can't log in to the system. What did I do wrong?*

A. When a user changes from one business unit to another, his or her security roles are automatically removed. This happens so you can explicitly select the appropriate role to fit her responsibility into the new business unit. To log in to the system, a user must have a security role. Ensure that the new business unit's security role is properly established.

Q. *One of my users left the organization, and I want to transfer all his records to the new person taking over his role. Can I do this in one procedure, or do I have to manually reassign each record?*

A. Records can be "assigned" individually or in bulk. On individual records, you can simply use the Assign option or just change the Owner attribute on the record itself. You can change bulk records by selecting multiple records in a list and choosing the Assign option in the ribbon. Transferring every record of one user to another is an option taken from the Actions menu when you have opened the user's record; you just have to enter the new user to whom all the records will be reassigned.

Q. *I need to add a new user, but I have run out of Microsoft Dynamics CRM licenses. I have a user in the system who recently left. How can I reuse her license?*

A. Navigate the list of users in the Administration section from the Settings menu. Select the users who have left the organization and, from the ribbon, choose

Disable. Doing so disables the users so that they will no longer be permitted to access the system, and it also frees up their licenses for reuse.

Q. *We have a new employee, and she is going to be doing both sales and marketing. Which security role do I give her: Salesperson or Marketing Professional?*

A. You can give her both roles. A user can be assigned multiple security roles where it makes sense to do so. If there are conflicts in security privileges between the assigned roles, a "least restrictive" rule applies. For example, if one role stipulates that a user cannot do something, and the other says he can, he will be permitted to perform the action.

Q. *I sometimes use temporary staff to do telesales. I have given them the Salesperson security role so that they can access the sales-related information. Because they are temporary staff, however, I don't want them to be able to export to Excel. Is there a way to achieve this?*

A. This is a great example of where a new security role could be created to achieve this business requirement. Navigate to the list of security roles from the Administration section from the Settings menu. Highlight the Salesperson security role, click the More Actions button in the toolbar, and select Copy Role. Enter the desired name for the new role (perhaps Telesales Temp Staff). When the new role opens, click the Business Management tab. Locate the Export to Excel privilege on the right side of the lower half of the screen; click the green dot, and it will change to a red circle (signifying None). Save and close the new security role. Any users who now have this security role assigned to them will not see the Excel button on any screen.

Q. *I have created a "personal view" of all the opportunities in my pipeline, and now a colleague also wants to use it. Can this be done automatically, or does my colleague have to set it up himself?*

A. From the Advanced Find screen (where personal views are created), click the Saved Views button in the ribbon and then select the Share button. The view can now be shared with other users or teams.

Quiz

1. Which of the shipped security roles permit users to see almost every record in the system and delete any records for which they are marked as the owner?

2. How do you regain the license from a user who leaves your organization to make it available for another to use?

3. How do you display a list of which users have been assigned which security roles?

Answers

1. Only the System Customizer has reduced access to core customer related records. While seeing everything in the system is not a big issue, it is worth-while reviewing what you will allow users to delete. Consider the scenario in which a disgruntled employee decides to leave your organization; you proba-bly don't want that person going through the system, deleting all their records. It is a better practice to get users to use the native feature of deactivating a record if it is no longer current/active rather than deleting records.

2. So that any history is maintained for your business, a user cannot be deleted from the system. However, you can disable a user via the Actions menu on the user record. When you disable a user, his or her license is released back into the available pool of licenses.

3. Unfortunately, no predefined feature provides this information. However, by using the Report Wizard, you can build the report easily. When you run the Report Wizard, make sure you select Roles as the primary record type and Users as the related record type.

Exercise

Let's look at a scenario of how you might need to control access to data and how you could implement that through the Microsoft Dynamics CRM security model.

Scenario

NYZ Company, a company based in San Francisco with sales offices in Seattle, New York, and Atlanta, has an Eastern sales manager based in New York and a Western sales manager based in San Francisco. Both can see all the opportunities of their respective regions but not nationally. They also have a marketing manager who is based in Atlanta and needs access to everything. The sales teams in each office is permitted to see the sales opportunities within their own office (so that the teams are not stepping on each other's toes), but a team is not allowed to see the sales opportunities in the other offices.

Possible Solution

To segregate the data between what the sales managers can see and what each salesperson can see, we need to establish a business unit hierarchy. Therefore, we have opted to create four additional business units under the default one, as shown in Figure 5.42. Hierarchically, we have also placed Seattle and Atlanta under San Francisco and New York, respectively; this is because we need the sales managers to be able to cascade down their respective branches of the hierarchy.

FIGURE 5.42
Possible solution for business unit hierarchy.

In this model, the sales staff will be assigned to each business unit related to where they work. Each will be given an appropriate security role; in particular, their roles must stipulate that they have Business Unit privilege for opportunities (so that they can only see any opportunities in their own business units).

The Eastern and Western sales managers will be assigned to the New York and San Francisco business units, respectively. They will also be assigned appropriate security roles; but in their cases, we must make sure that they have Parent Child Business Unit privilege for opportunities (to ensure that they can see all the opportunities in the business unit to which they belong as well as the opportunities in the business units below them).

The marketing manager could be placed in the Atlanta business unit (where he physically resides), or he could be placed in the top-level business unit (perhaps representing his position within the organization). The key here is that we must give him the appropriate privilege, depending on where we place him. If he is placed in the Atlanta business unit, he must have Organization privilege for opportunities, which allows global access to all opportunities in the system (because he will need to look up the organizational hierarchy as well as across it). If he is placed in the top-level business unit, he could be assigned the Organization or Parent Child Business Unit privilege for opportunities (because here, he really only needs to look down the hierarchy).

HOUR 6

Managing Leads

What You'll Learn in This Hour:

- ▶ A little history
- ▶ What data to capture and the import process
- ▶ Distributing leads
- ▶ A deeper look at leads
- ▶ From lead to account: conversion

Managing sales leads is the beginning of a sales process and one core reason for using a CRM application. In this hour, we dive into the world of leads and the meaning of leads in the world of Microsoft Dynamics CRM. Be patient for the first part of this hour is going to look at taking an outside list of leads (such as a list you might get from a trade show) and pulling this list of leads into Dynamics CRM. In general a lead is a person who is considered to be an unqualified prospect—as in sales has not talked to this person or they have had just a brief conversation. A lead has the potential to become a new customer, but this potential has not been qualified.

A Little History

As mentioned, a lead is an unqualified contact or person who is usually associated with a company. This unqualified contact can come from a number of places, including a business card, a purchased list, a referral, a trade show, a seminar, or a random phone call. In Microsoft Dynamics CRM, there is a special place in the system for these unqualified contacts (leads). There are two core reasons for the separation between qualified and unqualified contacts. The first is that many companies purchase large lists of contacts, and it is generally good practice not to put a huge list of unqualified contacts in with your nice clean qualified data. There is definitely something to be said for not having to sort through 50,000 extra Lead entity records when trying to run a sales funnel report.

The second reason is that Microsoft Dynamics CRM takes a multilayered approach to the tracking of everything that happens around relationships, and yet when data is collected from many other places and systems, it tends to be rather flat (or *normalized*, for you database gurus). Flat relates to a very small set of data that can all be captured in a small set of fields. This differs from a more hierarchical approach. The Leads entity of Microsoft Dynamics CRM allows for a flat company contact record to be converted to a more robust structure, including Account, Contact, and Opportunity entities, and all the associated activities, history, connections (a.k.a. roles and relationships), and notes.

One common way to create Lead entities is to import them from a purchased or an acquired list. If you are using Microsoft Dynamics CRM Online, you can also tap into the offered third-party Internet lead capture functionality, or perhaps when you rolled out Microsoft Dynamics CRM On-Premises or Online you added one of the advanced marketing options. The functionality to import leads into Microsoft Dynamics CRM is robust and an area of potential confusion, and yet given how often it is used, we take a good piece of this lesson to talk about importing new data into the Leads area of Microsoft Dynamics CRM.

Importing New Leads

The Import from Microsoft feature includes the ability to import from an XML-formatted spreadsheet (*.xml), a text file (.txt), a common separated text file (*.csv), and a compressed version of any of these (*.zip), but the easiest and most accurate way to work with import is to start by populating a template for data import. To do this, you select Templates for Data Import from the CRM Settings menu, under Data Management.

The template can be used to enter and upload bulk data for a particular entity via an XMLSS format. In addition to creating blank templates, you can bulk export the existing data for an entity into the XLMSS format from the Microsoft Dynamics CRM Database. Once you export the data, you can make changes and updates to the existing records or add additional records to the file and then import it back into Microsoft Dynamics CRM.

There is a template available for almost all entities within Microsoft Dynamics CRM 2011, as shown in Figure 6.1.

One example of a template for import is an Excel spreadsheet that has predefined columns for name, address, and telephone. Users who use this template then simply add their data to the Excel spreadsheet in the order in which Dynamics CRM expects it and then use this template to pull data into the Leads entity.

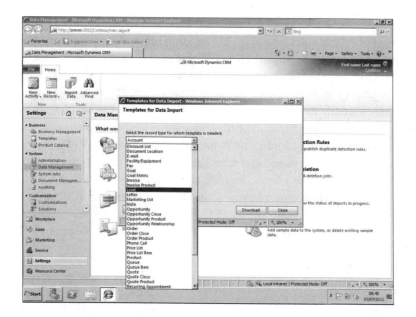

FIGURE 6.1
Templates for
data import.

An imported XML-formatted spreadsheet can be used as a basis for importing leads, as shown in Figure 6.2.

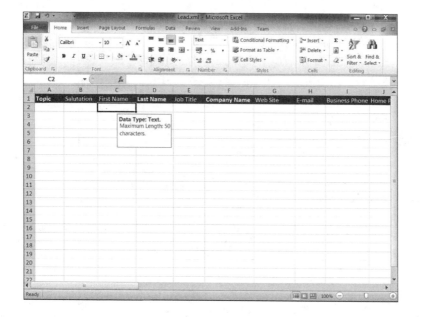

FIGURE 6.2
Lead template
for data import.

If you have recently purchased a list of leads from an external source, you can take advantage of a Microsoft Dynamics CRM tool that imports data from any file that is formatted as a comma-separated-value file. You will see people refer to this type of file as a "CSV" file, but the general gist is that all values in the file are separated by commas, and the set of data ends with a carriage return. The system and wizards can therefore understand where one piece of data ends and the next begins, as well as when one record of information ends and another begins. This file is also an industry standard, so if you purchase data from another company or if you get a list of leads from a trade show, you will most likely be getting that list in either Microsoft Excel or CSV file format. In addition, you can save any Excel file as a CSV file. If you use a field separator in your data, such as the comma in "Smith, Smith and Jones LLP," you must also enclose the field in a data delimiter, such as double quotes. The following example shows what a few lines of a CSV file might look like:

Name, Topic, Phone Number

John Doe, Interested in large purchase, 425-111-1111

"Smith, Smith and Jones LLP", Dropped by booth, 425-333-2222

Figure 6.3 shows that the Microsoft Dynamics CRM Data Import Wizard lets you choose what separators are used in your CSV file.

FIGURE 6.3
Choosing data separators.

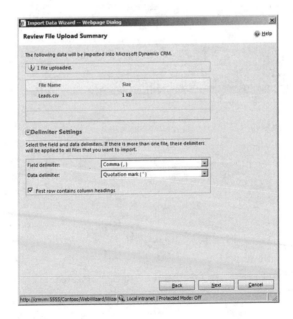

The other key item that you want to be careful of when preparing or reviewing your data for import is that the system cannot always digest special characters. For instance, @, #, &, and * often have other meanings to computer software, and if they are embedded in your data, they can cause the system to choke. International characters can have the same effect. Microsoft Dynamics CRM will check for characters that are not agreeable and will not upload data that does not fit.

What Data to Capture and the Import Process

There are a number of different drivers for putting data into Microsoft Dynamics CRM. These may range from entering basic contact information to logging specific areas of interest or market sector information. Among the benefits of importing data (either individual contacts or businesses) into the Lead entity is the ability to easily qualify and convert a Lead entity to a Contact entity or Account entity, with all the associated relationship information. Entering this information manually as Contact entities and Lead entities entails creating individual records for both and associating them as primary contact and parent account. We will cover this qualification and conversion process later in this hour.

As an example of when to import leads into the Microsoft Dynamics CRM system, imagine the need to import data after a trade show or when a list of potential leads has been purchased and the interest list can go on. There is often a need to import data when a new staff person is hired or when a merger or an acquisition occurs. With each need and interest, it is important to consider which tool to use to import data because each tool offers different advantages.

The Data Import Wizard: Data Mapping

The Data Import Wizard enables end users to map Microsoft Dynamics CRM data fields to fields represented in the import file. For instance, if you know that the first field in your import file is Company Name (because the first column in your Excel spreadsheet is Company Name), your map would associate the first field in the import file to the company name in Microsoft Dynamics CRM. Figure 6.4 illustrates this.

Another consideration is where in Microsoft Dynamics CRM do you want to import this data? There are numerous choices, but for this discussion, you are importing this data into Lead entities. You are actually mapping Company Name in your import file to Company Name in the Leads entity, as you saw previously.

FIGURE 6.4
Data mapping.

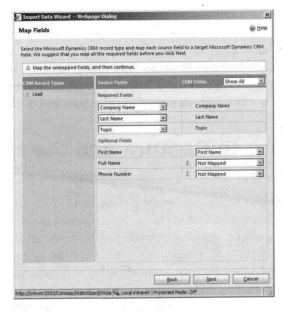

Let's look at a data mapping from the Data Import Wizard by following a process of importing a CSV file that contains two leads into the Leads entity in Microsoft Dynamics CRM:

1. From the Leads Records entity, select the Import Data drop-down.

2. Choose Import Data. You now see the import screen shown in Figure 6.5.

FIGURE 6.5
Starting a data import.

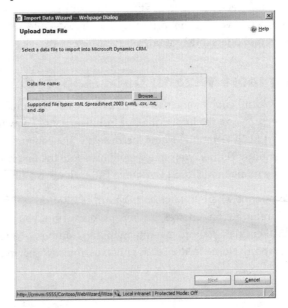

3. Tell the system the name of your import file and where it is located. The next screen confirms the file chosen and allows you to set how the data is delimited. Is the data separated by only commas or by commas and quotes? Are the quotes single quotes or double quotes? This screen also allows you to define the first row in your CSV file as the column headings row—and this is vital for the next stage of mapping.

4. You then proceed to the next screen (see Figure 6.6). This screen allows you to choose predefined mapping for import or automatic. In this case, choose Default (Automatic Mapping) and click Next.

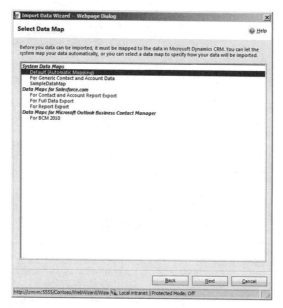

FIGURE 6.6
Selecting a data map.

5. Choose Leads for the record type to import to (see Figure 6.7).

6. Map the fields as shown in Figure 6.8. Essentially, this stage involves bringing together the two parts of the import—the CSV file and the Lead Entity record in Microsoft Dynamics CRM. Figure 6.8 shows the source columns from the CSV file and the CRM fields, some of which are already mapped! If the Source Data columns are identical to CRM fields, the import process automatically maps them.

Full Name

Notice that Full Name has been ignored. The source CSV file had a column containing the full name of the lead, along with columns for first name and last name. The lead record in Microsoft Dynamics CRM only contains these options, so you can safely ignore this column.

By the Way

FIGURE 6.7
Selecting a map
record type.

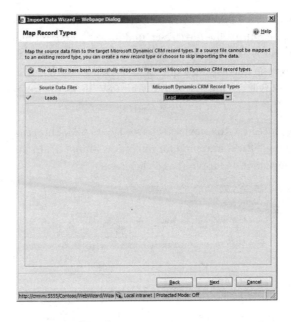

FIGURE 6.8
Mapping fields.

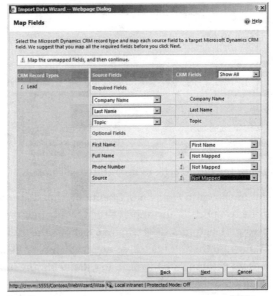

7. In Figure 6.9, map a piece of data called source in the data file to the Lead attribute (field) source, via a drop-down list. If the data does not exactly match items in the list, you must tell the system how the data in the source field maps to items in the source drop-down list attribute in Microsoft Dynamics CRM.

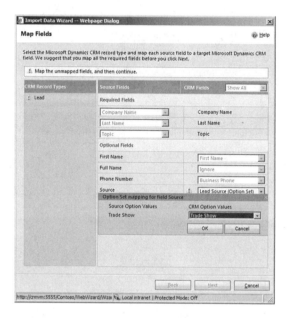

FIGURE 6.9
Matching drop-down list items.

8. Review the mapping and edit the mappings as needed.

9. Tell the system who will be assigned as the owner of the lead after data is imported and whether duplicate records should be included (see Figure 6.10). Note that almost every core record within Microsoft Dynamics CRM has an owner. This owner could possibly be a specific user or the system, depending on the type of entity. With regard to leads, the owner is a specific Microsoft Dynamics CRM user.

10. Save this map for future use. Call this map Trade Show Map because this might be the sort of data you import on a regular basis after trade shows.

You can view the import process results by navigating to Imports (see Figure 6.11). Figure 6.12 and Figure 6.13 show how the import process appears when completed.

FIGURE 6.10
Assign leads
and check for
duplicates.

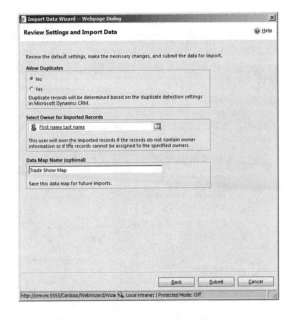

FIGURE 6.11
System mes-
sages: Import.

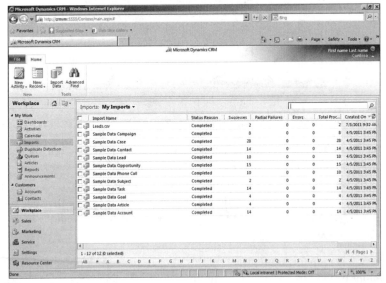

You can also display the new records as a list of new leads, as shown in Figure 6.12. Figure 6.13 shows the data that was entered into Microsoft Excel and how it looks in the Leads view.

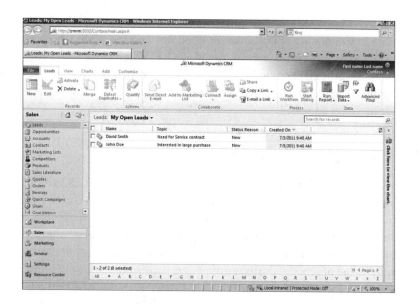

FIGURE 6.12
Leads: Import completed.

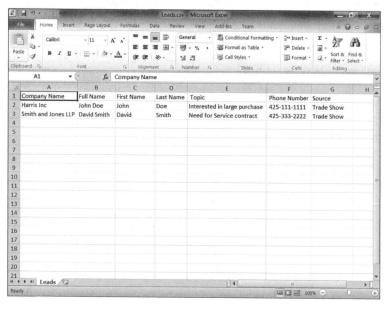

FIGURE 6.13
Original data in Excel 2007: Leads to import.

You can also select a specific lead and drill down into the details, change the details, or add to the details that were uploaded. After leads are imported, the sales process usually goes through a qualification process. After a lead is qualified, the Lead entity is converted to an Account entity.

Microsoft Dynamics CRM can also automate the process described here, using the features and functionality of the Microsoft Windows Workflow Foundation (WWF). Hour 16, "Workflows: Creating Simple Workflows," focuses on creating simple workflows, but it is worth mentioning here that the system can be designed to automatically kick off an automated sales process when a Lead entity is converted or when an Opportunity entity is created.

Distributing Leads

When a lead is entered into the system, core information can be used to distribute this lead to the appropriate salesperson. Microsoft Dynamics CRM can be configured with business rules using workflow functionality that kicks in when a lead is created. For instance, if a lead has a zip code that begins with a specific set of numbers, a workflow rule can automatically change the sales territory or owner of that new Lead entity to the appropriate sales territory or salesperson. Another example might be if a lead also includes the industry the lead is part of. In this case, you might have salespeople focused on managing leads for each industry.

Figure 6.14 shows an example of a simple workflow set up to associate all leads with a zip code starting with 05 to a specific salesperson.

When you get to Hour 16, remember this example. The concept of changing the owner and sales territory of Lead entities when they are created is a great workflow to start practicing with.

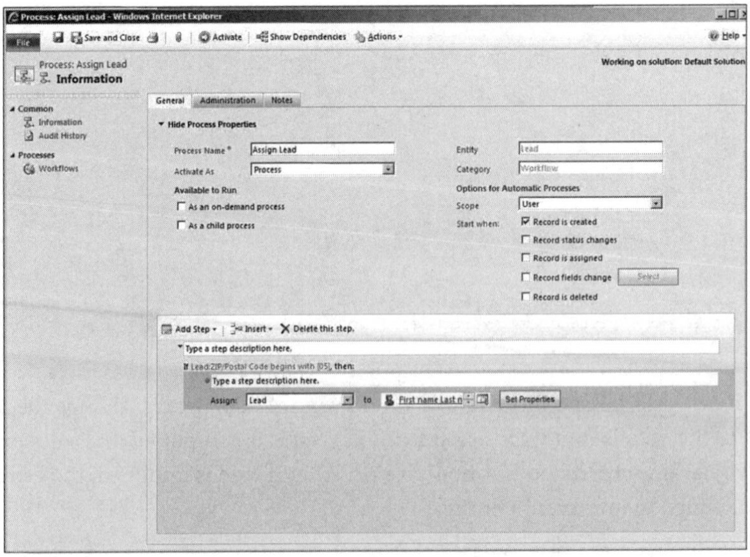

FIGURE 6.14
Distribution of
leads workflow.

A Deeper Look at Leads

After a lead is imported, the details can be fine-tuned and changed. Figure 6.15 shows the General section of a Lead entity. Before any configuration, the Lead form is made up of four sections: General, Detail, Notes & Activities, and Preferences. You can also add more sections, remove sections, or add more data fields to existing or new sections. There is also a section at the top of the form called the header that can contain a summary of information from other areas of the Lead entity for quick reference.

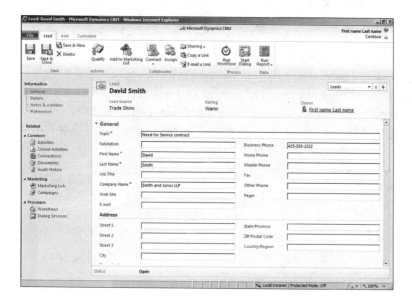

FIGURE 6.15
The General section of a Lead entity.

Let's discuss four fields on the Lead entity: Topic, Currency, Rating, and Details.

If you are looking at a long list of many leads, the Topic field helps distinguish two leads with exactly the same information. For instance, you might have two leads with different contacts, but perhaps they work in the same company. The Topic field can be renamed through system customization; however, it cannot be removed. Given that the Topic field is a required system field, some consideration is needed to decide how your company wants to use Topic. Some examples for Topic include where the lead came from, how the lead is categorized, and to what division the lead is assigned.

The next field worthy of discussion is the Currency field. In Microsoft Dynamics CRM, you can assign different currency to different Leads. This enables a global corporation to track local leads in the currency of the country where the lead is being worked. Currency also impacts other entities in the system that are associated with money, such as Opportunity, Quotes, Orders, and Invoices. When setting up system configuration within Microsoft Dynamics CRM, you can enter a currency-conversion rate table. The currency-conversion rate table does not automatically update, but it can be manually changed as needed.

The Rating field on the Lead entity has a drop-down that contains the options Hot, Warm, and Cold. The value on this field maps to the Opportunity entity during the conversion process. This rating helps a salesperson prioritize leads when making decisions regarding which lead to call first to qualify and flows through as an indicator on the Opportunity entity to offset the core sales funnel analysis fields, such as estimated close date, sales stage, and percent probability. If a lead or an opportunity is cold and the estimated close date is within a couple weeks or days, the sales manager might want to have an offline discussion with the salesperson.

Finally, there's the Details field. It is tempting to use the Details field for notes; however, the field is limited in size. The best use of the Details field is for a brief profile of the company with which the lead is associated. This profile might be a cut and paste from the company's website, or it might just be local knowledge. Figure 6.16 offers an example of the Details section of a Lead entity.

FIGURE 6.16
The Details section of a Lead entity.

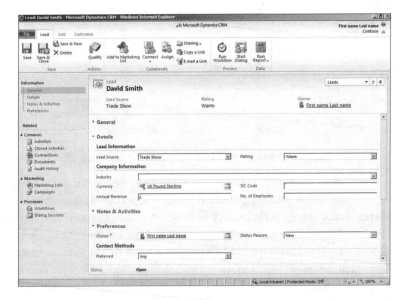

Notice that, in the Details section, the last field displayed is the Source field. This field is very important if you want to analyze where your leads came from. We recommend you move this field to the General tab and set it as required.

The next section we are going to look at is the Preferences section, shown in Figure 6.17.

FIGURE 6.17
The Preferences section of a Lead entity.

The fields in the Preferences section document business process compliance when in the qualifying stage—items such as whether the lead has requested that you do not call them but you are allowed to send them information via e-mail. This field can also document whether the lead should be flagged for a certain marketing campaign to heat them up a bit, or perhaps marketing materials have been sent to them and you want to flag and show the last campaign this lead was included in. In addition, if this lead was acquired through a new marketing campaign, the Preferences section displays what source campaign generated the lead.

Mapped Data

Activities and details on a Lead entity do not necessarily get copied to the Account or Opportunity entity during conversion. If you are going to be working on a Lead entity past the qualification phase, you should convert it so that your detailed activities, notes, and work are organized around the Account or Opportunity entity.

By the Way

From Lead to Account: Conversion

Figure 6.18 shows the change from Lead entity to the more complex Account entity and related entities.

Microsoft Dynamics CRM has a conversion process that takes a flat Lead entity and expands it to the dimensions needed to track a complex company and sales process. A Lead entity can be converted into an Account entity, a Contact entity, or an Opportunity entity. You have the choice of converting a Lead entity to all three or any combination of the three. Depending on the company, you might find that all three entities are used or that only one is used. Even within the Microsoft Dynamics CRM Community Discussion Forums, you will see many different debates on this subject.

FIGURE 6.18
From lead to
prospect.

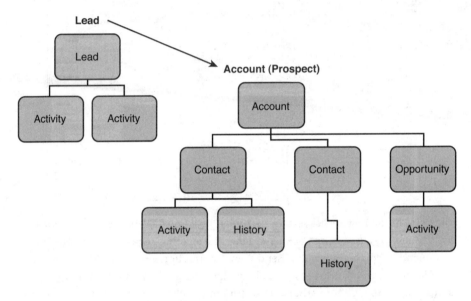

Once a Lead entity is converted, a sales process can kick off, a salesperson can add more contacts, and any other numerous activities can be associated. With regard to the Opportunity entity, you are kicking off an Opportunity entity that tracks the dollar value of the potential sale and other key sales information; this entity lives in the sales funnel until it is closed and relegated to history as won or lost.

Figure 6.19 shows the choices you have when converting a Lead entity.

In Figures 6.20, 6.21, and 6.22, you can see the Account, Contact, and Opportunity records that created from the conversion process of the Lead entity in Figures 6.18 and 6.19.

Although Microsoft Dynamics CRM enables users to import leads and then convert Lead entities to Account, Contact, and Opportunity entities, the feature does not have to be used as part of your sales process. You can enter an Account entity, select Contact from the left navigation pane, and enter the Contact (which can autopopulate with Account entity details). Later, when you are ready, you can create an Opportunity entity to track the promised deal.

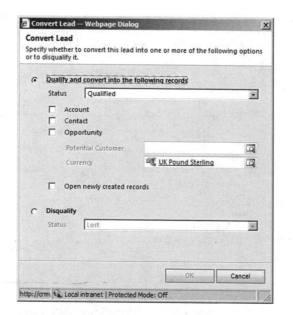

FIGURE 6.19
Converting a lead.

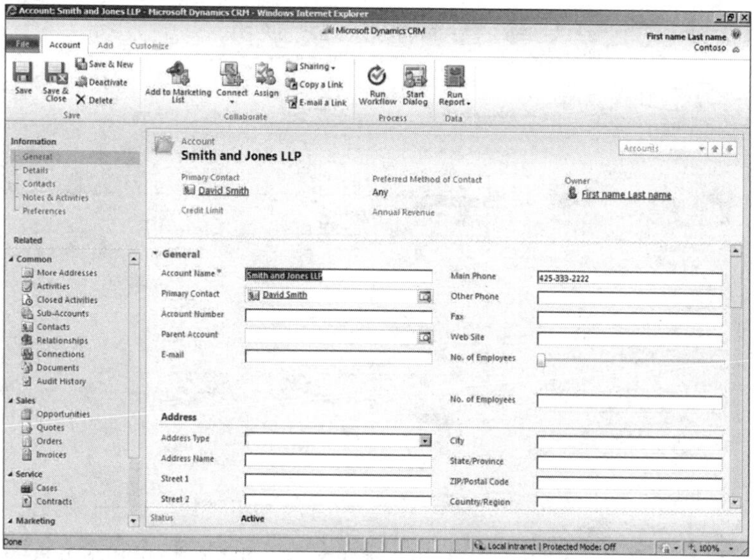

FIGURE 6.20
The created account.

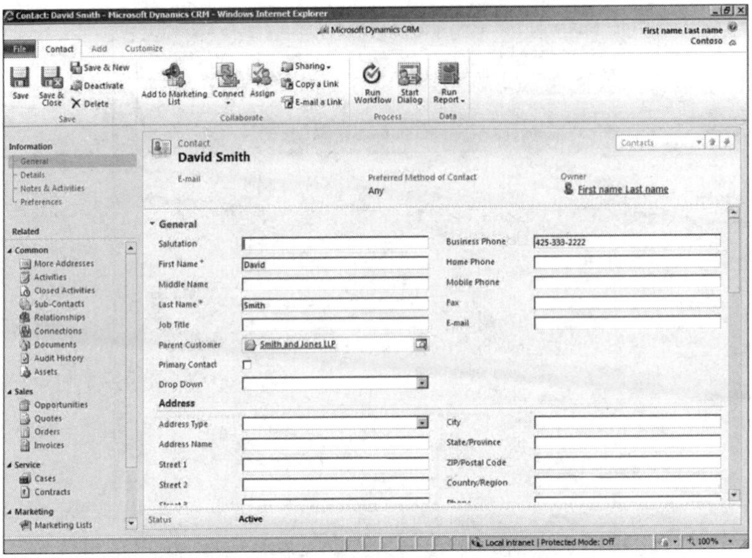

FIGURE 6.21
The created contact. Notice that the Topic field and the Description field in the Opportunity entity are populated with data from the Lead entity.

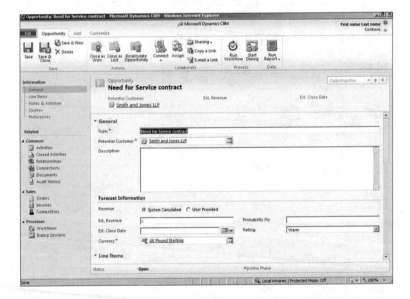

FIGURE 6.22
The created Opportunity entity.

The Lead entity feature offers a few key benefits. The first is the ability to keep the long, long list of unqualified leads separate from your shorter list of qualified accounts of type Prospect. The second is that it offers some efficiency around creating new Account, Contact, and Opportunity entities. It also offers a flat normalized table for data import that is similar to a user's experience with Excel and allows for field matching with a commonsense approach. The third reason is that this qualification and conversion process yields vital information with regard to your business process. It enables you to report on how many Lead entities were created and then qualified to Opportunity, Account, and Contact entities; what you find might, for example, indicate the benefit of a campaign.

Like many other Microsoft products, Microsoft Dynamics CRM gives you many choices when it comes to the business processes you decide to use.

It is important to note that while Lead entities can be seen as a temporary area to store potential sales, they should be treated with the same care as the more valuable Opportunity entities. For a sales manager, it is important that every lead coming into the company be processed and either qualified or disqualified. If a lead is disqualified, that the company should track the reason why it was disqualified so the next time a lead like this comes in, the sales team might be able to transform it into a win.

Workshop

Smith Incorporated is a company that sells manufacturing products to auto body shops around the world. On a regular basis, the marketing department at Smith Incorporated purchases lists of leads that include all the new auto body shops in the United States. The lists that it purchases are downloaded and are in text file format. The marketing department takes the list, opens it in Microsoft Excel, and adds a column labeled Source. It populates the Source column with the name of the list it purchased. The department also deletes one or two columns of the spreadsheet that contain data that it can immediately see is not of interest. When it finishes the review, the department saves the file as a CSV file and imports it into the Leads entity of Microsoft Dynamics CRM.

After the leads are imported, they are assigned to specific salespeople within Smith Incorporated, based on zip code. The salespeople schedule activities and start making their calls, or the built-in workflow system automatically creates a set of activities, prioritizing the calls based on the rate associated with each lead. When a salesperson completes a call, he or she completes the Phone Call activity and either schedules another call or converts the lead based on the conversation. When a lead is qualified through a phone call and a positive conversation with a contact, the Lead entity is converted to an Account, Contact, or Opportunity entity. If the Lead entity is disqualified through a conversation, the Lead entity is run through the conversion function, and it is closed as disqualified; the reason for disqualification is entered into the Lead entity.

New opportunities that are created kick off an automatic sales process, starting at the first sales stage, which has four associated activities: update estimated close date, probability percentage and rating, follow up with prospect by sending requested initial sales material, and confirm that the Lead received and reviewed the information and is ready for an appointment. The goal of the first sales stage is to start the sales process and further qualify the lead. The second sales stage includes activities associated with meeting the prospect face to face.

Q&A

Q. *Is it necessary to use Lead entities? Or can we bypass that feature?*

A. You can bypass Lead entities, but you might want to add a Source field to either the account or contact to capture where your new accounts or contacts came from. Traditionally, Source is part of the Lead entity.

Q. *I uploaded a spreadsheet into a Leads entity incorrectly, and I now want to delete everything I uploaded. Is there an easy way to do this?*

A. Yes. In Microsoft Dynamics CRM, if you have the right security you can select the first lead and the last lead you want to delete and then click the black X.

Q. *I did a data import, but all the data in my Excel spreadsheet is not in the Leads entity. What happened?*

A. Microsoft Dynamics CRM keeps track of which leads were uploaded and which were failures. Under Imports in the left navigation pane, you can change your view to Completed Imports. Then you can double-click an import to choose it and show more details, including documented failures.

Q. *We want our leads to be associated to a specific salesperson, depending on the state. Is this supported?*

A. Yes. Microsoft Dynamics CRM supports this scenario by offering users the option to define workflow rules that can be applied after an import is completed.

Quiz

1. What are the four fields on the General tab of a lead that are worth more consideration?

2. How do you use the Lead Topic field? What are some examples?

3. How does Lead rating relate to Opportunity rating?

4. Can data be imported into other record types?

5. Why does the system support a lead and a prospect, and why are they different?

6. What are possible data separators?

Answers

1. Topic, Currency, Rating, and Details are the four fields.

2. The Lead Topic field is used to help classify different leads (for example, two leads from different contacts at the same company).

3. The lead rating can map to the opportunity rating and can indicate how active, hot, or cold the lead is.

4. Yes, data can be imported into a variety of record types, including Account, Contact, and Lead entities.

5. A lead is an unqualified prospect. A prospect is a classification of a type of account and associated contacts. A lead is an entity.

6. Possible data separators are a comma or a comma and quotation marks.

Exercise

Create a data file using Microsoft Excel. Include the company name, contact name, contact address, telephone number, e-mail address, web page, and source. Save this file as a CSV file and import it into Microsoft Dynamics CRM. During the import, map each of your fields from your Excel file to fields within the Lead entity in Microsoft Dynamics CRM. Notice that you have to upload a sample data file and, if you have not added a header row to your Excel spreadsheet, the sample data file might be a bit tougher to map to the Lead entity. You might also notice that it is beneficial to have a first name column and a last name column in your data file because the Lead entity has the name split into three fields. For the Topic field, map the company name and the source. Notice that you can map two fields to create a merge effect.

After the leads are imported, check the system messages. Did all the leads get imported, or were there errors?

Now, open one of your new leads and populate a few more fields. Now try converting it to an Account entity, a Contact entity, and an Opportunity entity. What data gets moved during the conversion?

The Account Entity in More Detail

- ▶ Entering data: the Account form
- ▶ Account data
- ▶ How the Account entity relates to a few other entities
- ▶ What the Account entity can impact
- ▶ How the Account entity can be redefined

In this hour, you will master the framework and architecture used throughout the application for data capture through the use of a data entry form. In addition, you will learn what pieces of the form offer options for more usability and what areas connect to related data.

Entering Data: The Account Form

Figure 7.1 shows the initial Account form. This is what you will see when you create a new Account.

The details on an Account form include common information, such as address and telephone numbers, and also some very specific industry or audience niche information. Figure 7.1 shows an example, but let's dive into more detail.

The Account form is built with a number of different building blocks, all of which offer different options. Forms such as the Account form appear in their own window, and you can open many forms at once. This ability to open many forms at once is a difference between Microsoft Dynamics CRM and other CRM systems. In Microsoft Dynamics CRM, you can be working on many of the same entities or a combination of entities at the same time. If you want to enter three new Account entities, for instance, you can have three Account forms open. Microsoft Dynamics CRM gives you the option of the multiple-window experience when working with forms. You will grow to love this if you are a multitasker or if you leverage the power of instant messaging and carry on two, three, or four conversations at once. In addition, taking advantage of newer hardware technologies, such as using multiple monitors or using a new much larger monitors, really emphasizes the power of this feature.

FIGURE 7.1
The Account form.

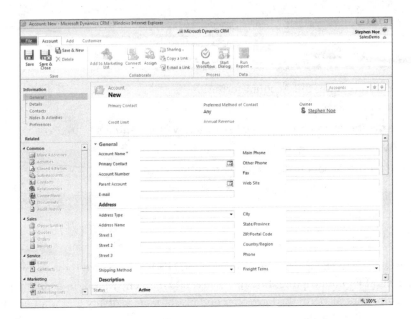

The ability to open many forms at once could confuse and frustrate you if you are not a multitasker and if you are only comfortable with having one window open at a time. You can avoid this confusion by understanding this feature and choosing to use it or to not use it.

The Left Navigation Pane

The first building block of a form is the leftmost menu, which is called the *left navigation pane* (see Figure 7.2).

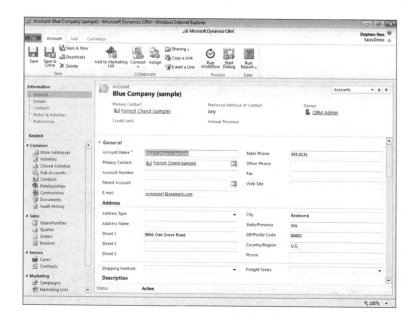

FIGURE 7.2
The left naviga-
tion pane.

The left navigation pane contains a list of all the related entities. (Remember that we discussed those entities [record types] in Hour 1, "What Is Microsoft Dynamics CRM?") These listed entities have a close and direct relationship to the displayed entity (Account), and these related entities are served up with a filter. When one of the left navigation pane entities is selected, the information that is available is specifically for the displayed Account entity. If you select Contact, the contacts displayed will be only those contacts associated with that account. In addition, if you select one of these entities and create a new entity, such as a new contact, all information from the selected account is available to the system, and the system prepopulates the related fields in the new entity. For instance, if you open an account and then select Contact, New, you will see that the contact's address is prepopulated with the account's address, and the parent account is prepopulated with the account name. This saves on data entry effort. An example of other related entities to the Account entity are Activity, Contact, Opportunity, Subaccount, More Addresses, and Case. Figure 7.3 shows the main entry form for the Account entity.

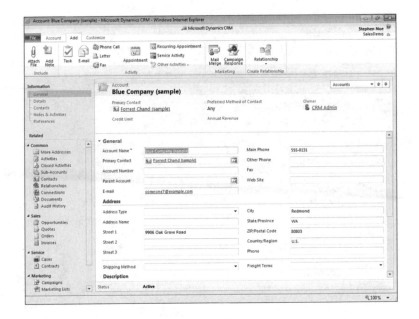

The Main Entry Screen

The second building block of a form is the main entry screen. This is your work area, where you enter data. The main entry screen displays a list of different fields for data entry. These fields are specific to the Account entity and include default fields that come with the system—such as Name, Address, Phone Number, and Parent Account—but can also include fields that were defined during the setup and configuration of your Microsoft Dynamics CRM system. Most default system fields can be turned off, and some default systems fields are available, but are not often used, and as such Microsoft ships them as not displayed. You can choose to display them when you configure the system. Figure 7.4 shows the Account form; notice the sections in blue in the top-left corner of the form, under the word "Information."

The main entry screen is a long, scrollable form that is also organized by sections, and each section can have different data fields on it. When the system administrator configures Microsoft Dynamics CRM, he or she can eliminate or add sections to each form. Each section within a form contains other sections of related data fields and can be configured to be open or closed when the main form is displayed.

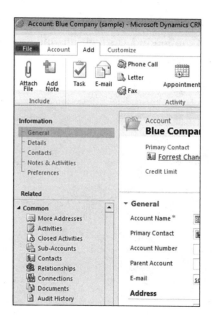

FIGURE 7.4
The Account form.

Account Data

Account data is divided up into a number of different sections. Let's take a look at each of them.

The General Section

The General section of the Account form is shown in Figure 7.5. This section contains specific fields that are worth a closer look. These include Parent Account, Primary Contact, Relationship, and Address Phone Number.

When it comes to data fields on the Account form, including the General section, a few require a good explanation. The first field in the General section that needs explanation is Primary Contact. In Microsoft Dynamics CRM, you can have an unlimited number of contacts associated with an account; however, for each account, you have the option of selecting only one primary contact. This primary contact displays on account-specific views and in other locations such as an account-centric report. The Primary Contact field can mean different things to different companies and can even be renamed. An alternative name might be Key Decision Maker, Primary Buyer, or Company Champion. The primary contact could be any number of different people, such as the main decision maker, the chief financial officer, or the key target. The decision about who to associate with the Primary Contact field in smaller clients is usually relatively simple; however, in larger prospects or clients, choosing just one primary contact for an account can be much more difficult. Not to worry: Microsoft Dynamics CRM offers a huge variety of options when it comes to configuring, customizing, and capturing and creating associations and relationships.

FIGURE 7.5
General section data fields of particular interest.

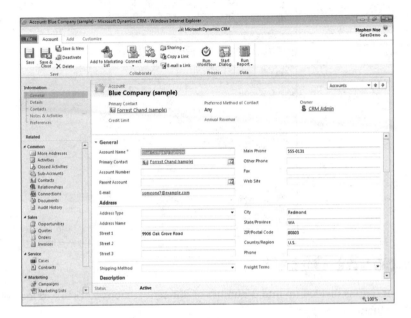

The next field that is worthy of mention and discussion in the General section is Parent Account. For any given account, there can be an assigned parent account. The Parent Account field is not required, but if entered, it offers a tree of related connections. Parent accounts are no different from accounts, so a listed parent account can also have a parent of its own. In this way, you can capture a hierarchy within a corporation or other hierarchies, depending on the situation. A parent account could be corporate headquarters, and the account could be a division office. A local store could have a parent account of regional headquarters, and a regional headquarters account could have a parent account of U.S. operations. The list is almost endless. As a paradigm shift, if you were capturing car dealerships and Car Manufacturing plants within the system, the parent account could be the Manufacturing Plant where the car dealership purchases the cars, and the current account could be the car dealership where a specific car is residing.

There is a Phone field listed under Address. This is the address phone number and is placed and captured here as references to the phone number a company, such as FedEx or UPS, would use when trying to deliver a package. The delivery fields in the General section can be turned off and are often not needed (depending on the model of the business using Microsoft Dynamics CRM).

Finally, the Description field is a little deceiving because it is a text field, but it is limited in size. If you were thinking of using the Description field on an ongoing basis to add notes, for instance, be aware that you will run out of space. The Description field is much more appropriate as a corporate profile or a place to put a brief summary of the account. Notes, on the other hand, are unlimited. We talk more about notes in a bit.

The Details Section

Figure 7.6 shows the Details section of the Account form. Within this section are some key fields worth further discussion, including Industry, Territory, Relationship Type, and Price List.

FIGURE 7.6
Details section data fields of particular interest.

The Details section also has a number of fields that are worth detailed discussion. Microsoft Dynamics CRM comes with a long list of industries for the drop-down list associated with the Industry field. Some examples include Eating and Drinking Places, Public Relations, Durable Manufacturing, Financial, Wholesale, and Social Services. The Industry field is similar to Standard Industry Codes (SIC) or North American Industry Classification System (NAICS), but it is more focused on the description you might use for the account as opposed to a recognized standard. SIC is also a default and available data field associated with the account. If Industry is important to your classification and firm, one option is to set up the industry drop-down list to correspond with the descriptions associated with the SIC code. Another option is to let Industry indicate how your sales team would classify the Account and then complement this with a SIC or NAICS classification. Industry, SIC, NAICS, and other similar fields tend to be used or not used depending on the company using Microsoft Dynamics CRM. When setting up Microsoft Dynamics CRM, it is important to ask the right questions to get input on this specific area.

Territories in Microsoft Dynamics CRM are defined by the company using Microsoft Dynamics CRM and are set up by selecting Settings, Business Management and then Sales Territories. Territories can be adjusted, added to, and changed. Territories are not just a defined acronym and association; each also has functionality and associ-ation to other information in the system.

More Details on Territories

Figure 7.7 offers a look at how territories are set up in the system.

By the Way

> **Territories**
>
> I want to take a slight detour and give you just a little more insight into territories. If you look at Figure 7.7, you will see that a territory has associated with it a terri-tory manager and an association to an unlimited number of members. Members are users in the Microsoft Dynamics CRM system, such as salespeople who are associated to a specific territory. So, a territory could be associated with a spe-cific account and a specific set of members (or salespeople). This association greatly expands what you can do with reporting or views, which we discuss in later lessons. You can also define specific processes and associate them with specific changes to territories. You can see the word *Workflows* in the left navigation pane in Figure 7.7. Workflow is the automation of a business process, and many com-panies have territory-specific workflow processes.

The Relationship Type field is a customizable drop-down list of options. From a pre-configuration standpoint, it contains the following default items: Competitor, Consultant, Customer Investor, Partner, Influencer, Press, Prospect, Reseller, Supplier, Vendor, and Other. The Relationship Type field allows you to describe what this account is with regard to how it relates to your company. The most common rela-tionship types are Prospect and Customer.

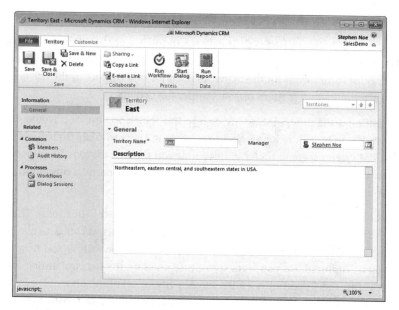

FIGURE 7.7
Sales territory
setup.

The Contacts Section

Figure 7.8 shows the Contacts section of the Account form. This section of the form assists user productivity by showing only the contacts within the specific account that are owned by the user viewing the form. You can also change the view selected in the grid by clicking the drop-down list to the right of the contact's icon at the top of the grid.

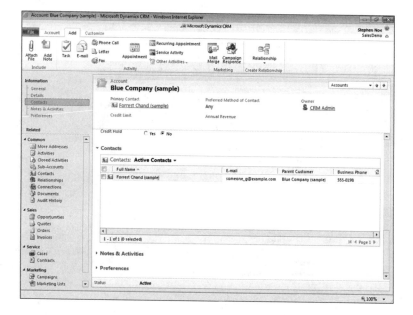

FIGURE 7.8
Displaying
all contacts
associated with
an account.

The Notes & Activities Section

The Notes & Activities section is definitely worth talking about. Microsoft has added an Activities list that displays the open activities for the account and related contacts. This list summarizes all the activities open for any contact in the account. Next, a scrolling panel of notes appears under the activities.

If you don't like the notes all the way over in this fourth section, or if would like the notes window to be a little larger, you can adjust it. Users who are accustomed to a flatter CRM system seem to prefer to have notes on the first section. The placement of notes within a form is not specific to an individual so consensus among the team using the form is required.

In true Microsoft fashion, Microsoft Dynamics CRM is packed with choice. This can make the system more complex but also more flexible. When it comes to choice in notes, you need to decide what your business process will be with regard to where notes will be captured. Do you want to capture notes on the Account entity, the Contact entity, the Opportunity entity, the Activity, or all of the above? Perhaps you want to only add profile type notes to the Account entity and you want to add very specific detailed notes to each Contact entity it relates to. You also have to decide between what goes into Description (or if Description is even turned on) and Notes. At the Account level, Description is a great place to put the account profile (often from the account's website), for instance, but at the Contact and Activity levels, it gets a bit more difficult.

Figure 7.9 shows an example of the Notes tab with two different notes entered.

FIGURE 7.9
Notes and
activities.

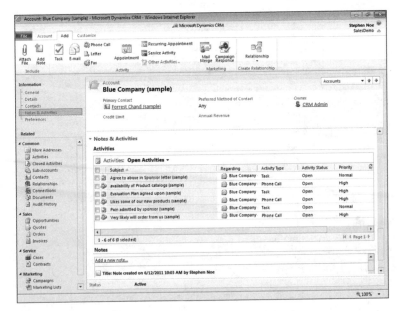

Can I Get an Executive Summary?

I can hear your question now: Is there an executive summary on the account that pulls all the associated notes from associated contacts, activities, opportunities, and more onto one display? The answer is yes and no. Microsoft Dynamics CRM does not currently come with an executive summary of all notes for a particular account; however, numerous third-party solutions offer this, and it is something that can be built with development resources if you want to build it yourself. In addition, with the right business process, it does not become an obvious need.

The Preferences Section

Figure 7.10 shows the Preferences section of the Account form. Fields worthy of further discussion in this section include Owner, Originating Lead, Price List, and Last Date Included in Campaign.

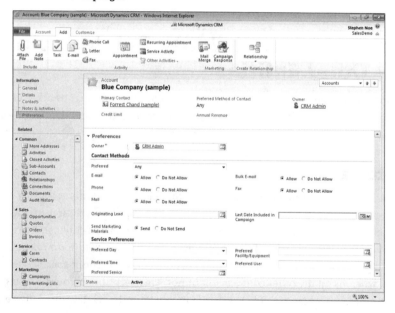

FIGURE 7.10
Data fields of particular interest in the Preferences section.

In the Preferences section, the first data field that jumps out is the Owner field. Notice that next to the owner is a small red asterisk (*). This red star indicates that this is a required field. The owner must be a Microsoft Dynamics CRM user or a staff member at the organization using Microsoft Dynamics CRM. The Owner field is one of the security controls that can be used to determine who has access to which Account entities. The Owner field also drives a number of reports and views. You can rename the field called Owner, but you cannot eliminate this field because it is required by the system. Some examples of renaming the owner might be to rename it to account manager or the primary salesperson, or the assigned customer service representative.

In earlier chapters, we talked briefly about a lead versus an account prospect. When a Lead entity is entered into the system, it can be converted to an Account, Contact, and/or Opportunity entity. The Originating Lead data field is a system field that displays where this Account entity came from if it came from a Lead entity. A system field is a data field that the software keeps updated automatically. As a reminder, the best way to think of a lead is as an unqualified contact.

Last Date Included in Campaign is another system field. When you use the Microsoft Dynamics CRM campaign features, the system captures and tracks the last date that this account was associated with a campaign. It then displays this field in the Administrative section of the Account form. This is useful when thinking about the account either because you want to include it in a new marketing campaign or you are interested in calling and following up with that account regarding the last material that was sent.

How the Account Entity Relates to a Few Other Entities

Account is a core entity in Microsoft Dynamics CRM. It has numerous other associations to other entities. Let's look at a few of these other entities and the relationship they have to Account.

Contacts

Account relates to a number of other entities, and each relationship is slightly different. The first, and possibly the most obvious, relationship is the relationship between an Account entity and its various Contact entities. An Account entity can have an unlimited number of associated Contact entities. In addition, within an Account is an optional primary contact. The primary contact appears on account-specific views and reports, whereas all the other contacts might not. This keeps the account reports and views cleaner and easier to read. Another feature within the relationship between Account and Contact is the ability for the Account entity to share information with a new Contact entity when a new Contact entity is created from the Account form. This reduces user data entry and maintains data integrity. For instance, when a Contact entity is created after choosing the Account entity, the account address details and account name are duplicated to the new Contact entity. If the Contact entity is created without the Account entity open, data will not populate.

Other Accounts: Parent Account and Subaccounts

Subaccounts can be used when setting up an account that is a subset of a larger account structure, such as an umbrella company or a very large corporation that has different accounting practices. Figure 7.11 shows an example of using subaccounts.

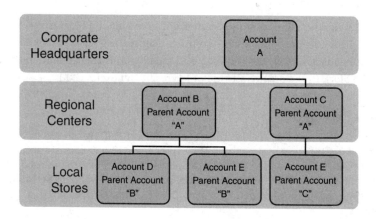

FIGURE 7.11
A subaccount
example.

You don't have to use subaccounts because you can set up an account as a parent, and each parent account can have a parent, and so on. Figure 7.12 shows an example of a parent account structure.

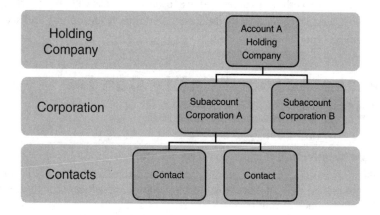

FIGURE 7.12
A parent
account
example.

What the Account Entity Can Impact

Account is one of the core entities within Microsoft Dynamics CRM, and it is related to many other entities. The Account entity has an impact on many other functions and features in Microsoft Dynamics CRM. Therefore, if you are thinking of renaming the Account entity, consider a few things.

First, consider the fact that features that you might not want to use today might be features you want to use tomorrow. If you decide to rename Account to Prospect and set up some other database structure for Client, for example, the entire service module prebuilt within Microsoft Dynamics CRM is semi-useless because it would be tied to Prospect rather than Client.

Other features and functions are also built on the core building block account, including the connections function, the contract features, the service calendar, and even such functions as duplicate checking and inactivation. The Account entity is a key building block in the greater scheme of Microsoft Dynamics CRM.

By the
Way

> **Introducing the GUID**
>
> The Account entity also has a globally unique identifier (GUID) which can be used to connect many different systems. It can be used to tie to an account-specific document folder created and maintained in Microsoft SharePoint to the account in Microsoft Dynamics CRM. It is also used by third-party independent software vendors (ISVs) who offer Microsoft Dynamics CRM plug-ins and add-on applications.

When working with Microsoft Dynamics CRM, it is easy to get lured into changing and adding everything. However, without good vision into the long-term impact, it is always good to talk with an experienced Microsoft Dynamics CRM architect first. At the very least, post your ideas to the Microsoft Dynamics CRM forums and see what type of feedback you get from the field.

How the Account Entity Can Be Redefined

Watch
Out!

> **Software Architecture Insight Could Be Helpful**
>
> The following text shows major changes to the Microsoft Dynamics CRM system that do not require the experienced skills of a software developer or software architect. Reproduce at your own risk.

The first two lessons of this book provide a few hints about how the Account entity can be redefined, but let's take a deeper dive now that you understand that changing the Account entity has wide-ranging impacts.

Say that a company purchases buildings and then hires a rental management company to handle the leasing of the offices within the buildings. In this particular case, the company wants to track all the buildings as the core building blocks of its system. After careful consideration by the Microsoft Dynamics CRM architect and review of the implications with the client, the Account entity is renamed Building.

In Figure 7.13, you see that when you rename the Account entity, the top of the screen displays the word Building, as opposed to Account. On the other hand, there are specific data fields, which still have the name Account, associated with them. In this particular example, the Microsoft Dynamics CRM system customizer would also have to rename each data field (attribute) that has the word *account* as part of the data field (attribute) name. There are only a few, but as you can see in Figure 7.13, they definitely need to be changed. In addition to changing the entity title, you need to consider the text associated with error messages, the names of any account-specific system views, and any reports that have *account* as part of any of the descriptive information. Although this seems like a lot of information, the name of the Account entity and all associated data fields can be changed fairly efficiently by using available tools and a dash of Microsoft Dynamics CRM experience.

FIGURE 7.13
Renaming Account to Building in system customization (with nothing else changed).

Workshop

A financial investment company, Wood Finance, has a staff of 10 financial planners. Each planner has many relationships, specifically with consumers who work with individuals from Wood Finance to manage their long-term and short-term investment portfolios. In addition, Wood Finance offers corporate discounts and corporate "lunch and learn" seminars to corporations that offer the services of Wood Finance to their staff members interested in more detailed financial planning.

Wood Finance uses Microsoft Dynamics CRM to manage its relationships. The Account entity captures corporation details, and it also captures a family surname so that families of individuals can be grouped and potentially viewed or reported on together. Wood Finance uses the subaccount, and it uses it rather creatively. The company uses the subaccount to capture the details of other surnames within a family tree. For instance, the Smith family has a master surname of Smith, which is an Account entity within Microsoft Dynamics CRM; however, Mr. and Mrs. Smith have two daughters who are both married. Wood Finance would like to track all that happens within the world of the married children, too, and it wants to track that the married children have a relationship to the Smiths. A Subaccount entity has been created for the James family in Microsoft Dynamics CRM for the James family because Mrs. James is Mr. and Mrs. Smith's married daughter.

Figure 7.14 shows an example of the building blocks in this family example.

FIGURE 7.14
If the Account entity is a family surname, the subaccounts contain related family surnames.

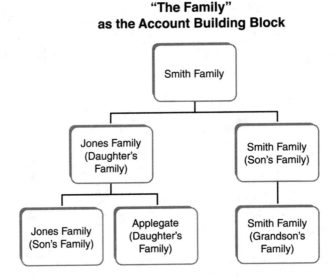

"The Family"
as the Account Building Block

Q&A

Q. *We track NAICS and SIC, but sometimes we just want to associate a general less standard industry. Is this possible?*

A. Yes, you can track other industry codes and you have two choices. You can use a drop-down list of industries that are common to your company, or you can create a text field to capture any combination of typed-in text that describes the industry.

Q. *Many of our accounts have a complex hierarchy of relationships to other accounts. How is this handled?*

A. An account can have a parent account, a parent account can have a parent account, and so on up the ladder. You also have the option of associating sub-accounts. Lastly you can use the Connections feature of Microsoft Dynamics CRM to associate an account to any other account.

Q. *We e-mail around a ton of attachments, but we do not necessarily want to capture those attachments within Dynamics CRM associated with e-mail tracking or notes. Can we turn off attachments?*

A. Yes, you can block attachments.

Quiz

1. What are some of the impacts of changing the name of an Account entity to something else?

2. Are Parent Account entities different from Account entities?

3. How are Territory entities related to an Account entity?

4. What are the four components of a form?

5. Why is the address phone number different from the main business phone number?

6. How many addresses are attribute fields within the Account entity?

7. How many sections can you create on the Account form?

8. Would you enter your descriptive notes in the Description field or the Notes field?

Answers

1. If you decide to rename Account to Prospect, for example, and set up some other data structure for Client, your entire service module prebuilt within Microsoft Dynamics CRM would be semi-useless because it would be tied to Prospect rather than Client.

2. Parent account entities are not different from account entities.

3. Every Account entity is associated with a Territory entity, and every owner of an Account entity is associated with a Territory entity.

4. The four components of a form include the Left navigation pane, the Form Assistant, the main entry form (orscreen), and sections.

5. The Phone Number field associated with the address is provided for delivery companies such as FedEx and UPS.

6. There are two addresses that are defined as attribute fields within the Account entity.

7. You can create more than eight sections on any specific form.

8. No, because the Description field is limited in size. The Notes field is not limited in size and is designed for an unlimited amount of notes.

Exercise

Using Microsoft Visio, paper, or a large white board, diagram the following scenario. The Wild Adventure Corporation (WAC) organizes tours of local nature preserves as a team-building exercise for large local corporations. The WAC needs to keep track of the nature preserves that it visits and the corporations that purchase its nature preserve tours team-building services. How would you use the Account entity in this scenario?

HOUR 8

The Sales Funnel

What You'll Learn in This Hour:

▶ Sales styles and choices
▶ Automating the sales process with workflow
▶ Editing an existing workflow

In this hour, you'll learn about the world of sales and how sales, sales processes, sales funnels, and overall sales styles are tied to Microsoft Dynamics CRM. This lesson dives into different industry sales methodologies, and it looks closely at what the sales funnel is all about, what it is used for, and why it is important.

Sales Styles and Choices

It is hard to talk, think, and learn about Microsoft Dynamics CRM without some discussion about personal working styles. It is even more difficult to talk about the application, as a true sales force automation or a customer relationship management application, without discussing the impact of sales styles.

Sales Cultures and Styles

There are many different approaches to sales and the sales process. Two approaches are to use a relationship-focused approach or to use a product-oriented approach. Relationship-oriented salespeople, approaching a sale from a prospect-oriented and personal perspective, place an incredibly high level of value on the relationships that they have with individual contacts. In fact, many relationship-oriented salespeople put the relationship above the immediate sale because they know that in the long term, the return will be higher. Relationship-oriented salespeople have a very specific need to protect and grow their trusted relationships. They also strive to keep all the details of all their various contacts organized and available so that they can work on the maximum number of accounts and contact relationships. They are interested in buzz and information about their prospect and customer accounts within the system that might come from other sources, such as social media sites. For instance, if a particular prospect is the subject of a Twitter conversation or the prospect has a long list of new press releases, this information is critical for a relationship-oriented sales person. Tracking this external data becomes a value add for any system. This arena of sales audience can gain benefit from integration of Microsoft Dynamics CRM with external sources, such as a data cleansing services or repositories of additional information on specific businesses, such as Hoovers (www.hoovers.com), Dun & Bradstreet (www.dnb.com), and others. They often also have an interest in integration with some of the social media and Web 2.0 toolsets, including websites such as LinkedIn (www.linkedin.com) and Twitter (www.twitter.com).

Technical sales style salespeople are experts on their product and work to educate and inform their prospects. Technical salespeople not only need to keep track of all their relationships, they also need to keep track of their product knowledge and product knowledge resources.

A product-oriented salesperson tends to be in tune with their products, with an ever-changing audience of prospects. They don't necessarily need a deep relationship with a prospect because a prospect might only be buying the offering once. Product-oriented salespeople are more interested in capturing all the details of their specific product, engineering and sales techniques for selling the product, their market, and the competition selling the same type of commodity product. Product-oriented salespersons need to keep track of their prospects or incoming sales calls, as volume tends to indicate number of sales, but they might also need Microsoft Dynamics CRM to keep all the product and competitor details organized and accessible. They might use the system to track weaknesses in comparable products on the market, competition specials, product defects and recalls, available inventory, and perhaps key knowledge on use and configuration (and additional details). They might also want to keep diagrams and schematics on their products, and they can use the integration to SharePoint to maintain details on unstructured product data.

Neither of these primary focus cultures is exclusive; in fact, many sales styles overlap. A person selling a set of commodity products might have a well-established network of clients that he upsells to in addition to incoming calls for orders, and a salesperson focused on selling services through relationships might also have a wide range of product offerings. Microsoft Dynamics CRM handles this overlap by offering support for both services and product cultures. The software offers a product catalog and quote, invoice, and order functionality, and it offers a robust company hierarchy to support complex relationships through the connections feature. The goal for you is to dive in and master the pieces of the software that best apply to your selling culture and methodology.

Corporate Selling Methodologies

For any given company, there are many different sales methodologies. These range from industry-standard methodologies, such as those used by Sandler Sales (www.sandler.com), Miller Heiman (www.millerheiman.com), Richardson (www.richardson.com), and Performance Methods (www.performancemethods.com), to custom (perhaps more industry-specific) sales process methodologies designed and matured within a specific company. One of the keys to success with Microsoft Dynamics CRM for a customer, partner, or third-party vendor is to understand the selling methodology and business process that are to be used with the product.

If your company does not currently have a formal selling methodology, it most likely has business processes in use that can give additional insight into how using Microsoft Dynamics CRM might work best within the environment. In our consulting days we would often work with companies that did not necessarily categorize how they sold into a "sales methodology"; however, with a bit of detective work and some business process diagramming, existing processes can easily be understood.

The Existing Sales Methodology Built into Another Application

If your company is currently using a CRM application other than Microsoft Dynamics CRM, you might have a methodology built into the software that was or is in use today. This methodology could be something that everyone loves or hates, and it could also be limited or crafted to fit the software in use. One of the key shifts when moving to Microsoft Dynamics CRM is to not only move existing sales processes, but to also consider these sales processes as they might mature and change based on new functionalities. Take, for instance, a company that uses the XYZ CRM application. In this software, you cannot define a sales process, but the software captures notes, contact details, appointments, and scheduled calls. It is robust enough, but it is not everything that the company needs. When this company moves away from the XYZ CRM application to Microsoft Dynamics CRM, it has the option to define a standard sales process because Microsoft Dynamics CRM offers it a place to define the process and the functionality to make the sales process more efficient.

The Ad Hoc Sales Method

What about a company that is not using an industry-level CRM application? An example might be a company heavily vested in using Microsoft Outlook for much of its day-to-day sales work. It might not have an existing CRM application, but through the use of Microsoft Outlook, it categorizes information, captures communication, organizes contact details, creates reminders, sets appointments, tracks tasks, and perhaps follows a routine that works for it. The company might also be supplementing Outlook with a variety of Microsoft Excel spreadsheets to forecast, set budgets, analyze open opportunities, and compare goals to actuals. It does not have a true collaborative environment, but it does have processes. Letters, mailings, and other efforts might be part of the process, perhaps supported by Microsoft Word. The reality is that technology is being used. It might not be the best technology for the job, but it is being used.

If you add in its collaborative need for a service department that captures details on what is going on with current clients and that this service department has ideas and efforts about selling additional product and services, this company really needs that one place to organize and collaborate.

Microsoft Dynamics CRM pulls all of this into a total solution, organizing and pairing technology with methodologies and business process and bringing a new dimension to the table, which offers different complementary layers of collaboration and organization. Microsoft Dynamics CRM takes all the pieces and applies the right piece to the right job, Outlook for e-mail, Word for letters, and Microsoft Dynamics CRM to collaborate on what needs to get done to close an opportunity. It also adds a layer of graphical visibility to what is being captured and reinforces requests to sales teams to enter data.

Opportunity Tracking

Earlier lessons talk about what makes up an opportunity. This section reviews what opportunities are used for. The opportunity is the core building block of most sales processes. It is the "object" or "the potential sale" that moves through the sales funnel and that is classified, won or lost, closed, analyzed, compared to goals, reviewed, and tracked. An opportunity has a life all its own, with a beginning, a middle, and an end. It is also associated with a prospect. The opportunity is not the prospect, but it is related. The opportunity starts with the awareness that a potential sale is within reach or worth going after and ends with the winning, losing, or postponement of that sales opportunity. Some companies also consider that an opportunity starts once a prospect is qualified, but this can be personal preference.

When courting a potential prospect, the loss of an opportunity does not necessarily mean that you will not try to sell that same prospect again in a year or so. The loss of an opportunity also does not mean that the prospect is not a prospect. The loss of an opportunity signals the end of a sales process, which was supposed to result in success or failure or perhaps the closing of an open door because of a locked-down budget or problems in the economy.

The other advantage of an opportunity is that for any given prospect, you could potentially have multiple opportunities, depending on your business model. For instance, you might have two departments that sell different products to the same company, or you might have a product division and a service division. The product division might have an opportunity to sell a specific set of products, and the service department might have a different opportunity to sell complementary services. Each opportunity can be unique and have its own close date and its own set of processes, and the success of each is independent.

Sales Percentages

The sales percentage or the probability of a win is related to the opportunity. Microsoft Dynamics CRM supports defining a probability of a win in any number of different formats. Many companies like to have a common definition of their probabilities and so will relate the percent probability to a stage within the sales process. Still other companies tolerate the free-will choices of their sales team and can interrupt the probability based on individual salesperson's style. Others offer three to six options, such as 0%, 10%, 25%, 50%, 75%, and 99% (or a similar series).

One of the key concepts with probability percentages is that the probability is generally used to offset the predicted and anticipated revenue in the pipeline. If there is a potential deal for $10,000 with a probability of 25 percent, the analysis determines this potential sale is worth $2,500 dollars (10,000 * .25).

When the anticipated revenue is offset based on the salesperson's or sales team's predictions, a CEO, board of directors, or even venture capitalists can better understand what sales will be successfully closed based on the sales teams predictions.

The probability can also be used to judge the risk level or temperature around a specific opportunity. The percentage can be a salesperson's assumption or even a manager's valuation, based on provided data.

Sales Stages

A sales process is made up of a set of sales stages. For each stage, there might be a set probability percentage, a set temperature or rating, and a defined set of actions. As actions are completed, you move closer and closer to the goal of moving a prospect to the role of new client or customer. As each step is completed, you move the opportunity through the sales funnel. For each set of actions completed, a sales stage is completed, and the sales process moves forward. The following is an example of a sales process:

▶ **Stage one**—Establish a dialog and an initial relationship with the prospect. Potential activity items for sales stage one include the following:

1. Phone call: Follow-up to initial conversation

2. Send letter with more details and further introduction

3. Phone call: Follow-up to letter

4. After connecting with the prospect, send a thank you e-mail or letter and an e-mail with promised info

5. Update sales stage and probability percentage

▶ **Stage two**—Understand and document the needs as defined by the prospect. Potential activity items for sales stage two include the following:

1. Prepare custom PowerPoint presentation (focused on prospect needs)

2. Outline your understanding of what they are looking for

3. Research prospect history for supporting information

4. Make appointment to meet

5. Meet face to face to reiterate what you have learned

6. Update sales stage and probability percentage

▶ **Stage three**—Validate to the prospect that you have heard their needs by communicating back your understanding of what they are looking for. Potential activity items for sales stage three include the following:

1. Meet face to face to reiterate what you have learned

2. Update sales stage and probability percentage

▶ **Stage four**—Share your company's culture, vision, and history with your prospect. Potential activity items for sales stage four include the following:

1. Follow-up to meeting

2. Update sales stage and probability percentage

▶ **Stage five**—Answer any questions your prospect might have about the company. Potential activity items for sales stage five include the following:

1. Phone call

2. Continue to build and mature your relationship with the prospect.

3. Update sales stage and probability percentage

▶ **Stage six**—Share with the prospect how your offering can meet their needs. Potential activity items for sales stage six could include the following:

1. Demonstrate the product
2. Update the sales stage and probability percentage

▶ **Stage seven**—Present proposal. Potential activity items for sales stage seven include the following:

1. Prepare proposal
2. Negotiate details
3. Update sales stage and probability percentage

▶ **Stage eight**—Close the deal. The activity item for sales stage eight is as follows:

1. Close the opportunity as won!

Each stage can have any number of activities, which can include a variety of different tasks, phone calls, letters, e-mails, and even specific goals. Stages can also call different workflows or have automatic functions that occur, such as the automatic generation of an e-mail message. In addition, Microsoft Dynamics CRM supports the ability to standardize and automate a sales process using the Microsoft Dynamics CRM Workflow engine. There is more about workflow in the next chapter; for now, let's look at a simplified example that was configured in Microsoft Dynamics CRM Workflow.

Automating the Sales Process with Workflow

In this section, we walk through setting up a piece of a full sales process and the end result. We start by accessing processes and creating a new workflow and then add the sales stages to this new workflow. Figure 8.1 kicks off the process.

Creating a New Workflow for the Sales Process

Figure 8.1 shows where to start creating a workflow for the sales process. This is how your window will appear when you are getting started.

FIGURE 8.1
Automated
sales process
(workflow).

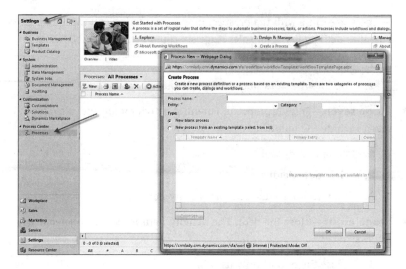

Next, you'll see how to set up the sales stages and the associated steps for a new workflow. You start by creating a new workflow, and because you are focusing on a sales process, you associate this new workflow with the opportunity record. Notice that you are not selecting a dialog; a dialog is a different type of process. As shown in Figure 8.2, you assign a name (CRMLady Sales Process) and select the opportunity entity from the entity list.

FIGURE 8.2
Creating the
new automated
sales process
workflow.

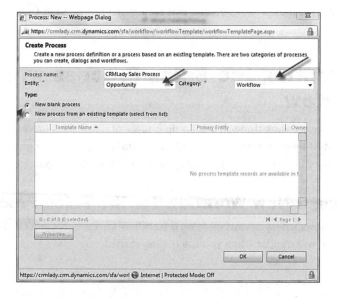

The scope of the new automated sales process should be organization. Figure 8.3 shows the scope in the upper-right corner.

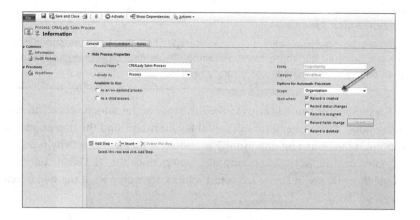

FIGURE 8.3
Sales process scope.

Adding Sales Stages

In Figure 8.4, you take your first step toward creating a sales process in the workflow: You start to add a stage. A stage categorizes a set of steps and often a set of activities and a section of the sales process. A stage can also indicate or help classify what needs to be done within a level or section of the sales funnel. Stages are optional, but they are fairly common when defining sales process workflows.

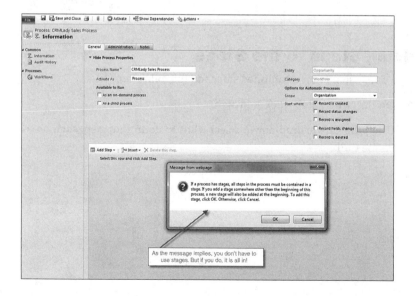

FIGURE 8.4
Adding a stage to the workflow.

Individual Sales Processes

You can create individual sales processes for specific subsets of salespeople for a less-standardized and more custom offering. Depending on your organization, this option might be embraced or strongly rejected.

Figure 8.5 shows how you add steps to the first stage of the sales process. This figure shows the stage "Stage One: Establish Initial Relationship" and the step phone call. The concept is that when an opportunity is created, a phone call activity is automatically created and added to the opportunity owner's to-do list. The label "Initial Reachout" that you see in Figure 8.5 is just a label describing what the step is actually doing.

FIGURE 8.5
Stage one: Establishing an initial relationship.

Adding Steps to the Stage

To add a new step to an established stage, do the following:

1. On the General tab, click Add Step.

2. Using the Create drop-down, select what to do in that step, such as Phone Call.

3. Click Set Properties and configure the properties of the activity.

4. Select Step Description and enter a description for the step.

Figure 8.6 shows an example with the phone call stage open.

You can now add more steps that create activities or update the prospect to sales stage one, or you can add another stage. For instance in sales stage two, you can set the probability percentage to 25%.

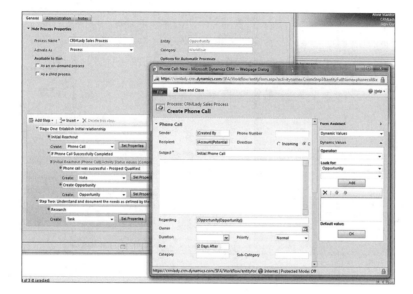

FIGURE 8.6
Sales Stage
One, Phone Call
Activity.

If the probability to close is less than 25%, set the probability to close to 25%, as shown in Figure 8.7. You do this so that any new opportunity that has had stage one completed will have a probability assigned. There are other ways to skin this beast, but this serves as an example of the condition option of workflow. Within any given step, you can add conditions that when true or false can be associated with activities or can update attributes in the opportunity.

Watch Out!

> **Async and Conditional Statements**
>
> You do not want to create a conditional statement that puts the system into an infinite or potentially infinite wait state.

FIGURE 8.7
Conditionally setting the probability on the opportunity to 25 percent.

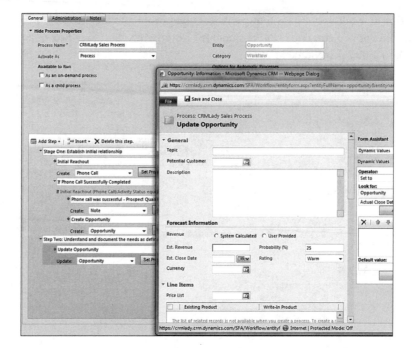

Using a Conditional Statement in a Step

Figure 8.8 shows how you add a new task to prepare a PowerPoint presentation. You go a bit further by showing that the task can also be customized to include details that might be important to remember and dynamic variables that pull data from the opportunity entity (record type) when the stage is activated.

By the Way

> **Form Assistant**
>
> You can add dynamic data by using the Form Assistant on the Set Properties page of the task.

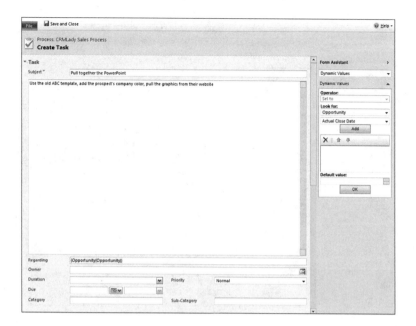

FIGURE 8.8
The task for preparing a PowerPoint presentation.

You can now continue to add an unlimited number of different types of activities by using Create Record, or you can add updates to other existing records by using Modify Record. You can also assign new or modified records to other people who are users of Microsoft Dynamics CRM, and you can complement them with conditions.

Publishing a Workflow

The sales process can be a set of simple tasks to get started, or it can be multilayered and complex. Start small by creating a two- to three-step sales process with one or two activities. After the sales process is created, you need to activate it to access and use it, or if it is automated, to have it start processing. You can make a sales process automatic or on demand manual. Manual allows you to control when the sales process starts, because you choose the Run Workflow option when you are ready to run the workflow.

Figure 8.9 shows the Publish option.

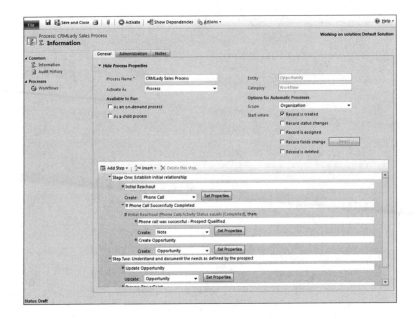

To activate, you select Activate from the top of the Create Workflow form or from the view of all workflow processes.

After the workflow is activated, it is available to run. In this example, the new manual workflow is available to run from the Opportunity screen. If it had been created as an automatic sales process, the process would run automatically when a new opportunity is created. Manual or automatic depends on the configuration choice when creating the workflow.

Figure 8.10 shows a new opportunity created and saved. Notice that after the opportunity is saved, you have the Run Workflow on top of the opportunity form. Figure 8.10 shows green check marks next to each step:

1. Select Sales.

2. Select Opportunity.

3. Select New.

In this example, if you choose to run the workflow, the entire workflow runs from start to finish, and you can see the final process. In the sales process workflow, you did not add any conditions (for example, requiring an activity to be completed to move to the next step) or wait states (for example, requiring a condition to be met to do the next action). The system does what it was told and displays what was accomplished and what is still pending in the sales process.

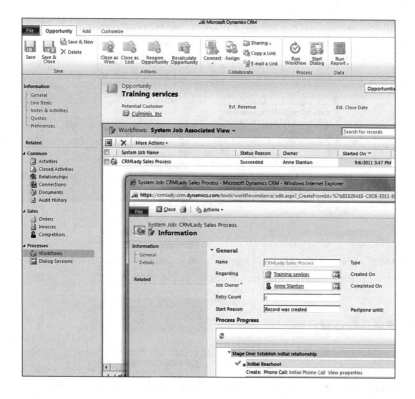

FIGURE 8.10
The opportunity workflow.

You now want to add in some timing logic and progress based on timing, dates, and the completion of activities. So, you need to build into your sales process workflow some wait conditions.

Wait States Can Be Dangerous

Wait states can be dangerous if they are not properly created because they can create a situation where the async process (the process that handles workflow processing) is waiting in a never-ending state. Always work with a knowledgeable CRM advisor on wait steps within a workflow.

Editing an Existing Workflow

If you want to change a workflow that has already been published, you need to do two things: Check the workflow and see whether it is actively running or waiting and then unpublish the workflow so that it can be edited. To unpublish, do the following:

1. Select Workflows.

2. Select the workflow of interest (for example, the sales process workflow).

3. Select the Unpublish option.

The status of the workflow is set back to Draft, as shown in Figure 8.11. To set a workflow back to Draft, you must choose to Deactivate it.

FIGURE 8.11
Workflow deactivation.

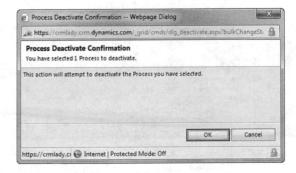

You'll learn about expanding this workflow to include wait states, more conditions, and dates in Hour 16, "Workflows: Creating Simple Workflows."

Workshop

Wild Landscaping is a landscaping company that specializes in native species. It focuses on bringing hardy and local plants to each area that it services, and it offers services and has offices all over the world. Each office has a variety of teams, including long-term maintenance, administration, planning and architecture, consumer sales, business sales, and the weekend dream makeover speed team.

The company sells its services to both businesses and consumers. Businesses often purchase the long-term maintenance plan, whereas consumers are more partial to the weekend dream makeover offering.

Wild Landscaping has a successful sales process that it has used around the world. It uses its sales process in two different ways with two different sets of associated activities depending on the audience. It uses its sales process as it applies to the business prospects and the business sales team, and it uses its sales process when approaching consumers.

The business sales team must ultimately find out who the key decision makers are within the company it wants to approach. It does this by starting with a warm referral to someone within the company, and then it leverages the relationship to learn more about the company.

Q&A

Q. *We use five different sales processes. Can we create these and then associate different sales processes with different accounts?*

A. You can create each of the sales processes as manual processes and then associate them as you need them. You can also automatically associate them if you have a clear business rule, such as the owner of the opportunity that helps the system to act on a specific set of conditions.

Q. *We use the Miller Heiman sales methodology. Is there a plug-in that automatically configures Microsoft Dynamics CRM with the Miller Heiman templates, worksheets, and configurations?*

A. Yes, there are third-party options that offer the Miller Heiman sales methodology as a plug-in to Microsoft Dynamics CRM. Check out the Microsoft Dynamics Marketplace.

Q. *We recently created a workflow, but it is not running. What did we forget?*

A. If your workflow is not working, then most likely you forgot to activate the workflow. A workflow stays in draft mode until it is activated.

Quiz

1. What is the probability to close used for as it applies to opportunity? Why would this variable be of value to a group of venture capitalists?

2. Name two sales methodologies that can be incorporated into Microsoft Dynamics CRM.

3. Can the system handle a sales process that is oriented around selling a specific set of services as opposed to a set of products?

4. How many opportunities can you have on any one given prospect?

Answers

1. The probability percentage on an opportunity is used for analysis to offset the estimated revenue based on a salesperson's interpretation or a step in the sales process. This offers a more realistic expectation of expected revenue.

2. Two of the many sales processes that can be incorporated into Microsoft Dynamics CRM are Sandler Sales and Miller Heiman.

3. Yes. Microsoft Dynamics CRM can automate, document, and follow a services-oriented sales process.

4. You can have an unlimited number of opportunities on any given prospect.

Exercises

Create a simple sales process that includes the following items:

1. Automatically create a new activity of type task to remind a specific salesperson to update the close date, estimated revenue, and probability to close on the opportunity.

2. Plan for and schedule a demonstration of a product.

3. Follow up on the demonstration.

Outline the sales process that Wild Landscaping might be using. Start with a warm referral to a person in a company in your area. What happens after that introduction? Can any of these steps be automated? Which steps? What are some of the other things you might have to do if you start with this warm lead?

HOUR 9

Marketing Campaigns

What You'll Learn in This Hour:

- ▶ The marketing campaign
- ▶ Creating and tracking a marketing budget
- ▶ Capturing the results
- ▶ Tracking the steps, activities, and tasks

Now that you have learned the different sales styles and how to track opportunities, it is time to learn about a component that helps drive sales: the Marketing Campaigns module. This module in Microsoft Dynamics CRM enables you to build, manage, track, and report on the efforts that your team has put into promoting a marketing event.

The Marketing Campaign

A campaign contains all the information related to a specific marketing effort over a period of time. One way to look at a campaign is as an umbrella over a set of information. Take, for example, all the details that are involved with putting together a trade show. These details include tasks that need to be done, budgets that need to be put together and tracked, mailings and announcements and the responses to these, and more. A full marketing campaign keeps track of all the planning tasks, the campaign activities, and the campaign responses. It also lets you add target products and sales literature to the campaign, which allows you to see all related information in one place in Microsoft Dynamics CRM. By having all the information in one place, you can see and understand the effectiveness of your marketing campaign.

Think of a campaign as a container that holds all the information related to a marketing activity. Full marketing campaigns manage more complex marketing efforts, where you want to create multiple activities, maintain several marketing lists, and keep track of planning tasks and responses.

To create a new campaign, follow these steps:

1. From the main menu, Navigate to the Marketing area of Microsoft Dynamics CRM by selecting Marketing from the Left Navigation.

2. Next, Select Campaigns from the left navigation menu.

3. Click New.

For an example, you will create a full marketing campaign to manage your company's annual summer picnic. On the Campaign entry form, as shown in Figure 9.1, do the following:

FIGURE 9.1
A new campaign.

1. Enter a name for your campaign.

2. Select the status reason. Because you are creating a new campaign, you can leave it at its default value, Proposed.

3. In the Campaign Type field, select the type of the campaign you are managing. In this case, select Event from the drop-down list because you are creating a campaign for an event.

4. In the Campaign Code field, enter your own code or leave it blank to have the system automatically generate a campaign code.

5. Save the campaign. After you save your campaign, you cannot change the Campaign Code field.

6. Leave the Currency field set to the default, your system base currency. In this case, it is set to U.S. Dollar.

7. Leave the Expected Response field set to its default of 100. This field holds the number of expected responses from managing this campaign.

8. Set the Proposed Begin Date and Proposed End Date fields for your campaign in the Schedule section.

9. Enter a description for your campaign in the Description field (optional).

10. When you are done populating the information on the General section, click Save on the menu bar to save the Campaign. After the Campaign is saved, you can add planning tasks, campaign activities, and campaign responses.

Quick Campaign Versus Campaign

Quick campaigns differ from full-blown campaigns in Microsoft Dynamics CRM. A quick campaign is a light version of a campaign. It contains only a single type of activity and works with a single marketing list. However, quick campaigns and campaigns can share the same marketing list and receive campaign responses. We look at quick campaigns later in this hour.

By the Way

Marketing Lists

One of the important tasks to do for a campaign is to define the marketing lists. A marketing list contains the list of members that are either Account, Contact, or Lead entities that will receive the marketing material.

Microsoft CRM 2011 has two types of marketing lists: static and dynamic. A static marketing list contains a group of leads, contacts or accounts (referred to as *list members*) that you manually add to the list by using one of CRM's search or query tools. Once these members have been added to a static list, the list will not change unless you add or remove members manually. In contrast, dynamic marketing lists are queries that always contain whatever members meet the criteria at the time you use the list. For example, you might create a dynamic marketing list of leads whose Lead Source field is set to Trade Show. Each time you use the list, it will dynamically refresh itself to include all trade show leads at that moment.

If you have already created marketing lists in the Microsoft Dynamics CRM system, you can use your existing marketing lists for your marketing campaign, or you can create a new marketing list. Because you are doing a new campaign, in this section, you'll create a new marketing list.

By the Way

> **Marketing List Members**
>
> Each marketing list can contain members from only a single type of record. If your campaign needs to be sent to all types of records, you need to create multiple marketing lists.

To create a new marketing list, follow these steps:

1. Navigate to the Marketing area of Microsoft Dynamics CRM.

2. Select Marketing Lists from the left navigation menu.

3. Click New.

4. On the Marketing List entry form, enter the name for your new marketing list.

5. Select the type of record (Account, Contact, or Lead) from the Member Type drop-down list.

6. Populate the Purpose, Cost, and Description fields (if desired).

7. Click the Save button on the menu bar to save the marketing list. After the marketing list is saved, as shown in Figure 9.2, you can add the Marketing List members.

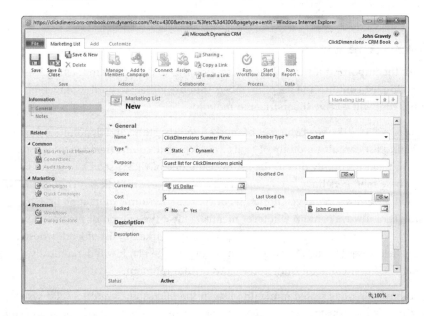

FIGURE 9.2
A new marketing list for existing contacts.

Marketing list members are existing contacts—that is, accounts or leads from within your Dynamics CRM system. If you want to add to your marketing list someone who is not currently a contact, you need to first add the person as a contact or lead before associating him with a marketing list.

Locking Marketing List

If you lock a marketing list by selecting Yes for the Locked field, as shown in Figure 9.2, you cannot add or remove members to the marketing list. To add or remove members, you change the value to No and save the marketing list. After you finalize your members, you can lock your marketing list by changing the Locked value back to Yes.

By the Way

The Marketing List Members navigation choice is now enabled on the navigation menu. To add new members, follow these steps:

1. Click Marketing List Members.

2. Click Manage Members on the View menu. A Manage Members window appears (see Figure 9.3).

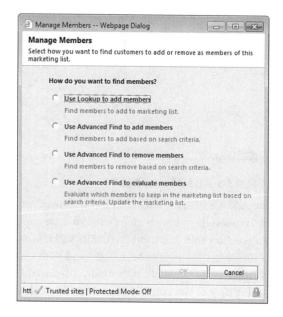

FIGURE 9.3
Manage Members options.

3. Choose an option to manage members. You have four different options: Use Lookup to Add Members, Use Advanced Find to Add Members, Use Advanced Find to Remove Members, and Use Advanced Find to Evaluate Members. As long as the marketing list is not locked, you can use the four options to change your members.

Use Lookup to Add Members

If you select the option Use Lookup to Add Members, a Lookup dialog box appears, enabling you to search for the records that you have identified in the Member Type field of your marketing list. With the Contact type selected, the system will perform the search against contacts, and the active contacts will be returned to you. To see this in action, follow these steps:

1. Select the contacts, as shown in Figure 9.4, and add them to the right pane.

2. Click OK after you add members.

FIGURE 9.4
Using the Look Up Records dialog box to add members.

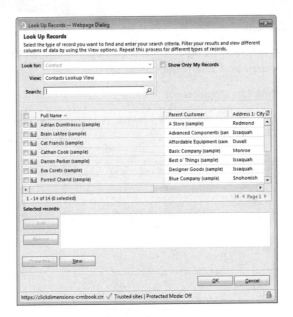

Use Advanced Find to Add Members

Use Advanced Find to Add Members is a feature that will be introduced a few times in this book. You use it to set up your own views with your own queries (see Hour 11, "Configuring Your Interaction with Microsoft Dynamics CRM") and working with Excel (see Hour 20, "Utilizing the Power of Microsoft Excel with CRM Data"). If you select Use Advanced Find to Add Members, a common Advanced Find dialog box appears, as shown in Figure 9.5. You can add your own filter criteria to identify the list of members as follows:

1. Choose your criteria: an attribute (field) and a value or range of values.

2. Choose View.

3. On the result page, select the members you want to include.

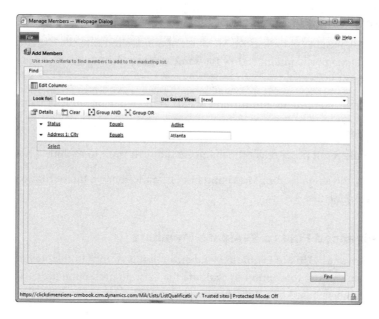

FIGURE 9.5
The Add Members dialog box for adding members.

4. Click Add to Marketing List to add the found people or accounts to your marketing list, as shown in Figure 9.6.

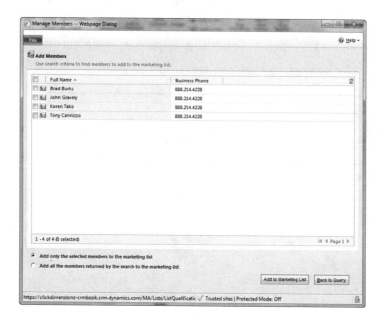

FIGURE 9.6
The result of using the Add Members dialog box for adding members.

Use Advanced Find to Remove Members

The Use Advanced Find to Remove Members option is similar to the Use Advanced Find to Add Members option. Follow the same steps to identify the list of members that you want to remove:

1. Choose your criteria: an attribute (field) and a value or range of values.

2. Choose View.

3. On the result page, select the members that you want to exclude.

4. Click the Remove from Marketing List button to remove them from your marketing list.

Use Advanced Find to Evaluate Members

The Use Advanced Find to Evaluate Members option is similar to the previous two options. You can use this option to evaluate the existing marketing list to add or remove members based on additional filtering criteria.

Add Marketing List to Campaign

After a marketing list is created, you can use it in your marketing campaign. To tie your marketing list to your campaign, follow these steps:

1. From the Left Navigation, Campaigns, Navigate to your campaign.

2. Select Target Marketing List from the navigation menu.

3. Click Add to add your marketing list (see Figure 9.7).

By the Way

Adding a Marketing List to Campaign Activities

The marketing lists must be added to a campaign before you can use them in your campaign activities.

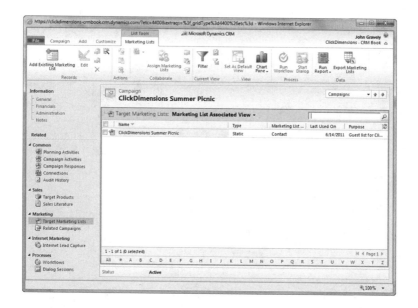

FIGURE 9.7
A new campaign's Target Marketing Lists quick view.

Planning Tasks

Planning tasks are activities of type Task. Think of them as your marketing campaign to-do list. After a planning task is created, you can assign the task to yourself or to others on your team to help launch the campaign. For example, if you are going to run a campaign for your company's summer picnic, you could create a planning task for booking the location, a task for ordering the food, a task for putting together the e-mail invitations, and so on.

To create a planning task, follow these steps:

1. Select Marketing.

2. Select Campaigns.

3. Find and open your campaign.

4. Select Planning Tasks on the navigation.

5. Click New from the ribbon.

6. Enter the information for the planning task, including Subject, Regarding, Owner, Duration, Due, and Priority, as shown in Figure 9.8.

7. Click Notes to add additional information or attachments related to this planning task.

8. When you finish, click Save and Close to save your planning task.

FIGURE 9.8
A new campaign's planning task.

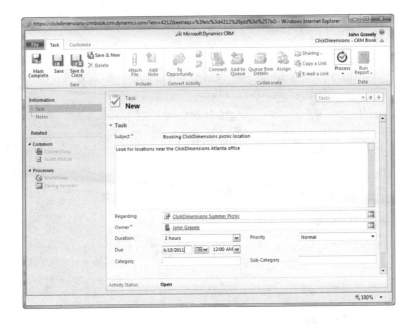

Creating a Planning Task

You can create a planning task by selecting a new activity of type Task and setting the Regarding field to a specific campaign.

Campaign Activities

Campaign activities are the core component of a campaign. They are not the same as regular Microsoft Dynamics CRM activities. They are the actions that make up the campaign, such as phone calls, appointments, letters, faxes, and e-mails. Campaign activities contain information, such as scheduled start date, scheduled end date, priority, budgeted cost, and actual cost of the activity.

A campaign can contain multiple campaign activities. For example, you can set up a campaign activity to send out an e-mail campaign and then follow up with phone calls. Campaign activities have two categories: channel activities and non-channel activities. Channel activities are communications such as a phone call, a letter, or an e-mail message that reaches the customer when the campaign activity is distributed. Non-channel activities are to-dos for you and your team during the campaign; a task will be created and added to the user's activity list. Campaign activities can share a single marketing list or use a different marketing list within a campaign.

To create a campaign activity, follow these steps:

1. From the left navigation, select Marketing.

2. Select Campaigns.

3. Find and open your campaign.

4. Select Campaign Activities from the navigation pane.

5. Click New from ribbon.

6. On the Campaign Activity form, select the channel from the Channel drop-down list, as shown in Figure 9.9.

7. Enter a subject for your campaign activity.

8. For the Type field, select the option that best describes the campaign activity that you are creating.

9. Verify the owner. The Owner field, by default, is you because you are creating the campaign activity. You can assign it to another user if that user will be responsible for it.

Non-Channel Activities

If you want to create a non-channel activity, select Other or just leave the Channel field blank.

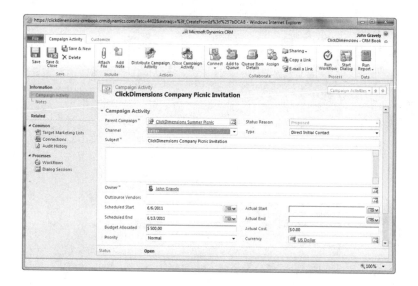

FIGURE 9.9
A new campaign's new campaign activity.

10. Assign an outsource vendor if your campaign activity involves an outside vendor. Enter the scheduled start, scheduled end, budget allocated, and priority information.

11. Under the Anti-Spam setting, exclude marketing list members if contacted within a set time period and enter the number of days you want to pass before a member in your marketing list can be contacted again.

12. Click Save to save the campaign activity.

Every campaign activity must have at least one marketing list. Because you added the marketing lists to the campaign earlier, you can add that to your campaign activity.

To add a marketing list to the campaign activity, follow these steps:

1. Click Target Marketing Lists in the navigation pane.

2. Click Add from the ribbon.

3. In the Look Up Records dialog box, as shown in Figure 9.10, click the search icon to get the lists of available marketing lists.

4. Add the marketing list by moving it to the pane on the right.

5. Click OK to add the marketing list to the campaign activity.

6. Click Save to save the campaign activity.

FIGURE 9.10
A new campaign's Look Up Records dialog box.

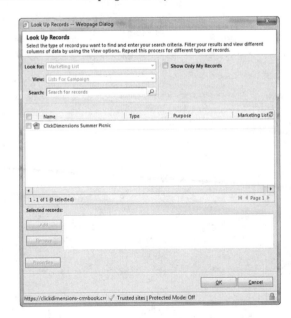

Distributing Campaign Activities

After you create a campaign activity, your next step is to distribute the campaign activities. Distribution of a campaign activity kicks off and assigns the campaign activity to the specific people who need to accomplish it and links the activity to the associated Account, Contact, or Lead entities. To distribute a campaign activity, click Distribute Campaign Activity on the menu bar. A form opens, based on the channel type that you specified. For example, if you select E-mail, a New E-mail form shows up. If you select Phone Call, a New Phone Call form shows up. In this example, a letter was selected in this campaign activity, so a New Letters form appears, as shown in Figure 9.11. You can see that some of the fields on the form are disabled because the system automatically populated those values.

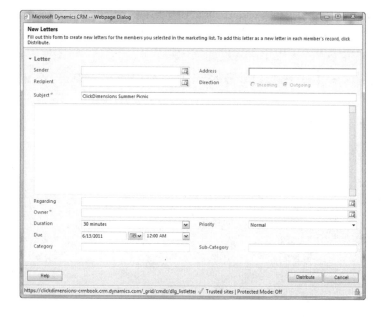

FIGURE 9.11
Distributing a campaign activity.

After a campaign activity is distributed, the activity owners can view the open activities under Activities in their workplace. They can then complete the activity, such as making phone calls or sending the e-mail.

Campaign Activity Status

After a campaign activity is successfully distributed, the status reason for the campaign activity changes from Proposed to Completed.

Campaign Templates

Over time, you will invariably conduct similar campaigns. Instead of re-creating a campaign every time, Microsoft Dynamics CRM offers you the option to create a campaign and save it as a template. Then, the next time you run a similar campaign, you don't have to re-create the same tasks and activities. This saves you time in planning your marketing campaigns.

There are two approaches for creating a campaign template. The first approach is to create a new campaign template by going to Campaigns and clicking the New Template button on the ribbon. When the new campaign form appears, fill in the necessary information and then click Save and Close to save the template. The second approach is to create a template from an existing campaign. Just open your existing Campaign, click the Action menu, and select Copy as Template, as shown in Figure 9.12. This second approach is the most popular way to create a campaign template.

FIGURE 9.12
Creating a campaign template from and existing campaign.

> **Campaign Template**
>
> To identify a campaign template, it's a good idea to include the word *Template* in the name.

Quick Campaigns

A quick campaign is a light version of a full-blown campaign. It can contain only a single type of activity and works with a single marketing list. The marketing list can be a group of Account, Contact, or Lead entities. After you decide what type of activity you are going to create and the owner of the activity, creating the quick campaign is easy.

First, identify a list of recipients through the Advanced Find tool, as shown in Figure 9.13, or through one of the Account, Contact, or Lead views. In this example, you will launch a quick campaign from the search result of contacts through Advanced Find, as shown in Figure 9.14.

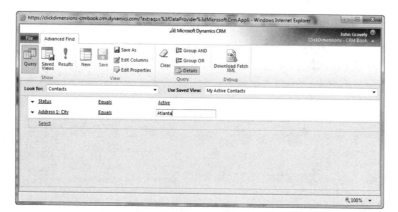

FIGURE 9.13
An advanced find for contacts in Atlanta.

FIGURE 9.14
Advanced Find result.

On the results screen, click the Create Quick Campaign button on the ribbon and then select one of the three available options: For Selected Records, For All Records on the Current Page, or For All Records on All Pages. In this case, you are going to select all records. On the next page, enter the name of the campaign and then click the Next button to continue, as shown in Figure 9.15.

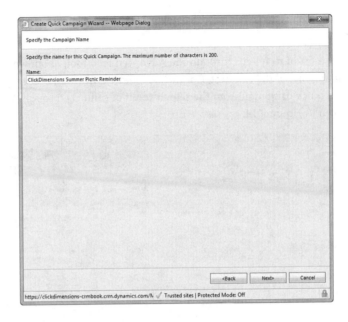

On the Select the Activity Type and Owners page, as shown in Figure 9.16, choose the type of activity that you want to create and select the owner of the activity. The available activity types are Phone Call, Appointment, Letter, Fax, and E-mail. If you select E-mail, you have the option to have Microsoft Dynamics CRM send out the e-mail message and automatically close the e-mail activities.

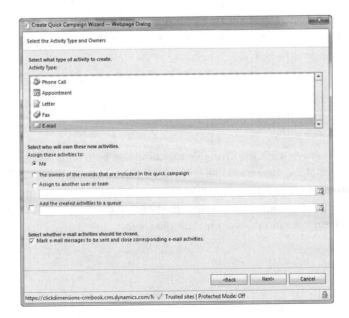

Based on the activity type you select, the corresponding activity form opens. Populate the necessary information for the activity and then click the Next button to continue. After confirming the details, click Create to create the quick campaign; the activities are distributed immediately.

Creating and Tracking a Marketing Budget

The budget and the actual cost of a campaign are located in the Financials section, as shown in Figure 9.17. You can enter the Budget Allocated amount, Miscellaneous Costs amount, and Estimated Revenue amount for a given campaign. The Budget Allocated field indicates the dollar amounts that you have dedicated to this campaign. The Miscellaneous Costs field contains the dollar amounts that are not incurred by the campaign activities, such as the cost of the marketing lists. The Estimated Revenue field contains the dollar amounts that you expect to generate from this marketing campaign.

FIGURE 9.17
The Campaign Financials section.

Total Cost of Campaign Activities and the Total Cost of Campaign have been disabled on the campaign by default because Microsoft Dynamics CRM will automatically calculate the values based on the financials from the campaign activities that are tied to the campaign, as shown in Figure 9.18. The calculation of the total cost of the campaign activities amount is based on the actual costs of all the campaign activities. The calculation of the total cost of the campaign amount is based on the total cost of campaign activities plus the miscellaneous costs recorded for the campaign.

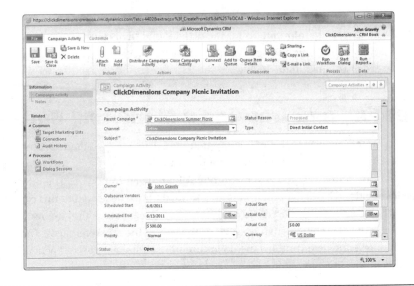

FIGURE 9.18
Campaign activity; notice the Budget Allocated and Actual Cost fields.

Refreshing Campaign Activity

If you don't see the Total Cost of Campaign Activities and Total Cost of Campaign values change after you update the financial fields on the associated campaign activities, refresh the campaign by closing and reopening it.

Capturing the Results

After you have distributed the activities to your customers, the customers will start responding to your campaign. Their responses will be captured as campaign responses in Microsoft Dynamics CRM. The total number of responses for the campaign will be one of the ways to measure the effectiveness of the campaign. After the campaign responses are generated in the system, you can convert the responses into leads, quotes, orders, or opportunities.

There are multiple ways to capture the results in Microsoft Dynamics CRM. You can manually create the campaign responses from within the campaign or create an activity and convert it to a campaign response. If you are not connected to Microsoft Dynamics CRM, you can still record the responses of your campaign in a text file and then import the records when you have access to your Microsoft Dynamics CRM system again. In addition, if e-mail tracking is enabled in your Microsoft Dynamics CRM settings, incoming e-mails in response to your campaign can automatically be created as a campaign response in Microsoft Dynamics CRM.

Manually Creating a Campaign Response

To manually create a campaign response, follow these steps:

1. Open your campaign.

2. Click the campaign responses on the navigation menu.

3. Click New on the ribbon. A new Campaign Response form displays for you to enter information, as shown in Figure 9.19.

4. Indicate the customer's response by populating the Response Code field on the Campaign Response form.

5. Associate this response to your existing Account, Contact, or Lead entity in Microsoft Dynamics CRM by clicking the lookup icon next to the Customer field.

6. When you finish with this screen, click Save to save your campaign response.

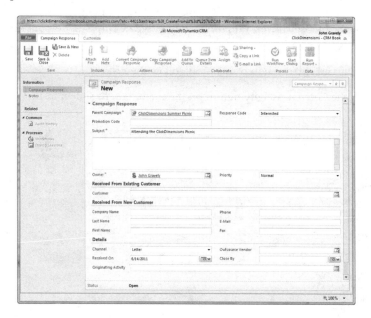

FIGURE 9.19
The Campaign Response form.

More Options for Converting an Activity to a Campaign Response

An activity, such as an incoming e-mail, can be converted to a campaign response. Additionally a completed phone call or other type of activity can be used as a campaign response.

Creating a New Customer

You might have to create a new customer by populating the Company, Last Name, First Name, Phone, E-mail, and Fax fields in the Received from New Customer section. Optionally, you can also populate the Details section here.

Creating a Campaign Response

Another way to create a campaign response is to create a new activity and chose Campaign Response as the activity type. This can be done anywhere within the system that you can create a new activity.

By the Way

Response Code Values

Your system administrator can customize the Response Code values to use the terminology that fits your business.

When you are working with a specific activity, such as a phone call that you received, you can also convert it to an activity of type Campaign Response by associating it with a source campaign.

To convert an activity through association, follow these steps:

1. Click the Convert Activity button on the menu bar, as shown in Figure 9.20.

FIGURE 9.20
The Phone Call Activity form; notice the Convert Activity button on the menu bar.

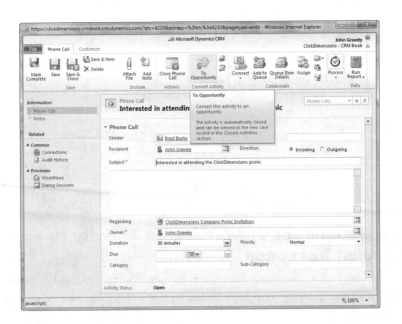

2. Select To Opportunity from the available options. The Convert Phone Call to Opportunity dialog box appears, as shown in Figure 9.21.

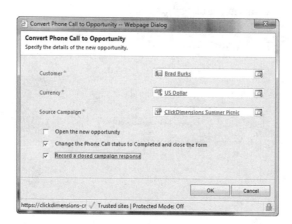

FIGURE 9.21
The Convert
Phone Call to
Opportunity dia-
log box.

3. Populate the Customer and Source Campaign lookup fields.

4. Check Record a Closed Campaign Response.

5. Click OK. A new Campaign Response is created for the source campaign that you specified.

Create Campaign Response

You can convert the following activities into campaign responses: Appointment, Letter, E-mail, and Fax.

By the Way

Importing Responses

To import campaign responses into Microsoft Dynamics CRM, you have many options. You can leverage the default Microsoft Default CRM data import tool, as described in Hour 6, "Managing Leads," or you can use a third-party import tool.

After the campaign responses are created, you can perform several tasks. You can assign the campaign response to another user on your sales team or assign it to a queue. You can convert the response into a lead, quote, order, or opportunity. Also, you can close the campaign response as completed or canceled.

Tracking the Steps, Activities, and Tasks

After a marketing campaign is under way, you can track the status of each step in the campaign and view the progress of the activities in Microsoft Dynamics CRM. To view the status of the campaign activities, go into the specific campaign and select Campaign Activities in the navigation area, as shown in Figure 9.22. You will see a list of the activities and the status for each of them.

FIGURE 9.22
A campaign's
Campaign
Activities view.

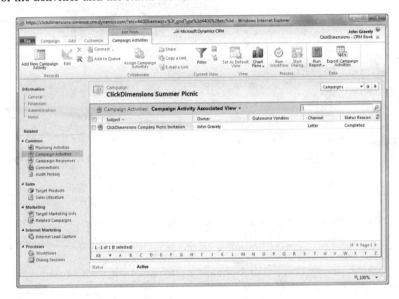

In addition, Microsoft Dynamics CRM provides three reports to track the progress and effectiveness of your campaigns. Based on the information provided in these reports, your company can decide which campaigns should continue to run, which should stop, and which should be modified.

The reports available in the Reports section are Campaign Activity Status, Campaign Comparison, and Campaign Performance. If the default reports don't contain the information you are looking for, you can create an Advanced Find query or a Report Wizard report to get the data you need. For more information on finding, analyzing, and reporting, see Hour 20 and Hour 21, "Reporting and Query Basics."

Summary

In this lesson, you learned the essentials of marketing campaigns in Microsoft Dynamics CRM. You should be able to create a marketing campaign, create a marketing list, manage cost, capture responses, and track activities in a marketing campaign. Now, you can see that the Microsoft Dynamics CRM Marketing Campaigns module is a great tool for your company.

Workshop

Dragon Financials is a brokerage house that sells financial products and services to customers across the country. To get investors interested in its financial products and services, it participates in several national financial events every year. In addition to the national financial events, Dragon Financials hosts monthly online seminars to educate investors about the different financial products and trading platforms it offers. The marketing department at Dragon Financials has leveraged the Marketing Campaigns module in Microsoft Dynamics CRM to help it to plan, keep track of activities and costs, and measure the effectiveness of its marketing activities.

Dragon Financials mainly focuses on the yearly national financial events. There are many things to prepare before attending the show. The marketing team creates a full marketing campaign to manage those events. The team uses planning tasks to lay out the action items that it needs to do for the event, such as reserving the booth space, preparing the booth, printing the brochures, making travel reservations, and inviting its top-rated customers to the financial events. Because its top-rated customers consist of private investors and institutions, the team creates two marketing lists for its campaign in Microsoft Dynamics CRM. After the marketing lists are created, the marketing team creates and then mails the invitations to investors. Next, it follows up with them on a phone call after two weeks to make sure that they have received the invitation and to confirm their attendance. So, it has created two campaign activities: one for the invitations and one for the follow-up phone call. After marketing receives the confirmation of attendance, it creates a campaign response and associates it with the campaign. The marketing team also uses the financial functions in the campaign to keep track of its campaign costs and report them to upper management when the campaign ends.

In addition to the yearly national financial events, Dragon Financials hosts online seminars to educate investors. It needs to notify its potential investors and current customers about these seminars and to keep track of the registrations. It leverages the quick campaign feature in Microsoft Dynamics CRM to create an e-mail campaign to notify its investors. Because Dragon Financials has the Microsoft Dynamics CRM tracking setting turned on, all the e-mail replies are automatically converted to campaign responses. After a campaign response gets into the system, Dragon Financials then assigns it to a salesperson to follow up with the investor.

As you can see, Microsoft Dynamics CRM provides the marketing features that Dragon Financials needs. It helps the company organize many marketing events and streamline the process for maintaining constant communication with its investors.

Q&A

Q. *Does the financial data in a full campaign synchronize with my accounting software?*

A. No. Currently, the marketing campaign financial features do not integrate with any Microsoft ERP packages. A Microsoft Dynamics Partner can provide more information on available third-party solutions to integrate your two systems.

Q. *Does a contact have to exist in the system for me to add it to a marketing list?*

A. Yes. If a contact does not exist, you need to first create the contact as a contact, account, or lead and then associate it with your marketing list.

Q. *Why must I distribute campaign activities?*

A. Campaign activities have an extra feature built into their functionality to allow a marketing department the flexibility to fully organize all the necessary activities associated with a full campaign prior to actually assigning them to specific people to get accomplished.

Q. *Can I create a new campaign from an existing campaign?*

A. Yes. You can use an existing campaign as a campaign template to create a new campaign.

Quiz

1. What is the difference between a full campaign and a quick campaign?

2. What record types can be used in a marketing list?

3. What is a channel campaign activity? What is a nonchannel campaign activity?

4. True or False: A campaign response can be converted to a Lead entity.

5. True or False: The total cost of a campaign is calculated automatically.

6. What default reports in Microsoft Dynamics CRM help a marketing manager track the progress of a campaign?

Answers

1. A quick campaign is a light version of a campaign. It contains only a single type of activity and works with a single marketing list. It is geared toward use by a salesperson at the end of the month or a sales department doing a quick announcement, special, or alert. A full campaign is geared toward use by the marketing department, which has more coordination needs around complex events.

2. Account, Contact, Lead, and Opportunity can be used in Marketing Lists.

3. A channel activity is an external activity, such as an e-mail message, a letter, or a phone call, that initiates contact with a customer when the campaign is distributed. A non-channel activity is an internal activity act, such as to-do list items to track actions that must be performed during a campaign.

4. True. A campaign response can be converted to a Lead entity.

5. True. The total cost of a campaign is calculated automatically.

6. Campaign Activity Status, Campaign Comparison, and Campaign Performance help a marketing manager track the progress of a campaign.

Exercise

Imagine that you are the marketing manager for a real-estate company, and your company is going to host a presales event for a new residential building. You have to ensure that the location of the event is booked, identify the list of guests you want to invite, send e-mail invitations, and call the guests to confirm the registration after they respond that they will attend the event. You have been given $10,000 for this sales event. Upper management wants to know the actual cost and effectiveness of this marketing event after it's over.

Use the information provided here to create a campaign in CRM to manage this marketing campaign.

HOUR 10

Entering Data as a Salesperson

What You'll Learn in This Hour:

- ▶ A month in the life of a salesperson
- ▶ Capturing a lead and entering a lead
- ▶ Converting a lead to an account and contact
- ▶ Final planning

This lesson looks at how a salesperson might use Microsoft Dynamics CRM during a typical day and the following weeks. We will follow a scenario from day to day as a lead moves from being a lead to being a new customer.

A Month in the Life of a Salesperson

David Daily works at a small company that locally roasts specialty organic coffees and processes dried organic tea leaves. The company, Semi-Roasted, Inc., sells specialty coffees that it locally roasts and organic tea leaves that it dries. It also sells associated hot drink items, such as coffeemakers, coffee cups, teapots, and other tea accessories. David's is a consultative sales representative and coffee aficionado, and his position requires that he find new sales prospects. He manages his existing customers while continuing to sell them more value-added product.

To find new prospects, David participates in a national coffee roasters' event in which representatives from all the global coffee distributors present on the latest in the coffee farming industry in their respective countries. Attendees at the conference tend to be restaurant owners, wine and cheese shop buyers, consumers, and other food and beverage industry people. David's goal at the conference is to meet people who have a high-end audience of consumers and an appreciation for both organic and locally roasted product.

By the
Way

Different Ways to Create a Lead

There are many ways to create a lead or a new contact in Microsoft Dynamics CRM. These include entering directly into a mobile phone by using a Microsoft Dynamics CRM Mobile client; scanning the information into a third-party scanning plug-in to Microsoft Dynamics CRM; typing the information into the mobile device contacts and synchronizing with Outlook Contacts, which then can synchronize to CRM contacts; and accessing Microsoft Dynamics CRM from any web-enabled machine and typing in the new lead details directly.

Semi-Roasted, Inc., also regularly sends out mailings to its current customers and the people in its prospect list to promote their subscription service for the coffee bean of the month and for their local tasting events.

Semi-Roasted, Inc., places a high value on its existing relationships with its customers. It manages a prerelease new product club and often has private tastings for local VIPs.

In the next few sections, we sit on David's shoulder and walk through a day, a week, and a month in his life at Semi-Roasted, Inc.

Capturing a Lead and Entering a Lead

David attends the national coffee roasters' event and, at lunch, he meets Janice, a woman from a town near where Semi-Roasted, Inc., is located. After further discussion, David learns that Janice is the owner of a local restaurant called The Coffee House, which serves recipes cooked from seasonal locally grown fruits and vegetables for breakfast and lunch.

David and Janice exchange business cards because Janice is interested in adding locally dried teas and locally roasted organic coffees to her menu. Janice then has to rush to another session.

David has a few minutes and he has his laptop, so he enters Janice's contact information directly into his Microsoft Dynamics CRM system. In Figure 10.1, David starts Microsoft Dynamics CRM and chooses Sales and then Leads.

In Figure 10.2, David creates a new Lead entity, and in Figure 10.3, he enters the details from Janice's business card. He first enters contact details into the General section.

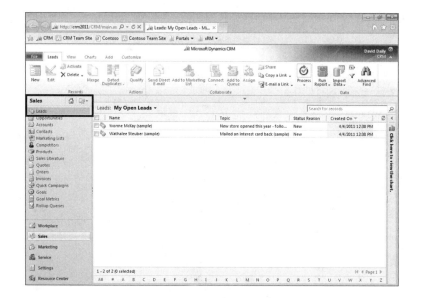

FIGURE 10.1
Creating a new Lead entity.

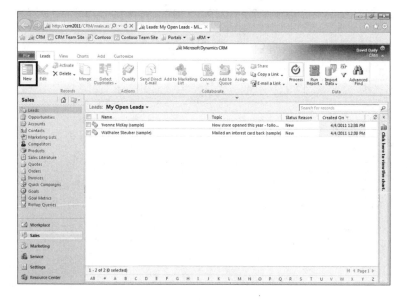

FIGURE 10.2
Entering the details.

David is a fast typist, so he does not mind typing in the information. He also enjoys the chance to further think about and memorize some of Janice's information. He uses a few memory tricks, including noting the color of her hair and associating it to her company name. She has blonde hair with a small green braid, and he associates green braid with local produce, green and organic.

FIGURE 10.3
Entering the
general details
for a Lead
entity.

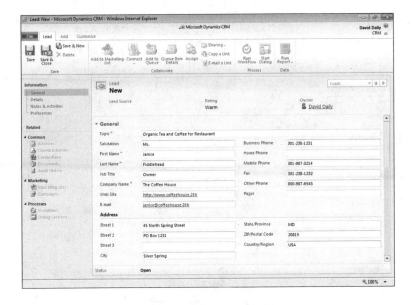

FIGURE 10.4
Entering the
address
details.

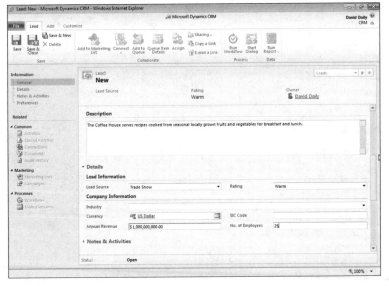

David continues to enter information, as shown in Figures 10.4 and 10.5.

Finally, David wants to capture a few notes while the conversation is still fresh in his mind. He will meet a number of new people throughout the day, and if he does not take notes now, he might forget some details. In Figure 10.6, David has entered some notes on the lead.

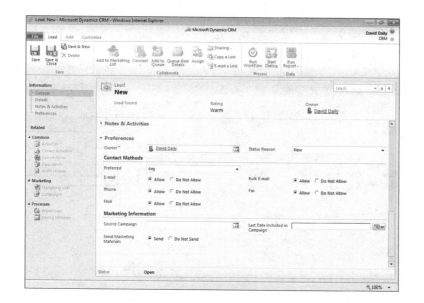

FIGURE 10.5
Entering the administrative and marketing information.

FIGURE 10.6
Entering notes.

Now that Janice Fiddlehead has been added to David's Microsoft Dynamics CRM system, he can continue with the show. He runs to his next session.

Later that night, David decides to further qualify and follow up on his conversation with Janice. He jumps back into his Microsoft Dynamics CRM system to send Janice an e-mail.

David uses the Microsoft Dynamics CRM search features to quickly find Janice in his long list of leads. He types Janice into the search box at the top of the Leads view, as shown in Figure 10.7.

FIGURE 10.7
Searching for
Janice.

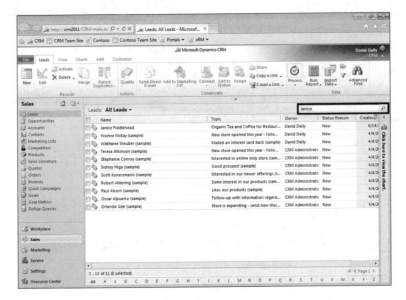

Once he opens Janice's record, he navigates to the Notes & Activities area from the left navigation pane and then uses the ribbon to create a new activity of type E-mail, as shown in Figure 10.8.

FIGURE 10.8
Creating an
e-mail message
using Dynamics
CRM.

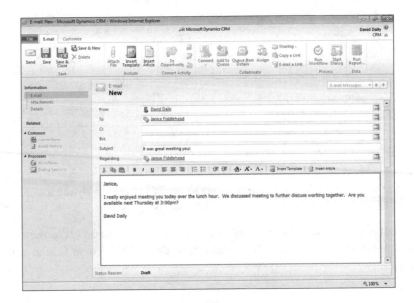

> **Another Option**
>
> David could also send an e-mail to Janice from his Microsoft Outlook e-mail client and associate it with Microsoft Dynamics CRM if he is currently connected to his internal network or the next time he is connected to the network.

Converting a Lead to an Account and Contact

David finishes up his week at the conference and is back in the office the next Monday morning. In the office, he enters many other leads that he met at the conference and schedules and makes decisions regarding what he needs to do to qualify each of them.

> **Another Option**
>
> David could also upload a list of leads from Excel, or he could use a third-party tool that supports scanning business cards into electronic Microsoft Dynamics CRM format to scan the business cards he collected.

Later in the day, he receives a response to his e-mail from Janice. She is available on Thursday at 3:00 p.m. David converts Janice's Lead record to an Account entity and a Contact entity, now that a solid base of conversation has continued and Janice has agreed to meet. To make this change, David opens Janice's Lead entity. Then he selects Qualify from the ribbon at the top of the form. Finally, he chooses Account and Contact.

David is not ready to create an Opportunity entity for The Coffee House yet because he is not comfortable defining an estimated close date and the probability of close until after his first meeting.

Once the Lead entity is converted, David creates an appointment in Outlook for Thursday at 3:00 p.m., and he relates that to Janice's contact record in Microsoft Dynamics CRM (see Figure 10.9).

David does a little research and discovers that there are a few other people associated with The Coffee House. He finds Jack Wilkes, the CFO, by searching for The Coffee House on the Internet. He finds a couple of articles where Jack has been profiled, and he finds a Yellow Pages listing with a few primary contact people. David adds these contacts to the account, as shown in Figure 10.10. To do so, he opens the Account and selects Contacts, Add New Contact from the ribbon, then he enters the information he has found. Figure 10.10 shows entering a new contact from the prospect. Because David first selects the account and then Contacts, Add New Contact, all the address details are automatically populated.

FIGURE 10.9
Associating an
Outlook
appointment
with Microsoft
Dynamics CRM.

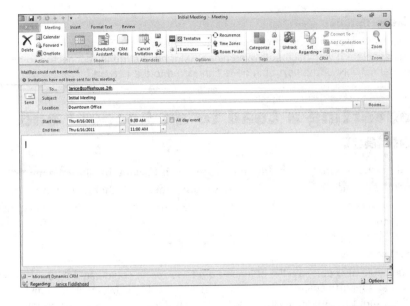

FIGURE 10.10
Adding a new
contact to a
prospect
account.

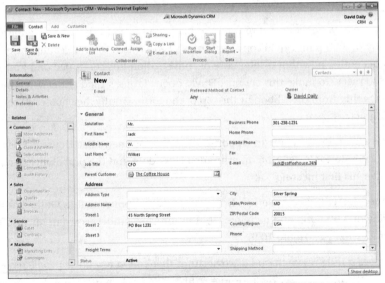

Figure 10.11 shows a list of the new contacts David entered and that are associated
with the new account The Coffee House. Notice that the list is filtered and shows
only contacts associated with The Coffee House.

David considers his options and decides that he wants to offer Janice and some of
her associates a taste test of his product. He is not going to do this until after his first
meeting with Janice, but by planning ahead, he can mention in his meeting the

option for a follow-up. He also knows that there is a delicate balance between too few meetings and too many meetings. Using the sales process that he has configured in Microsoft Dynamics CRM, David has a well-used and rehearsed plan.

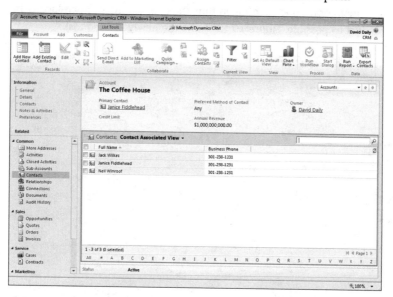

FIGURE 10.11
All the new contacts on the account of The Coffee House.

David completes each activity in the sales process by filing the activity away to history, and he date and time stamps it for future reference (see Figure 10.12). David's appointment with Janice is an activity, but he also needs associated activities that help him prepare for his appointment.

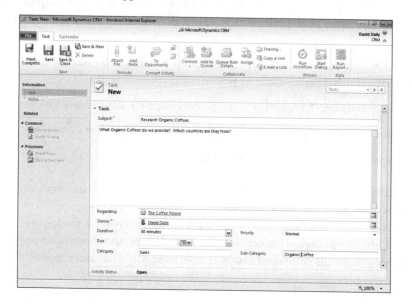

FIGURE 10.12
New task (activity): Check out Organic Coffee offerings.

David sets up a task activity to research which of the coffees that Semi-Roasted, Inc., provides are organic. He sets up another task activity to research the most environmentally friendly coffee-producing countries and adds a note to double-check for the closest provider. Janice had mentioned that she tries to buy as much locally produced product as possible. Figure 10.13 shows the newly created task.

FIGURE 10.13
New task (activity): Check out environmentally friendly countries.

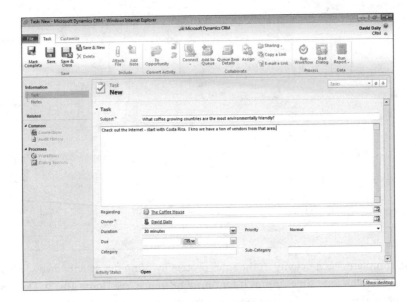

After David adds these two tasks, he runs to a meeting, confident that he won't forget to prepare for the appointment he has with Janice now that he has captured the two things he wants to do before their meeting. Figure 10.14 is a list of all David's open tasks.

When David returns, he completes the first of the two assigned tasks. He can mark an activity as completed in three ways:

▶ From Outlook, check off the task as completed from the Outlook task list.

▶ From Microsoft Dynamics CRM, open the activity and select Complete.

▶ From Microsoft Dynamics CRM, open the activity and select Close Task.

Figure 10.15 shows the detailed completed task activity. Completed activities have a status of Completed and show up under all activities and the Completed Activities option associated with the account. If you display all of David's activities, you get Figure 10.16. If you choose the account The Coffee House and choose Completed Activities, you get the completed activities associated with The Coffee House.

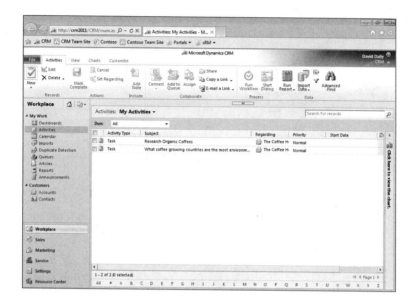

FIGURE 10.14
David's open
task activities.

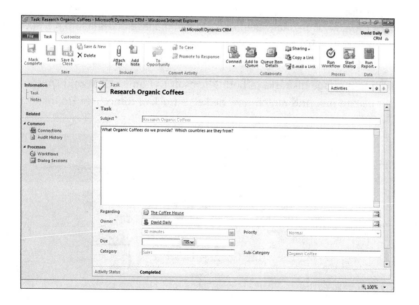

FIGURE 10.15
Detailed completed task
activity.

Options for Managing Activities

Microsoft Dynamics CRM provides several ways to manage your activities. You can manage activities from Outlook, with Outlook tasks synchronizing to Microsoft

By the Way

FIGURE 10.16
History display
from the
account The
Coffee House.

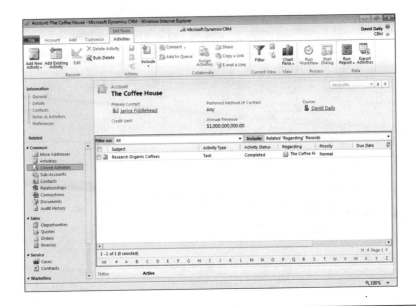

FIGURE 10.16
History display
from the
account The
Coffee House.

Dynamics CRM task activities. You can manage activities by selecting Microsoft
Dynamics CRM, My Work, Activities. And you can manage activities from a specific
account by selecting the account and then selecting Activities.

David likes to manage his tasks in both Microsoft Dynamics CRM and Outlook. He
loves that he can mix and match how he keeps track of things (see Figure 10.17).

FIGURE 10.17
Activities dis-
playing with a
completed
activity.

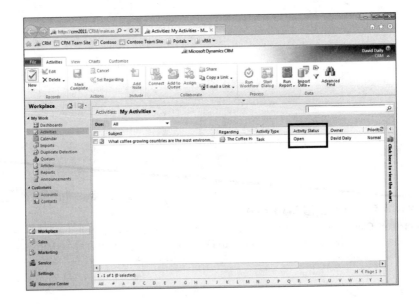

The Appointment

Thursday comes, and David is ready. He is looking forward to meeting with Janice again, and he feels confident that he has products that meet her needs.

David and Janice talk for an hour. David spends a good amount of time listening to Janice's explanation of her business, goals, and needs. He asks a few questions to support his internal efforts to ensure that her company is going to be a good long-term customer and that funds and budget are available, but in general, he mostly listens. At the end of the meeting, David fills Janice in on the Semi-Roasted, Inc., philosophy that matches some of what she has mentioned, and he sets up a meeting for the entire team to try some of David's coffee and tea offerings. David specifically wants a chance to meet a few other people at the company so that he has good depth of buy-in and some extra internal champions.

When David gets back to the office, he jumps into Dynamics CRM and prepares a follow-up letter using a template he has used in the past. To do so, he opens the account for The Coffee House. Then, from the menu bar, he selects Add. Finally, from the ribbon, he selects Mail Merge. The screen shown in Figure 10.18 appears.

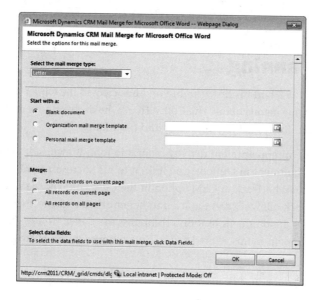

FIGURE 10.18
A mail merge follow-up letter form for Janice at The Coffee House.

David realizes that he has a good chance of closing this deal within the next 60 days, and he decides to set up a new Opportunity entity with an estimated close date of July 31, 2011. He calculates that the approximate revenue will be

$1,000/quarter and that this account is positioned for a long-term reoccurring revenue model, if handled correctly. David creates the Opportunity entity as shown in Figure 10.19.

FIGURE 10.19
Creating an Opportunity entity.

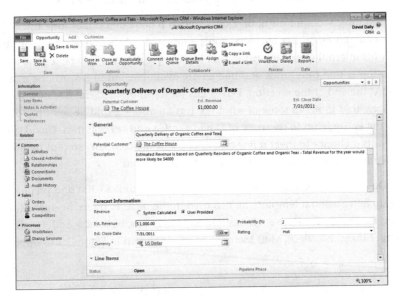

Final Planning

Now that David has had his first meeting and has created the Opportunity entity and captured some details about The Coffee House, he decides to meet with his sales manager to talk about his final approach and technique.

David sends out an appointment activity request to John Brown, sales manager. He creates this appointment in Outlook and links it to his Microsoft Dynamics CRM calendar by choosing the Track in CRM option in the CRM Outlook client. He also sets a regarding, which allows David to pick another entity to relate to the appointment. He associates the appointment to John's company, the Coffee House. This helps David capture appointments related to The Coffee House in the Microsoft Dynamics CRM history.

John Brown is notified that David has requested a meeting. He accepts, and the response updates David's Outlook calendar item.

David and John meet and decide on the following action plan for The Coffee House:

1. The coffee/tea tasting

2. Follow-up call to the tasting, offering a reference (or two)

3. Introduction to Mel Robinson, owner of This Little House of Cookies (an existing client from a neighboring state)

4. Follow-up call on how the discussions with Mel went and scheduling of the revenue meeting

5. A revenue meeting/discussion with Janice, with some sharing of statistics related to potential profit that The Coffee house can generate from offering high-quality good-tasting coffee

6. Follow-up call to the revenue meeting to answer any remaining questions

7. Close-the-deal meeting to sign final paper work and possibly an introduction to the new account/customer service representative

Now that the plan has been decided, David adds these items to his calendar and task list. They become activities in Microsoft Dynamics CRM (Outlook synchronizes from tasks and Outlook calendar), and they are dated with a pending date that balances all that needs to be done prior to July 31, 2011.

As the weeks go by, David completes each phone call, each appointment, and each task, resulting in a closed deal on July 31, 2011. After returning from his last appointment, David closes the Opportunity entity in Microsoft Dynamics CRM as a win, as shown in Figure 10.20.

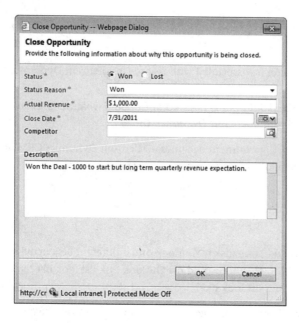

FIGURE 10.20
Closing a won opportunity.

Workshop

Semi-Roasted, Inc., has a marketing department, which is run by Jackie Grand. Jackie is excited that David has closed The Coffee House because it is one of her favorite local restaurants. Jackie makes a point to introduce herself to Janice Fiddlehead the next time she is in the restaurant. As they are talking, Jackie mentions that she is looking for a few new case studies for some of the marketing efforts she is working on. Janice jumps at the chance for some free advertising and volunteers to be written up as a case study for Semi-Roasted, Inc. Janice creates a new marketing campaign called Case Studies and defines a number of specific activities associated with this campaign. These activities include sorting and finding a list of happy existing clients, reaching out and talking with the clients, scheduling interviews with the clients who have volunteered, writing and editing the case studies, and sending a follow-up thank-you gift. Janice has been given a budget for these activities, and she adds this to the marketing campaign.

Q&A

Q. Is it possible to pull leads into Dynamics CRM from an Excel Spreadsheet?

A. Yes. Microsoft Dynamics CRM offers Excel templates that can be populated and then uploaded into Dynamics CRM.

Q. Can David associate his notes on Janice with her record in Microsoft Dynamics CRM?

A. Yes. Notes can be associated with records in Microsoft Dynamics CRM.

Q. When an appointment is created in Outlook, what does it look like when synchronized with Microsoft Dynamics CRM?

A. An Outlook appointment becomes a Microsoft Dynamics CRM activity of type Appointment. It displays on the activity views.

Quiz

1. Can David add one task to Outlook and a different task activity to Microsoft Dynamics CRM? What would his Outlook task list look like? What would his open activities list look like?

2. What does David do in Microsoft Dynamics CRM when he gets a new lead at the national coffee roasters' event?

3. What are David's options for entering a new lead in Microsoft Dynamics CRM?

4. Why does David close activities when they are done?

5. Can Jim Brown, sales manager, see David's activities? Is such transparency valuable? Why?

Answers

1. Yes, David can add tasks to either Microsoft Dynamics CRM or Outlook. His task list will include all tasks.

2. He enters the lead as a new Lead in Microsoft Dynamics CRM.

3. One option for David is to enter leads through his mobile device using the Microsoft Dynamics CRM mobile client or a third-party mobile option. He can also use his laptop, as long as he has Internet access or, if he is offline, he can use his laptop and sync with the corporate network later.

4. David closes activities so that they are filed to history and removed from his active list of things to do.

5. Depending on how security is set up, Jim Brown can see David's activities.

Exercise

Create a marketing campaign that Jackie can use to keep track of her need to capture and create a number of case studies. What are other tools within Dynamics CRM that Jackie can leverage to make creating these case studies easier? Set up a marketing list and then use it to invite people to participate in the case study effort. When people respond, where do you capture their responses? Associate the responses with the marketing campaign.

HOUR 11

Configuring Your Interaction with Microsoft Dynamics CRM

What You'll Learn in This Hour:

▶ Basic configurations

▶ Web Resources

▶ Default fields

In this hour, you will learn how to modify Microsoft Dynamics CRM to better fit your business needs. You will learn how to add new fields to the data entry forms and modify existing fields. You will also learn how to move fields from section to section. Finally, you will learn about including iFrames and adding form-specific scripts to the system.

Basic Configurations

When it comes to designing the entry forms for getting data into Microsoft Dynamics CRM, Microsoft delivers a robust offering. In this section, you start by making just a few changes and then expand out into the world of really changing a user's interaction with Microsoft Dynamics CRM without writing a single line of code.

Figure 11.1 shows the top of the default data entry form for an account.

Figure 11.2 shows the bottom of the default data entry form for an account.

Every entity (record type) has at least one form, and you can change a number of different things on these forms. You can add or remove fields, you can add or remove sections, and you can add or remove tabs. You can also modify the values of a drop-down list either by adding to them, changing them, or deleting them. You can also add an iFrame. (We discuss what an iFrame is in later sections of this hour.)

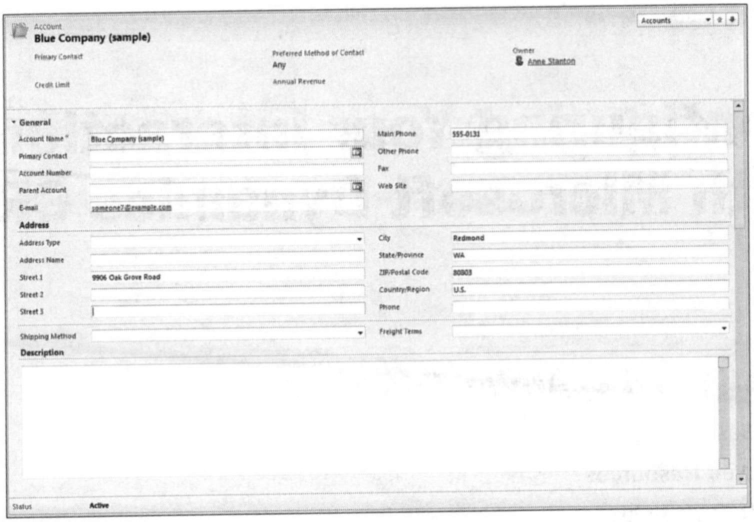

FIGURE 11.1
The top of the default account data entry form.

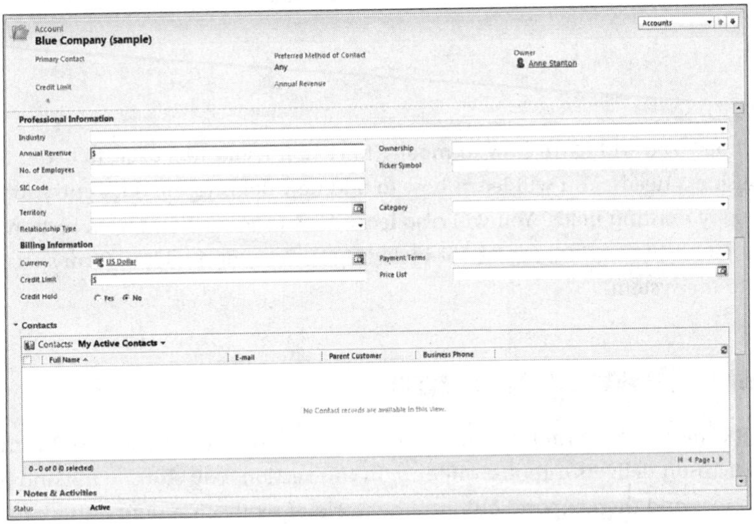

FIGURE 11.2
The bottom of the default account data entry form.

You are now going to change the look of this default data entry form by changing fields.

Removing Fields

You can remove a number of fields from the forms shown in Figure 11.1 and Figure 11.2.

To remove fields and change the default form, you need to do the following in Microsoft Dynamics CRM:

1. Choose Settings.

2. Choose Customization. (If you do not have this option on your menu, you probably do not have the correct security privileges to perform this function. Talk with your Microsoft Dynamics CRM administrator.)

3. Choose Customize the System.

4. Choose Components, Entities.

5. Choose Account.

You now see a list of items that are related to the specific Account entity (record type). These include the core setup information, the forms and views functionality, account fields, a series of different types of relationships that can be created, charts, and the account-specific system messages and error code descriptions. As discussed in earlier hours, an account is an entity that is built from a number of fields. To modify the data entry form for an account, select Forms and Views.

How Many Forms Can You Have for Each Entity?

For any given entity, you can have a main form and a mobile form.

By the Way

Figure 11.3 shows the area where you select the account form. Figure 11.4 shows the form as it looks when editing. Notice that you have a number of new choices, including a new Common Tasks pane.

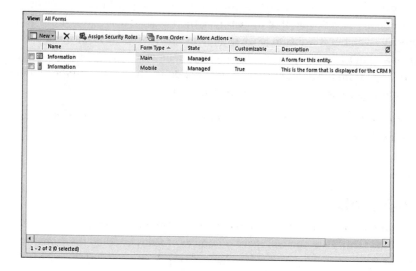

FIGURE 11.3
Choosing an Account form.

FIGURE 11.4
Changing an
Account form.

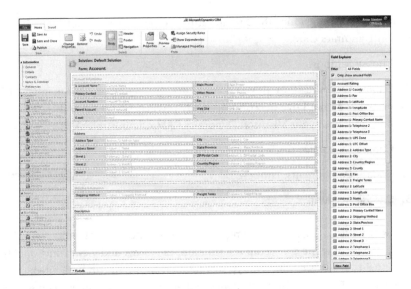

To remove a field from the account form, follow these steps:

1. Select the field using your mouse. You can tell the field is selected because a solid box appears around the field.

2. When the field is selected, remove it by choosing the Remove button in the ribbon. This process does not remove the field from the database, nor does it delete data. It simply removes the field from the data entry form.

Consider, for instance, a company that decides to only capture address information at the contact level. This method has various disadvantages, but it is an example. This company also decides that there is no e-mail address associated at the generic company level, but it wants to leave its options open for later. To encourage the adoption of this business process, the company removes the address fields and the e-mail fields from the account form. It does not delete the fields from the database. If the place to enter data is not available, data will not be entered.

Figure 11.5 shows exactly the same account data entry form in edit mode minus the address fields and the e-mail field.

Moving Fields

Now that you have removed a number of fields, you might also want to move fields around the form. Here you will move a number of fields by using the mouse to drag

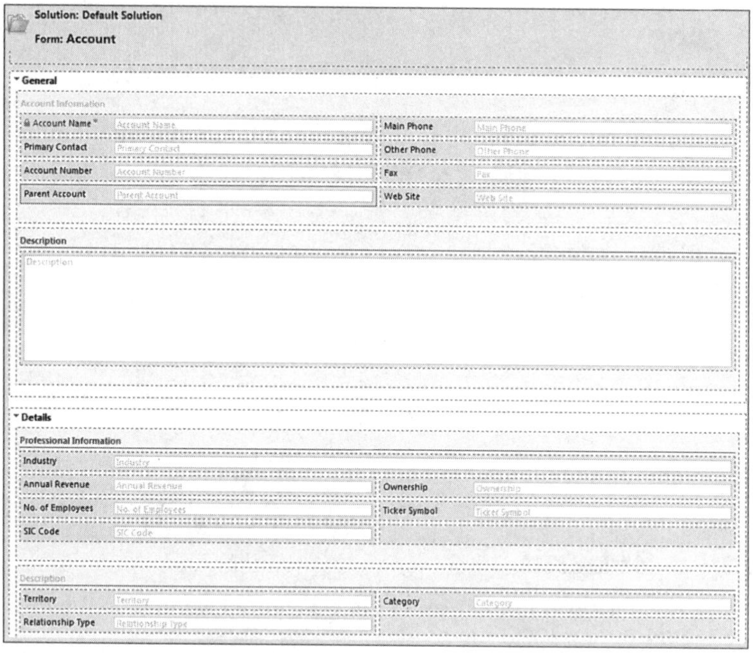

FIGURE 11.5
Removing the address fields: editing the form.

and drop the fields. Figures 11.6 and 11.7 show the fields moved to new locations. Notice that you need to choose the section you are editing, including the header, the footer, and the body.

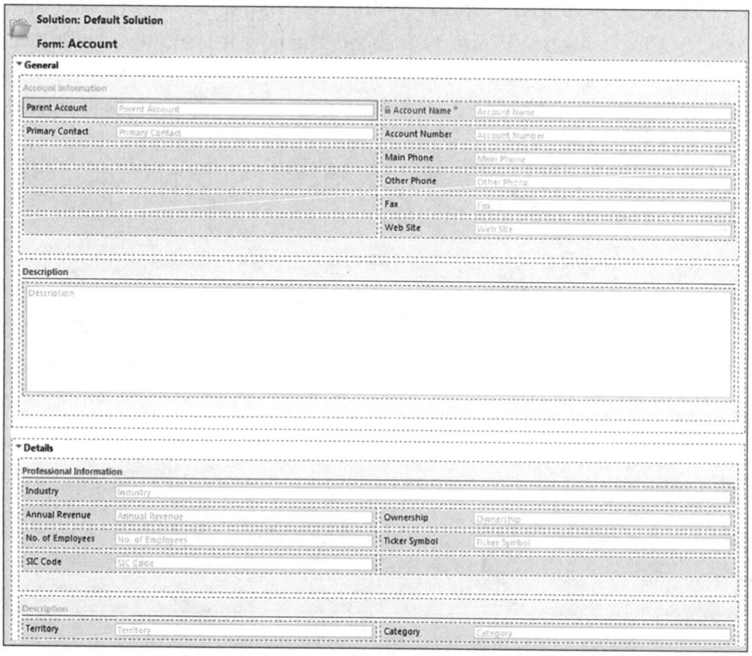

FIGURE 11.6
Moving fields: editing the form.

FIGURE 11.7
Moving fields:
the user
perspective.

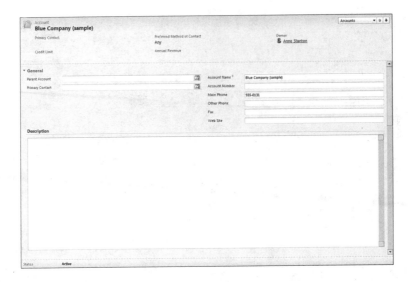

Adding a Subgrid

You can add and modify a form by using some advanced features on the Insert tab. To add a subgrid, do the following:

1. Choose Insert from the upper-left corner.

2. In the ribbon, click Sub-Grid.

3. As shown in Figure 11.8, add a subgrid to the account form to hold international details. Adding a subgrid requires choosing a format of either one, two, three, or four columns. Figure 11.9 shows the new International subgrid.

FIGURE 11.8
The Insert
options.

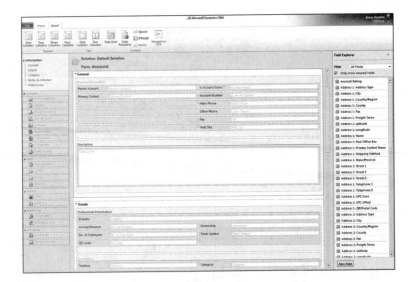

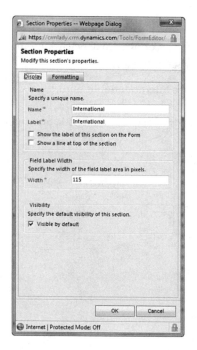

FIGURE 11.9
Adding a
subgrid:
International.

Figure 11.10 shows the process for adding and moving fields:

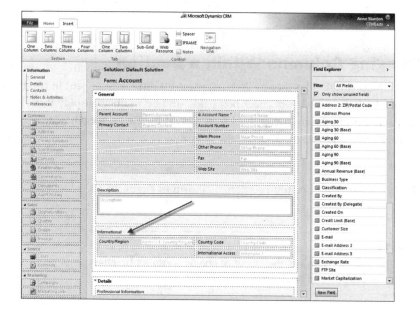

FIGURE 11.10
International
section fields.

1. Move any fields that are internationally oriented to the International section.

2. Add a new field such as Country Code by clicking the New Field button in the bottom-right corner of the form.

3. Turn on fields that are international in nature.

Figure 11.11 shows two fields added: Country Code and International Access.

FIGURE 11.11
The new International section on the account form.

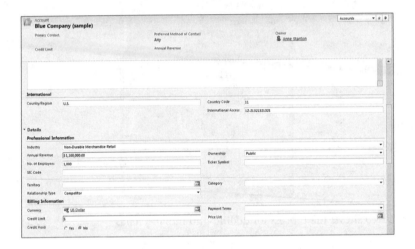

Changing Columns Within a Section

Mr. Jack BlackHat decides that he does not want his display to appear in two even columns. He has a number of check box fields, and he wants to display them in four columns to get maximum use of the screen real estate. He wonders how to change this. To change this, Jack needs to do the following:

1. Select Insert.

2. Insert a new four-column section, as shown in Figure 11.12.

By the Way

Once Saved

Once the section is saved, the layout of columns cannot be changed unless you delete the section and set up a new one.

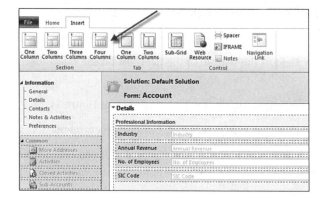

FIGURE 11.12
Inserting a four-column section.

After Jack creates the section as four columns, he can add fields to this section. Jack has already created a number of fields to represent colors. In Microsoft Dynamics CRM 2011, you can create an option set of colors and then you can use this option set for each field you create. Jack is a magician who makes balloon animals at parties, and he always asks his clients what their favorite colors are. Jack has added these color selections to the account form. Notice that the choices in Figure 11.13 are all the boxes.

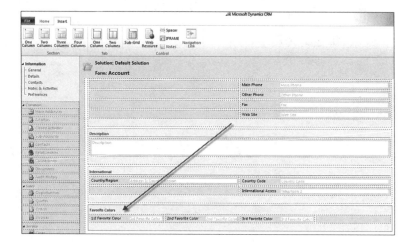

FIGURE 11.13
Check boxes.

How Did Jack Add New Fields?

As you are building a form, you can add new fields as follows:

1. Click New Field at the bottom of the fields list on the right-hand side of the screen.

2. Choose a display name for the field, as shown in Figure 11.14.

3. Choose whether the field is required, business recommended, or optional.

4. Choose a type for the field, such as Option Set. If you choose Option Set, then choose the option set you want to use, as shown in Figure 11.15.

FIGURE 11.14
Choosing a new field's display name.

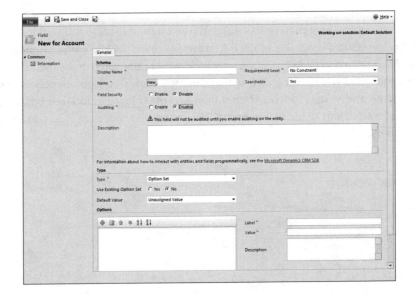

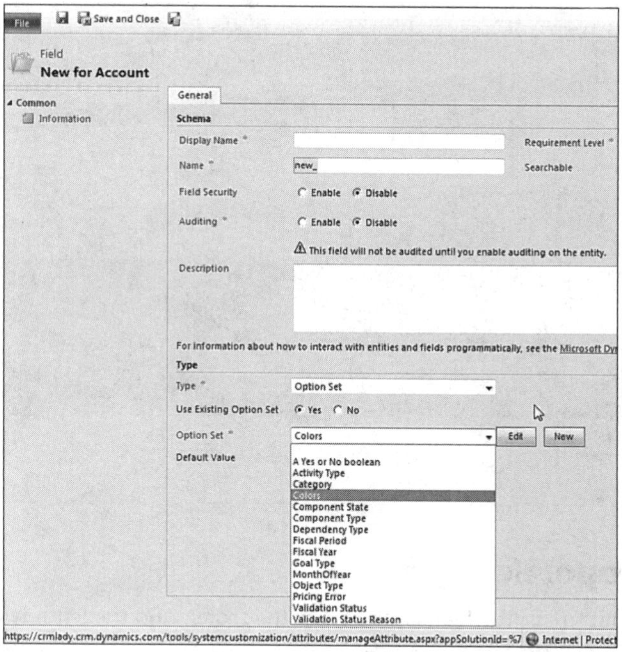

FIGURE 11.15
Choosing a
new field's
option set.

Adding the Internet to a Form: An iFrame

An iFrame is a frame that allows you to display content from other places within Microsoft Dynamics CRM or from the Internet, within an entity form in Microsoft Dynamics CRM. *iFrame* has an official definition, but it's rather technical. For those readers who live and breathe technical terms, well, you either know what an iFrame is already or you can search online for iFrame to satisfy that technical desire to add it to your vocabulary.

Jack BlackHat wants to search for content on specific accounts each time he is looking at the details of an account. He thinks that a tab that offers him some search capability would be wonderful. He is in luck: Microsoft Dynamics CRM supports this interest. Look at Figure 11.16. It shows a new field that offers search, as well as an iFrame added to the new favorite color section. In addition, the properties of the iFrame include Microsoft's search decision engine's website (www.bing.com).

In the following section, you will dip your toe into a bit of programming, or at least you are going to visit the area of forms that programmers can have fun with.

FIGURE 11.16
www.bing.com
shown on the
account form
in the Color
section.

Form Properties

A form has four areas: the header, the body, the footer, and the left navigation pane. Figure 11.17 shows the form with most of the sections removed out of the body of the form for clarity.

FIGURE 11.17
Form sections.

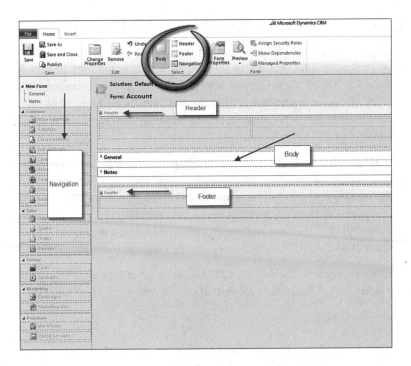

For any given form in the system (and each entity has at least one form), you can run a script OnLoad or OnSave of the form. To access this feature, choose Form Properties, as shown in Figure 11.18.

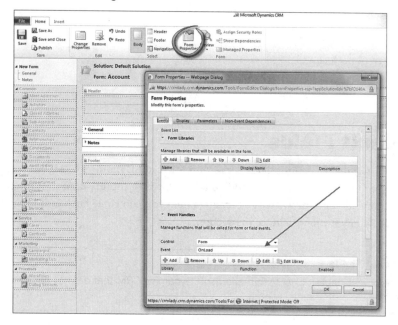

FIGURE 11.18
The Form Properties screen.

You can now access your libraries by using OnLoad or OnSave.

Web Resources

In addition to iFrames, you now also have a new item called Web Resources. This was necessary given that in the world of online you can limit yourself to custom pages hosted in the same web server in which CRM was running. As the web tools have expanded, so has Dynamics CRM.

In addition, Web Resources prevent you from having to copy and paste the same Jscript over and over again on various onChange, onLoad, and onSave events.

Josh Beal sums it up in one really nice statement: "It is not a matter of can I do it...it is a matter of should I do it." He also indicates that hacking away at some .JS files on a web server is a risky venture and potentially not upgradable.

There are now a number of Web Resources that developers can use to expand the user experience. These include many of the following (although this list doesn't not include all the options):

- ▶ HTML web pages
- ▶ CSS style sheets

> ▶ Script (JScript)

> ▶ Data (XML)

> ▶ Images (PNG, JPG, GIF, or ICO)

> ▶ Silverlight (XAP)

> ▶ XSL style sheets

> ▶ ASPx.net Pages

Default Fields

A certain number of default fields come with Microsoft Dynamics CRM, but you are not limited to just these. You can add your own fields to capture data that might be specific to your company. After you create a field you can circle back and update the form and add your new field to any section.

By the Way

Optional Fields
Numerous attributes exist within Microsoft Dynamics CRM that are not necessarily displayed on the initial forms.

Adding Fields

To add or change fields, you go to the Customize Entities page. Here's how you add some fun fields to the contact entity to complement Jack BlackHat's business model:

1. Choose Custom Entities.

2. Choose the entity you want to add attributes to (for example, Contacts).

3. Choose Fields.

In Figure 11.19, you can see the list of default contact fields. Some of them are already displayed on the form, and others can be used as needed. If the field that you want to create is not in the list, you can create it. When creating a field, you must make a number of decisions. As an example, you will create a field called Likes Magic? that will allow Jack BlackHat to mark each contact as either liking or disliking magic. This field has an answer that is one of two answers, Yes or No, so you want to choose the field type Bit. Figure 11.19 shows the list of default fields for Microsoft Dynamics CRM. Figure 11.20 shows the first screen you see when creating a new custom field.

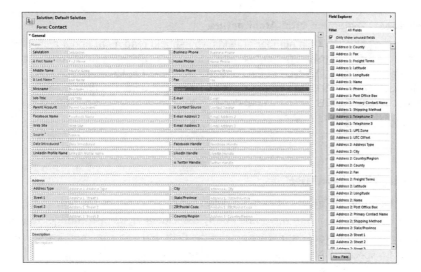

FIGURE 11.19
Contact fields.

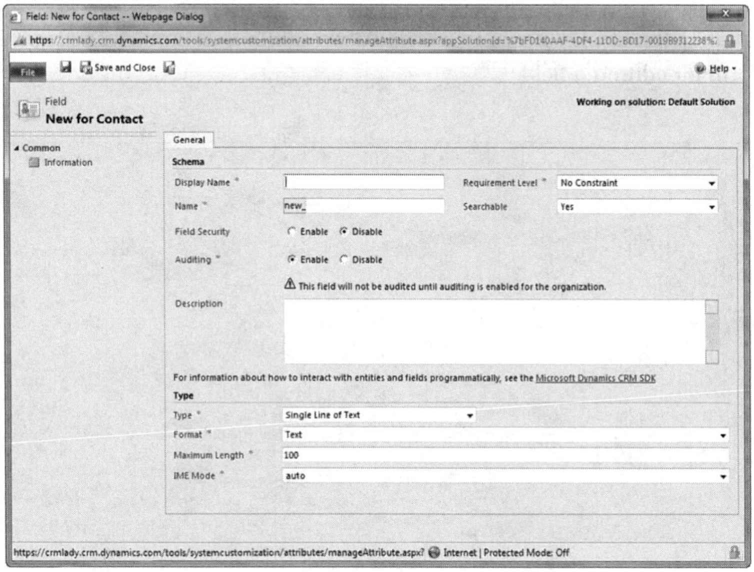

FIGURE 11.20
Creating a new attribute: Likes Magic?

Fields can be of all different types. The Type field within the attribute is not only a drop-down list of choices, but when you make your choice, the formatting of the actual details change based on the type you select. For instance, if you choose that the field you are adding is an Int (for integer), your formatting choices will include how many decimals and the maximum and minimum values.

Microsoft Dynamics CRM Architecture

If you are going to add a number of fields, you should read more about architecting Microsoft Dynamics CRM or talk with a Microsoft Dynamics CRM specialist before proceeding. The type of field and the creation of fields affect the entire Microsoft Dynamics CRM framework and database structure. Adding a new field is not always the best architectural decision to solve a business need for a specific type of report or display.

Changing Names

You can change the names of existing fields. When you change the name of a field, the name on the form and the name in any associated views also change. You cannot change the internal database name of the field, but you can change the display name of a specific field. To change a field name, follow these steps:

1. Select a specific field.

2. Select the field.

3. Change the display name to a name of your liking. Figure 11.21 shows the form for editing a field.

FIGURE 11.21
Editing a field.

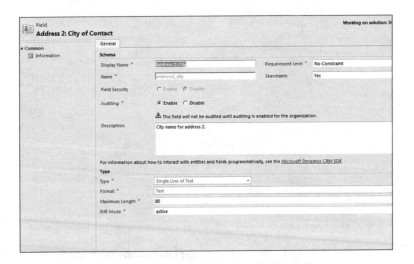

Field Internal Names

Although you are changing the field display name, the name that appears in reports will be the original.

Adding and Modifying Drop-Down List Values

Another common change to fields is to modify or add drop-down values to fields that are of type picklist. If you choose the field role on the Contact entity, you can add to the default picklist values, as shown in Figure 11.22.

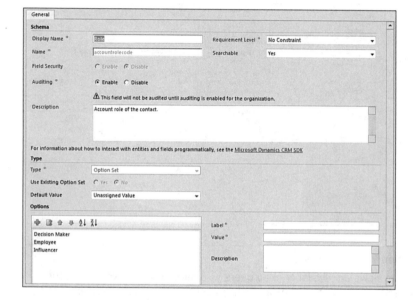

FIGURE 11.22
Adding to the drop-down list values.

You now know how to change and modify a form and add and change existing fields. You can add drop-down values to drop-down fields, and you can create sections on a form. You also have the power to add your new fields to the existing form. You have also learned how to add a simple iFrame that serves up an external web page. These web pages could be a search engine or even a mapping application for easy access to maps.

Views

A list of system views is available on every entity you select. System views include items such as My Accounts, Active Accounts, My Activities, Closed Activities, Leads Open Last Week, and more.

To create system views, you can start by looking at the Account entity System Views option under Customization. Figure 11.23 shows a list of the system views under Forms and Views associated with the Account entity. In addition to what you will learn about Advanced Find and creating ad hoc user-specific views in later hours, here we examine how you can modify existing system views and set up new system views.

FIGURE 11.23
Forms and views.

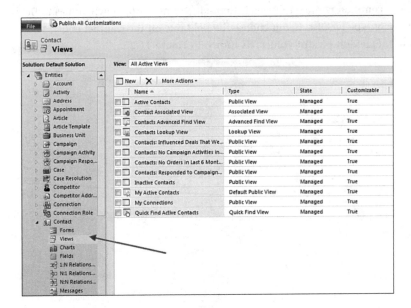

System Views

System views are available to all users who have access to your Microsoft Dynamics CRM system. You can have an unlimited number of system views per entity.

Modifying an Existing System View

To modify a view, follow these steps:

1. Select the system view you want to change (Figure 11.24).

2. Choose a column.

3. Use your mouse to control the common tasks green arrows to move a column to the right or left (see Figure 11.25).

4. Select Common Tasks, Add Columns to add existing fields to the view.

5. Select Common Tasks, Change Properties to change the width of the column you have selected.

6. Use Configure Sorting to select a field as the default sort (see Figures 11.24 through 11.26 for examples).

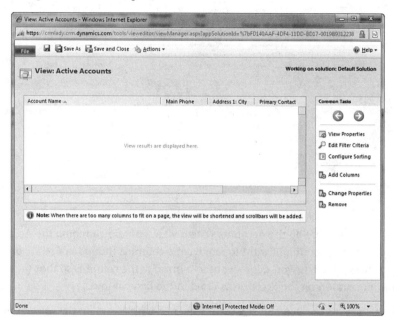

FIGURE 11.24
A system view.

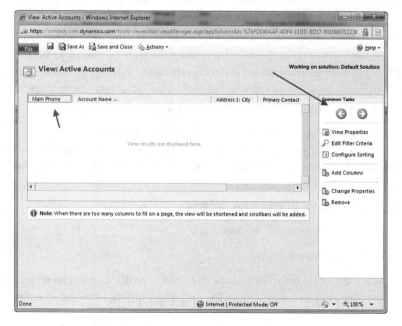

FIGURE 11.25
Modifying green
arrows.

FIGURE 11.26
Modifying the
Accounts sys-
tem view.

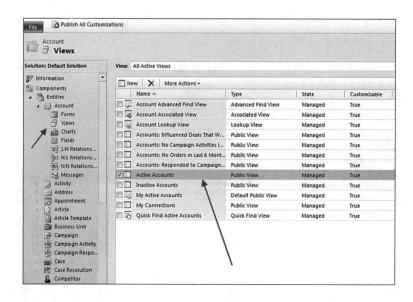

When you are modifying the Accounts system view, you are changing the Accounts view for all users. You might want to remove the columns that do not really apply to your business model, or you might want to rearrange the columns so that the most critical information on the accounts is listed in the first column.

When you use a view, you can sort by any column by clicking on the column header, but a review and a change of the default sort saves a step.

The width of the column can also make a difference. If your business has long account names, ensure that the Account Name column is as wide as possible. On the other hand, if your account names are relatively short, shorten the Account Name column to take advantage of more screen real estate. Also, you can manage the white space to make the display more user-friendly.

Columns that you select for your view are also columns of data that will appear in your interaction and use between Microsoft Dynamics Excel and views of data. You will learn more about this in Hour 20, "Utilizing the Power of Microsoft Excel with CRM Data."

Adding a New System View

To add a new system view, follow these steps:

1. Choose Customize Entities.

2. Choose the entity associated where you want to create a new system view. For example, you can create a new view associated with the Phone Call entity.

3. Choose Forms and Views.

4. Click New (see Figure 11.27) and give your new view a name and description (see Figure 11.28).

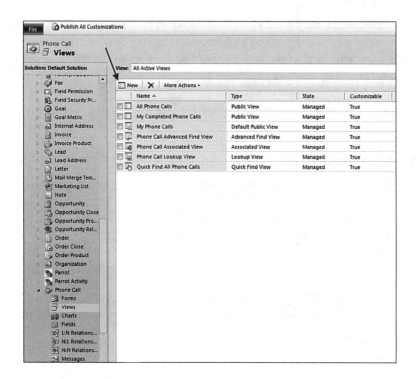

FIGURE 11.27
Forms and Views.

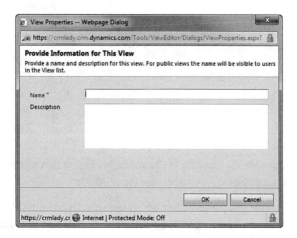

FIGURE 11.28
Creating a new system view.

You can now proceed to select columns, adjust the width of those columns, and arrange those columns to your liking. After you finish, click Save.

Adding a Filter

You might want to limit the data that displays when your new view is selected. For instance, say that you are creating a phone call view that only shows phone calls that start with 401. To filter the data in your new system view, follow these steps:

1. Choose Filter Data Criteria (see Figure 11.29).

2. Using the power of query, select your filter criteria.

3. Choose Phone Number.

4. Choose Contains and Enter 401.

FIGURE 11.29
Filtering data criteria.

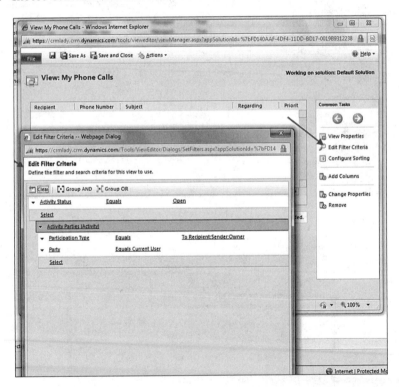

Adding new system views is just one of the many ways you can use views. For more details on creating custom ad hoc views, see Hour 20.

You have now changed your interaction with Microsoft Dynamics CRM and have added additional ways to interact with and display all the data that has been captured in the system.

Workshop

Jack BlackHat has a small business called BlackHat Magic, which offers magic performances to individual families for birthday parties and celebrations, and to large corporations for trade shows and employee festivals. Jack uses Microsoft Dynamics CRM to track specific details on the contacts he works with and the families and companies who engage him. Jack has added a number of custom fields to his version of Microsoft Dynamics CRM so that he can track the different preferences of his contacts as well as the various associated birthdays, anniversaries, and special events. Jack also likes to remember everyone he meets, so he spends extra effort to capture details that helps him remember his hundreds of contacts. These details include hair color, eye color, and favorite outfit.

Jack also keeps track of how different families are related to each other. He uses the Parent Account field in Microsoft Dynamics CRM to create a family tree type of association. Jack also uses the Microsoft Dynamics CRM relationships feature to capture associations between kids that play on the same sports teams and their parents so that he can pass out his business cards and ask for appropriate references.

Q&A

Q. Are there fields available to use that are not displayed on the default forms?

A. Yes. Microsoft Dynamics CRM comes with a large number of fields that are not included on the initial default screens. These can be used as they are or renamed.

Q. How do I add values to the drop-down lists?

A. You add values to the drop-down lists by editing an attribute that is of type picklist, you can also associate option lists with picklist fields.

Q. I want to offer the entry of an account number on two different sections in the account form. Can this be done?

A. Yes, you can display the account number field on different sections of the form multiple times.

Q. *How do I create a personal view that is not available to other users in the system?*

A. You can use Advanced Find. For more details on using Advanced Find, see Hour 20.

Q. *Can I share a personal view with other people?*

A. Yes. You can create a personal view and share it with a team or with specific users.

Q. *Can I delete an existing system view?*

A. Yes, but doing so deletes it for all users of your Microsoft Dynamics CRM environment.

Quiz

1. What are three fields that Jack needs to add to his Microsoft Dynamics CRM system? What type of fields are they?

2. Do you see any example within Jack's business where an iFrame would prove useful?

3. How many forms does each entity have?

4. What needs to be changed on the form to allow for four columns?

5. Can you display a field more than once on any given form?

6. After you create a new system view, who has access to it?

Answers

1. Likes Magic? of type Bit, Favorite Color of type Picklist, and birthday of type DATETIME with the option of Date only selected.

2. Jack BlackHat travels often. Easy access from within the account to one of the mapping applications, such as Live Maps, is extremely helpful.

3. Each entity can have more than one form.

4. The properties of the section need to be changed to add four columns.

5. You can now display more than one of the same attribute on any given form.

6. System views are available to all users of Microsoft Dynamics CRM.

Exercise

Add the fields that Jack BlackHat needs for his BlackHat Magic company, including fields to track each critical event on the contact form and the details to help Jack remember each contact's unique features. These might include height, character, and eye color. In addition, create the color fields of type Bit and then add these to a section of the account form. Set each field to a check box and display it in four columns.

Check Boxes Are Not Usually the Answer

Check boxes are not the answer for a good number of business situations. There is a more historically appropriate solution in the use of activities. Discuss your choices with an experienced Microsoft Dynamics CRM architect.

HOUR 12

Contacts and Activity Capture

What You'll Learn in This Hour:

- ► Capturing contact information
- ► Related contacts
- ► Leveraging and using activities

In this hour, you will learn about contacts and associated activities. In addition, this hour gets into the details of relating contacts to each other and to other accounts.

Capturing Contact Information

In Microsoft Dynamics CRM 2011, you capture contact information through the Contact form, which is separated into different sections. We are now going to look at the different sections of the Contact form.

The General Section

As introduced in Hour 2, "The Basic Vocabulary of CRM Functionality," a contact is a specific person. A contact also has related information, such as the activities a staff person might have promised to complete for a person and the relationships that a person has with other people and companies. Depending on the industry and business, and even the country culture and rules, various levels of detail can be captured about a specific person in the Contact form in Microsoft Dynamics CRM 2011.

Contacts Are Not Always People

A contact does not have to be a person: It can be renamed just like any other customizable entity in Microsoft Dynamics CRM. Rename offers you the full contact functionality whereas a custom entity would not. If you are in a unique industry, you can rename and use a contact for a piece of clothing associated with an outfit, a farm animal associated with a farm, an area of a sign associated with a sign, or a type of wine associated with a wine cellar.

Contacts in Microsoft Dynamics CRM have a number of nuances of interest for discussion. For instance, capturing details on a person isn't always just about the technology. In certain countries, it is not culturally acceptable to track certain types of personal information within business electronic databases, such as personal habits, favorite hobbies, golf scores, and more. If you are configuring Microsoft Dynamics CRM for another company, you might want to check on some of these types of business and cultural rules.

Figure 12.1 shows the default General section of the Contact form. The following looks at some of the important fields in this section.

FIGURE 12.1
A contact's general details.

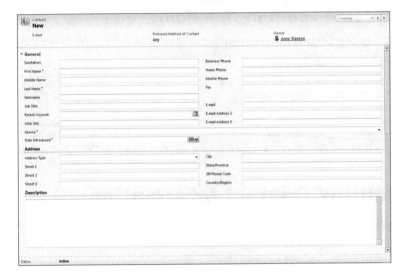

The Name Fields

Notice that in Figure 12.1, the name is displayed using three different fields: First Name, Middle Name, and Last Name. This format for capturing allows for sorting and for granular views based on three specifically unique and yet related pieces of information. The system is also designed to offer a full name display if it has access to these three core data fields. There is also the option to totally skip this separation of name and use the full name only, with JScript populating the required Last Name field.

Salutation

Salutation is a field for capturing all the different terms you would use when writing a letter or addressing someone other than by his or her first and last name. These can include Mr., Mrs., Ms., Dr., and more, depending on the country or style in which your company addresses contacts. This field can also be used with mail merge when you are using a generic Dear field such as Dear Sir.

Did you Know?

> **Salutation**
>
> By default, the Salutation field is a text field, but if you have a long list of options, you may want to hide the default Salutation field and add your own custom field of type Picklist to ensure a higher level of consistency in spelling and form over time.

Job Title

One of the default fields for a contact is Job Title. Job Title is an open text field, so a user can enter any derivative of job title as fits. Text fields can be a problem for data quality and as such you might want to replace this field.

Did you Know?

> **Data Quality**
>
> If you want to control consistency of spelling and job title options, you might want to make this a drop-down list (using the Picklist attribute). On the other hand, in this day and age, you can come across some rather creative job titles, and you don't want to frustrate yourself or users if they want to add something creative.

Parent Account

For any given contact, there is one parent account. The parent account relationship is a special one in Microsoft Dynamics CRM. Just as an account can have a primary contact, a contact can have an association to a specific account (or customer). The association to a customer is a lookup on the Account entity. If the account doesn't exist, this field can be left empty, or a new account can be entered when the contact is entered.

Did you Know?

> **Lookup**
>
> A lookup is when the system has an association between two entities and the system uses this association to look up data that is related via a key or primary field. This can also be thought of as a one-to-many, many-to-one, or many-to-many relationship between entities.

Currency

Every contact can have a unique association to a currency from the currencies defined in Microsoft Dynamics CRM. Currency is a required field for a contact because it is used in many other places in Microsoft Dynamics CRM. However, if you have only one currency, you can move this field to a different section and set your currency as the default.

Figure 12.2 shows the currency lookup.

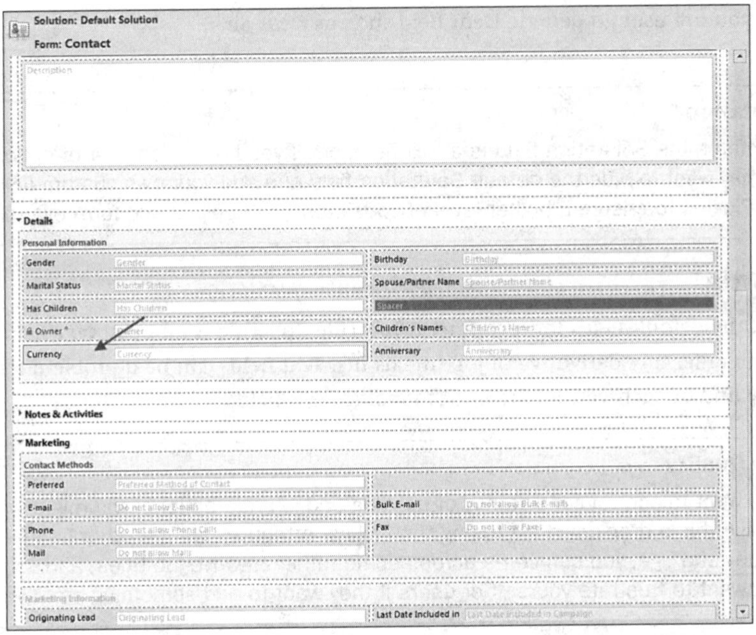

FIGURE 12.2
The currency
lookup.

Phone Numbers

Each contact has spaces for a number of different phone numbers, by default a set of telephone numbers are named Business, Home, Mobile, and Fax. This sixth phone number is a delivery address phone number for reference to shipping forms that require a phone number. There are default phone numbers, but that does not mean you can't add more or take away some that might not be useful. You can also change the phone number format by creating new complementary attributes for extension and area code. You can use a small piece of code as part of the OnChange event to the phone number attribute for formatting. For more information on OnChange, OnLoad, and OnSave events, check out Hour 24, "Microsoft Dynamics CRM as a Development Framework."

The Address Fields

The Contact form includes a primary address, but you can add an unlimited number of addresses for a contact by using the More Addresses option in the left navigation pane. If you create a contact after selecting its account, the address will be prepopulated with the account's address; otherwise, it will be blank. The primary address also includes an address name (which might be something like "corporate headquarters").

Other Fields in the General Section

Other fields worth noting include Address Type (which includes Bill To, Ship To, Primary, and Other by default), Shipping Method, and Default Freight Terms. If you are in a service industry and you don't ship product, you might want to turn off some of these fields by selecting System Configuration, Customization to offer a cleaner interface.

Description

The text in the Description field is limited to approximately 2,000 characters, so you should carefully consider how to use it. One use of the Description field is to summarize a general profile for a contact, or you can select the contact's profile from a website and paste it into this space. The Description field should not be used for regular historical notes because if it is used in this manner, a user might run out of space. (See the section "The Notes and Activities Section," later in this chapter, for information on historical notes.)

The Details Section of the Contact Form

Figure 12.3 shows the common fields found in the Details section of the Contact form.

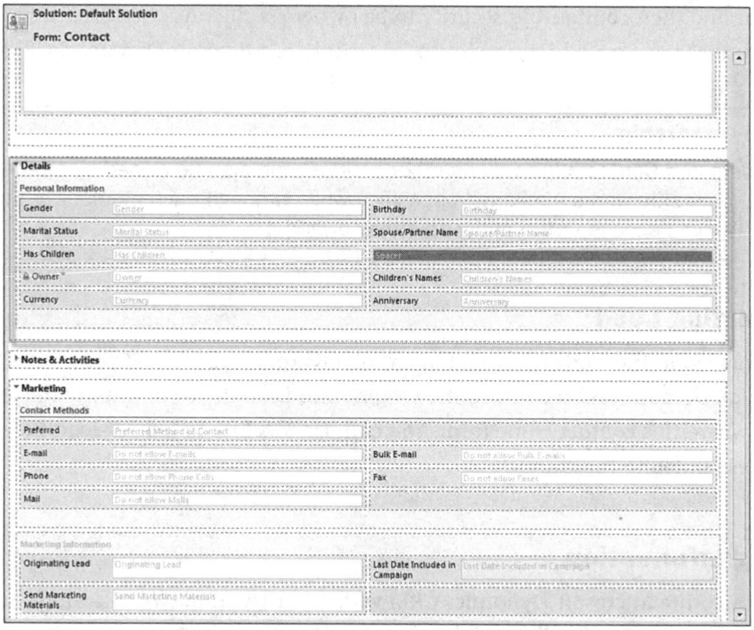

FIGURE 12.3
Contact details.

Department

Department is descriptive only and is not used in other parts of the system. It can be helpful, however, when extending Microsoft Dynamics CRM or when creating ad hoc reports.

Role

Role is a drop-down field that supports a user's interest in classifying the true role of a contact (for instance, influencer, decision maker).

Owner

The owner of the contact affects many things in Microsoft Dynamics CRM. It is a key field that helps control data access and role-based security. It can also be used to focus and filter data for views and reports. Every contact in Microsoft Dynamics CRM must be assigned an owner, and the owner of the contact must be a licensed Microsoft Dynamics CRM user of the system. This also applies to the owner of the account. The owner of the account and the owner of the contact do not have to be the same.

For instance, perhaps you want to limit who has access to specific contacts. You can do this by assigning the proper owner to each of the contacts associated with an account and then configuring security to be owner specific. As you learned in Hour 5, "Security," you can add many layers of security to Microsoft Dynamics CRM.

> **Team Ownership**
>
> Accounts and Contacts (as well as other entities) can also be owned by a team. Team ownership works similarly to specific owner although each member of the team is given access to the entity as if they owned it.

Originating Lead

If you are using the leads feature of Microsoft Dynamics CRM, and you convert a lead to an account and a contact, the Originating Lead field will display the lead record where this contact came from. You can use this link to look at lead notes and activities related to the contact.

Billing Information

If you integrate Microsoft Dynamics CRM with other Dynamics applications, such as the accounting software Microsoft Dynamics NAV, Microsoft Dynamics GP, or

Microsoft Dynamics AX, some of the billing information will be automatically populated. If your accounting software is not integrated with Microsoft Dynamics CRM, the Billing Information field is a place to capture billing details that might be of interest to the sales team. In addition, if you are using Microsoft Dynamics CRM to create quotes, orders, and invoices, the default price list defined on the contact will be the default price list used when creating quotes, orders, and invoices for this contact. If you are not using Microsoft Dynamics CRM for any type of accounting, you might want to remove this field from the form.

Contact Methods

To help support anti-spam regulations and compliance with these regulations, Microsoft Dynamics CRM provides a place to capture the marketing wishes of your contacts. When creating marketing campaigns, when sending email (including bulk email), and when doing mailings, Microsoft Dynamics CRM checks the settings on the contact and alerts the user of any mailing issues. For instance, if you set a contact to not allow email, Microsoft Dynamics CRM will not allow you to send email to that contact. If you have the account set to Do Not Allow and the contact to Allow, the Account takes priority, and your mailing will be blocked.

Marketing Information

As you learned in Hour 9, "Marketing Campaigns," Microsoft Dynamics CRM has a campaign management system that allows for detailed tracking of activities associated with specific marketing efforts. When looking at specific contacts, you can see the last campaign that a specific contact was included in, and you can set whether you want a specific contact to be included in future marketing campaigns.

Service Preferences

Service Preferences is a section associated with the scheduling and service functionality in Microsoft Dynamics CRM. If you are not using service and scheduling functionality, you can remove this field or this entire section from the form (although you might find some of the fields useful).

In terms of service, as you will learn in Hour 19, "Scheduling," scheduling is a detailed and robust function in Microsoft Dynamics CRM, but it is also quite particular when it comes to wanting specific details. If you plan to use scheduling, you definitely want to choose and set the right specifics on your contact with regard to preferred service, preferred equipment/facility, and preferred user. This will make using the scheduling feature a lot smoother. Defining the preferred fields within a contact when a contact is added eliminates the need to go back and update all contacts with the preferred settings.

The Notes and Activities Section

Notes and Activities are available on many different entities, and you can capture notes and activities on all or a subset of entities, but it's important to consider how notes will be used. If you want to aggregate all notes from all entities into one central place, you need either a report, a custom application, or a third-party add-in to Microsoft Dynamics CRM. By default, Microsoft Dynamics CRM serves up notes as they relate to a specific entity. There is definitely good reasoning behind this, but it also can trip you up. For instance, to see all the notes and the total set of conversations you have had with a specific contact, choosing the Notes section on that contact will show you a good running history, unless you also have contact-specific notes on an account, an activity, or the opportunity.

It is important to decide on a good business process with regard to notes. You can also offer more freedom in note taking (ultimately capturing more corporate details) if you add in a note display or report.

Figure 12.4 shows an example of the Notes section with three captured notes.

FIGURE 12.4
The Notes and Activities section of the Contact form.

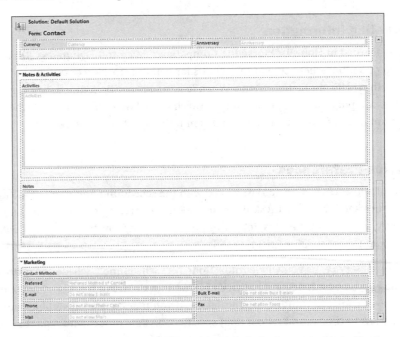

Notes are unlimited in terms of how many words you can type in them. You can have a long note or a series of short notes. You can also associate attachments with notes, although these attachments are more for historical reference than for long-term collaboration and editing. If you want a true document library where you can search, check out, edit, and check in documents, you really want to leverage the integration between Microsoft Dynamics CRM and Microsoft SharePoint. They make a natural partnership, and with a tiny bit of work, you can have the correct SharePoint account-specific document library appear as a section in the account or contact record of Microsoft Dynamics CRM.

By the Way

Unstructured Data Such as Documents

SharePoint is a great solution for unstructured data, and Microsoft Dynamics CRM works well as SharePoint's partner with structured data.

For more information about your chosen architecture for Microsoft SharePoint with Microsoft Dynamics CRM, talk with a local Microsoft Partner who specializes in SharePoint and Microsoft Dynamics CRM. Additionally you will want to leverage the integration to SharePoint that is delivered with Dynamics CRM v2011.

By the Way

Where to Put Notes

If your teams are good at business processes, a simple rule of thumb could be to organize the free-form notes captured by all the different people in your organization. If each person at your company has a unique and creative style, however, you might want to leverage technology to summarize and organize the free-form notes captured.

Related Contacts

If you have many different relationships that you want to track or if you want to capture the relationships that a given contact has to other contacts or accounts, you might want to take advantage of the relationship-tracking feature of Microsoft Dynamics CRM. There are two different options here: relationships and connections.

Tracking Relationships

The relationship-tracking feature offers a chance to define relationship roles, such as association and association member or vendor contact and reseller contact. The relationship-tracking feature of Microsoft Dynamics CRM exists because it was available in earlier version, but in v2011 is being replaced by connections. The relationship tracking feature is accessible from the left navigation pane of the Contact form, the Account form, and the Opportunity form.

Figure 12.5 shows the new relationship form, as accessed from by selecting Relationships on the Contact form.

FIGURE 12.5
Adding a new
relationship.

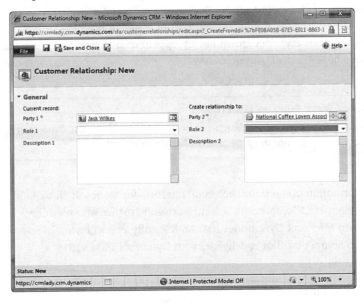

Figure 12.6 shows the details of a completed relationship. In this example, Jack Wilkes is a member of the National Coffee Lovers Association.

FIGURE 12.6
An added rela-
tionship.

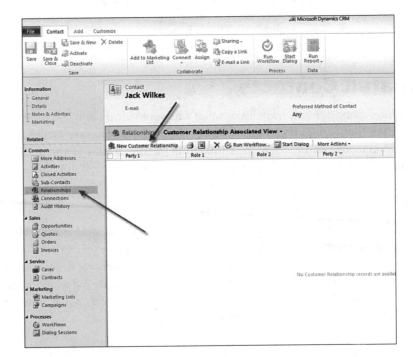

Tracking Connections

The second option when it comes to tracking who is connected to whom is to track connections. Connections are unique entities that track relationships between different accounts and relationships between different contacts. In fact, you can even use connections to track the complex relationships between other entities.

Unlike the relationship feature discussed in the preceding section, connections offers a lot more long-term depth of feature and functionality. For instance, when you create a connection between a person and an account, you can define the specific role the person has within that relationship. You can also capture when the relationship started and when the relationship ended (if it ended). So a contact can be connected to an account, but it can also be connected to an opportunity, a lead, or another contact.

When you are using connections, you can use different views to determine such things as who is influencing a specific sale or who manages a specific budget. Figure 12.7 shows a connection on a contact associated with an account. In this specific situation, the account is not the contact's employer but is a vendor with which the contact does business. The contact has this connection because he was a former employee of this vendor. We can capture that John Smith worked at Greenfield Vendor prior to holding his current position with ABC Company.

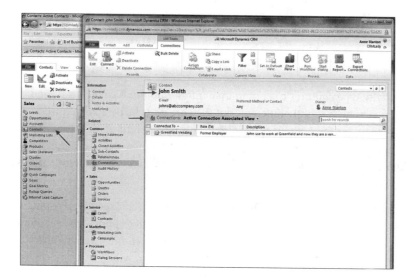

FIGURE 12.7
Contact connections.

Leveraging and Using Activities

As you learned in Hour 2, activities are classified as one of the following: tasks, faxes, phone calls, e-mails, letters, appointments, and special case service activities or marketing campaign activities. The special activities are discussed in Hour 9 and Hour 19. Figure 12.8 shows the full list of activity types.

FIGURE 12.8
Activity types.

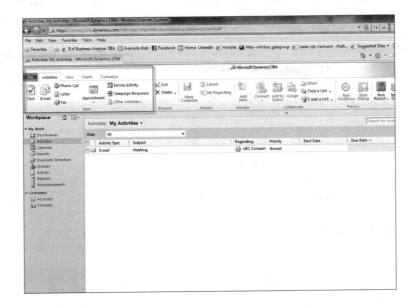

Each activity type captures a set of unique information and core details, and therefore each activity is slightly different, but they are all considered activities and are aggregated under the Activity entity views. This means that all activities can be shown under the activities view usually found in Workplace, and all your activities can be seen in the view My Activities (see Figure 12.9). We talk more about special types of activity views later in this hour.

Additionally if you select a specific contact or if you select a specific account, you will see listed in the left menu that you have an Activities option and a History option. In these two areas, History is another name for completed activities.

Activities as a Key Indicator

Activities are the key indicator for tracking who did what and when within the system. When the Save as Completed option is chosen, an activity is locked into history, and the system stamps it with a user, date, and time. This stamp allows you to view or report on the actual completed date and on the created date and last modified date.

By the Way

FIGURE 12.9
The My Activities view.

Task Activities

Figure 12.10 shows the details of a Task activity. You can configure a Task activity to synchronize with Microsoft Outlook tasks. This synchronization means that, if you check off the task as completed in Outlook, it also shows up as completed in Microsoft Dynamics CRM, and if you complete the activity in Microsoft Dynamics CRM, it shows up as completed in Outlook tasks. Activities of type Task are the only activities that synchronize with Outlook tasks.

You can associate an attachment with a task activity, as shown in Figure 12.11.

FIGURE 12.10
A Task activity.

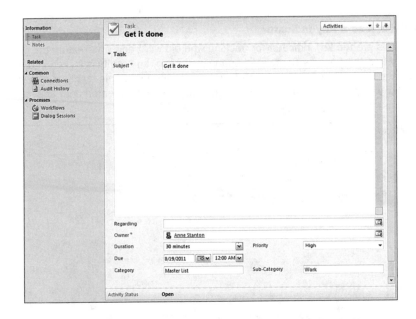

FIGURE 12.11
The task activity attachment window.

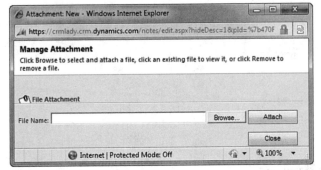

By the Way

Attachments

Attachments are unstructured files of various sizes, and although Microsoft Dynamics CRM can be configured to limit attachments to sizes within a limit, you should consider the risks and rewards of inserting attachments before building this feature into your business process.

Fax Activities

Figure 12.12 shows a Fax activity. A Fax activity does not send faxes; it tracks that a fax was sent. It includes an area for you to indicate what number and to whom the fax was sent. In a Fax activity, notice that there are some unique fields, such as Fax Number, Recipient, and Sender. Fax activities do not synchronize with Outlook, but

they can be viewed under the Activities view (see Figure 12.13). You can also reach
the Activities view via the Activities folder in Outlook.

FIGURE 12.12
A Fax activity.

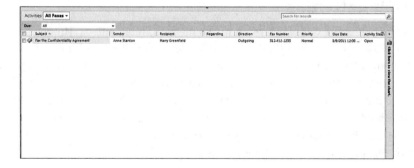

FIGURE 12.13
The Fax
Activities view.

Phone Call Activities

If you create a new activity of type Phone Call after you have chosen the contact,
the Phone Call activity automatically populates with the contact's main phone
number and the correct contacts for both the contact and the CRM user. Figure
12.14 shows an example.

FIGURE 12.14
A Phone Call
activity.

In addition, if you change the Outgoing and Incoming radio buttons on the Phone
Call activity, the names will be automatically swapped.

E-mail Activities

E-mail activities are completed when tracking e-mail from Outlook. However, from
within Microsoft Dynamics CRM, you can create an e-mail message and save it to
be sent later. You can also create an e-mail message and associate it with someone
else so that the other person can send it when ready. Perhaps someone wants you to
create a first draft and he then wants to do a final edit and send it. You can also create and send an e-mail message immediately. E-mail messages created and sent
from Microsoft Dynamics CRM are not tracked in Microsoft Outlook. This is by
design. Figure 12.15 shows an E-mail activity.

E-mail activities have an option to allow you to format an e-mail message using
rich text commands, insert a standard e-mail template that might include data
fields from Microsoft Dynamics CRM, or insert one of your Knowledge Base articles.

FIGURE 12.15
An E-mail
activity.

If you do want to associate an attachment with an e-mail message, you first need to save the e-mail message (which you can do without exiting) and then associate the attachment to the created E-mail activity.

As you learned in Hour 9, you can also send e-mail messages as part of a full marketing campaign or a quick campaign.

E-mail messages that are tracked from Outlook and e-mail messages that are sent from Microsoft Dynamics CRM would appear under a contact's history and under the staff members' activities. In addition, you can set a "regarding" within an e-mail message and associate it with another entity, such as an invoice, an opportunity, or a service case.

Letter Activities

A Letter activity can track when letters are sent to a prospect or customer. A Letter activity is a classification that includes an area to indicate which address to send a letter to or the address to which a letter was sent. Figure 12.16 shows an example of an activity of type Letter.

FIGURE 12.16
A Letter activity.

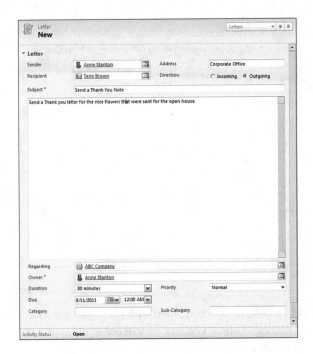

Appointment or Recurring Appointment Activities

An Appointment activity shows up on the Microsoft Dynamics CRM calendar in the My Activities view of Microsoft Dynamics CRM. If you are synchronizing all appointments to Microsoft Outlook, they also appear in your Outlook calendar. You can also selectively connect Outlook appointments to Microsoft Dynamics CRM from Outlook. When you do this, the items appear as Appointment activities in Microsoft Dynamics CRM. See Figure 12.17. Recurring activities can also be tracked, although they are tracked as a unique activity of type recurring.

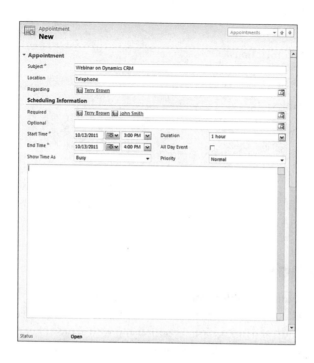

FIGURE 12.17
An Appointment
activity.

Custom Activities

You can create custom activity types if the other options do not fit your business
model. To create a custom activity type, you need to create a new entity and select
the option to make the new entity an activity (see Figure 12.18). Here's how you do it:

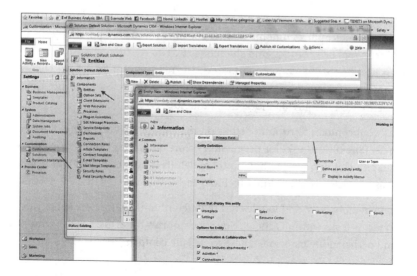

FIGURE 12.18
Creating a cus-
tom activity.

1. Select Settings.

2. Select Customizations.

3. Select Customize the System.

4. Select Entities.

5. Select New.

6. Select Define as an Activity Entity.

After you define a custom activity entity, the choice of types of activities list will be updated. For instance if you select New from My Activities, the list of choices will now include your new type.

Workshop

Janet runs a boutique clothing store, and she uses Microsoft Dynamics CRM to manage her marketing efforts and her relationships with customers. Given that Janet's store is a boutique, she has a special relationship with some of her most loyal clients, and Janet makes a point of remembering what they like. Janet captures each visitor who visits her store and who signs up for her regular mailings. Janet also uses Appointment activities to capture meetings for private showings of new clothing lines and to mark on her calendar her quarterly board meeting. Janet has rearranged the Contact form to fit her business model. She has created a new section and a set of attributes to capture details, such as favorite clothing color sets, sizes, and notes on buying history.

Janet does not capture job titles on her contacts, but she does use much of the other information. She captures a home address, business address, and, if unique, a shipping address for each contact, and she makes sure to capture at least two phone numbers and (if possible) an email address. She also notes if one of her clients does not want to receive mailings or e-mail messages. There is a low tolerance among her audience for unrequested marketing materials.

Janet uses subcontacts to capture details on the children of each of her elite member customers. (She always asks for permission before doing this.) Janet plans to expand her children's clothing line, so having these details is helpful. When capturing details on contacts' children, Janet includes the birth date.

Janet is incredibly busy and juggles many different to-do items. She keeps track of these items as tasks within Outlook. She synchronizes these tasks with Dynamics CRM and occasionally associates these to specific contacts.

Q&A

Q. *We are thinking of using contacts for items other than "people." Is this a problem?*

A. Renaming contacts and using the entity differently is not a problem; it is commonly done in some industries.

Q. *We want to be able to fax from Microsoft Dynamics CRM. Is this what the Fax activity is for?*

A. No. The Fax activity does not send a fax; it is designed to remind you to send a fax or track that a fax was sent.

Q. *We have a drop-down list for salutation. Can we change the Salutation field to a drop-down list?*

A. No. The Salutation field in Microsoft Dynamics CRM cannot be changed, but it can be taken off the form and replaced with your own salutation attribute (field).

Quiz

1. If Janet, whose boutique is described earlier, creates an activity of type Letter, will it show up in Outlook's Tasks list?

2. If you create and send an e-mail message from Microsoft Dynamics CRM, will it appear in Outlook's Sent folder?

3. Why is the owner of a contact so important?

4. Where would you recommend that Janet capture her notes on the buying habits of her customers? Where should she capture notes about on the buying habits of the children? What are some of the advantages and disadvantages of the various choices?

5. When will an activity of type Phone Call be automatically populated with the phone number from the account or contact?

Answers

1. Letters will appear in Outlook's Tasks list if Janet configures letters to synchronize with Outlook.

2. No. E-mail sent from Microsoft Dynamics CRM does not synchronize with Outlook.

3. The owner of a contact is a key field for security and for views and reporting.

4. Buying habits can be captured in the notes of each contact. You potentially lose a summary view of all notes on the entire account, but with code or a third-party add-on, you have options.

5. The activity of type Phone Call gets automatically populated with the phone number if you have an account or contact in context and then create a new activity of type Phone Call.

Exercise

Create two activities of each type and associate them with a specific contact. Create one activity from Activities from the Workplace navigation bar. Create the other activity after selecting a specific contact and then selecting Activity from the left menu of the Contact form. What happens differently when you create each of these activities in these two different ways?

Go to the Activity view and change the view type to each of the unique types. Notice how the views change, based on the type of activity you choose.

HOUR 13

Sending E-mail from Microsoft Dynamics CRM

What You'll Learn in This Hour:

▶ Capturing e-mail
▶ Sending one quick message
▶ Sending multiple e-mail messages
▶ CAN-SPAM Act compliance
▶ The Microsoft Dynamics CRM Outlook address book
▶ Configuring e-mail based on your preferences

In this hour, you will learn how e-mail works in Microsoft Dynamics CRM. You will also learn how to associate e-mail in Microsoft Outlook with records in Microsoft Dynamics CRM.

Capturing E-mail

Many of our conversations these days are captured in e-mail, and yet we often don't manage to get these e-mails saved and associated with other company information. When only storing e-mail in our personal Outlook folders, we lose the chance to categorize and associate e-mails with specific service cases, sales opportunities, and marketing campaigns. Microsoft Dynamics CRM resolves this issue by offering a number of configuration choices when it comes to e-mail.

Choices include the following:

- **Track all incoming Outlook e-mail in Microsoft Dynamics CRM—** This tracks all e-mail for the specified user in Microsoft Dynamics CRM as e-mail activities, and a link exists between all e-mail-associated people in the To and From fields.

- **Track only incoming e-mail that was sent in response to an e-mail originally sent from Microsoft Dynamics CRM—**When e-mail is sent from Microsoft Dynamics CRM, a tracking token is associated. When this e-mail is responded to, Microsoft Dynamics CRM can link the response to the original via the tracking token.

- **Track only e-mail related to your accounts, contacts, or leads—** E-mail that you send or that is sent to you is tracked if it came from an account, a contact, or a lead with a matching e-mail address within Microsoft Dynamics CRM for which you were designated as owner.

- **Manually track e-mail you specifically choose—**You can manually track selected messages from Outlook in CRM by using the Track in CRM option in the Microsoft Outlook ribbon.

- **Manually Track a set off e-mails in Microsoft Dynamics CRM—**If you select a set of e-mails and then choose track the system will manually track each one.

- **E-mail messages from Microsoft Dynamics CRM Online records that are e-mail enabled—**E-mail messages are tracked from all record types, including custom record types, that contain an e-mail address field.

After e-mails are tracked you can also change which records those are associated with, either by associating them or changing their association.

Sending One Quick Message

Say that you want to send a message from Microsoft Dynamics CRM. As you learned in Hour 12, "Contacts and Activity Capture," you can do this by creating a new activity of type E-mail. To send a quick e-mail in this way, follow these steps:

1. Select Activities.

2. Select E-mail (a type of activity).

3. Look up and associate the recipient.

4. Add your e-mail content or template and content.

5. Click Send.

Figure 13.1 shows an e-mail being sent directly from Microsoft Dynamics CRM.

FIGURE 13.1
An E-mail activity in Microsoft Dynamics CRM.

Now, let's say you want to send a quick e-mail from Outlook, and you want to track this e-mail in Microsoft Dynamics CRM. To send an e-mail message in this way, follow these steps:

1. Create an e-mail message in Outlook.

2. Click the Track in CRM button at the top of the message.

3. Click Send.

Figure 13.2 shows an e-mail message with the Track button in Microsoft Outlook. When sending an e-mail via Microsoft Outlook or when opening an existing e-mail, you have the option to click this Track button. This button also has the option to set a "regarding," which enables you to associate an e-mail from Outlook with more than just the sender and selected receivers. It also lets you associate the e-mail with other specific records in Microsoft Dynamics CRM.

FIGURE 13.2
An Outlook e-mail message.

Sending Multiple E-mail Messages

In Hour 9, "Marketing Campaigns," you learned about marketing and the ability to do quick campaigns and full marketing campaigns. If you are interested in tracking a blast of e-mails, you have three choices. You can do a quick campaign or full campaign with e-mail campaign activities from Microsoft Dynamics CRM (options 1 and 2), or you can send an e-mail to multiple people (option 3), either from Microsoft Dynamics CRM or from Outlook with Track selected.

If you choose to send a single e-mail to multiple people, the single e-mail message will be captured in Microsoft Dynamics CRM and will be available for lookup on all valid contacts in Microsoft Dynamics CRM who received the message.

In Figure 13.3, one e-mail record is associated with different contacts. This represents the sending of an e-mail to multiple contacts. In Figure 13.4, three different e-mail records are created, and they are all exactly the same. This represents the sending of e-mail from bulk mail or marketing campaigns where a unique E-mail activity record is created for each and every person the e-mail message is sent to.

Bulk e-mail creates and stores multiple copies of the same e-mail message, each associated with a different contact. This allows the system to capture the responses of each individual and to copy and save the responses against the unique e-mail

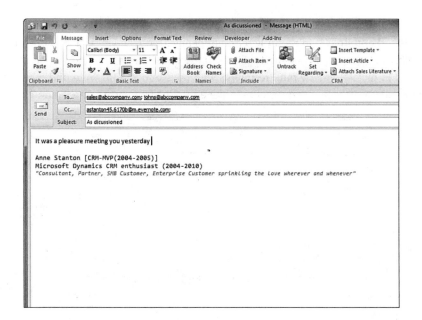

FIGURE 13.3
Mail sent to multiple recipients from Outlook.

FIGURE 13.4
Mail sent to multiple recipients from Dynamics CRM.

and contact. Sending one e-mail message to multiple recipients saves one copy of the e-mail and links it to multiple different people. If a recipient is not a contact within CRM, the contact's e-mail address in the e-mail activity record will be highlighted in red. All other e-mail recipients who are contacts with valid and associated e-mail addresses will appear in blue in the e-mail activity record (see Figure 13.5).

FIGURE 13.5
An E-mail activity with a valid contact e-mail address.

To further clarify, in the first situation, if you delete one e-mail message, all other e-mail messages are retained. In the second situation, if you delete the e-mail message, it will not be available to any recipients.

Creating and Sending Bulk Mail from a Quick Campaign

If you decide to do a bulk e-mailing from a quick campaign, you have two choices. The first is to use Microsoft Dynamics CRM to create the e-mail message that will be sent. Figure 13.6 shows the Create Quick Campaign Wizard. To complete the process, follow these steps:

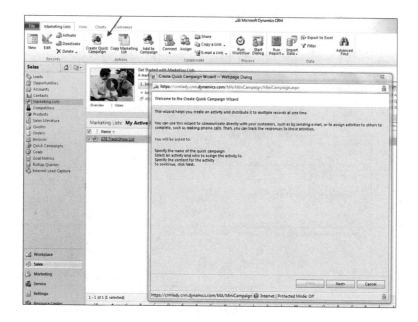

FIGURE 13.6
The Quick
Campaign
Wizard.

1. Select or create a marketing list to which to send your e-mail campaign. (See Hour 9 if you need a refresher.)

2. Choose Create Quick Campaign and follow the Quick Campaign Wizard.

3. Choose the type of item that Microsoft Dynamics CRM will generate when the campaign is kicked off. Figure 13.7 shows an example of choosing E-mail from the drop-down list.

4. Create the e-mail message, as shown in Figure 13.8. You can use rich text to make the e-mail look the way you want, and you can insert Microsoft Dynamics CRM data fields that will populate when you create and kick off the campaign. Write the body of the e-mail message.

5. Kick off the campaign by clicking the Create button (see Figure 13.9).

Another way to do a bulk e-mailing from a quick campaign is to do a Microsoft Word mail merge (see Figure 13.10 and there is more in Hour 14, "Microsoft Word Mail Merge"). Doing a mail merge offers different choices than those you have when building the e-mail from within Microsoft Dynamics CRM.

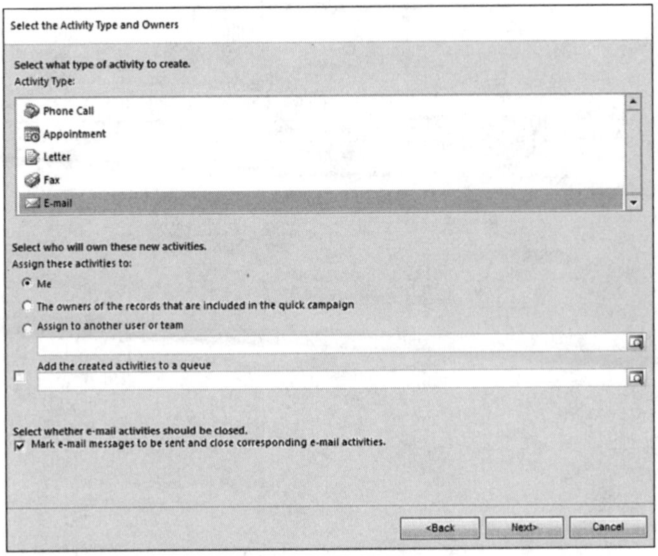

FIGURE 13.7
Selecting E-mail.

FIGURE 13.7
Selecting E-mail.

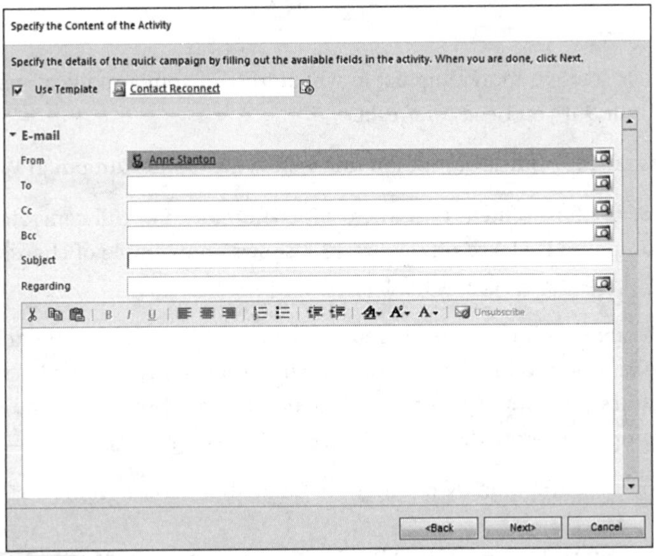

FIGURE 13.8
Creating the
e-mail message
body.

When you open the Select the Mail Merge Type drop-down, you have a number of choices, as shown in Figure 13.11.

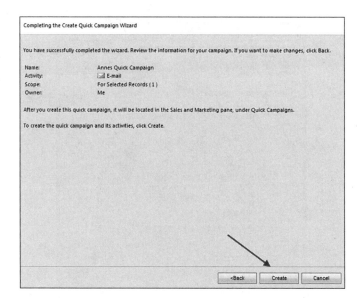

FIGURE 13.9
Completing a
quick campaign.

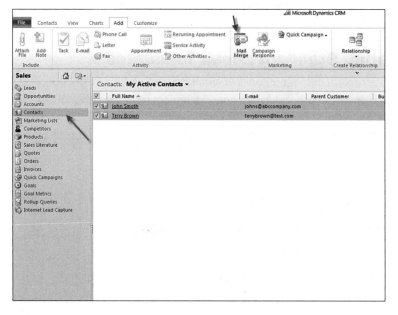

FIGURE 13.10
A mail merge
on contacts.

To proceed with creating a quick campaign mail merge of type E-mail, follow these steps:

1. Select either an organization e-mail template or one of your own personal mail merge templates.

2. Select the data fields you want to include.

3. Click OK. The Word mail merge template opens on your screen.

FIGURE 13.11
Selecting a mail
merge type.

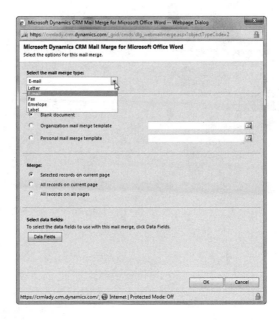

Creating Standard E-mail Templates

There are two different repositories of templates and options for creating e-mail messages. These include an individual e-mail template from the personal templates and an organizational template from the company templates. You can create standard organizational e-mail templates that can be used by everyone on your team in Microsoft Dynamics CRM by following these steps (see Figure 13.12):

1. Select Settings.

2. Select Templates under Business Administration.

3. Select E-mail Templates from the list of template options.

4. Select New E-Mail Template.

5. Choose Global, as in a Global template to be shared.

6. Create the e-mail template details.

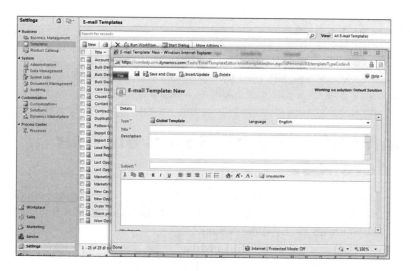

FIGURE 13.12
Creating an
e-mail
template.

CAN-SPAM Act Compliance

As you learned in Hour 7, "The Account Entity in More Detail," and Hour 12, you can mark individual accounts or contacts at your clients so that you don't send e-mail to them.

You can also send bulk e-mails and track the responses from those e-mails, as you learned in Hour 9.

To understand the Federal Trade Commission's (FTC's) CAN-SPAM Act and to ensure that your e-mails are in compliance with this act, see http://business.ftc.gov/multimedia/videos/complying-can-spam-act.

Now that you have learned the ins and outs of e-mailing from Microsoft Dynamics CRM, you might want more functionality when it comes to marketing, particularly as it relates to advanced marketing. Third-party solutions are available, and many of them plug right into Microsoft Dynamics CRM.

The Microsoft Dynamics CRM Outlook Address Book

Microsoft Outlook has a concept called the Personal Address Book, which is what you see when you drill down on To in Outlook. This is different from Microsoft Outlook Contacts. Microsoft Dynamics CRM offers a complementary personal Outlook address book with Microsoft Dynamics CRM data for use when choosing the To field when sending messages from Outlook. The Microsoft Dynamics CRM address book includes accounts, contacts, facilities/equipment, leads, queues, and users.

Did you Know?

Address Book Security

The Outlook address book is saved on the local drive of the Outlook user. If the security of local data is of concern, you might want to discuss this external data with your Microsoft Dynamics CRM partner or your technology advisor. Having data on your local drive puts it at risk when a laptop is stolen.

Configuring E-mail Based on Your Preferences

Some configuration settings are unique to every user of Microsoft Dynamics CRM. One of these configuration options is the choice of how your Outlook address book is handled. Figure 13.13 shows the options.

To display the user preferences in Dynamics CRM 2011, you need to select File, Options.

FIGURE 13.13
E-mail choices.

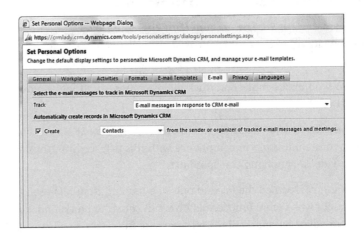

There is also an E-mail tab, as shown in Figure 13.7. It's worth thinking hard about how you want to track e-mail because there are advantages and disadvantages to all the e-mail tracking options. For instance, consider the option to automatically track all e-mails. The benefit: The most robust capture of corporate intelligence is controlled by the system, eliminating human choice and error. The disadvantage: Personal e-mail and e-mail that staff do not want tracked are captured, tracked in Microsoft Dynamics CRM, and seen by other Microsoft Dynamics CRM team members.

Workshop

A small medical practice called Just in Time Advice has just installed Microsoft Dynamics CRM. Just in Time Advice provides answers to common medical questions via the Internet and telephone. Questions that cannot be answered are referred to a local physicians' network. Justin Brown is the CEO of Just in Time Advice. Justin wants to expand the number of physicians in Just in Time Advice's physicians' network. Justin starts his efforts by using e-mail to reach out to his connections from various previous positions. He reviews his contacts and selects 30 different people. He writes a personal e-mail message to each contact. The message is written and then saved in Microsoft Dynamics CRM for future reference. The message is also set with a specific medical practice using the "regarding" feature, which is the medical practice that exists in his database as an account that each physician is associated with.

Justin also asks his marketing coordinator, Mary Mill, to send out a bulk e-mail to all contacts, announcing a new e-newsletter. Mary uses a quick campaign to send this announcement.

Q&A

Q. *We send a lot of e-mail. Does Microsoft Dynamics CRM track who has requested not to be contacted?*

A. Yes. Each contact can be optionally marked as Do Not Send or can be further refined and limited by being set to Do Not Send Bulk E-mail.

Q. *Can we track the responses to e-mail messages that have been sent?*

A. Yes. You have numerous ways to capture responses to e-mail messages.

Q. *Some people at our company want all of their e-mail messages tracked, and others want only selected e-mail messages tracked. Is this difference of choice an option in Microsoft Dynamics CRM?*

A. Yes. E-mail tracking is configured at the user level.

Quiz

1. What is one advantage to tracking e-mail in Microsoft Dynamics CRM?

2. What are the three choices for tracking e-mail responses in Microsoft Dynamics CRM?

3. When you send an e-mail message from Outlook, copy five contacts, and track the message in CRM, how many copies of the e-mail are saved in CRM?

4. What is one reason you would not want to use the Microsoft Dynamics CRM Outlook address book?

5. In the scenario described previously, what are Mary's choices when creating her announcement about the new e-newsletter?

Answers

1. Tracking e-mail in Microsoft Dynamics CRM allows you to be more organized by associating e-mail messages with accounts and contacts. In addition tracking e-mail messages, Microsoft Dynamics CRM lets all users see the message, rather than just the user who created the e-mail conversation.

2. You can track all incoming Outlook e-mail in Microsoft Dynamics CRM, track only incoming e-mail that was sent in response to an e-mail originally sent from Microsoft Dynamics CRM, and track only e-mail related to your accounts, contacts, or leads.

3. One copy of the e-mail is saved in CRM.

4. There is a higher security risk when data is stored locally.

5. Mary can create an E-mail activity and send it to multiple people, or she can use the quick campaign feature of Microsoft Dynamics CRM to send a bulk mailing.

Exercise

Create Mary Mill's e-newsletter announcement e-mail. To get started, set up a marketing list for all active contacts. After the list is created, follow the steps for creating a quick campaign using the Quick Campaign Wizard. Get creative with what you want to say in the e-mail and insert some of the Microsoft Dynamics CRM fields. You can also insert a Microsoft Dynamics CRM e-mail template.

HOUR 14

Microsoft Word Mail Merge

What You'll Learn In This Hour:

▶ Mail merge templates
▶ Creating a template using an existing Word template
▶ Managing templates
▶ Managing data fields
▶ Enabling macros in Microsoft Word 2010 or 2007

The ability to merge data from Microsoft Dynamics CRM into familiar tools, such as Microsoft Word, is a big plus for business professionals. This hour explores a topic that many business professionals struggled with before finding Microsoft Dynamics CRM. Workers often spent hours designing or creating business letters or complex Word documents each time their data changed or a new, slightly different need arose. Using data stored in Microsoft Dynamics CRM and templates reduces the redundancy of repeatedly creating something new.

Microsoft Dynamics CRM can work with what you have, allowing much of the data from Microsoft Dynamics CRM to be merged into a template or different templates that can then be used to quickly create finished Microsoft Word documents.

Let's now look at the available templates and familiarize ourselves with our options.

Mail Merge Templates

Various management templates are available in Microsoft Dynamics CRM. For instance, several templates relate to major business building blocks (entities) within the software (quotes, letters, marketing events, and leads, to name just a few). Figure 14.1 shows the gateway to templates.

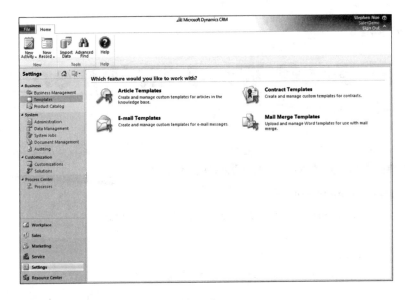

To reach the mail merge templates, follow these steps:

1. Choose Settings.

2. Choose Templates.

3. Choose Mail Merge Templates. The screen shown in Figure 14.2 appears.

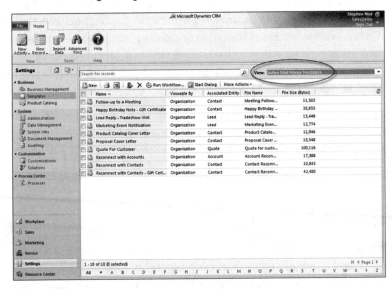

These templates were designed for both new and experienced users, and the list can
be expanded as you get more comfortable with the application. In Figure 14.2, by

default, the Word templates have the .doc extension (representing the Microsoft Word 2003 format). This extension gives the templates the most versatility for working with all versions of Word and backward compatibility with Microsoft Word 2003. It also allows them to work with Microsoft Word 2010 and 2007.

The default system view when you select Templates is a list of all active mail merge templates, which also includes any customized templates. Customized templates do not default to having the .doc extension. In Figure 14.2, you can see that the customized template filename differs from the filenames of the default templates that come with Microsoft Dynamics CRM. Customized templates use the current Microsoft Office Extensible Markup Language (XML) format when they are created. There are two reasons for this: The XML format is a new standard that is compatible with many other applications and the XML format is nonproprietary.

Other views, including the following, are also available to see all or a subset of available templates from this area:

▶ Active Mail Merge Templates

▶ All Mail Merge Templates

▶ Inactive Mail Merge Templates

▶ My Active Mail Merge Templates

All templates that you create and that are active are listed in the My Active Mail Merge Templates view (see Figure 14.3).

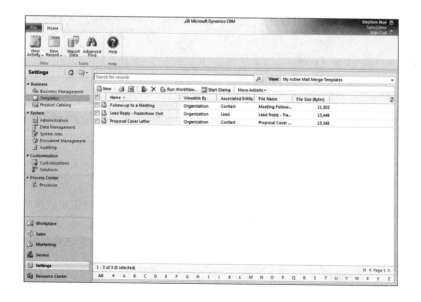

FIGURE 14.3
My Active Mail Merge Templates view.

Creating a Template Using an Existing Word Template

To add an existing Microsoft Word XML template to Microsoft Dynamics CRM, choose New from the menu bar. Figure 14.4 shows what you see at this point. Basically, you take a standard Microsoft Word 2007 template in XML format and save it into Microsoft Dynamics CRM as a new Microsoft Dynamics CRM mail merge template.

FIGURE 14.4
Creating a new mail merge template.

Give your template a name that will make it easy to find and descriptive enough that others with whom you share it will readily know what it was designed for.

For example, you can create a template, named Business Casual Letter Template, that enables you to easily write business casual letters. You can associate this template with the Contact entity because it is meant for a specific contact.

Then, you can associate this template with the Word XML template file created earlier. Figure 14.5 shows the results of all this.

After you complete these steps, you can further edit the original XML file by inserting Microsoft Dynamics CRM data references into the Microsoft Word XML template by using the Data Fields button on the template screen.

FIGURE 14.5
A mail merge template populated with answers.

After you click the Data Fields button, a list of all available contact data fields (attributes) appears (see Figure 14.6). Note the Record Type drop-down list at the top of this screen. This list allows you to select data fields from related entities for your merge in addition to the contact data fields, such as the company name from the parent account.

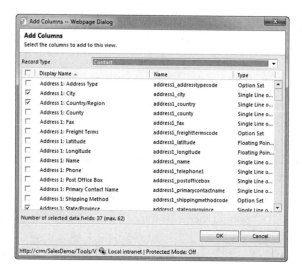

FIGURE 14.6
Available data fields.

By checking the checkbox next to an attribute, you can choose the extra data fields that suit your modifications. When you have done so, click OK.

Managing Templates

Templates can be individual, shared, or available for everyone in an organization. In this section, you'll open up an existing template and look at some of the options for sharing and managing it. When you create a template, you are the owner of it by default. The new template is individual, available under My Active views, and not seen by others within the company.

What if you create a template that everyone in the office will benefit from? You have the option of making this new template available to your entire organization. Or you can select to assign the template to only one other Microsoft Dynamics CRM user in your organization. You also have the option to share the template with a team or list of users. Figure 14.7 shows the Assign Mail Merge Template dialog.

FIGURE 14.7
Assigning a template.

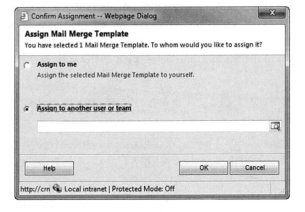

As shown in Figure 14.8, you can make a template available to the entire organization. The figure shows the options you see when you click the Make Available to Organization button.

Now that you know how to associate an existing XML file so that it becomes a Microsoft Dynamics CRM mail merge template, let's look at the internal data fields of a specific template.

FIGURE 14.8
Assigning a
template to an
organization.

Managing Data Fields

Each Microsoft Dynamics CRM entity has many data attributes (fields). The basic templates have default attributes (fields) chosen, but you can add or remove data attributes (fields) that you want within the template. Just click the Data Fields button to see those fields (see Figure 14.9).

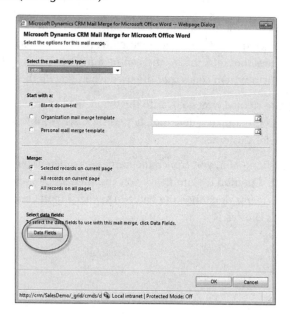

FIGURE 14.9
The Data Fields
button.

One use of a template is to prepare professional-looking quotes. You can take data from a quote entered in Microsoft Dynamics CRM and merge it into a Microsoft Word document, using a template to merge it into a final Word document that includes your logo, choice of fonts, colors, and the data fields of your choice.

A limit of 62 data fields applies when using mail merge templates. Therefore, mail merge templates might not always be the best solution. Figure 14.10 shows the warning that the system displays.

FIGURE 14.10
Note the 62-field maximum for customized templates.

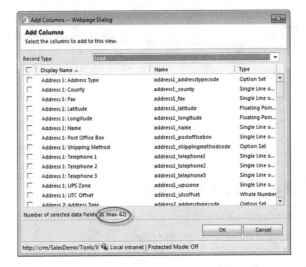

Figure 14.11 shows an example of a quote template, and Figure 14.12 shows the resulting mail merged quote. In the quote template, notice that there are a lot of commands and codes that look messy and can be fairly bewildering. These are Microsoft Word macro system codes that are used when you do the final merge.

To use the template created, you go over to the Quote feature under Sales, Quotes. From the top of the Creating a Quote dialog, you click the Word icon next to the words Print Quote for Customer.

When you get the hang of it, you can create numerous different templates in a variety of formats with a myriad of data fields. You can then share these formats with individual users or teams or change the value in Ownership to Organization and increase everyone's choices.

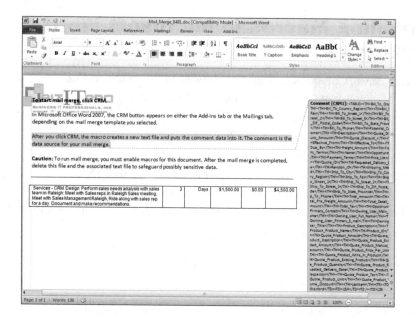

FIGURE 14.11
A quote template.

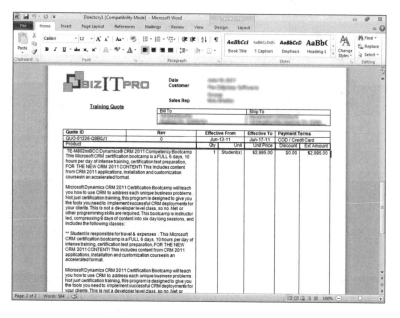

FIGURE 14.12
A quote.

Enabling Macros in Microsoft Word 2010 or 2007

In some network environments, security administrators disable the use of macros within Microsoft Word to protect the network from macro viruses. You need to look at how to allow macros to work in Microsoft Word if Microsoft Dynamics CRM templates are going to be of any use to you.

In Word 2010, click the File tab at the upper left of the Microsoft Word interface. In Word 2007, click the large Microsoft Office button at the upper left of the Microsoft Word interface. There are many controls you can use to customize your Microsoft Word environment. You get to them through the Trust Center by following these steps:

1. In Word 2010, choose Options; in Word 2007, choose Word Options.

2. Click Trust Center.

3. Click Trust Center Settings.

4. Click Macro Settings. The dialog shown in Figure 14.13 appears.

FIGURE 14.13
Enabling macros.

In the Macro Settings dialog, you are interested in the last two settings:

▶ Disable All Macros Except Digitally Signed Macros

▶ Enable All Macros (not recommended; potentially dangerous code can run)

Your security administrator will be happy to learn that the Microsoft Dynamics CRM macro is a signed macro. Therefore, you can choose the first option; you don't have to discuss the second option with the rest of the IT staff.

When you first work with a template, the macros are displayed and are technical looking. You need to get to the CRM button, as displayed at the top of the Word document. Figure 14.14 shows add-ins where you can find the CRM button to perform the merge.

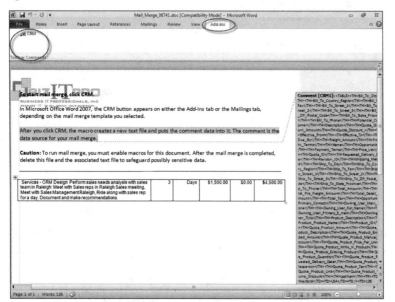

FIGURE 14.14
The CRM macro is digitally signed. You can find it under Add-Ins.

Try It Yourself

Using a Letter Template with a Lead

In this section, you'll test run a merge using a template. Say that there is a lead in Microsoft Dynamics CRM whose name is Walter Horton. He stopped by your booth at a recent trade show, and you want to send him a follow-up letter.

You can use one of the default templates for leads to do this. To choose a default template and apply it to a specific lead, you follow these steps:

1. Select Sales.

2. Select Leads.

3. Highlight Walter Horton.

4. Click the Add tab on the top of the ribbon.

5. Click the Mail Merge icon on the ribbon to start the mail merge (see Figure 14.15).

6. Click the Organization Mail Merge Template radio button.

FIGURE 14.15
The Word icon
starts the mail
merge.

7. Click the lookup icon to the far right of the Organization Mail Merge Template radio button. Microsoft Dynamics CRM prompts you to choose a template (see Figure 14.16).

FIGURE 14.16
Selecting a
template.

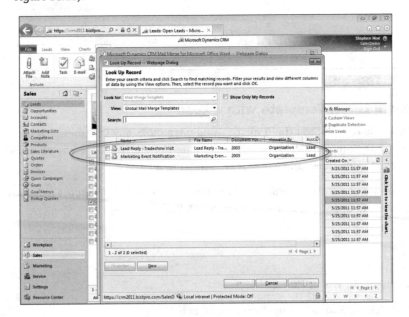

Templates by Entity

Notice that Microsoft Dynamics CRM is aware that you are using the Lead entity and it therefore displays only the lists of templates for leads. This feature expedites the process because you don't have a lot of unnecessary options that might slow you down.

8. Choose a template from the list and click OK (see Figure 14.17).

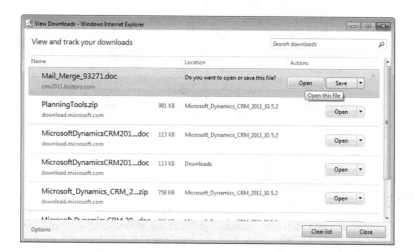

FIGURE 14.17
Starting a mail merge.

9. If you see a Protected View bar at the top of Word where the ribbon is supposed to be, click the Enable Editing button to continue. If a security warning stating that macros have been disabled is displayed, click the Enable Content button. When you start the merge, Microsoft Word opens, but it may look different from what you're used to (see Figure 14.18).

FIGURE 14.18
Opening
Microsoft Word
for a merge.

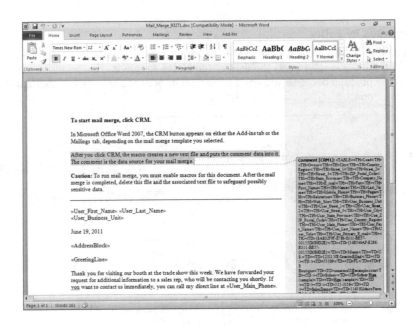

Leveraging the Power of Word

Here is what is happening: Microsoft Dynamics CRM is using a Microsoft Word macro to perform the merge. The data entered into the document can be understood as formatting from the template. The fields are referencing the data fields chosen for the template and, essentially, you are hooking into the data stored in the Microsoft SQL tables of the Microsoft Dynamics CRM databases. You can ignore all the noise.

Ignore all the potentially bewildering noise and just run the Microsoft Dynamics CRM macro, as follows:

1. Click Add-Ins from the Microsoft Word ribbon (see Figure 14.19).

2. Click CRM. The screen shown in Figure 14.20 appears.

3. When prompted to do so, add recipients to the document, as shown in Figure 14.21.

4. Scroll to the right, and you see all the fields that will be included in the merge. Click the OK button in the bottom right of the dialog box. The sidebar offers many of the mail merge options in Microsoft Word. Preview the letter by selecting Next: Preview Your Letters in the lower-right area of the screen. The letter is displayed, as shown in Figure 14.22.

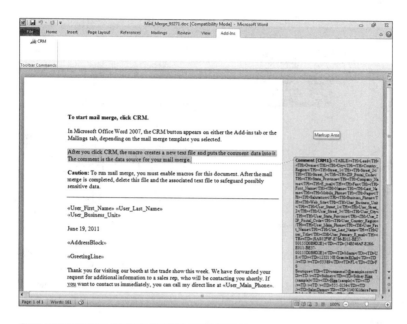

FIGURE 14.19
A mail merge document being created.

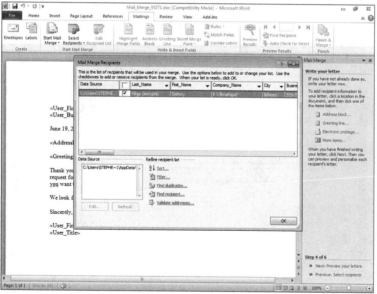

FIGURE 14.20
A mail merge document started.

A Basic Template

Because this is the basic template, you might find this a bit lackluster for a business document. To spruce it up, you can edit the document template to include a company logo and other text within the template itself or you can edit the document while in this process. Both options allow you flexibility.

FIGURE 14.21
Adding recipients to the document.

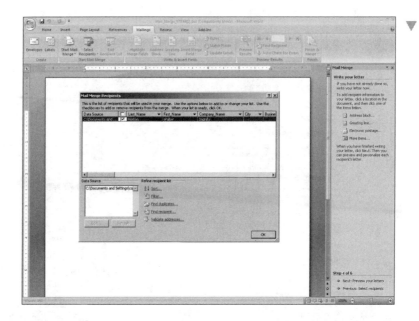

FIGURE 14.22
The letter.

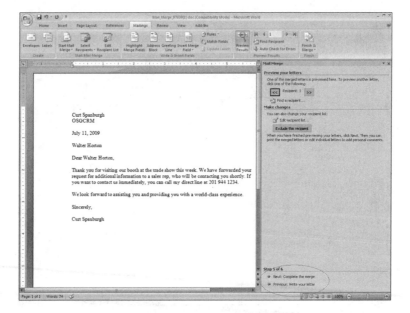

5. Click Next: Complete the Merge in the lower-right area of the screen. You now have the option to print or to edit individual letters.

6. Click Print, and you are done.

Try It Yourself ▼

Creating a Document with Merged Data from an Account

Now, let's work without a template to help clarify how Microsoft Dynamics CRM works with Microsoft Word. Follow these steps:

1. Select Sales.

2. Select Accounts.

3. Highlight a specific account. (Figure 14.23 shows an example.)

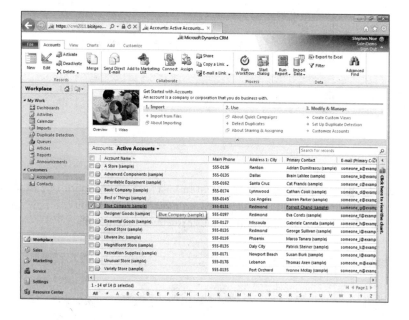

FIGURE 14.23
Creating a new document for an account with Microsoft Dynamics CRM data.

4. Choose the Add tab on the top of the ribbon.

5. Click the Mail Merge icon on the ribbon to start the mail merge.

6. When asked to choose from a list of personal or organizational templates or create your document from a blank document, choose Blank Document (see Figure 14.24).

7. Click Data Fields and select the data fields to use in your document. Notice that company fields related to the name and address are already selected for you. ▼

FIGURE 14.24
Creating a new
document for
an account.

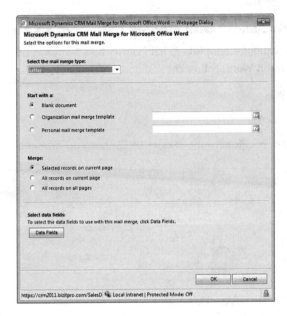

8. Click OK.

9. Click Open to open the new document in Microsoft Word. Figure 14.25 shows a
blank document with the Microsoft Word macros enabled. You can now add
any number of data fields and various associated text or tables.

FIGURE 14.25
Inserting a
mail merge.

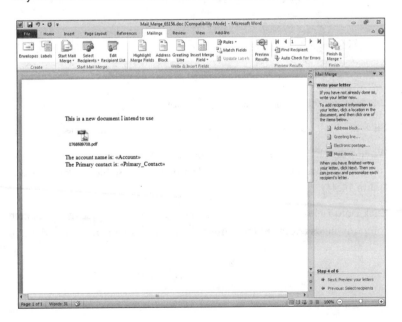

10. Choose the Add-Ins tab of the ribbon.

11. Click the CRM button on the Add-Ins tab.

12. Select the Mailings tab of the ribbon.

13. Use Insert Merge Field to insert any of the Microsoft Dynamics CRM data fields that are of interest to your document (refer to Figure 14.25). If desired, type any text into the document and format it as you would in any Word document.

Using the Match Fields Option

You can also use the Match Fields option to match Microsoft Word merge fields to Microsoft Dynamics CRM merge fields. If you do this, you can use the Microsoft Word wizards.

By the Way

Figure 14.26 shows an example of the document with a few of the merge fields embedded in the text.

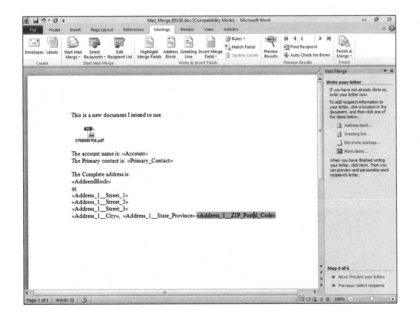

FIGURE 14.26
A Word document with merge fields.

▼

Try It Yourself

Using the Reconnect with Contacts - Gift Certificate Template

As a final example, you'll run through using one of the standard templates for a specific contact. Follow these steps:

1. Choose Sales.

2. Choose Contact.

3. Highlight a specific contact.

4. Click the Add Ins tab on the top of the ribbon.

5. Click the Mail Merge icon on the ribbon to start the mail merge.

6. Choose Organizational Mail Merge Template.

7. Choose the last template in the list: Reconnect with Contacts - Gift Certificate.

8. Choose Selected Records on Current Page (see Figure 14.27).

FIGURE 14.27
Merging into an existing template.

9. Click OK. The recipients are displayed, as shown in Figure 14.28.

10. In the Mail Merge Recipients dialog, click OK.

11. In the Mailings tab of the ribbon, choose Finish & Merge (see Figure 14.29).

▼

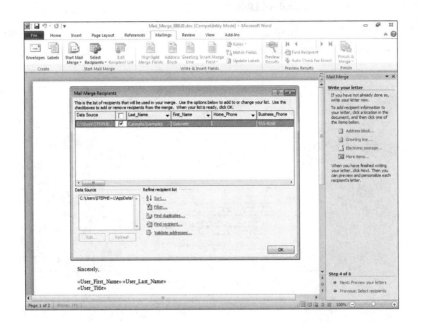

FIGURE 14.28
Merging into a
letter.

FIGURE 14.29
Merging.

12. Choose Edit the Individual Document.

13. Click OK. The document appears on the screen, as shown in Figure 14.30, and you can print, edit, or change it.

FIGURE 14.30
The end result of the mail merge.

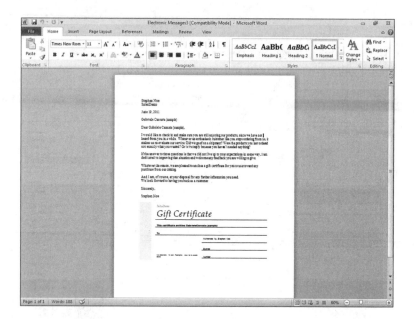

Workshop

A bridge builder's architectural firm spends a great deal of time looking at potential sites for new bridges. When it looks at a site, the employees gather a lot of unique data about soil types, distance, risk factors, and more. They enter all this data for an account that represents that particular site. The firm then uses Microsoft Dynamics CRM to put together all the site details into a Word document that can be shared with all the interested parties. It also uses Microsoft Dynamics CRM to prepare complex proposals if the firm decides that a project makes sense.

Given that the bridge builder's architectural firm is using Microsoft Dynamics CRM, it has also added to the system all the products it uses and the contractors it depends on. The employees add notes and data for the contractors to capture what each contracting firm specializes in, and they use the product catalog when they are preparing proposals and quotes.

Each generated proposal is unique, but every proposal is based on 1 of 15 different proposal templates and the existing quote data in the system. The bridge builder's architectural firm uses the data within the system and a Word mail merge with the appropriate organizational proposal template to complete any proposal needs.

Q&A

Q. *My company has strict rules about Word macros. Can we use the mail merge feature without enabling macros?*

A. No. The Microsoft Word macros need to be enabled for mail merge to work; however, the Microsoft Dynamics CRM macro is a signed macro.

Q. *Does Microsoft Word 2010 make much of a difference? We are currently on Microsoft Word 2007.*

A. Microsoft Word 2007 is the first version of Word to support the standard XML format. This format offers more flexibility and options with mail merging. Microsoft Word 2010 takes this one step further and offers you even more capabilities.

Quiz

1. Is there a way to see all mail merge templates in a system?

2. Is there a default template for creating a letter?

3. Can I use my own Microsoft Word XML file as a Microsoft Dynamics CRM mail merge template?

4. In the scenario described previously, what does the bridge builder's architectural firm need to do to set up its proposal templates?

Answers

1. Yes. You can select Settings, Templates, Mail Merge Templates and then choose the All Active Templates view.

2. Yes. There are a couple different default letter templates.

3. Yes. You can associate any Microsoft Word XML document with Microsoft Dynamics CRM.

4. The firm needs to save its existing proposal templates into XML format and then associate them to Microsoft Dynamics CRM.

Exercise

On your own system, set up a number of new mail merge templates. For instance, you can create a template for each of the major building blocks within the system, such as accounts, leads, contacts, opportunities, and quotes.

After you have created some templates, use one or two of them to see how they work. Be patient but be ready to be dazzled.

HOUR 15

Outlook Integration

What You'll Learn in This Hour:

▶ Microsoft Dynamics CRM for Outlook options
▶ The synchronizing architecture
▶ Synchronizing data
▶ Mobility
▶ What to watch out for: troubleshooting Microsoft Outlook

Microsoft Dynamics CRM integrates with Microsoft Outlook in a number of different places. There are numerous choices when it comes to Outlook integration. In previous hours, we touched on a few of them. This hour examines the options that relate to data in Outlook, Microsoft Dynamics CRM 2011 data, and data on your mobile device synchronizing with Outlook.

Microsoft Dynamics CRM for Outlook Options

Microsoft Dynamics CRM has many configuration settings, but only one set applies uniquely to each user. To get to these unique settings, you select File, Options to open the Set Personal Options window. Figure 15.1 shows the General tab in this window.

FIGURE 15.1
Personal
options.

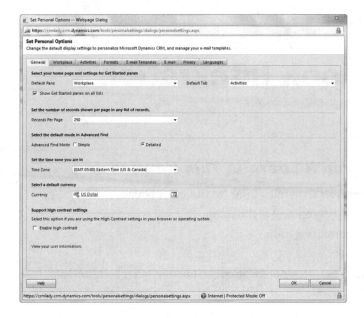

The Synchronizing Architecture

In the world of Microsoft Dynamics CRM, you have a number of choices when it comes to where data is stored and what is shared between various potential repositories, including Microsoft Exchange, Microsoft Outlook, the centralized corporate Microsoft Dynamics CRM databases, and the local offline Microsoft Dynamics CRM Outlook client. Figure 15.2 shows a diagram that indicates where data could *possibly* be located as it relates to the Microsoft Dynamics CRM Outlook client.

Notice the word *possibly*. There are significant configuration choices with regard to this subject, as discussed in Hour 4, "Infrastructure Choices."

All data is stored in the central Microsoft Dynamics CRM database on the server, with some exceptions. Sometimes, users want access to their CRM data when they are not connected to the Internet such as when they are on a plane. Therefore, a subset of the master data needs to occasionally be available offline. In addition, in some companies, users have control over which of their Outlook data is stored in the centralized database, so some data from Outlook is in both Outlook and Microsoft Dynamics CRM. There are advantages and disadvantages to each choice.

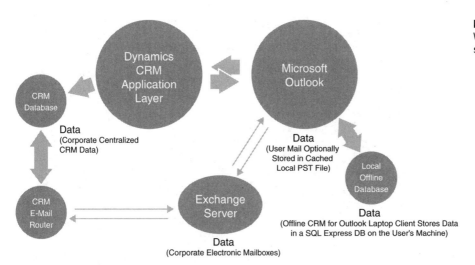

FIGURE 15.2
Where data is stored.

Synchronizing Data

When there is data in Outlook (such as Outlook tasks, Outlook appointments, and Outlook contacts) that is also in Microsoft Dynamics CRM, you may want to have this data related from one application to another, but you might not want to synchronize all the different pieces of data. To make the synchronization choices, you open Outlook and select File, Options, CRM (see Figure 15.3). Then, on the Organization Information screen, you click Synchronize. The Synchronization tab appears, as shown in Figure 15.4.

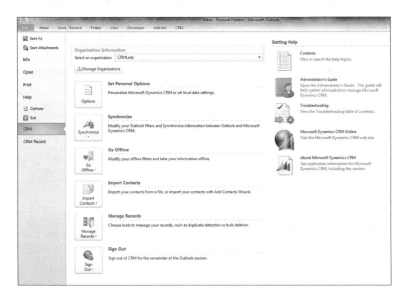

FIGURE 15.3
Selecting File, Options, CRM in Outlook.

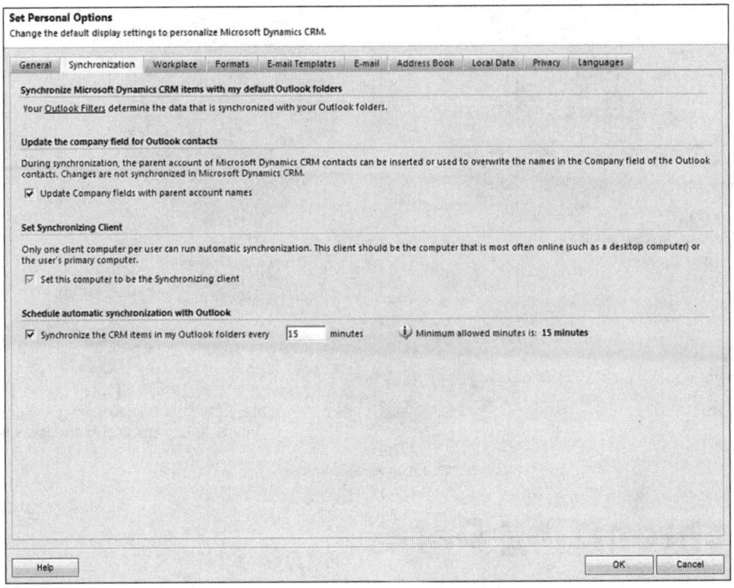

FIGURE 15.4
The
Synchronization
tab.

FIGURE 15.4
The
Synchronization
tab.

Tasks

You can map and synchronize Microsoft Outlook tasks to Microsoft Dynamics CRM
Task activities. If these two items are mapped, actions against one impact the other.
This synchronization is so seamless that when you complete a task in Microsoft
Outlook (by checking the Complete box), the activity in Microsoft Dynamics CRM is
completed. In addition, if you add an activity of type Task in Microsoft Dynamics
CRM, the task will appear on the Microsoft Outlook task list. If you follow the steps
to close an activity of type Task in Microsoft Dynamics CRM, the task will be com-
pleted in Microsoft Outlook. Figures 15.5 and 15.6 show the tasks as viewed from
Microsoft Outlook and Microsoft Dynamics CRM.

To complete a task in Outlook, do the following:

1. Select Tasks.

2. Choose the task you want to complete.

3. Click the check box to the left of the task.

To complete an activity in Microsoft Dynamics CRM, follow these steps:

1. From the main menu choose, My Work, select Activities.

2. Open a specific activity by double-clicking it.

3. Select Actions, Close.

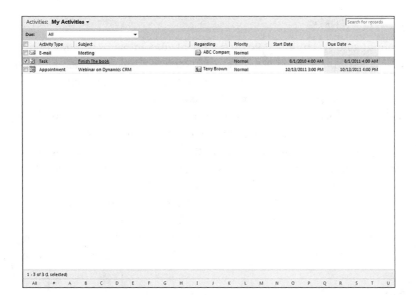

FIGURE 15.5
My Tasks selected for synchronizing.

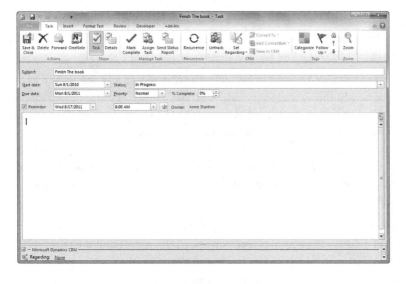

FIGURE 15.6
Microsoft Dynamics CRM activities of type Task.

4. Choose Status and accept the default, Completed.

5. Close the window.

By the Way

Synchronizing Task Activities

Only Task activities and, optionally, Phone Call activities from Microsoft Dynamics CRM synchronize with Task activities in Microsoft Outlook. Appointments and other types of activities do not synchronize to tasks because they are related to other areas of Outlook.

Appointments

You can map and synchronize Microsoft Outlook appointments with Microsoft Dynamics CRM Appointment activities. If appointment synchronization is turned on for the user's personal options, and then when they create an appointment in Microsoft Outlook, an Appointment activity is created in Microsoft Dynamics CRM. In addition, the Appointment activity is associated with the same person on whose Outlook calendar it originated. Thus, five different Microsoft Dynamics CRM users who are creating different appointments in their Outlook environment for possibly the same account have one place, Microsoft Dynamics CRM, to go to see all appointments associated with a specific account (but only if the contact on the account was invited to the appointment). Appointments are a special situation because they can be synchronized only if they relate to an appointment between two people. Recurring appointments from Outlook are also supported. Recurring appointments are a special type of activity, but they also show on the CRM calendar if they are tracked.

E-mail

E-mail is the reason Microsoft Outlook exists. Capturing e-mail from Outlook to Microsoft Dynamics CRM is so important that it is difficult to explain exactly what a turning point this can be for some companies.

The communications between teams and clients or teams and prospects contain a wealth of insight into a company's relationships. This information also represents private conversations between two people. Needless to say, making these private communications more public may present conflicts. Microsoft Dynamics CRM offers a couple different choices for tracking e-mail. From an Outlook perspective, you can synchronize all e-mails or you can choose which e-mails you are composing or that you have received that you want to manually push from Microsoft Outlook to Microsoft Dynamics CRM.

When you synchronize e-mail, the e-mail shows up in Microsoft Dynamics CRM as an E-mail activity. The e-mail is associated with the sender and the receiver in the database. If either of these people is not a contact with the same e-mail address in Microsoft Dynamics CRM, the e-mail address will appear red in CRM to indicate that it needs resolution. Figure 15.7 shows an e-mail address in red.

You can resolve a red e-mail address by doing the following:

1. Double-click the e-mail address highlighted in red. The Resolve Address window appears (see Figure 15.8).

2. Resolve the e-mail address by associating it with an existing contact or by creating a new contact and associating it with that.

FIGURE 15.7
A Microsoft
Dynamics CRM
unassociated
e-mail address.

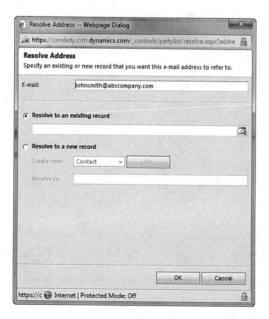

FIGURE 15.8
Resolving
e-mail: Clicking
the e-mail
address.

> **Deleting Outlook Business Rules**
>
> You can delete e-mail messages in Outlook, and they will not be deleted automatically in Microsoft Dynamics CRM. Therefore, you can file and store e-mail associated with accounts and contacts and still keep your Outlook inbox small, clean, and neat.

Contacts

Contacts can be a tough subject because many people actually use the Microsoft Outlook contacts in their current daily business processes, and they must therefore change their habits and business process to take into consideration the new options with Microsoft Dynamics CRM. Take Microsoft Dynamics CRM out of the picture and just think about Microsoft Outlook and contacts; Microsoft Outlook has a contact system that is represented in two different ways. We start from this baseline before looking at how the Microsoft Dynamics CRM Outlook client changes the picture with more choices.

Figure 15.9 shows the Microsoft Outlook Contact template. Notice that you have some core basic information, including name, job title, addresses, e-mail addresses, and notes.

FIGURE 15.9
Microsoft
Outlook Contact
template.

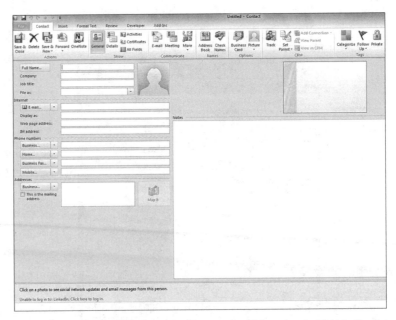

Figure 15.10 shows the Microsoft Outlook contacts address book. This is the list of contacts you access when you select and click the To field in a new e-mail message.

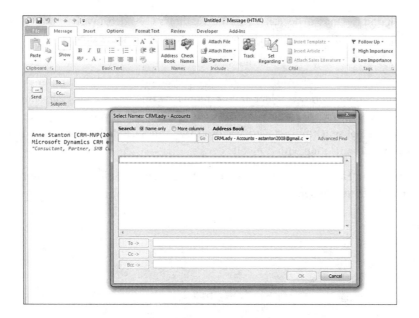

FIGURE 15.10
Microsoft
Outlook
address book.

In Microsoft Outlook, you have some duplication. If you synchronize your Outlook contacts with your mobile device, you have two places where your contact names reside within Outlook and on your mobile device. If you then introduce CRM, you add a third place within the CRM database on the network. Wow! And yet it works. What happens when we introduce the Microsoft Dynamics CRM Outlook client? Microsoft Dynamics CRM offers three additional choices:

▶ Direct access to the Microsoft Dynamics CRM central database of contacts via a Contacts folder right from within Outlook

▶ A new Microsoft Dynamics CRM Outlook address book that complements the Microsoft Outlook address book and is available when you double-click the To field when sending a new e-mail message

▶ Synchronization and mapping between the Microsoft Outlook contacts and the Microsoft Dynamics CRM contacts (You can synchronize either all contacts in your main Outlook Contacts folder or an individual selection of a specific contact.)

Figure 15.11 shows how contacts can move from Microsoft Dynamics CRM to Outlook and then to a mobile device and back again. In this example, the connection from Microsoft Outlook to the mobile device is specifically between Microsoft

Outlook and the mobile device. Microsoft Dynamics CRM gets involved only because it is talking to Outlook. In the next section, we talk more about other mobile options.

A key concept is that Microsoft Dynamics CRM synchronizes with the main Microsoft Outlook Contacts folder. If you create a second folder called Personal, you can move your personal contacts to this second folder. When you do so, personal contacts are not synchronized with Microsoft Dynamics CRM. But this might also prevent synchronization with a mobile device.

Notice how, in Figure 15.12, there are three Outlook contact folders in addition to the main Contacts folder.

FIGURE 15.11
Contacts synchronized.

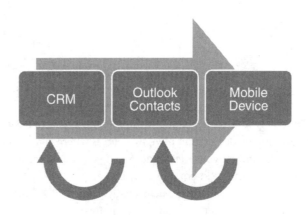

FIGURE 15.12
Contact folders in Outlook.

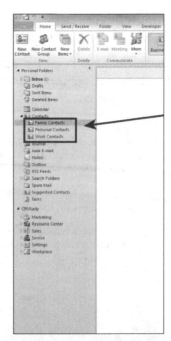

Another option is that many companies that use Microsoft Dynamics CRM do not use Microsoft Outlook contacts. They get a piece of software for their mobile device, or they use the default mobile client within Dynamics CRM, and they just stop using the Microsoft Outlook Contacts feature altogether.

Mobility

Microsoft Dynamics CRM lends itself to mobility, and as mentioned in earlier lessons, it includes a mobile option. One concept with mobile and the mobility options for Microsoft Dynamics CRM is that if you can get to the web, you can access your Microsoft Dynamics CRM data in a form that fits on a phone. This type of option totally eliminates the complexity of moving or copying or synchronizing data between three places (the server, the laptop, and the phone). Data is stored on the secure corporate network, and access to that data is either via the Microsoft Dynamics CRM Outlook client, the Microsoft Dynamics CRM web interface via Internet Explorer, or a mobile client running on any number of different mobile devices.

The second concept in the world of mobility is to have a subset of the data copied to the mobile device and then resynchronized at regular intervals. This allows access to this data even when the Internet is unavailable, such as when you are on an airplane or underground. A number of third-party companies offer this complex offline capability, particularly with enterprise security. An example is www.cwrmobility.com.

Keep in mind that Microsoft Dynamics CRM uses an authentication model that might not be compatible with the operating system or the browser that you use on your phone. In such cases, software specifically designed for Microsoft Dynamics CRM is usually required.

What to Watch Out For: Troubleshooting Microsoft Outlook

Given the complexity of moving data (such as contacts) around between multiple places and the handling of this data by many different applications, such as Microsoft Outlook and mobile synchronization, there are a few key things to watch out for.

Consider that Microsoft Outlook can be modified by many different applications and plug-ins, such as toolbars and other products, and you see that there are a number of variables. If you experience any difficulty with the Microsoft Dynamics

CRM Outlook client, you might look at what else is installed as an add-in to Outlook.

Microsoft has upgraded and developed a number of tools to complement the Microsoft Dynamics CRM Outlook client software and help reduce and check for potential issues in a variety of environments. The tools are part of the installation of the Microsoft Dynamics CRM Outlook client, and they have options and preferences for troubleshooting.

Some of the areas that the Microsoft Outlook CRM tool helps to diagnose are address book synchronization and Outlook synchronization.

If you are using Outlook to send all CRM e-mail, then you want to check the following:

- Send e-mail
- Track e-mail
- Automatic e-mail tagging
- Offline data updates (for laptops/offline clients)

You can also delete temporary Microsoft Dynamics CRM client files and create an output file for Microsoft.

The Conversion Feature

Microsoft Dynamics CRM offers a conversion feature that allows users to convert an e-mail to an opportunity, a lead, or a case. This greatly reduces the setup time required by a person who wants to quickly take a new incoming e-mail message and track a potential sale or service call. You also have the ability to connect an e-mail message to a connection. Take, for instance, an incoming e-mail message from a specific prospect contact. Tracking this e-mail message ties it to the prospect contact, but you can also connect it to a different relationship such as a vendor or third-party partner.

On troubleshooting the Microsoft Dynamics CRM Outlook client, The Power Objects team has a great blog post. It has expanded some of Microsoft's tips and added its own insight with supporting pictures (http://blog.powerobjects.com/2009/06/02/outlook-crm-client-troubleshooting-a-guide-for-the-rest-of-us/).

You might also find an eight-step guide to getting started with the Microsoft Dynamics CRM Outlook client interesting reading. To access this guide, go to the Microsoft Dynamics CRM Resource Center at http://rc.crm.dynamics.com/rc/regcont/en_us/live/articles/10stepstoOC.aspx.

Workshop

Jack Green is the CEO of an engineering company. His firm does a wide variety of sketches, drawings, inspections, and other architectural work for businesses all around his area. One of Jack's goals is to actively network at a variety of association meetings. He runs into numerous people he knows well, but occasionally he finds himself talking with someone he can't quite remember. Jack wants to be able to excuse himself and check his database of contacts and notes. To do this, Jack uses the mobile client for Microsoft Dynamics CRM. He can quickly search his contacts, and he has also set up a view to sort by a few key characteristics.

Jack also uses a combination of Microsoft Dynamics CRM and Microsoft SharePoint to organize and store the architectural drawings that are produced and their associations to certain accounts. With enterprise search, he can quickly find any document needed without having to define account-specific folders.

Q&A

Q. *I want to delete a bunch of contacts out of my Outlook folder. What happens in Microsoft Dynamics CRM when I do this to synchronized contacts?*

A. Contacts deleted in Outlook are not deleted in Microsoft Dynamics CRM. This also applies to e-mail messages.

Q. *I have a limit on the total number of e-mail messages that I can keep in Outlook. Can I delete items from Outlook without deleting them from Microsoft Dynamics CRM?*

A. Yes. Any e-mail message that is synchronized with Microsoft Dynamics CRM can be deleted from Microsoft Outlook without impacting Microsoft Dynamics CRM.

Q. *I receive a number of attachments. What happens to my e-mail attachments when I synchronize with Microsoft Dynamics CRM?*

A. Attachments can be stored with e-mail messages in Microsoft Dynamics CRM; however, they can accumulate and eat a lot of database space. Given this, larger Microsoft Dynamics CRM installations often have an alternative option for the storage of associated attachments, such as integration with SharePoint, which is a document library.

Quiz

1. In the scenario described previously, what else can Jack use from his Microsoft Dynamics CRM system to help him remember details about different people he meets?

2. Mary wants to keep her personal contacts out of Microsoft Dynamics CRM, and yet she needs some of these key details at work. How can Mary keep her personal contacts separate if all contacts are synchronized?

3. Do you have to use the Microsoft Dynamics CRM Outlook client to access Microsoft Dynamics CRM?

4. Will Microsoft Dynamics CRM Phone Call activities synchronize with Microsoft Outlook Task activities?

5. Where do Outlook appointments synchronize?

Answers

1. Jack can use the account feature of Microsoft Dynamics CRM to associate accounts with his contacts. He can then search by account or contacts.

2. Mary can create a new Outlook contacts file called Personal. This personal file does not have to synchronize with Microsoft Dynamics CRM.

3. No. You do not need to use the Microsoft Dynamics CRM Outlook client.

4. Yes. Phone calls will synchronize with tasks if you choose to synchronize phone calls.

5. Outlook appointments synchronize with Microsoft Dynamics CRM Appointment activities. They do not show up in the Outlook task list.

Exercise

Create a new Outlook folder of type Contacts. Move a couple of your contacts to this folder. What happens to these contacts? Can you associate these contacts with Microsoft Dynamics CRM? Try synchronizing a few e-mail messages. What happens to e-mail messages that have multiple recipients? Are these messages available on each and every contact?

Workflows: Creating Simple Workflows

What You'll Learn in This Hour:

▶ What is a workflow?

▶ Internal alerts based on specific criteria

▶ Using a workflow to automate a process

This hour takes a closer look at the world of workflows and how workflows help you automate simple processes. We touched on workflows in earlier hours—specifically, on how they relate to the sales process. However, workflows can be used for much more. This hour is a primer that will help get you started working with Microsoft Dynamics CRM's automatic workflow creation features. One of the goals of this lesson is to get you started with workflows without overwhelming you, so we approach the topic from a simple step-by-step. You want to increase your understanding of workflows slowly so that you can first master an understanding of a single workflow and then multiple and perhaps parallel workflow processes that can be kicked off.

What Is a Workflow?

A workflow is an automated process. A process that is automated is often associated with conditional statements, such as business rules that have multiple choices. Depending on the choice, an action can occur. (For instance, if an e-mail is received, a task activity called follow up is automatically created.)

So, if a condition within a business rule is true and an action can occur, a workflow can empower the system to automatically do this action, such as create or close tasks, appointments, e-mails, or other activities. A workflow can also call a small program, based on a set of conditions. Additionally a workflow can be designed to be extremely simple or more complex, such as the simple step of identifying when an Account record is created or the more complex series of steps of when a set of interrelated tasks are completed.

You can have a personal workflow that streamlines your own tasks, or there may be workflows that everyone in your organization uses to ensure that business processes are consistent.

A workflow can be about back-office processes or directly related and responsive to actions that a user might perform.

When setting up a specific workflow, it can also apply to either the needs of a developer extending Dynamics CRM or to a CRM administrator automating a process, two very different audiences.

By the Way

> **A Workflow Is Asynchronous**
>
> A workflow contains asynchronous processes, which means that a request is created, and then, depending on what is pending and happening at the same time, the request is processed when resources are available. Programmers and CRM administrators need to make sure a workflow is the right tool for a particular situation.

The following are a few examples of workflows:

- ▶ When an opportunity is closed, send the sales manager an alert that indicates whether the opportunity was won or lost.

- ▶ When a new lead is entered, assign that lead to the appropriate territory manager.

- ▶ If a value is added to a specific field that is incorrect, send an e-mail to the user (or to the user's manager) to correct the value.

- ▶ If a client exceeds his credit limit, set that client's account to "on hold."

- ▶ If an estimated close date has passed, send an alert to update or close the opportunity.

- ▶ If an appointment is scheduled with one of the company's top 100 C-level executives, send an e-mail to the account manager and to the regional manager.

- ▶ If the system generates an error and posts to a log file, send an alert to the CRM administrator.

Key benefits of workflows include the following:

- ▶ Increasing efficiency

- ▶ Standardizing processes

- ▶ Training new users on existing process

- ▶ Controlling well-established routines

- ▶ Improving existing process

- ▶ Providing an audit trail

- ▶ Streamlining steps

- ▶ Doing parallel processing to increase data throughput

- ▶ Increasing user adoption

- ▶ Improving internal communication and collaboration

Key areas to watch out for when working with workflows:

- ▶ Automating can generate unwanted or misunderstood transactions.

- ▶ Workflows with wait states can wait forever without the right logic.

- ▶ Automation does not guarantee compliance.

The best way to learn about workflows in Microsoft Dynamics CRM is to set up a few. You'll do this next.

Shared Workflow Technology

Microsoft Dynamics CRM uses the same Microsoft Windows Workflow Foundation as Microsoft SharePoint Services. This consistent technology continues to support the long-term goal of a totally integrated experience between Microsoft Office SharePoint Services (MOSS), Windows SharePoint Services (WSS), Microsoft Dynamics CRM, and Microsoft Office.

In the following pages, you will create a few simple workflows. You'll then move to creating a slightly more complex workflow.

As shown in Figure 16.1, you start the process by selecting Settings, Processes, New and choosing Workflow as the category.

FIGURE 16.1
Creating a new
workflow.

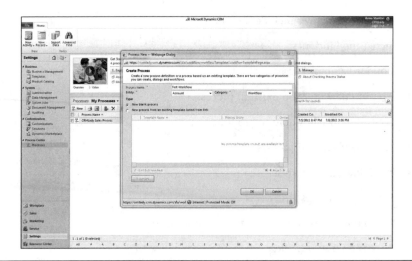

Access to Settings

Configuring a workflow is considered an administrative task, although workflows
are designed to allow either automatic or manual user processing.

If you do not have access to setting up workflows, talk with your Microsoft
Dynamics CRM administrator about getting your security role changed.

Figure 16.2 shows the screen you use to set up a new workflow. In this case, you are
going to set up a workflow that sends an e-mail alert when an appointment activity
is created.

FIGURE 16.2
Creating the
steps in a
workflow.

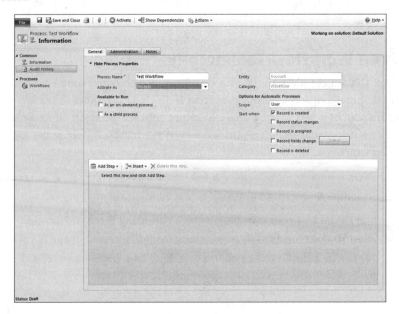

To create this new workflow, you need to choose a name and pick the correct entity:

1. Enter Appointment Alert Workflow.

2. Choose Entity Appointment.

Note that you are creating this workflow from scratch as opposed to using a predefined template. You can set up templates later in the process, after you are using many different, yet perhaps similar, workflows.

Figure 16.3 shows the next screen you use to create a workflow. At this point, you can indicate whether this is a workflow or a workflow template, and you need to choose the scope. In this example, you are going to create a personal workflow, so the scope is User. This scope limits the workflow access. The other choices include setting the access to this workflow to Business Unit, Child Business Unit, or Organization.

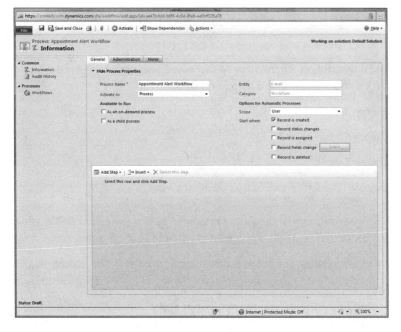

FIGURE 16.3
Defining workflow properties.

You are going to create an alert when an appointment is created and, therefore, you can leave the default Start When setting (that is, Record Is Created). The next step is to add the condition and the step:

1. Choose Add Step.

2. Choose Check Condition. (Figure 16.4 shows the condition statement.)

FIGURE 16.4
Adding a
condition to
a workflow.

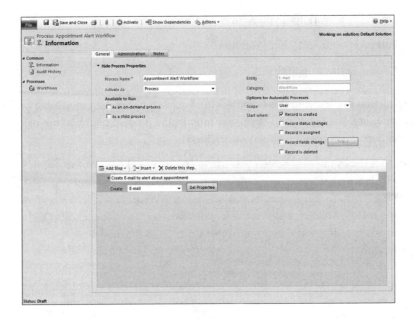

3. Add a description for the step. At this point, you have added a description, but you have not added a step or an action.

4. Choose Add Step.

5. Choose Create Record.

6. Choose E-mail.

7. Select Set Properties to Edit and create the e-mail.

Figure 16.5 shows a copy of the e-mail template. Notice the yellow fields, which indicate dynamic values that will be populated when the e-mail is generated.

Now save your workflow. For the workflow to work, it must not be in draft mode, so you need to publish it. To do so, choose Publish at the top of the Workflow, Settings form.

The new workflow will now automatically run every time an appointment activity is created in the system.

To test the workflow you've just created, make a new activity of type Appointment and assign it to yourself. In a minute or two, you will get an e-mail message, alerting you to the fact that a new appointment was created.

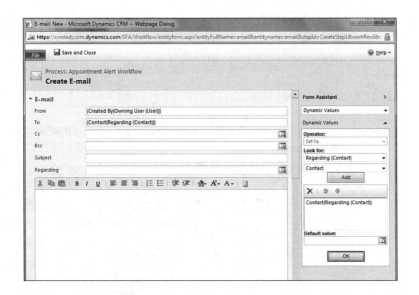

FIGURE 16.5
Creating a step
to create an
e-mail message.

Internal Alerts Based on Specific Criteria

You've already created a simple workflow to send an e-mail message when an appointment activity is created, but perhaps there is something more critical that you want to make sure does not slip between the cracks. What if a company does not want to go after any sales opportunities of less than $100,000 because it thinks that these opportunities are not worth the expense it takes to close them? Now, let's expand the scope of this example and say that the sales force for this company is all over the world. It is hard to resist the temptation to go after a hot deal. Perhaps an opportunity has estimated revenue of $90,000, and all the salesperson has to do is make a few phone calls to close it. Do you think that salesperson is going to follow the company policy and walk away?

To automatically alert management that such opportunities have been created, you can use a Microsoft Dynamics CRM workflow to alert a few key people when a new opportunity is added that is less than $100,000. Here's how you set up this new workflow:

1. Select Settings.

2. Select Workflow.

3. Select New.

4. Give the workflow a new name, such as Opportunity Less Than 100,000 Alert.

5. Select the Opportunity entity.

6. Click OK.

7. Select Add a Step.

8. Select Check Condition.

Figure 16.6 shows where you are so far. You have created a new workflow of type Opportunity with the desired description.

FIGURE 16.6
New workflow:
Opportunity
less than
100,000 alert.

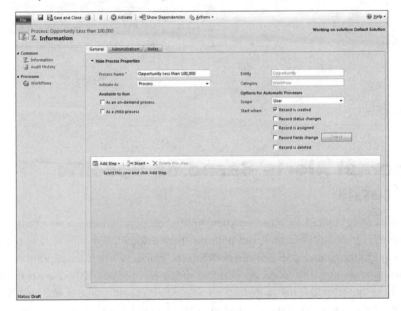

Now, you are going to set the variables associated with the condition. You should double-click the blue words that look like this: <condition>. Click to define.

Figure 16.7 shows the first screen for setting the condition. Notice that it looks almost exactly like the Advanced Find screen you have seen in other lessons.

In this particular case, you are inserting a condition which says that the opportunity estimated revenue is less than or equal to $100,000, and if this condition is true, the system will send an e-mail to the big boss. Figure 16.8 shows an example of an e-mail message that could be sent in this situation. Notice that you can use colors (for example, the word *alert* in red). You can also insert dynamic data fields, as shown in Figure 16.8 in yellow. These fields would be populated from the data in the created opportunity record.

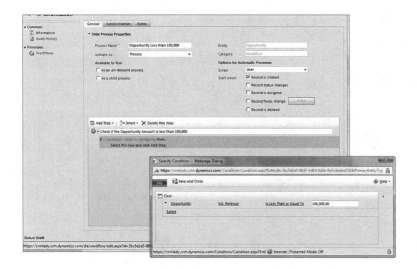

FIGURE 16.7
Inserting a business rule or condition.

FIGURE 16.8
A sample alert e-mail.

Figure 16.9 shows the completed workflow. If your condition is false, you are not going to do anything, so you do not need to enter a condition and action if your original rule is false.

You do, however, have to publish the workflow for it to start working on the next saved opportunity.

FIGURE 16.9
The finished
alert.

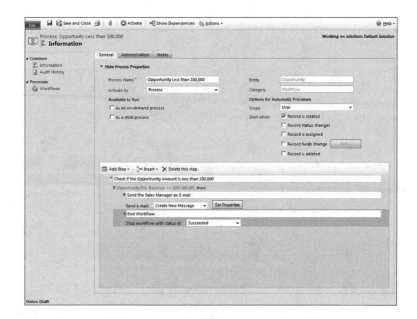

Warning

Published workflows should be stopped and unpublished before applying updates to any environment. If they are not stopped, a partially running workflow could be poorly interrupted.

Running `OnCreate`

Your new workflow is set to run `OnCreate`, and therefore this workflow will not run retroactively on already saved opportunities.

Setting a Workflow to Run

You do not have to choose On Demand or Child Workflow for the workflow to run automatically upon creation of a new opportunity.

Using a Workflow to Automate a Process

To this point, you have worked with some fairly simple workflow rules that either have no condition or only one condition or, if that condition is true, they do only one thing. What about a more complex workflow, designed to automate a complete process? We tackled the sales process in earlier hours, but workflow automation is not limited to sales. What if you have a process that requires three people doing things at different times? Take, for instance, a simplified version of the process involved in completing a book chapter for a publisher. Each chapter has to be written, reviewed, edited for format and content, and reviewed by the author. Table 16.1 shows this flow of information.

TABLE 16.1 Book Chapter Process

1.	Author: Write chapter.
2.	Publisher: Distribute to reviewer.
3.	Reviewer: Review chapter.
4.	Publisher: Receive reviewed chapter back from reviewer.
5.	Publisher: Send to author to confirm changes.
6.	Author: Confirm reviewer changes.
7.	Author: Send chapter to publisher.
8.	Publisher: Receive finalized chapter.
9.	Publisher: Publish.

You can create a workflow that tracks these steps and, after a step is completed, the workflow can create the next action for the appropriate person. Here's how you create the workflow:

1. Choose Settings.

2. Choose Workflow.

3. Choose New.

4. Enter a name, such as Book Chapter Process.

5. Choose Task. (You are going to track a series of tasks, so your base entity is Task.)

6. Under Options for Automatic Workflow, make this an organization workflow so that the workflow will kick off anytime someone creates a task that meets the specified conditions. Figure 16.10 shows the new workflow before you've added any steps.

7. Set this to an On Demand (manual) workflow so that the user can start the write chapter process when he or she kicks off the process. The other choice would be to set a condition that checks whether a new task was created with either a specific subject line or a specific category or any other business-type rule that can be communicated through the data that the user would be entering.

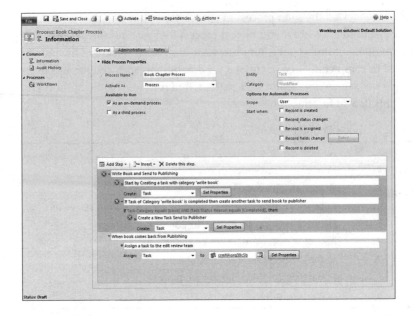

8. Set Available to Run to On Demand.

9. Add a step.

10. Create a record. Make this a Task record.

11. Set the task to Write Chapter. The workflow should create the Task activity to write the chapter. You should give the writer three days to complete this task. He or she can adjust as necessary, but you can use the system to set the due date as three days after the creation date.

Figure 16.11 shows the configured task record. Notice the items in yellow.

To create a due date of three days after the creation date, you can use the Form Assistant to the right of your form:

1. Place your cursor in the Due Date field.

2. In the Form Assistant, choose Operator 3 Days.

3. Choose After.

4. Set Look For to Task and Created By.

5. Click Add.

6. Click OK.

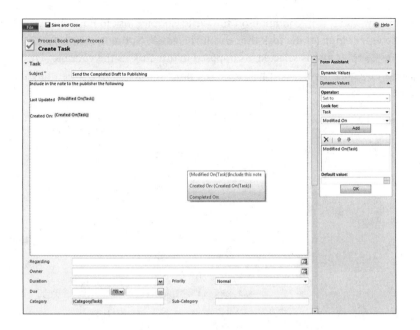

FIGURE 16.11
A configured task.

Figure 16.12 shows an example of the Form Assistant and your choices. The default value can also be set, but it is necessary only if there is a condition in which the data you selected would not be available.

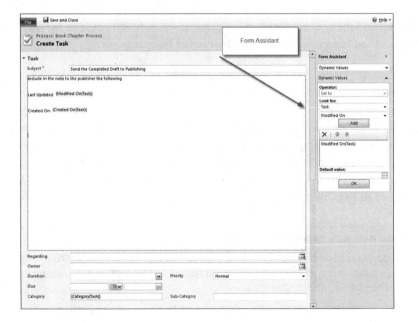

FIGURE 16.12
Adding a dynamic data field.

You can now add a wait condition on the Write Chapter task to have the system wait until the user completes the task that was just created. Notice in Figure 16.13 that the Write Chapter task is selected, as opposed to just Task as the variable. This is important because if you select just Task, the process will continue when anyone completes a task.

FIGURE 16.13
New Wait Stage condition in Workflow.

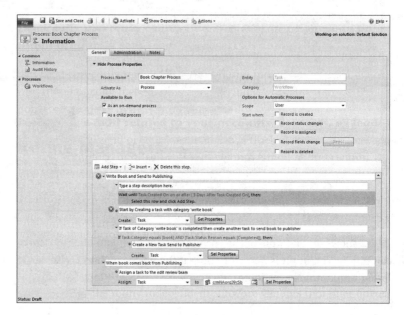

After you add the wait condition, you must add what the system is to do when the wait condition is met, which can be either of the following:

▶ Add a step.

▶ Add a stage.

The system will give you a warning to indicate that this particular workflow is more complex and that, if you add a stage in the middle, you must start the process with a stage. You can add the stage Chapter Completed and rename the automatically inserted stage to Write Chapter. Figure 16.14 shows where you are so far: You have added two stages, one task, and one wait condition.

Did you Know?

Who to Assign a Task To?

If you don't know who to assign a task to, you can use the Microsoft Dynamics CRM Queue feature and assign tasks to a queue. In this example, however, you know who is going to do what.

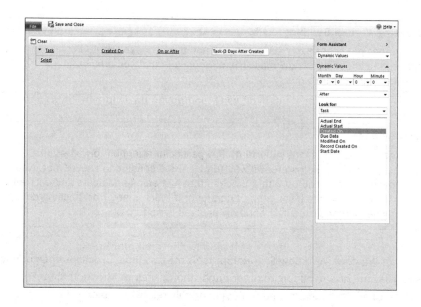

FIGURE 16.14
Wait condition.

Now you need to add the step to edit the chapter:

1. Select Add Step.

2. Select Create Record.

3. Give this step a name, such as Edit Chapter.

4. Select Create Task.

5. Select Set Properties.

When setting properties, you can assign a record to a specific publisher who will be doing the editing. In this example, you have only one publisher, which makes this setup easier.

You also need to create a draft e-mail for the writer. The writer working from his or her own activity list will see the draft e-mail and can then attach the chapter and send it. Here's how you do this:

1. Select Add Step.

2. Select Create Record.

3. Select Create E-mail.

4. Select Modify E-mail Properties.

Creating Versus Sending

Notice that you choose to create a record and then choose Create E-mail as opposed to choosing Send E-mail. The difference is that you are creating a draft e-mail for the chapter writer.

Wait States

Warning Two (yes, it is that important): Pay particular attention to wait states within a workflow. A wait state will wait forever if the condition is never met. Needless to say, you can end up with a process that just spins and spins and eats all the machine resources if you are not careful or if there is an error. Tracking down a poorly defined and executed workflow process is no fun.

Microsoft Windows Workflow Foundation tools are available in Microsoft Dynamics CRM. They are also available in other applications, such as Microsoft SharePoint Services. In addition, there are resources available related to architecting proper workflow functionality. Microsoft has a section on architecting workflow, at http://msdn.microsoft.com/en-us/library/bb955348.aspx, that is worth reading and mastering, but there are also more out there.

Workshop

The Polar Bear Publishing Shop has a number of complex tasks that need to be completed in a certain order. Completion of these tasks is interdependent, requiring that one person do what he or she needs to do and then hand off to the next. The Polar Bear Publishing Shop wants to document and standardize some of these sets of tasks.

John Brown, CIO of the Polar Bear Publishing Shop, architects a set of processes. He first documents what the processes are and then lays them out in a business process diagram. After the process is validated and approved by his peers, John uses Microsoft Dynamics CRM to automate different sets. He sets up a workflow process for book binding and for editing and review. He also sets up the process around working with a particular set of vendors who supply paper and ink for his presses. John finds that the flexibility of Microsoft Dynamics CRM allows him to review and redo processes regularly.

John also uses the workflows he has designed as training tools. This reduces the classroom and e-learning requirements that would otherwise be needed for his staff.

Q&A

Q. *I want to emphasize my alert e-mails. Can I use different-colored text?*

A. Yes. You can use any number of text colors in the body of an e-mail message.

Q. *I have a process that involves many different people, and I don't always know to whom to assign a task. How can I set up this workflow?*

A. You need to use the Microsoft Dynamics CRM Queue feature, which allows you to assign an activity to the queue. For more information on queues, see Hour 17, "Support Management." You can also use the team concept.

Q. *Can I use Microsoft Dynamics CRM without using the workflow functionality? I am just not ready to automate anything yet.*

A. Yes. You can use Microsoft Dynamics CRM without workflows, and you can add workflows when you are ready.

Quiz

1. When you are changing the properties of a task within a workflow, what do the yellow fields represent?

2. Why is it important to be aware of wait states?

3. What is an example of a process that could be automated with a workflow?

4. What are three benefits of mastering and using workflows?

5. Where is a good place to learn more about workflows?

Answers

1. The yellow fields represent dynamic data fields that are populated when a task is actually created by the workflow.

2. Wait states have the potential to wait forever and so may cause a process that spins and spins and spins forever. A workflow that just stops with new requests getting added and without old requests being processed can cause significant system issues.

3. Here is but one example: If a value is added to a specific attribute that is incorrect, you could send an e-mail to the user or to the user's manager to correct the value.

4. Any three of the following:

- ▶ Increasing efficiency

- ▶ Standardizing a process

- ▶ Training new users on an existing process

- ▶ Controlling a well-established routine

- ▶ Improving an existing process

- ▶ Providing an audit trail

- ▶ Increasing user adoption

- ▶ Improving internal communication and collaboration

5. Microsoft provides more information at http://msdn.microsoft.com/en-us/library/bb955348.aspx.

Exercise

Create some of John Brown's processes on paper or with a Microsoft Dynamics CRM workflow. Take, for instance, the steps that John must go through to manage the ordering of a new supply of paper. He works with his CFO or the accounting department to first look at prices and to refresh the research regarding rates and quality. He then needs to select both the quality and the price point that works for the company. He or a team member reaches out to the vendors for more information and real-time pricing, and then the order gets placed. When the order is received, the teams have to update inventory and store the new supplies.

Support Management

What You'll Learn in This Hour:

▶ Creating and using contracts

▶ Maximizing support profitability and effectiveness

▶ Leveraging the subject line in a case

▶ Utilizing the Knowledge Base

We've covered a lot of information in the past 16 hours. However, we haven't yet talked about one particular department—the support department—that can use Microsoft Dynamics CRM for non-sales-related needs. A typical support department might need to keep track of customer service, support contracts, incoming questions, and problems and solutions surrounding incoming calls. This lesson delves into the world of support management using Microsoft Dynamics CRM.

What does a support department need? The functions within Microsoft Dynamics CRM that are key for a support department include contracts, cases, queues, the Knowledge Base, and scheduling. We cover scheduling in Hour 19, "Scheduling," so we touch on it here only briefly.

Creating and Using Contracts

A support contact consists of all the details of the agreement between your company and a client to provide support. The contract also includes management over what you sold to the client with regard to either the total number of calls, the total number of incidents (or cases), or the total number of support hours. Depending on how you offer support, the contracts feature of Microsoft Dynamics CRM can manage incoming use of services against a specific defined contract. Let's set up a contract to examine this further. Figure 17.1 shows where you need to go to get started. You get there by following these steps:

FIGURE 17.1
Contracts.

1. Select Service.

2. Select Contracts.

3. Select New. The Contract form shown in Figure 17.2 appears.

You'll populate the fields in the Contract form in the following pages.

In the following steps, you can start with a Service contract template (see Figure 17.3):

1. Select Service Contract.

2. Enter a name for the contract.

3. Choose a customer.

4. Choose a contract start date on which the contract will be effective and when it ends. Figure 17.3 shows an effective date of August 1, 2011, and an end date of July 31, 2012. This does not necessarily have to be the creation date. Contracts can be created and become effective at another time (such as the last day of the previous month).

5. Choose the contract address for both contract address and bill-to address or leave the address blank to use the customer's default address.

6. Confirm the billing information.

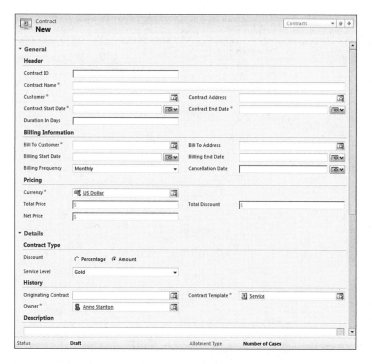

FIGURE 17.2
The Contract form.

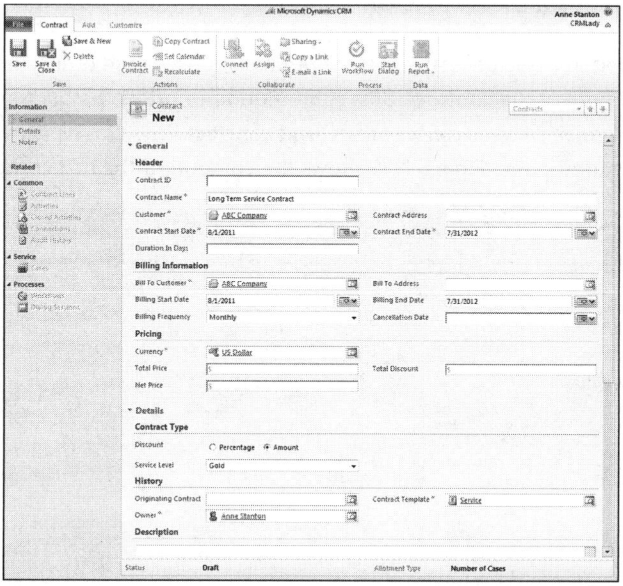

FIGURE 17.3
Creating a new contract.

7. When the basics are entered, save the contract but do not leave the screen. When you save the contract, you create the framework to associate other key Microsoft Dynamics CRM entities to the new contract (see Figure 17.4).

FIGURE 17.4
A new contract
with general
details that has
been saved.

Next, you need to associate some specific products, prices, and other specifics that
make up the bulk of the contract. This combination of prices, products, quantity,
and more are referred to as *contract lines*, and contract lines can be accessed from
the left navigation pane. Figure 17.5 shows the creation of the first contract line.

FIGURE 17.5
Creating a con-
tract line.

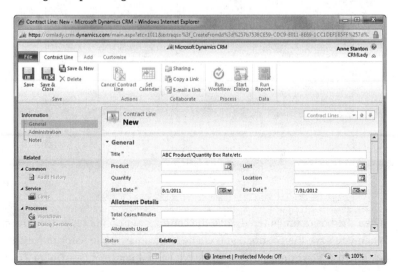

Finance Department

Many times, contracts are part of the finance or accounting department's paper-work, and finance creates them. Typically, the support department uses contracts in CRM. There is a relationship in CRM between contracts and cases that can reduce the total allocated tickets or time on a contract.

Contract Lines

Contract lines make up the body of a contract. They define what is covered under the contract terms. To create a new contract including adding contract lines, follow these steps:

1. Choose New.

2. Enter a title for the contract line. The example in Figure 17.5 is a contract line that covers a product called ABC Product, which is bundled in a box rate, and the title is ABC Product/Quantity Box Rate/etc.

3. Select the product from the Product list.

4. Enter the quantity.

5. Enter a value for Unit. Unit defines what quantity relates to. (For instance, a unit could be a box, an each, or a bundle.)

6. Enter the allotment details. The system will keep track of how many cases or minutes are used, but you need to enter what the contract covers.

7. Enter the price.

8. Choose Save and Close from the Ribbon to save the contract line.

A contract can have an unlimited number of contract lines. After you add the contract lines, you should save the contract. However, to make the contract available for case or activity association, it needs to be marked as invoiced. Contract lines can include a set of service hours, a yearly maintenance and tune-up, a number of phone calls to ask questions, and so on.

Associating Cases with a Specific Contract

You can associate cases with a specific contract. You do this when you are working on a specific case, and usually the person working the case is not the person who created the contract. The Case option in the left menu under service offers a view of all related cases.

When you associate a case with a contract, the data within the case can be used to reduce a set value in the contract. For instance, if you sell a service contract for 10 hours of service, you can have the system keep track of how many of the 10 hours have been used by the data within an associated closed case. You can also associate specific activities with either a case that is related to the contract or directly with the contract. Figure 17.6 shows the Case form. Notice the area related to contracts.

Cases can be associated with a contract or with specific lines within a contract. The example in this section associates the case with a specific contract and a specific contract line. In Hour 18, "Contracts, Cases, and Capturing Time," we look more in depth at using cases.

FIGURE 17.6
Associating a case with a contract.

Maximizing Support Profitability and Effectiveness

Let's jump away from the Microsoft Dynamics CRM software a bit and consider how we might significantly increase the profitability of support. In many situations, support and good customer service is a necessary expense, but it can also be a real profit center.

To maximize the profitability of support, you need to define what services you are offering. These could be different levels of telephone support or specific services that are performed in the office. You might also have some proprietary knowledge that is valuable. Take the time to really define and bundle these offerings. When you bundle the offerings, consider the following:

- ▶ What are you offering?
- ▶ What is the market value of these offerings?
- ▶ How should an offering be marketed?
- ▶ What terms can you use to classify and brand the offering?
- ▶ How can you differentiate the offering from the offerings of your competition (particularly if the competition is offering a similar service for free)?
- ▶ If you were to list the offering on a price list, what would you call it?
- ▶ What skills are needed to provide the service?

Each of these considerations can help you determine and sell a specific service. Customers will buy value and will pay a premium for something they need. You can also offer a certain amount of added value for free; however, if you offer something for free, make sure the clients understand that they are getting a fixed amount of something for free. Don't forget to remind them occasionally with a letter that indicates how much they have used your service/product and how glad you are that they depend on you.

Consider, for example, the following service: unlimited tier-one support to help you refine and fine-tune and occasionally solve your technical problems. Tier-one support can be a service offering that helps further define a specific problem. The tier-one team can be less experienced in a technology but more experienced with capturing the finite details that make solving the problem easier. These specific service offering details can be used as a win for your own company and a win for the client. A client's easy questions are efficiently answered, the problems are organized, and data is collected without the expense of spending hours with a tier-three support resource.

You now have two services you can sell:

- ▶ Unlimited tier-one support
- ▶ Limited and more expensive, yet more efficient, tier-three support

When your services are properly marketed and bundled, you end up with profit, and your customers end up with efficient and accurate answers to their problems from the right source.

The key concept to take away is that it is important to plan and design the services you are offering. This is especially critical in this age when information is a valuable asset. When information is shared, there is value in return. This value can be in dollars or in more information increasing the knowledge base and information asset pool.

As you work toward refining and defining your services, look at the Service Design Network (www.service-design-network.org) for guidance. The Service Design Network offers predefined offerings, bundles and templates that you can leverage within your own business.

There are other resources, too, but the key point is that marketing, branding, and selling can bring much-needed profit and client satisfaction to your service offerings. Microsoft Dynamics CRM can support your efforts to standardize your offerings and as such can almost pay for itself.

Leveraging the Subject Line in a Case

Let's go back to talking about how Microsoft Dynamics CRM can help you organize and bundle your services. You face a small requirement with an impact within Microsoft Dynamics CRM: the configuration of subjects. Subjects are used in a number of different places within Microsoft Dynamics CRM. For instance, each case can have a related subject; and sales literature, products, and articles can have subjects. The subject tree should be set up with some thought, and it should support both reporting and the general organization of a number of different areas of data. To define your subjects, follow these steps:

1. Choose Settings.

2. Choose Business Management.

3. Choose Subject. The screen shown in Figure 17.7 appears.

Subjects are categories used in a hierarchical list to correlate and organize information. Subjects can be used to organize products, sales literature, and Knowledge Base articles. Earlier in this lesson, you already defined both parent subjects and child subjects. Creating subjects offers one way to organize entities within a system.

This lesson's example has a subject called Bikes and child subjects of all the different types of bikes. Via the creation of subjects, you can organize your cases by category of bike. You can also get reporting by subject, which enables you to determine how

FIGURE 17.7
Setting up subjects.

many cases are being generated for what type of bike. You can then make business decisions based on that information, such as choosing not to carry the line of bikes that requires the most support.

Utilizing the Knowledge Base

The Knowledge Base is an area of Microsoft Dynamics CRM where you can both store your own Knowledge Base articles (KBAs) and manage the review process that creates your Knowledge Base articles. Look at Figure 17.8. One of the advantages of storing Knowledge Base articles within Dynamics CRM is that you can associate Knowledge Base articles with specific cases. If you use the Microsoft Dynamics CRM customer portal, you can also share these articles with your customers.

One of the most frequently asked questions when it comes to the Knowledge Base is whether it's possible to associate a Microsoft Word document with a Knowledge Base article. However, doing this breaks the model. The model is meant to organize data in structured, searchable templates. If you associate a Word document with it, you are not using a structured template, and you are bypassing the ability to search. If

FIGURE 17.8
Knowledge
Base article
status.

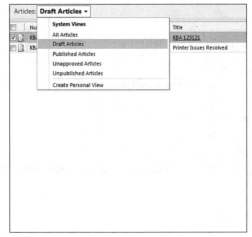

you would like a knowledge base of Microsoft Word documents, you might consider
using the integration with Microsoft SharePoint, which is built to manage unstructured data, such as Microsoft Word documents and document libraries.

Notice that you have Draft, Unapproved, and Published as options for articles.
Support personnel can write Knowledge Base articles and submit them for review.
You can also build a workflow to support the effort.

Templates help your support department capture information that is stored in standardized formats. If you create a new Knowledge Base article, you are instructed to
capture a title, a subject, key words, a summary, and more comments (see Figure 17.9).

FIGURE 17.9
Template
choices.

This standard format gathers a bunch of different information into a standard searchable library. By following a template, you can quickly create a new Knowledge Base article (see Figure 17.10).

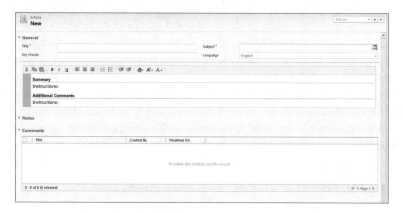

FIGURE 17.10
A new draft
Knowledge
Base article.

To submit a new article for publishing consideration, do the following:

1. Select Actions.

2. Select Submit.

Once submitted, the article is in the unapproved bucket. To publish the article, complete the following steps:

1. Select Actions.

2. Select Approved.

After the article is approved, it appears in the list of published articles and can be used as a reference throughout the company. Knowledge Base articles can be associated with cases, for instance, or shared with clients through e-mail.

Figure 17.11 shows a list of published Knowledge Base articles.

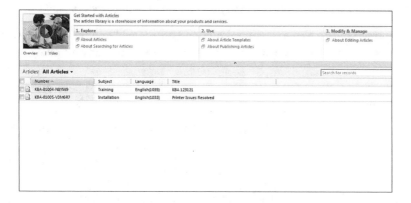

FIGURE 17.11
Published
Knowledge
Base articles.

Workshop

Technology Titans is a technology company that offers IT services. It sells service contracts based on a number of cases (incidents), and it also offers ad hoc hourly billing. Technology Titans sells products, too, and organizes its products in the Microsoft Dynamics CRM product catalog. Technology Titans is particularly keen on utilizing Microsoft Dynamics CRM to keep track of how many cases are getting used by a variety of clients. To do this, it sets up service contracts in Microsoft Dynamics CRM for each client. Each service contract is completed and then double-checked against its accounting software to confirm that it has been billed. After the contract is set up, the contract is activated. The teams are also trained that, to offer a service, they must create a service case. Each service case created is associated with the appropriate client contract.

Technology Titans also has a certain number of recurring cases. The solutions to the recurring cases are documented and saved in the Knowledge Base library in Microsoft Dynamics CRM. The company reviews these Knowledge Base articles on a scheduled basis to confirm that the information remains correct. It is also diligent about not putting everything in the Knowledge Base area. In addition, the company wants to save and store only items that recur regularly.

Q&A

Q. *We have the standard services that you might find at any technology company. How can we give these zing and the right marketing?*

A. The first step is to understand the value you are offering and your audience. You are also a consumer of technology services; what would make you feel great about spending money on these services? For example, you would probably pay a lot for a real expert in a specific technology because you could learn and potentially resell some of this expertise.

Q. *Are subjects that important? We have not set up a hierarchy of subjects.*

A. Subjects offer a way to organize cases and associated literature and Knowledge Base articles. They also potentially offer a reporting category for analytics.

Q. *We want to associate a Word document with a Knowledge Base article. Can we do so?*

A. No. By design, you cannot associate a Word document with a Knowledge Base article.

Quiz

1. Why does a contract have contract lines? What are they used for?

2. How does a case relate to a contract?

3. Can you search Knowledge Base articles?

4. Name three areas to consider when bundling support services to sell.

5. Does the Knowledge Base section of Microsoft Dynamics CRM offer standardization?

Answers

1. Contract lines define the specific services or products covered by the contract.

2. A case can be associated with a contract, and the hours or incident that the case represents can reduce the total available incidents left.

3. Yes. There is extensive search capability associated with Knowledge Base articles.

4. You could consider any of the items listed in this hour. The following three are examples: What terms can you use to classify and brand the offering? What are you offering? What skills are needed to provide the service?

5. Yes. One of the key features of Microsoft Dynamics CRM Knowledge Base is the standardization of information so that it's searchable.

Exercise

Using the earlier example about the Technology Titans, set up two different Knowledge Base articles for the company. Would "How to Configure Outlook" be a valuable addition to its library? Now, set up a contract for a new client who wants unlimited support. Should Technology Titans offer 24x7 support coverage? What would be the cost of doing this right, with the right level of skilled labor? Can this service be profitable?

Contracts, Cases, and Capturing Time

What You'll Learn in This Hour:

▶ Why use cases; what's in it for me?

▶ The hierarchy of contracts, cases, and time

▶ Working with cases and activities

▶ Proactive versus reactive capturing of time

▶ Distributing work: Users, teams, and queues

▶ Adding a workflow to close a case

This hour spends more time on cases and looks at the concept of capturing time against activities in Microsoft Dynamics CRM. It also explores methods of assigning cases for completion, using queues and teams.

Why Use Cases; What's in It for Me?

A service case record (also called an incident record) is a building block of any process geared toward issue resolution. That issue may be a service or support incident, a warranty repair, a help desk question, or a return merchandise authorization (RMA). Case records have several key features that make them work very well in this area:

1. Each case has a unique identifying number.

2. Each service case can be linked to a service contract and an associated contract line to track work delivered on service agreements.

3. Each case can roll up multiple individual activities into a single billable-time activity.

It is important to understand that case records can be modified and configured with additional fields, data relationships, and processes that meet your organization's requirements.

The Hierarchy of Contracts, Cases, and Time

Figure 18.1 shows the hierarchy of how the entities relate to each other in time related sequences. Time is captured on an activity in the duration field, and activities that are related to cases can map this duration into an actual case duration bucket. When a case is closed, time can be accumulated.

In Figure 18.1, the five-pointed star represents the capturing of time on a specific activity, and the seven-pointed star represents the potential of accumulation of actual time on a closed case.

FIGURE 18.1
Contract, cases, and time hierarchy.

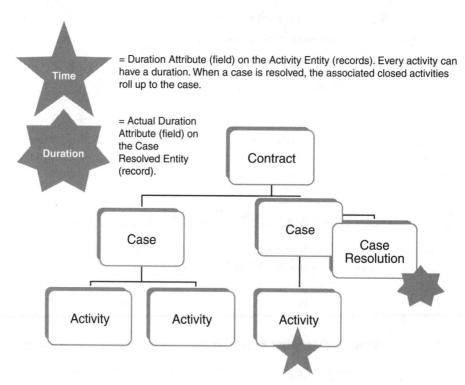

Time = Duration Attribute (field) on the Activity Entity (records). Every activity can have a duration. When a case is resolved, the associated closed activities roll up to the case.

Duration = Actual Duration Attribute (field) on the Case Resolved Entity (record).

The general concept is that every activity can capture the amount of time spent on that activity (the duration). When completed activities are associated with a case, the case will be updated with the actual accumulated duration of each activity.

You can also capture start and end dates on each activity. Then, by using the Report Wizard, a view, or an export into an Excel PivotTable, you can quickly get a list or picture of time for any given set of activities.

Using CRM to capture billable time for support cases lends itself very well to organizations where individuals are engaged with many different customers, projects, or issues on a given day. However, most professional service firms use timesheets to capture and track time and frequently have additional requirements related to auditing those time entries. If that sounds like you, then the good news is you can do that with CRM.

If you need timesheet functionality for your organization, you can customize the CRM system to meet your needs, or you can simply install a third-party customization that fits your needs. There are several solutions available in the Microsoft Dynamics Marketplace (http://dynamics.pinpoint.microsoft.com). Some, like Assistance PSA for Microsoft Dynamics CRM 2011, are general PSA tools and others, such as CRM4Legal, are targeted at specific industries.

Let's get back to really looking at capturing time within Microsoft Dynamics CRM without third-party tools. Figure 18.2 shows the time-oriented fields that are available in a Task activity.

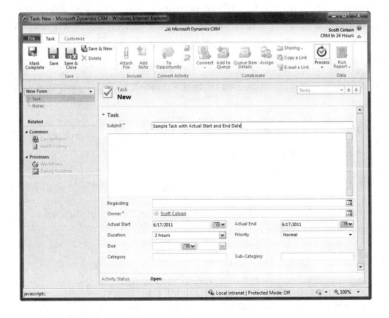

FIGURE 18.2
A task with Date and Duration fields.

Figure 18.2 shows how two hours of work completed on June 17, 2011, would be documented. The Duration field contains the amount of time spent, and the Actual End field documents the date the work was completed.

> **Fields and the Task Form**
>
> All these fields will not show up on the Task form unless you configure the form to show them. The only field that shows up automatically is the Duration field. By default, the Actual End field will be set to the date when you marked the activity as complete unless you show it on the form and actually enter a different date.

If you link a task to a case, the associated time can be reported on, viewed, or exported with relationship to the contact or account associated with the case.

Working with Cases and Activities

When working with cases and activities, it is possible for an activity record (task, phone call, and so on) to get generated before the case record, but it is also possible for a case record to be made first. Let's work through a typical scenario that demonstrates both ways of connecting an activity to a case. In this scenario, you will capture the phone call from a customer, create a case, link the phone call to the case, and then create a second task from the existing case.

There are many ways to create a new Phone Call activity record in CRM. For simplicity, you can start from the contact record because it is very easy to search for contacts based on either the first name or last name. For this exercise, you should use George Sullivan, a record created as part of the sample data load available in Microsoft Dynamics CRM 2011.

To create a Phone Call activity record from the contact record, follow these steps (see Figure 18.3):

1. Open the contact record.

2. Select the Add tab of the ribbon.

3. Click the Phone Call option in the Add tab.

Now you can use the phone call record to capture details about the call and then create a case from the phone call record (see Figure 18.4):

1. Enter the subject of the call.

2. Change the direction from Outgoing to Incoming.

3. Enter some notes for the call in the description field.

4. Update the Duration field to document the amount of time spent on the call.

FIGURE 18.3
Creating a phone call from an open contact.

FIGURE 18.4
A new Phone Call activity record.

5. Save the call by clicking the Save button.

6. Select the Convert to Case option on the Phone Call tab of the ribbon. The Convert Phone Call to Case dialog appears (see Figure 18.5).

7. Click OK.

> You can change the customer and optionally define the subject of the case from the CRM subject tree as part of this process.

FIGURE 18.5
The Convert
Phone Call to
Case dialog.

At this point, you are looking at a new case record. Now you can create a task to schedule future work to resolve the issue for the customer. You create the new task as follows (see Figure 18.6):

1. Select the Add tab of the ribbon.

2. Click the Task button in the Add tab.

Fill out the missing information in the task form to schedule the task for future completion (see Figure 18.7):

1. Enter a subject for the task.

2. Enter the due date and time.

3. Enter the expected duration.

4. Click Save & Close to save and close the task record.

FIGURE 18.6
Adding a new task to a case.

FIGURE 18.7
A new task.

At this point you have a new case record in CRM and two activities associated with the case. Figure 18.8 shows the open activity records associated with the case, and Figure 18.9 shows the closed activity records associated with the case. You can open each activity by clicking the activity name link or by double-clicking in the row.

FIGURE 18.8
Open activities
for the case.

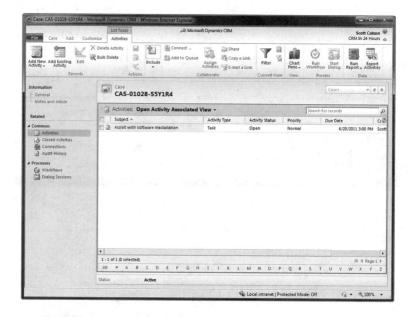

FIGURE 18.9
Closed activities
for the case.

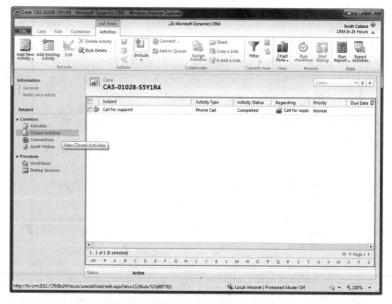

Once the issue associated with a service case is corrected, you want to mark the case as resolved. If you tried to mark the case as resolved at this point, however, you would get the error message shown in Figure 18.10 because you have an activity associated with the case that has not been marked as complete.

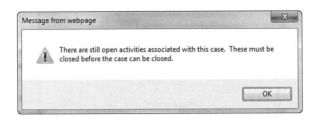

FIGURE 18.10
The open activities error message.

So to resolve the case, you first need to mark each open activity as complete. To do so, you select the Activities view in the related navigation section of the case form to see a list of all open activities associated with the service case (refer to Figure 18.8). Then you open and update each activity with any missing notes or time spent on the activity. Finally, you click the Mark Complete button to save the changes and mark the activity as completed.

When all the activities are closed, it is time to update the case to show that the issue has been resolved. To do so, you select the Case ribbon tab and then click Resolve Case in the Case tab (see Figure 18.11).

FIGURE 18.11
Resolving a case action.

When you complete this action, a Resolve Case dialog box opens, displaying the accumulated time spent on all activities related to the case (see Figure 18.12). To finish closing the case, you adjust the billable time if needed and enter a brief description in the Resolution text box. Then you click the OK button.

FIGURE 18.12
The Resolve
Case dialog.

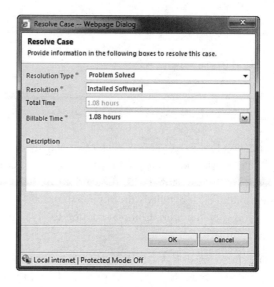

When the case is resolved, you see a Case Resolution activity in the Completed
Activities view for the case. This record contains the resolution information and the
billable time you entered when you resolved the case (see Figure 18.13).

FIGURE 18.13
A resolved case
with a Case
Resolution
activity.

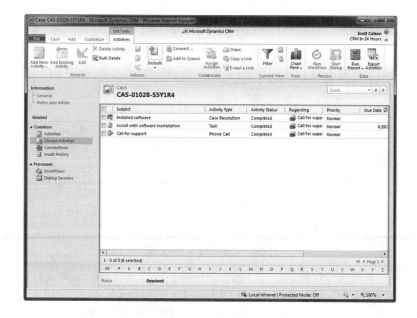

Proactive Versus Reactive Capturing of Time

The preceding example demonstrates using CRM cases in both a reactive way (generating a case when you take a phone call) and using CRM cases in a proactive way (scheduling a task for a future time). How you use CRM depends a great deal on your business and the processes you are implementing.

If you are constantly planning your schedule and proactively creating tasks, phone calls, and appointments that need to be completed in the future, Microsoft Dynamics CRM can help you track completion of those activities and give you a way to document how much time you spent on each activity as you close them out. On the other hand, if you live in a highly reactive world, and the work you do each day is somewhat dependent on what happens that day, you may find that it makes more sense to use a CRM case record to capture the thing that needs to get done. You can then create CRM activity records when you find time to work on the issue, and you can capture your time then.

Most organizations will be somewhere between these two scenarios. Lots of people want to jump on the proactive wagon. It's a good idea to be realistic about what your organization can do in this area and that you define a business process around CRM so that everyone uses the system the same way. This process can be as simple as a rule which states that no work will be done to resolve an issue until after a case that documents the issue has been made. This simple business rule ensures that everyone in the company who has CRM access has a way to know about the issue and therefore assist in resolution of the issue.

Distributing Work: Users, Teams, and Queues

Now that we have gotten into some details around linking cases to activities and tracking time, let's look at managing cases and workload in more detail. Chances are that you will have more than one person involved in resolving cases, and many issues will not be resolved in a single session or interaction.

Each case or activity in CRM can be owned by a single CRM user or a CRM team. From the standpoint of the system, an owner may have certain rights to modify that record that other users do not have. From the standpoint of getting the work done, the owner is typically responsible for doing the work or at least ensuring that the work gets done.

Although teams have been defined in CRM since the beginning, Dynamics CRM 2011 is the first version that actually supports ownership of a record by a team rather than an individual user, and this change has a big impact. Consider a scenario where you want only users who are qualified on a certain technology or process to work on issues related to that technology or process. You now have the ability to assign those cases to a defined team of users who have the required qualification, and you can give all members of that team the access they need to update the case record.

When distributing work in your organization, you have the option of distributing individual activities (a very proactive service model) or distributing service cases and allowing the case owner or team members to decide the best action to take (a more reactive model). You distribute this work directly by assigning the case or activity directly to an individual or a team, or indirectly by adding the case or activity to a queue.

Queues allow you to advertise specific activities or cases to a group of users as opposed to a specific person or team. Visibility to items in a queue can be given to a department, a subset of people, or everyone in the organization. The difference between adding an item to a queue or assigning it to a team is very subtle. The first thing to understand is that items added to a queue will remain in the queue until accepted or added to a different queue, and ownership of the case or activity does not change until someone specifically accepts the item from the queue. The second thing to understand is that queues, by definition, represent information in a FIFO (first-in, first-out) format so that the item that has been in the queue the longest is at the top of the list. The last significant thing is that queues can be set up to automatically process inbound e-mail to a specified e-mail address (for example, support@crmin24hours.com).

In order to understand this subtle difference, you'll next create a queue and a team and show how to distribute a case to a queue and to a team. First, you create a queue as follows:

1. Choose Settings.

2. Choose Business Management.

3. Choose Queues.

4. Click the New button to open a new queue window.

5. Enter the following information in the queue window (see Figure 18.14):

   ▶ Enter a unique queue name (in this case, Support).

   ▶ If your queue will process inbound e-mail, enter an e-mail address.

   ▶ Set the E-mail Access Configuration settings based on your system requirements.

6. Click the Save button.

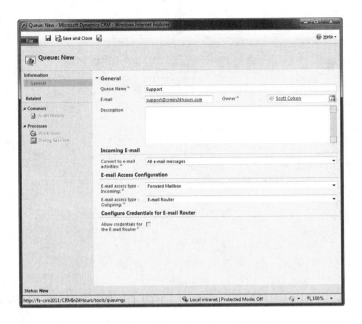

FIGURE 18.14
Creating a new queue.

Now you create a CRM team and assign yourself as a member as follows:

1. Choose Settings.

2. Choose Administration.

3. Choose Teams.

4. Click the New button to open a new team window.

5. Enter the following information in the team window (see Figure 18.15):

   ▶ Enter a unique team name (in this case, Support Team).

   ▶ Set yourself as the administrator.

6. Click the Save button.

7. Give the team the Customer Service Representative Role, using the steps as follows:

   ▶ Click the Manage Roles button in the Team tab of the ribbon.

   ▶ Check the Customer Service Representative role.

   ▶ Click the OK button.

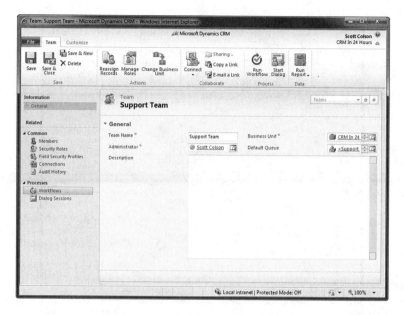

8. Add yourself as a member of the team as follows:

 ▶ Choose Members under the related item's section in the form navigation.

 ▶ Click the Members button on the Users tab of the ribbon.

 ▶ Check your name in the list of users.

 ▶ Click the OK button.

9. Click Save & Close to save and close the team window.

Now it is time to create a case that you can use to test your various methods of distributing the work to others. You create a case as follows:

1. Choose Service.

2. Choose Cases.

3. Click the New button.

4. Enter a case title and customer and then click the Save button to save the case but leave the form open.

In a first scenario, you should distribute this work to the support queue you just created (see Figure 18.16):

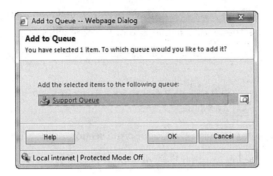

FIGURE 18.16
The Add to
Queue dialog.

1. Click on the Add to Queue button in the Case tab the ribbon.

2. Select the support queue in the Add to Queue dialog.

3. Click the OK button to complete the action.

Notice that you are still the owner of the case, as shown in the Owner field in the case form. Now you need to verify that the case has actually been assigned to the support queue (see Figure 18.17):

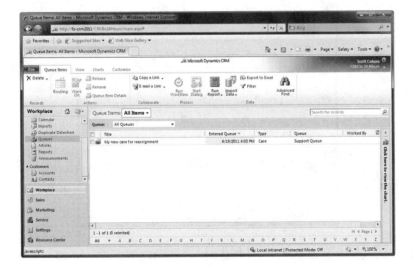

FIGURE 18.17
The case in the
support queue.

1. Choose Workplace.

2. Choose Queues.

3. Change the Queue Items view to All Items.

4. Note that the case you created is sitting in the support queue.

At this point, anyone who has been granted access to view queues can see this service case sitting in the queue, and ownership of the case will not change until a user accepts the queue item by clicking the Work On button in the Queue Items tab of the ribbon.

In the following steps, you'll assign the case to a team. You start by opening the case record and then proceed as follows:

1. Click the Assign button in the Collaborate section of the ribbon.

2. Select the Assign to Another User or Team option.

3. Click the Search button to the right of the dialog text box to open the Look Up Record dialog.

4. Change the Look For drop-down item from User to Team (see Figure 18.18).

FIGURE 18.18
The Look Up
Record dialog.

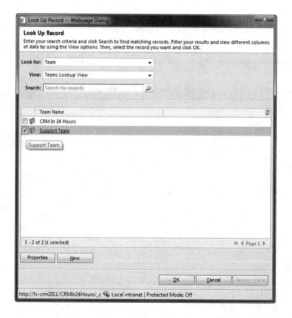

5. Select the support team you created earlier and click the OK button.

6. Click the OK button on the remaining dialog.

Note that the Owner field on the case has changed from you to the support team.

Adding a Workflow to Close a Case

When major functions occur, such as the closing of a case, great opportunities to have the system react with some automation present themselves. Consider, for instance, a need to alert the customer that a case has been closed. The system can generate an e-mail message, using a template that merges information from the service case to create the final e-mail. Figure 18.19 shows an existing e-mail template. Notice that the case number and the title have been included in this e-mail template.

FIGURE 18.19
An e-mail template.

Editing the E-mail Template

You can edit the e-mail template by choosing Settings, Templates, E-mail Templates and then selecting the Closed Case Acknowledgement e-mail template.

Did you Know?

This e-mail message gets sent by a workflow when there is a change in the case and the status of the case is set to Resolved. In this example, the e-mail is sent from a specific service person and sent to the customer associated with the case. However, many organizations send the e-mail from a common e-mail address, such as support@crmin24hours.com, so that any replies go back to an existing queue. To make this change, you set the e-mail sender to a queue that has the desired e-mail address.

The workflow to check the status of the case upon a change and to send an e-mail if the status is equal to Resolved is a workflow with two steps. Figure 18.20 shows this workflow.

FIGURE 18.20
An active work-
flow process.

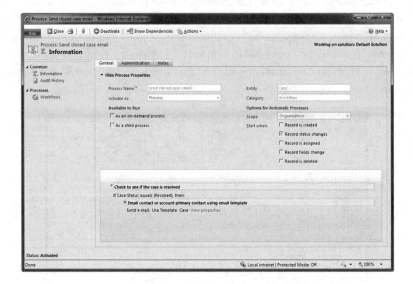

Notice that the options for automatic workflow are set to occur on record status changes, as opposed to when the record is created. You are capturing when a case changes and then reviewing the change with a condition statement to check whether the change resulted in the status being set to Resolved.

What is another situation where you might want a workflow on a change to a case? Here are some examples:

▶ When a case closes for a high-profile client, you might want to send an e-mail or create an activity to the internal support department manager or the CEO for a personal follow-up.

▶ When a case includes a value in the Follow-Up By field, you might want to schedule an activity to follow up for the appropriate support person or the incident manager.

▶ When a case changes and the status changes to high priority, you might want to create an appointment with a due date. The appointment would synchronize to Outlook and pop up an alert at the set time.

▶ When a case is resolved and the satisfaction level is very dissatisfied, you might want to kick off a special workflow process called Turning Around a Dissatisfied Customer.

The list can get even more interesting if you add a few layers or a bit of code. For instance, consider the following examples:

▶ When a case closes, you might want to send an e-mail to the client to say that his case is closed and include three questions. When he responds to this e-mail, you could capture the response and update the case with his input to the specific questions.

▶ When a case is updated, you might check whether there are any associated activities and whether those activities are open. If the activities are open and it has been a certain amount of time, you can determine who the owner of the activity is and alert his manager.

▶ When a case is updated, you might want to determine whether there are any other open cases for the same customer. If there are, you can check whether the subject has similar words that might indicate a possible duplication.

Workshop

Silver Streak Developers is a company that writes software for municipal governments. It has a number of developers, a quality assurance department, and a support department that takes incoming calls. Silver Streak Developers also has a sales department that sells the company's software to municipal governments all over the country. Silver Streak Developers uses Microsoft Dynamics CRM. The support department uses all the service components of Microsoft Dynamics CRM. Each of the company's clients has a support contract that is either a Gold or Silver level. The Silver level offers 24 incidents equally, approximately 24 calls a year, and the Gold level support contract offers 50 hours of service. Customers of Silver Streak can send e-mail messages to support@silverstreak.com, and a support person accepts requests from the support queue as soon as he is available. The support person creates a case, associates the e-mail message, and tracks all that he does to resolve the problem. When the problem is resolved, the support person closes the case.

Q&A

Q. *We want to capture all our time and then bill for it. Can Microsoft Dynamics CRM handle this?*

A. Yes. Microsoft Dynamics CRM can support capturing time against activities and the viewing of these activities, with their duration. Time can then be billed either from your accounting software or via an invoice that you enter in

Microsoft Dynamics CRM against a service product. If you need robust project billing, practice management, write-up/down auditing, or other features, you should look for an add-on to Microsoft Dynamics CRM or integrate a practice management or time and billing or project billing application with Microsoft Dynamics CRM.

Q. *We use RMAs and need to track when a product is returned under an RMA number. How well does Microsoft Dynamics CRM handle RMAs?*

A. The structure of Microsoft Dynamics CRM actually works extremely well for the management and handling of RMAs. In this scenario, the unique case number becomes the RMA number.

Q. *We have all our legal contracts set up in Microsoft Word. Can we associate a Word contract with the contract feature of Microsoft Dynamics CRM?*

A. No. File attachments cannot be associated with contracts in Microsoft Dynamics CRM. Okay, this is not really correct; yes, you can associate a Word contract with a saved note associated with the contract entity, but doing so is not recommend because Microsoft Dynamics CRM is not designed to be an incredible document library for unstructured data. For associating unstructured data, such as Word documents, with Microsoft Dynamics CRM, look into the incredible integration points for Microsoft SharePoint.

Quiz

1. Identify two places where time can be captured in Microsoft Dynamics CRM.

2. How are contracts related to cases in Microsoft Dynamics CRM?

3. Why would you want to use a queue?

4. If you are a proactive person, is it fairly straightforward to capture time on your activities as you complete them?

5. Name two ways to close an activity in Microsoft Dynamics CRM.

Answers

1. Time can be captured on an activity, and time can be captured on a case as a function of the attached activities.

2. Cases can be associated with a specific contract, and the time on a case can reduce the available time on a contract.

3. Queues allow you to assign activities or send e-mail to a generic bucket, such as a support queue or a support e-mail address.

4. Yes. When you complete your planned activities, you can add the duration when completing.

5. You can save the activity as closed or you can use the Close Activity option on the Action menu.

Exercise

Set up the Gold and Silver contracts that Silver Streak Developers uses with its customers. In addition, set up the support queue. When the contract and queue are created, create some new activities and assign them to the queue. Then try to send an e-mail to the queue's e-mail address. Also try to create a case and assign it to the contract you just created.

HOUR 19

Scheduling

What You'll Learn in This Hour:

- ▶ Scheduling in general
- ▶ Getting started with scheduling
- ▶ Viewing and managing scheduling conflicts
- ▶ Setting up scheduling

This hour focuses on scheduling people, places, groups, shared facilities, and equipment. This is a robust set of features worthy of deep thought and consideration. If scheduling is a core piece of your business, set aside extra time to master and read other material on this subject. Scheduling can be used for onsite visits, training facilities, equipment, and people who use equipment or places interactively.

Scheduling in General

Microsoft Dynamics CRM offers the ability to schedule, find conflicts, assign people, and juggle in-demand equipment and locations, such as conference rooms and training facilities.

Before we dive into scheduling, let's set some context. Some features and functions in Microsoft Dynamics CRM are more complex than others. The silver lining is that the complex functions complement more complex long-term functionality.

Scheduling is one of these more complex features, particularly when it comes to getting it all configured. So, in this lesson, you will first learn how scheduling works and all the great things you can do with scheduling. Then you will learn about the key areas of Microsoft Dynamics CRM that need to be set up for scheduling to work smoothly.

Getting Started with Scheduling

The world of Microsoft Dynamics CRM scheduling uses the term *service* as a specific item. A service is made up of a number of unique variables, including associated resources, times, and durations. In fact, you can use scheduling to organize and manage service teams, service people, service appointments, service activities, and service equipment.

The Service Calendar

The service calendar is a unique centralized calendar for services, service activities and appointments that is configured and displayed in a manner to support conflict resolution and filtering. Service activities also show up on a specific staff member's assigned calendar, which the staff member accesses by selecting My Work, Calendar.

Figure 19.1 shows the Service Calendar accessed in Microsoft Outlook.

FIGURE 19.1
Accessing
the service
calendar.

Service activities are unique items that apply to the management of service-specific activities. They are not the same as standard activities of types such as Task, Phone Call, Appointment, for example. One way to think of a service activity is as a supersized and complex appointment.

The service calendar is located on the Service menu, and you get to it as follows:

1. Select Service.

2. Select Service Calendar.

When you open the service calendar, you see a list of all resources in the left menu bar. These resources consist of all Microsoft Dynamics CRM users and other resources that were created, such as groups of users, equipment, or facilities. What displays in the left navigation pane is controlled by the Type drop-down menu option at the top of the calendar. Figure 19.1 shows the initial service calendar.

A Programmer's Option

You cannot customize the service calendar or change the default view in Dynamics CRM Scheduling. However, with a bit of programming expertise, you can edit the ISV.config file (which is an XML configuration document used to update the navigation structure of Microsoft Dynamics CRM Online, including adding custom buttons, tabs, and menus to entity forms) to change the colors of the time blocks.

Items that are scheduled on the service calendar include service activities and appointments. Before you can schedule a service activity, you need to create the service activity. After you create the service activity, the system immediately gives you the option to schedule it. A service can also be created which groups a set of service activities into a logical unit.

Creating a Service and a Service Activity

To create a new service, follow these steps:

1. Select Services from the left navigation.

2. Then select Services.

3. Now select New (see Figure 19.2).

For each service you might also have a set of activities to perform so the following shows how to create a new specific service activity.

Example of Service vs. Service Activity

An example of a service and service activity includes a situation where you might have a service called Repair and then a set of service activities that had to be complete for the full repair to be completed.

To create a new Service activity, follow these steps:

1. Select Service from the main menu.

2. Select the Service Calendar.

FIGURE 19.2
A service.

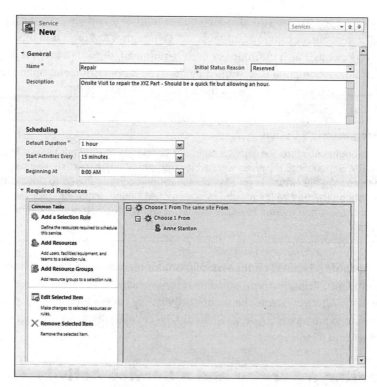

3. Select New Activity from the top of the service calendar form (see Figure 19.3 for the Service Activity form).

FIGURE 19.3
Service activity.

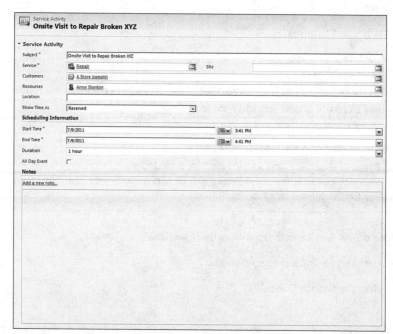

The subject field of the service activity is required. This field can be used as a category to help classify this particular service activity from a list of many other similar service activities.

Perhaps you want to create a service activity for inspecting a corporate office. Your subject could become Inspect the Corporate Headquarters. Your service is the standard service you created, called Inspection. Customer or Customers are the customers who require this service activity. Resources are resources that are not only available but also follow business rules. For instances resources are available within a specific chosen site or sites is selected.

If all the fields are not properly set up, you will receive an error message when trying to save the service. To fix this type of error, you select each of the lookup items and look at the details behind them. In this example, the resource was not associated with the selected site, and the business rule requires that the resource be a resource from the configured and selected site. When it comes to scheduling, the setup can trip up users, so it's important to make sure you review all of your setup. This includes sites (even if you have only one), users, and resources.

When scheduling a service activity, you have a number of choices to consider. During scheduling, you can check whether the selected resources are available and what the available times are. If you enter a specific time, you can select the option Check Available to search and determine whether the resources are available at the time selected. You will be presented with a list of available options that you can then select from for scheduling. Figure 19.4 shows a list of available times.

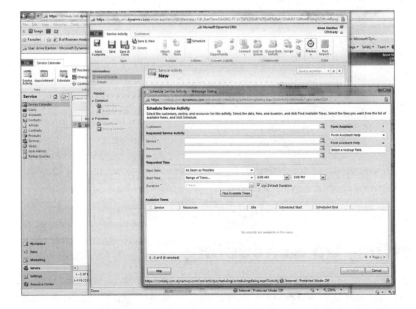

FIGURE 19.4
Scheduling a service.

Notice that in Figure 19.4 you can see three different windows. This occurs during scheduling when you are trying to schedule a service activity that does not exist. The system prompts you for scheduling information, and it prompts you for the information for the service activity that you are scheduling. A more logical approach is to create the service activity and then schedule it.

Viewing and Managing Scheduling Conflicts

After service activities are created and scheduled, you can use the scheduling calendar to check for conflicts:

1. From the scheduling calendar, choose the view of data you are interested in.

2. Click the Show Conflicts icon at the top of the screen, as shown in Figure 19.5. Conflicts in people's schedules show up in the calendar with a red box around them.

FIGURE 19.5
Scheduling
conflicts.

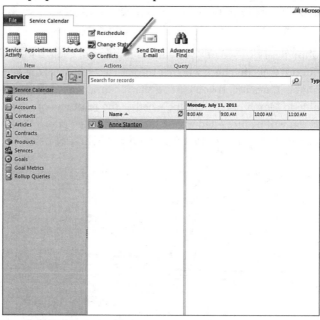

3. Choose View Service Activities from the Type drop-down to view conflicts between specific service activities.

4. Confirm that Show Conflicts is turned on (see Figure 19.5).

Setting Up Scheduling

Setup does not have to be done more than once, and for those working with a Microsoft Dynamics CRM partner, part of your project might be finalizing and configuring the scheduling functionality of Microsoft Dynamics CRM. In case it is not, this section goes through each section of Microsoft Dynamics CRM system configuration that needs to be configured for scheduling to work smoothly.

Defining Staff Availability

The first step in setting up scheduling is to double-check and configure staff people's work hours. To do so, follow these steps:

1. Choose Settings.

2. Choose Administration.

3. Choose Users.

4. Choose a specific user.

5. From the left menu bar, select Work Hours (see Figure 19.6).

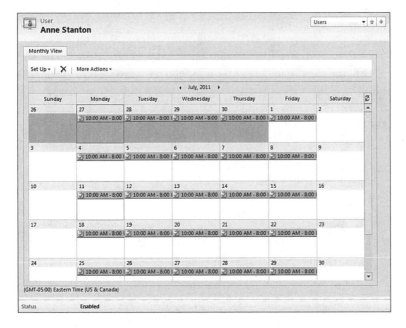

FIGURE 19.6
The work hours calendar.

Figure 19.7 shows the work hours calendar as it appears when first accessed. To configure work hours, follow these steps:

1. Select Set Up.

2. Choose New Weekly Schedule.

3. Drill down on the blue words Work Hours.

4. Enter the Work Hours for the user's workday.

FIGURE 19.7
Specifying the
work hours.

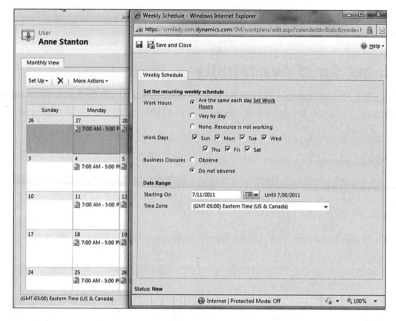

In Figure 19.8, the work hours are entered as 7:00 a.m. to 5:00 p.m., with 1/2 an
hour for lunch.

FIGURE 19.8
Entering breaks
and hours.

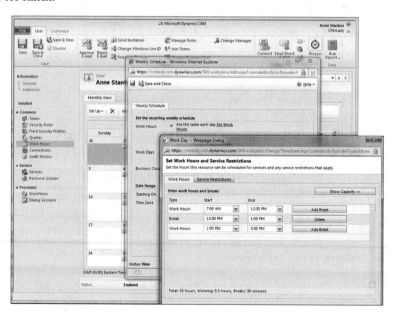

The point of adding in work hours for people you want to schedule is that, once this
is configured, scheduling becomes much more intelligent. If you try to schedule
someone during her break, the system will notice this and warn you.

By the Way

Quick Exercise

Spend some time adding some unique work hours to your system for practice. Consider this your warm-up and stretching exercise for the following sections. If you find that the system is being uncooperative, don't forget you can exit the work hours calendar and then return.

Defining Resource Groups, Equipment, and Locations

After the staff is correctly configured for scheduling, the other items referenced from the scheduling functions need to be set up. Let's tackle resource groups. A resource group is made up of any combination of users, equipment, facilities, and teams. To set up a resource group, follow these steps from the main menu:

1. Select Settings.

2. Select Business Management.

3. Select Resource Groups.

4. Click New.

Figure 19.9 shows getting started defining a resource group. When creating a new resource group, you are selecting from users, facilities, equipment, and teams, so if you are going to create groups that include facilities, equipment, and teams, take a minute and set these up as well. Figure 19.10 shows the resource group defined and saved.

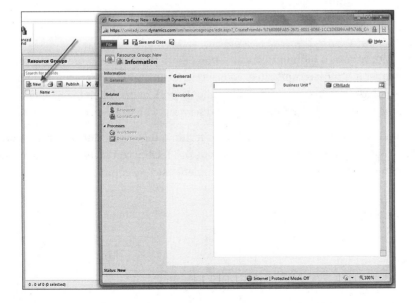

FIGURE 19.9
Resource groups.

FIGURE 19.10
A resource group defined and saved.

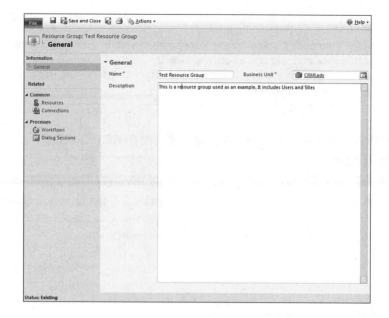

Setting Up Facilities and Equipment

To set up facilities and equipment, follow these steps:

1. Select Settings.

2. Select Business Management.

3. Select Facilities/Equipment.

4. Click New.

Figure 19.11 shows a brand-new facility, and Figure 19.12 shows more details on the facility after it has been configured. Notice that facilities and equipment also have a number of associated items, including available work hours (when the facility or equipment is available for scheduling) and services, which also need to be configured.

The configured facility in Figure 19.12 is a training center associated with the corporate headquarters. Resources associated with this facility can include a specific team of staff members, training materials, equipment (such as a projector), and more.

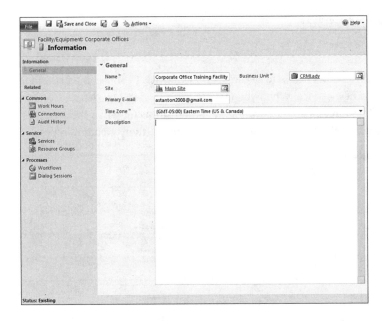

FIGURE 19.11
A brand-new facility.

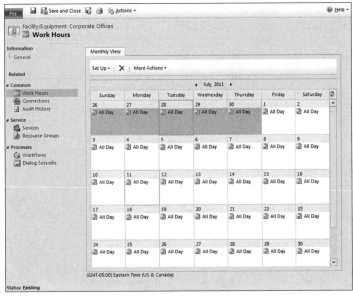

FIGURE 19.12
Configured facility with work hours defined.

Set Up Services

To set up services, follow these steps:

1. Choose Settings.

2. Choose Business Management.

3. Choose Services.

4. Click New.

Figure 19.13 shows access to services, and Figure 19.14 shows the first tab used in creating a new service. When you create a new service, you define associated required resources, default duration, a default status for when the service is applied to a specific schedule activity, and the scheduled activity creation interval.

FIGURE 19.13
Accessing
services.

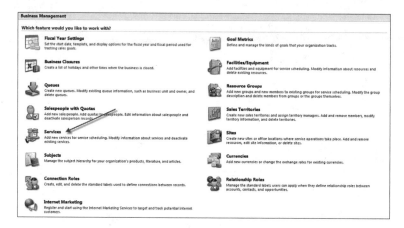

FIGURE 19.14
Creating a new
service.

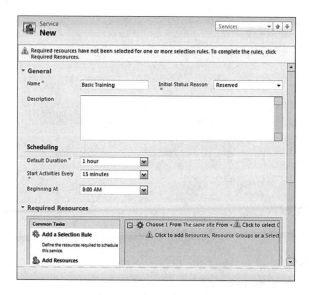

Figure 19.15 shows the second tab used in creating a new service. This form is more difficult, but you can master it. The system is looking for a few variables to associate with some business rules. When you're adding this service to a schedule, where are resources found? From what site are they drawn? If you click the word *site*, you can choose the total number of sites to look at and how many resources to select from that site. Figure 19.15 shows what the entry looks like.

FIGURE 19.15
How many resources are there, and from where?

Choose one resource from the same site. In this example, you can associate this rule with the corporate training center, and there is only one corporate training center, which is not located at multiple sites.

In Figure 19.16, you associate a resource group of trainers and determine that, when scheduling this service, a person must choose three trainers out of a group of five different people (users).

When you select the specific people (users) and try to save, the system asks if these particular people (users) should be saved and associated with a resource group.

FIGURE 19.16
Other
resources.

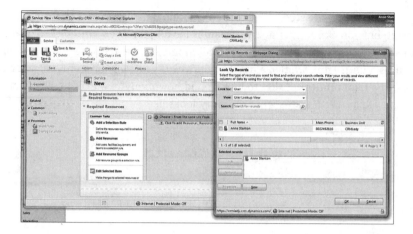

FIGURE 19.16
Other
resources.

Now that you have created one service, you should take some time to set up a few more services. Examples include the following:

▶ **An onsite visit to fix something**—What is being fixed? Who and what skills do they need to fix it? What tools are needed? Where are the tools located? If your company has a service truck that includes an inventory of tools, for instance, then scheduling either the truck or an associated tool might be of interest.

▶ **A demonstration**—This service requires a special demonstration laptop, a projector, a sales engineer, and a salesperson.

▶ **A cleaning service**—This service requires cleaning supplies, a company-owned vacuum cleaner, and a cleaning person.

Figure 19.17 shows a list of services.

You can deactivate a service, or you can delete services in bulk. Therefore, you have some flexibility in how you initially set up services. Just be careful that you don't use a service that you then delete because the system will prevent you from deleting services that have already been used.

Figure 19.18 shows the specific settings that need to be configured in order for scheduling to function properly.

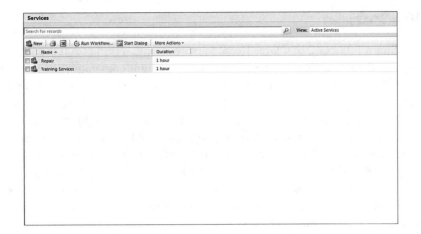

FIGURE 19.17
A list of services.

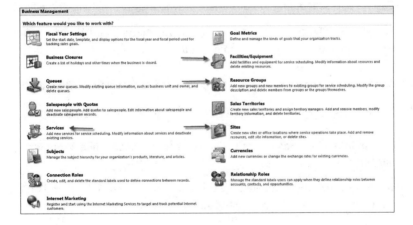

FIGURE 19.18
Scheduling setup items.

Workshop

Carla Brown is the CEO of a large cleaning business with a staff of 200 people. Her company, Corporate Cleaning Inc., specializes in cleaning corporate offices all over the city. Corporate Cleaning Inc. has a fleet of trucks, including one rug-cleaning truck, and various equipment that is used to service customers (for example, vacuum cleaners, bundled cleaning buckets that include various rags, brushes, and small brooms, and cleaning supplies for wood and glass). In addition to the equipment needed to service its clients, Corporate Cleaning has both full-time and temporary staff. In addition, it has students who work hourly, mostly during the summer months. Carla Brown uses Microsoft Dynamics CRM to keep track of all 200 staff members and their associated equipment, assigned vehicles, and when staff are unavailable to work at a client site.

Q&A

Q. *We have a team of five people who often handle work orders in the field. Can we use scheduling to keep track of who they are visiting and when?*

A. Yes. Microsoft Dynamics CRM's scheduling functionality allows you to track who is where and when and who needs to be where and when.

Q. *Can resource groups have more than just people associated with them?*

A. Yes. Resource groups can include people, facilities, and equipment.

Q. *We ran into numerous errors when trying to use scheduling. What is happening?*

A. You have likely not completed the configuration for scheduling, and all the pieces that you need for your schedules are not available.

Quiz

1. What is unique about a service activity?

2. Do you have to set up work hours if you are not using scheduling?

3. What items are scheduled on the service calendar?

4. Can you delete a service activity that has been scheduled and completed?

5. Name three different categories of things that can be scheduled.

Answers

1. The service activity has additional attributes (fields) that are scheduling oriented. One way to think of a service activity is as a supersized and complex appointment.

2. No. You do not need to set up work hours if you are not using scheduling.

3. Items that are scheduled on the service calendar include service activities and appointments.

4. No. You cannot delete a service activity that has been scheduled and completed.

5. People, equipment, and facilities can be scheduled in Microsoft Dynamics CRM.

Exercise

Set up the equipment and 10 of the staff resources that Carla Brown uses in her business. Create the carpet-cleaning truck and a few staff resources, including at least two students whose schedule are different from 9 a.m. to 5 p.m. Set up a student, Jackie Tee, who works only on Tuesdays and Wednesdays from 5 p.m. to 12 a.m.

Configure the rest of the requirements for scheduling, based on Carla Brown's business model. After scheduling is configured, schedule Jackie Tee to clean a specific office every Tuesday evening from 6 p.m. to 9 p.m. and a different client's office from 9 p.m. to 12 a.m.

Utilizing the Power of Microsoft Excel with CRM Data

What You'll Learn in This Hour:

- ▶ Key concepts and caveats
- ▶ Exporting the right data: Using Advanced Find
- ▶ Exporting a static worksheet
- ▶ Exporting a dynamic worksheet
- ▶ Exporting data for PivotTable analysis
- ▶ Adding outside data
- ▶ Reusing and sharing your spreadsheets
- ▶ Using a dashboard
- ▶ Using Excel to edit and clean up records

Now that you understand how to enter data in Microsoft Dynamics CRM, it's time to learn how to get that data out. This hour covers using the power of Microsoft Excel to work with data from Microsoft Dynamics CRM.

Key Concepts and Caveats

There are many reasons for analyzing data. Microsoft Dynamics CRM makes it easy to specify criteria for which records to include and then export the list to a Microsoft Excel worksheet or PivotTable. After the data is in Excel, all the power of Excel is there to analyze your data. When you're ready to export a list of data to Excel, Microsoft Dynamics CRM offers some basic choices: static or dynamic and table or

PivotTable. A static spreadsheet has no connection to Microsoft Dynamics CRM after it is created. The data is extracted and saved, and a user can't tell that it was created from Microsoft Dynamics CRM. A dynamic spreadsheet, on the other hand, retains its connection to Microsoft Dynamics CRM. It refreshes the included data from Microsoft Dynamics CRM when it is opened, and it maintains the data security that exists in Microsoft Dynamics CRM.

An export to a Microsoft Excel spreadsheet can be either static or dynamic:

▶ **Static**—A static spreadsheet is a snapshot of the data at the moment you created it, and it does not change when data in Microsoft Dynamics CRM changes. Static spreadsheets are great for one-time tasks and for capturing data at the end of a reporting period. They are also useful when you need to present the data to someone who is not a Microsoft Dynamics CRM user.

▶ **Dynamic**—A dynamic spreadsheet is connected directly to Microsoft Dynamics CRM data. When data in Microsoft Dynamics CRM changes, the data in the dynamic spreadsheet also changes. Dynamic spreadsheets are useful when you want to do the work to design the spreadsheet once and then analyze or share the data as the data changes.

Because of the security built into Microsoft Dynamics CRM, the data in an exported spreadsheet includes only records that the person who exports the data has permission to see. This is a key difference between the two types of spreadsheets:

▶ In a static spreadsheet, anyone who opens the spreadsheet can see the data, whether or not the person has access to Microsoft Dynamics CRM. You therefore need to be careful if you create a static spreadsheet with confidential data: Anyone who can open the file can view the data. A static spreadsheet does not require a connection to the CRM server.

▶ In a dynamic spreadsheet, only Microsoft Dynamics CRM users with the right security can view the data. When a dynamic spreadsheet is opened, users are prompted to refresh the data. Only data they have permission to see is included. This means that one dynamic spreadsheet can be used by many people, so someone with more Excel experience can design a complex PivotTable or worksheet, and each user can use it to analyze his or her own data. It also means that the data is refreshed whenever the user wants, allowing a user to use the spreadsheet as a report independently of the CRM interface. A dynamic spreadsheet requires a connection to the CRM server to run properly.

Excel has two ways of presenting data: tables and PivotTables. Either can be turned into a chart:

▶ A table provides a flat view of your data, using rows and columns.

▶ PivotTables are interactive: They are designed for the viewer to experiment with alternative ways of looking at the data.

Every time you export to Excel, Microsoft Dynamics CRM asks you to make a choice between exporting to a worksheet (table) or a PivotTable. Figure 20.1 shows the difference between these two formats.

This hour doesn't make you an expert on Microsoft Excel, but it does help you figure out how to get information into Microsoft Excel.

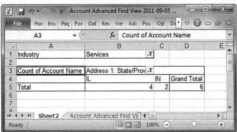

FIGURE 20.1
An Excel worksheet and an Excel PivotTable.

Required Software

If you use Microsoft Dynamics CRM Online, to export to dynamic spreadsheets or PivotTables, you must also use the Microsoft Dynamics CRM Outlook client. This is available as a free download for all Microsoft Dynamics CRM users.

By the Way

Finding Your Way in Microsoft Dynamics CRM

You need to know where the Advanced Find button is and where the Export to Excel button is. These buttons are in the same spot no matter what entity (record type) you are looking at. Figure 20.2 shows the location of these buttons.

FIGURE 20.2
Location of the
Advanced Find
and Export to
Excel buttons.

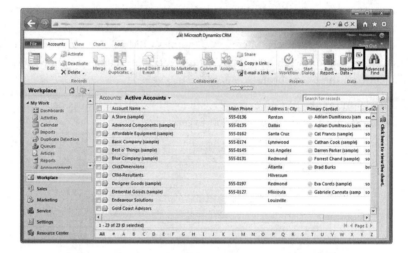

Exporting the Right Data: Using Advanced Find

If you're not exporting the right data, no fancy Excel trick will get you useful information. To get the right data, you need to learn how to use Microsoft Dynamics CRM Advanced Find to do two things:

▶ Filter data to exactly the data you want

▶ Display all the columns you need

▼ Try It Yourself

Limiting the Data Displayed

When exporting to Excel, you can limit the data you export, or you can export all data and filter it in Excel after the data is there. The approach you take will vary, depending on the amount of data you have and the specific analysis task you're working on.

Here's how to limit the data in Microsoft Dynamics CRM before you export.

▼

By the Way

Using Advanced Find

The easiest way to use Advanced Find is to go to a preexisting view that is close to what you want and then click Advanced Find. This defaults to that existing view and offers you the chance to modify it because most of the Advanced Find criteria you need will already be defined.

From anywhere in Microsoft Dynamics CRM, you can click the Advanced Find button to open Advanced Find.

To limit the data displayed, you select the primary entity (record type) to search and then specify search criteria. You can have criteria on the entity (record type) you are searching, such as only records with a status of Open, or you can have criteria based on related entities (records), such as entities (records) that have open activities associated.

You can be specific in your search. For example, if you were getting organized for a business trip to businesses with zip codes starting with 980, you could use the query shown in Figure 20.3 to look for active contacts that you own that are in a zip code beginning with 980 that have activities due in the next four weeks.

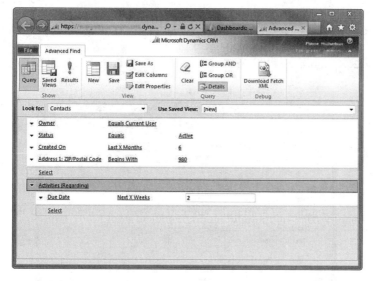

FIGURE 20.3
Query showing active contacts in zip code 980*.

There are several things to note about specifying criteria. First, each criteria line has three possible parts:

▶ **Field to search**—For example, in the second line, you're looking for records that have a Status field with Active as the value.

▶ **Operator**—In the third line, the operator is Last X Months, and in the Value column, you specify the number of months.

▶ **Value**—This is displayed in the third column. If the operator includes the value in it, such as the Equals Current User operator in the first line, no separate value part is displayed.

Second, notice the shaded area labeled Activities (Regarding). This shaded bar indicates that any criteria below it are from different entities (record types). In this case, the criteria are from the Activities entity (record type), and you're looking for activities due within two weeks that are associated with the contacts.

By searching for criteria from multiple entities (record types), you can find exactly the data you need.

You need to know a few details about specifying criteria:

▶ You can group criteria.

▶ Group AND specifies that all the grouped criteria must be true.

▶ Group OR specifies that only one of the grouped criteria must be true for a record to be included.

▶ You can add multiple values in one criterion. These are processed as an OR; if a record has any of the multiple values, it will be included in the results.

In Figure 20.4, notice the little arrow next to each criteria row. Select it to see the options.

FIGURE 20.4
Selecting or deleting a criteria row.

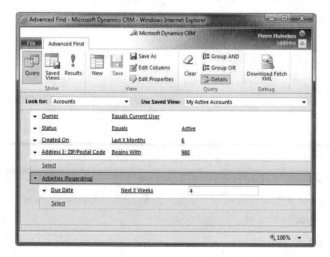

After you select a row, you can group it with other rows. Figure 20.5 shows the two City clauses grouped together.

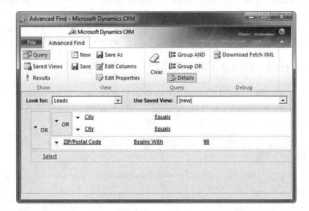

FIGURE 20.5
Grouped criteria.

If you are selecting criteria from a list, multiple values can be separated with a semi-colon. Figure 20.6 shows grouped criteria.

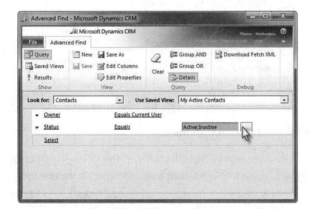

FIGURE 20.6
Entering multiple values in one criterion.

Task: Displaying the Exact Columns You Need

How you specify columns depends on which export method you choose:

▶ For static worksheets, select columns in Advanced Find before exporting.

▶ For PivotTables, select columns in Advanced Find first or click Select Columns in the Export dialog box.

▶ For dynamic worksheets, select columns in Advanced Find or click Add Columns in the Export dialog box.

First, we'll look at how to select columns in Advanced Find.

For example, perhaps you are preparing print mailing labels for a selected set of lead records collected from a trade show. Here's what you do:

1. From the Leads area, open the Open Leads view and click Advanced Find.

2. Add your criteria for Lead Source.

3. Click Edit Columns, Add Columns to add the columns necessary for a mailing. Figure 20.7 shows the Add Columns dialog.

FIGURE 20.7
Selecting additional columns to display.

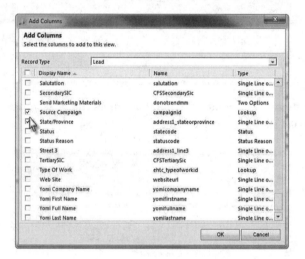

4. Click OK to select the lead columns.

5. Click Add Columns again, but this time, in the Record Type drop-down list, select a type of record. (Notice that you can select from the main record type you already picked or from related record types.) Select the Owner record type, select the First Name column, and click OK.

By the Way

Data from Multiple Record Types

You can select columns from multiple record types to include in the output. For example, if you are exporting leads, you can include the name of the source campaign or the name of the referring account.

The order of the columns in the Advanced Find results is the order in which the data will be displayed in Excel, so you might decide to reorder the columns using the green arrows, shown in Figure 20.8. While you're at it, you should delete any columns you don't need in your spreadsheet. Don't worry about sorting; that's easier to do in Excel after you export your data.

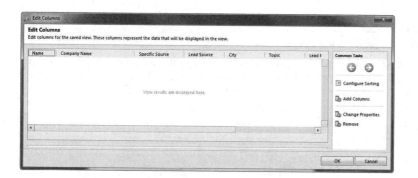

FIGURE 20.8
Reorganizing or
removing
columns.

Exporting a Static Worksheet

Now that you have exactly the data you want to analyze in your Advanced Find
results, it's time to export the data to an Excel spreadsheet. You might do this, for
example, to organize mailing information for a bulk mailing.

Try It Yourself ▼

Exporting Data for a Bulk Mailing

After you have the columns you need, such as name and address information for
mailing labels, follow these steps:

1. Click the Export to Excel button.

2. Examine the choice of options.

3. Select Static Worksheet with Records from This Page or select Static Worksheet
   with Records from All Pages in the Current View. (The choice here depends on
   what records you want in the spreadsheet.)

Figure 20.9 shows all the choices possible when you export to Excel.

FIGURE 20.9
Selecting the
type of Excel
file to create.

▼

Watch
Out!

Don't Panic on Message

When you click Open, don't panic when you get the dialog box shown in Figure 20.10: It will happen every time you open an Excel file you exported from Dynamics CRM. Dynamics CRM actually exports an XML file that Excel knows how to open. Save the file and then open it.

FIGURE 20.10
Warning about file type.

You'll see a dialog box prompting you to open or save the file.

When your data is in Excel, the column header will show you when the data is from a related record type. For example, the First Name (Owner) column comes from the Owner record type.

Figure 20.11 shows you the output in Excel.

FIGURE 20.11
Source of data displayed in column heading in Excel.

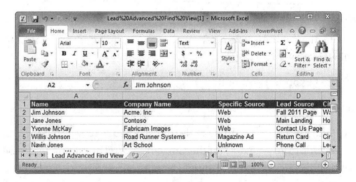

Now that the data is in Excel, you can do a mail merge to Microsoft Office Word to print letters or labels. You can even sign each letter with the lead owner's first name because you included that in the columns you exported.

Watch
Out!

Selecting the Right Format

When you save any spreadsheet created by exporting from Microsoft Dynamics CRM, by default, it is saved in XML Spreadsheet 2003 (*.xml) format. When you save it, if you're using Excel 2007, save it in the format Excel Workbook (.xlsx), or if you're using Excel 2003, save it in the format Excel 97-2003 Workbook (.xls). This will prevent you from getting a warning message every time you open the spreadsheet.

▲

Exporting a Dynamic Worksheet

If you want to create a spreadsheet that you can reuse as data changes in Microsoft Dynamics CRM, create a dynamic worksheet. A dynamic worksheet updates the contained data from Microsoft Dynamics CRM each time you open it. This is helpful when you want to put some time into formatting a worksheet and don't want to have to redo this work each time new data is added. It's also an essential feature if you're creating a dashboard that shows current data whenever it is viewed.

Task: Exporting Data to Chart

To export data to a dynamic spreadsheet, follow these steps:

1. Start from an Advanced Find view that includes all the records you want to export. For example, if you want to see a chart showing opportunities grouped by size, you could start by exporting the My Open Opportunities view.

2. Select the Dynamic Worksheet option. Notice that the Edit Columns button becomes available.

3. Click Edit Columns.

4. Select and order the columns you want in your table.

5. Click Export after your columns are set.

Before you see your data, there are three more sequential steps:

1. You'll be prompted to open or save the file. Go ahead and open the file and click OK when you see the message that the file is in a different format than specified by the file extension.

2. With some versions of Excel and some operating systems, you might see a message "Security Warning: Data connections have been disabled," and no data will be visible. If you receive this message, click the Options button and select Enable This Content.

3. If you are using Microsoft Dynamics CRM Online, the first line of the spreadsheet will say, "To view and refresh dynamic data, Microsoft Dynamics CRM Outlook Client must be installed." If you have the Microsoft Dynamics CRM Outlook client installed, click the Data tab and then click the Refresh from CRM button.

After you have the data exported, you can use Excel to create whatever charts you need. Each time you open your worksheet, the data will refresh from Microsoft

Dynamics CRM, or you can use the Refresh from CRM commands on the data ribbon to refresh the data.

Figure 20.12 shows a dynamic spreadsheet with the Refresh from CRM ribbon.

FIGURE 20.12
Refresh from
CRM on the
Data ribbon in
Excel.

Exporting Data for PivotTable Analysis

Dynamic PivotTables provide a way to slice and dice your data in different ways to quickly discover patterns.

Task: Exporting a Dynamic PivotTable

By default, all the columns in a view will be available to use in a PivotTable. If you want more columns, you can either add them to your view before you export or click the Select Columns button.

When you open the exported file, you'll see your standard blank PivotTable, ready to select the data to pivot. To select the data to pivot, do the following:

1. In the security message, click Options to enable viewing the content.

2. On the Data tab, click Refresh from CRM.

You are now ready to explore your data by using the PivotTable.

Two sheets are created for each PivotTable: Sheet1 contains the PivotTable, and the second sheet contains the raw data used by the PivotTable.

In Figure 20.13, by pivoting on the estimated close date and estimated revenue, you can see the projected income.

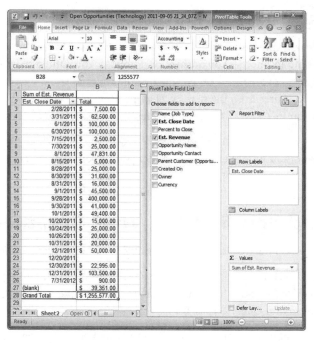

FIGURE 20.13
PivotTable for
opportunities.

Now you're free to use Excel to analyze and format your data, knowing that the
work you put into getting it just right will be usable each month as you forecast revenue from your opportunities. Figure 20.14 shows the sample PivotTable turned into
a PivotChart.

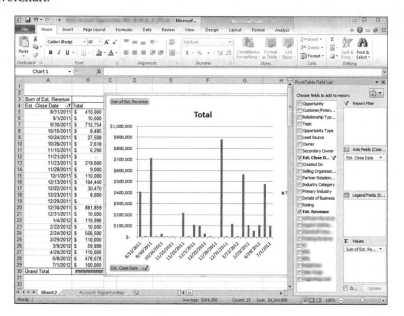

FIGURE 20.14
PivotChart for
opportunities.

Adding Outside Data

When you have a spreadsheet or PivotTable saved, you might want to connect the data in it to data in another spreadsheet or database. You can do so by using the advanced features of Microsoft Excel, which support establishing a data connection to another data source from the new Excel worksheet. This chapter's focus is on Microsoft Dynamics CRM, so the advanced features of Excel are not outlined.

For example, your department might have a budget model in Excel. You could connect it to your opportunities to assess whether you are on track to meet the budget numbers.

Reusing and Sharing Your Spreadsheets

To make your Excel file available to other people, you have several options:

▶ Add the Excel file to Microsoft Dynamics CRM as a report. This report can be available for you or for other people in your company. (See Hour 21, "Reporting and Query Basics.")

▶ E-mail a static or dynamic spreadsheet to other people or save it in a shared file system.

▶ Put the Excel file on an intranet site, such as a SharePoint dashboard.

By the Way

Accessing Data

Remember, if you e-mail or save a dynamic spreadsheet, only other Microsoft Dynamics CRM users can see the data in it. And they might see different data when they open it, because they will see results based on the records that they have permission to see.

By the Way

Making It Your Own/Customizing

The following tasks typically require system administrator or system customizer security roles:

▶ The columns that are displayed in Advanced Find by default can be customized. This changes the columns for all users in your organization.

▶ New system views can be defined and made available to all users.

▶ A Microsoft Dynamics CRM dashboard can be created using dynamic Excel spreadsheets and added to Microsoft Dynamics CRM as a report or as a web page.

Using a Dashboard

There are many ways to make a dashboard. Which one you choose depends on the needs of your company, such as how frequently you change what information you want to monitor, and whether the dashboard is used by all users or just a few. If you do not have the Excel and other tool knowledge in your company to create a dashboard, ask for help from a Microsoft Certified Dynamics CRM partner.

Using Excel to Edit and Clean Up Records

CRM 2011 adds a new feature when working with Excel. You may export to Excel, modify, and then reimport into CRM. This is commonly referred to as *data enhancement*. By using Excel's native formulas, you can improve or correct CRM data in Excel and then import the corrected data on top of the incorrect data, enhancing the quality of the information displayed in CRM. To access this function, follow these steps:

1. Navigate to the Advance Find or other view of data you would like to enhance.

2. Click Export to Excel.

3. Choose Static Worksheet.

4. Check the box Make Data Available for Re-importing by Including Required Column Headings.

5. Save the export to a local file.

6. Open the file.

7. Make modifications to the Excel spreadsheet data.

8. Save the spreadsheet, keeping the .xml 2003 format when you are prompted about whether to maintain the format.

If your export includes option sets (pick lists), you are given drop-down options. If the data is numeric, Excel formats your cells as numbers. Lookups are handled as simple text. As CRM puts data in hidden columns, it is important that you not change the layout or modify the columns in any way. Once you have cleaned up the spreadsheet data, you are ready for importing. Follow these steps to import to update existing records, using Figures 20.15 and 20.16 as a reference:

FIGURE 20.15
Making data
available for
reimporting.

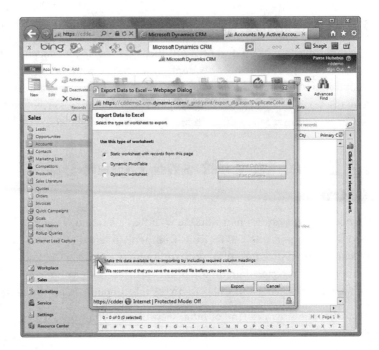

1. Choose Import Data from the ribbon.

2. Browse to the file. CRM will understand that this file is an update to existing records so no mapping will be required.

3. Submit. Within a few minutes, the data is updated.

Template for Import

In Microsoft Dynamics CRM 2011, a new feature has been added that allows you to download an Excel spreadsheet that contains a column for each of the fields associated with each record type. There is a data import template for each record type that can be imported. Excel data types enforce the type of data values you can add. This template also shows what columns are required fields in CRM.

To access this template, navigate to the record type you want. Then click Import and choose Import Template.

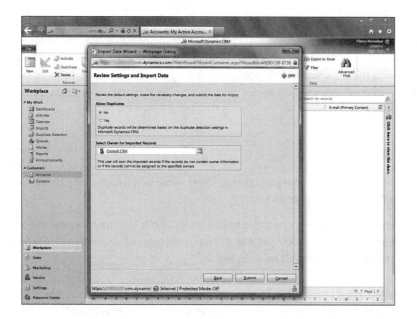

FIGURE 20.16
Updating existing records.

Workshop

John Brown, the sales manager from Hour 10, "Entering Data as a Salesperson," is getting ready for his quarterly meeting with the CEO. John wants to analyze patterns in how opportunities are won or lost in his territory so he can clearly communicate to his boss and so he can improve the results of his team. He creates a custom view in Advanced Find and exports it to an Excel PivotTable. After experimenting with various pivots, he finds one that clearly shows the data and turns it into a PivotChart. He fusses with the details to make it look exactly how he wants it for his PowerPoint presentation. The chart shows the three top factors in successfully winning opportunities, with the main factor being a response to the lead within 24 hours.

John saves his dynamic PivotTable in Microsoft Dynamics CRM as a report so that he can use it on a regular basis, and he embeds it in a PowerPoint presentation.

John's boss gives great feedback about his presentation and asks him to make it available to all the sales managers in the company. John shares the spreadsheet with the other managers and the CEO and decides to share it with all the salespeople. Because of the way data security is set up in the company, when each sales manager views the report, he sees just his own territory's data. When the CEO views the report, she sees the data for the entire company. When each sales representative views the data, all he sees is his own data.

Because the point of analyzing data is to learn what to do differently to improve results, the sales managers get together to determine best practices based on what they have learned. They decide to implement a new sales process using workflow to make sure the recommended procedures are followed. A simple workflow is implemented that sends an e-mail to the manager if a lead hasn't been followed up within 24 hours.

Q&A

Q. *When I share my dynamic spreadsheet with my manager, why does she see different numbers than I do?*

A. Each person who opens the spreadsheet sees data that matches records that she has permission to view in CRM. If your manager can see more records than you, more records will be included.

Q. *If I'm using Microsoft Dynamics CRM Online, why do I need the Microsoft Dynamics CRM Outlook client to export dynamic spreadsheets?*

A. Microsoft Dynamics CRM Online doesn't offer you the option of dynamic worksheet or dynamic PivotTable unless the Microsoft Dynamics CRM Outlook client is installed.

Q. *How many record types can I export at once?*

A. In any Advanced Find view, there is one primary record type. You can include columns from related record types. So, you can have data from many record types displayed, but only if they relate to the primary record.

Quiz

1. What type of spreadsheet should you use for confidential information: static or dynamic?

2. For which types of export do you need to select columns in Advanced Find before clicking the Export to Excel button?

3. Why should I save the Advanced Find view I used when exporting the data?

Answers

1. A dynamic spreadsheet contains data that you have permission to view in CRM. After data is in the static spreadsheet, anyone who views it can see the data.

2. This isn't relevant for PivotTables because you have to specify where you want the data when you open the file. If you're exporting a static or dynamic worksheet, organizing your columns in advance is important only if you plan to reuse the Advanced Find search because you can always reorganize the data in Excel.

3. Saving the view lets you know what the criteria were for the records in the spreadsheet. It also makes it easier to do the same or a similar export again.

Exercise

In your Microsoft Dynamics CRM or a demo version, export contact records to Excel to do the following:

▶ Create an Advanced Find search that includes just the columns you need to create mailing labels.

▶ Create a PivotTable that you can use to analyze the city and state where your customers come from. Determine whether the percentage for each state is the same in each month.

HOUR 21

Reporting and Query Basics

What You'll Learn in This Hour:

▶ Getting started with reports
▶ Using reports
▶ Creating your own reports with the Report Wizard
▶ Sharing a report with other users
▶ Adding a file or web page as a report
▶ Creating report snapshots (On-Premises only)
▶ Tips for keeping reports organized
▶ Creating custom reports without the Report Wizard

An important part of any deployment of Microsoft Dynamics CRM is working out not only what data needs to be entered into the system but also ensuring that your system captures the right data so that you can create the required reports.

Getting Started with Reports

When we use the word *reports*, we mean formatted representations of data, with information either grouped or charted. A report is typically used for getting a quick overview of patterns in your data so that you can make a business decision or for communicating performance to other people, such as capturing end-of-quarter results.

Microsoft Dynamics CRM comes with 25 predefined reports. Depending on how much Microsoft Dynamics CRM has been customized for your organization, these reports may or may not be useful for you.

Microsoft Dynamics CRM also comes with the Report Wizard, which makes it easy to create your own reports that include charts or tables for presenting your data.

Reporting

Reporting is one area where there are significant differences between Microsoft Dynamics CRM Online and On-Premises. Several features are available only to On-Premises users, such as the following:

▶ Modifying the default reports

▶ Scheduling snapshots of reports to run at specific times

▶ Creating your own reports, using Microsoft SQL Server

▶ Using reporting services or other ODBC reporting tools and adding the reports directly to Microsoft Dynamics CRM as a report

The default reports are divided into four categories:

▶ Sixteen sales reports show information about accounts, competitors; quotes, orders, and invoices; neglected accounts and leads; sales history and pipeline; activities and product data by account or by contact.

▶ Three marketing reports show information about campaigns and lead source effectiveness.

▶ Four service reports show summaries of cases, information on neglected cases, service activity volume, and top Knowledge Base articles.

▶ One administrative report shows data on Microsoft Dynamics CRM users, such as names, titles, phone numbers, and Microsoft Dynamics CRM security roles.

By the
Way

Defaults

The default reports use the default names of record types and fields in Microsoft Dynamics CRM. Any customizations, such as renaming cases to tickets (or adding, renaming, or removing fields), will not show up in the default reports.

An important task when you're planning to use Microsoft Dynamics CRM is to evaluate the default reports and determine what additional reports are necessary.

By defining what reports you need, you'll also think through what data you need to capture. For example, if you want to track opportunities by sales stage, you have to make sure your sales process tracks sales stage.

Using Reports

To get started with reports, you need to know where to find them, the basic anatomy of a report, and which security roles can do which report-related tasks.

Finding Your Way to Microsoft Dynamics CRM Reports

There are three ways to get to reports:

▶ From the Main menu:

1. Select Workplace.

2. Click Reports.

3. Set your View to All Reports. Most of the default reports are available from this location.

▶ From a view:

1. Select the Entity View of data you are interested in.

2. Click the Reports button on the menu bar of the view for reports that are in context of the records being viewed.

   Some reports, such as Sales History, make sense only when run on all the records. Others can be run on one or a group of records.

▶ From a form or specific record:

1. Select the entity of data you are interested in.

2. Specifically select one record and display the form.

3. Click the Reports button on the menu bar of the record for reports that make sense for the current record.

Figure 21.1 shows the options you get when you click the Reports button in the Active Accounts view. Only reports that make sense for accounts are displayed.

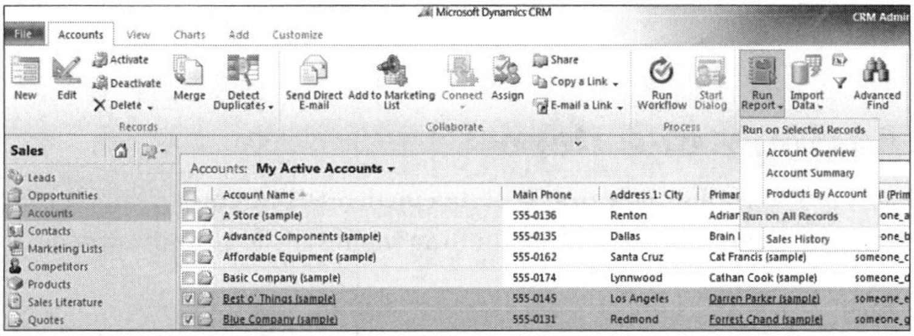

FIGURE 21.1
The reports menu, shown from a list of account records, with two accounts selected.

You are offered a choice of how to run the report, as shown in Figure 21.2.

When you select The Selected Records, the report will run on just the two records you highlighted. Click Run Report to see the results.

Figure 21.3 shows the Run Report menu from within a record. When you select a report this way, the report is run just on the open record.

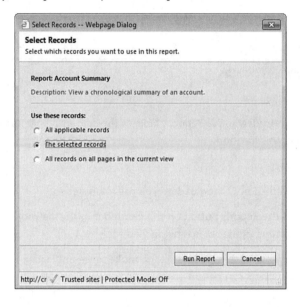

The Anatomy of a Report

Each report has a default filter that contains predefined criteria for which records to include. Typical default filters include limiting the results to records owned by you or to records modified in the past 30 days.

When you run a report, the Report Filtering Criteria screen is displayed before you see any data so that you can modify the filter. This lets you change the filter every time you run a report. The less data that is in a report, the faster it will run, so you should use the filtering criteria to limit the data to just what you need to see.

The report filter uses the same user interface as Advanced Find. For each criteria row, you enter a field name, an operator, and a value. Figure 21.4 shows a typical default filter, specifying records that have been modified in the past 30 days.

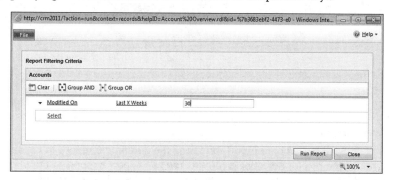

FIGURE 21.4
The Report
Filtering Criteria
screen.

After you run a report, it's helpful to know the filtering criteria used to generate the report. This is handy before printing the report because it ensures that when you look at the printout later, you can still tell what's included. Figure 21.5 shows the summary for the previous filter.

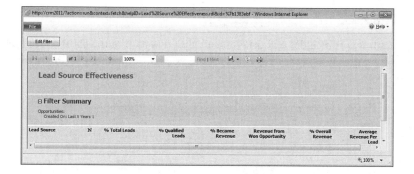

FIGURE 21.5
An expanded fil-
ter summary.

If the default filter doesn't match how everyone in your organization typically uses a report, your system administrator or system customizer can change the default filter.

Navigating in a Default Report

Most of the navigation to explore a report is at the top of the page, including buttons to page through the report and a search box to search for data in the report.

Many reports have grouping or display options at the top. When you run a report, the default grouping or display option will be used. You can select another option and click View Report to refresh it. Figure 21.6 shows these options for the Account Summary report.

FIGURE 21.6
Grouping and
display options.

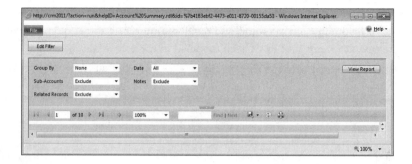

No Save Button

There is no Save button on a report for saving the data in the report. In Figure
21.6, notice the box for selecting a format. You can export a report to other formats, such as PDF and web archive, and save these files. These formats are useful for capturing specific results at a specific time period.

Exporting from a report to Excel exports a formatted report. This is typically not useful for analyzing data with Excel.

Viewing Data in a Default Report

If a default report includes a chart, you can click a section of the chart to see the
data behind the chart section. Figure 21.7 shows a chart produced by the Activities
report.

FIGURE 21.7
A chart pro-
duced by the
Activities
report.

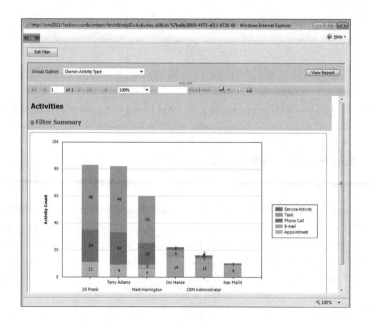

To see all the data used in the chart, you click Show All at the bottom of the chart. There is no easy way to get back to the chart; to do so, you need to rerun the report.

In the table of data, you can click any record to go right to the full record in Microsoft Dynamics CRM.

Who Can Do What with Reports?

Several permissions control who can do report-related tasks. These are defined in the Microsoft Dynamics CRM security roles:

▶ All default security roles give all users permission to run reports. When a person views a report, she can see only data on records that she has permission to view.

▶ All default security roles give all users permission to use the Report Wizard to create new reports for their own use.

Report Layout

Report users cannot change the layout of reports. The orientation, page size, font, and contents of reports are predefined.

Organizations that use the On-Premises version of Microsoft Dynamics CRM can have a system customizer modify these aspects of default reports, but the layout cannot be modified for reports created using the Report Wizard.

By the Way

▶ Most default security roles do not have permission to make reporting changes for all users at a company, such as adding a report for all users, renaming reports, or changing the default filter for default reports.

There are two types of reports:

▶ *Organization-owned reports* are visible to all the Microsoft Dynamics CRM users in your organization. All the default reports are, by default, organization owned.

▶ *Individual-owned reports* are visible just to the owners of the reports. As with other records in Microsoft Dynamics CRM, the owner can share individual-owned reports with specific users or teams.

Properties of a Report

Each report is stored as a record in Microsoft Dynamics CRM and has properties that define how it can be used. If you plan to add reports using the Report Wizard, you use these properties to hook up your report to the user interface so that you can run it from where you want.

First, let's look at the General tab (see Figure 21.8) for the Account Overview report.

FIGURE 21.8
The General
tab.

The Source area defines the source for the report. There are three options: Existing File, Link to a Web Page, and Report Wizard Report.

The Details area provides a name and description.

The third area, Parent Report, is used by only some default reports and by report customizers using On-Premises installations of Microsoft Dynamics CRM. Some complex reports have subreports, and this field keeps a subreport and parent report connected.

The most interesting area is the Categorization area. This is where you determine where in the user interface a report will be visible:

▶ You can select which forms and lists should include the new report on the Reports menu. If you put a value in Related Record Types, the report will be available on the Reports menu in that area of Microsoft Dynamics CRM.

▶ The Display In selection controls whether the reports are available in forms, records, or the main reports list. In Figure 21.8, the report will show up in the Reports area, on the Report menu in the Accounts area, and in the Report menu on an account form.

The Administration tab defines ownership settings for the report (see Figure 21.9). If you create a great report that everyone might benefit from, you can ask your system administrator or system customizer to make it organization owned.

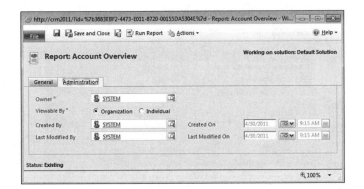

FIGURE 21.9
The Administration tab.

Creating Your Own Reports with the Report Wizard

It's late, and you are just about to head out the office and go home when your manager opens your door and asks you to create a quick report. Thanks to the Report Wizard, you can create a quick report and still make it home in time for dinner.

The Report Wizard lets you create charts and tables that summarize your data. In this example, you'll use the wizard to create a chart of opportunities by state.

To start the wizard:

1. Move to the Reports area.

2. Click New.

3. Choose to run the Report Wizard.

On the first page of the wizard (see Figure 21.10), select Start a New Report.

You can also use the wizard to modify a report that was created with the Report Wizard.

Default Report Exception

You cannot use the Report Wizard to modify a default report.

Watch
Out!

FIGURE 21.10
The Get Started page of the Report Wizard.

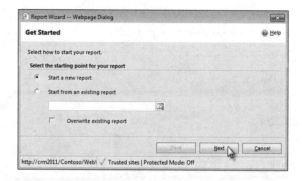

On the next page of the wizard, after specifying a name and description, you select which records to include in the report (see Figure 21.11). For this example, you can use the Opportunities record type.

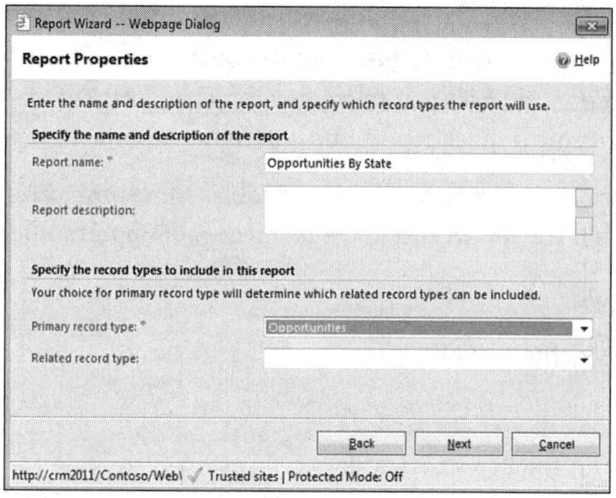

FIGURE 21.11
Specifying the record types to include in a report generated by the Report Wizard.

The next page of the wizard (see Figure 21.12) prompts you to define the default filter for the report. In this case, added a filter for opportunities that close in the next six months.

The next page, Layout Fields, is the most important page of the Report Wizard. This is where you select what data to put in your report and how to organize the data. The first step is deciding the big buckets for the report: how to group the information. Figure 21.13 shows grouping the report by state.

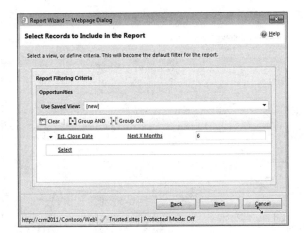

FIGURE 21.12
Selecting
records to
include in a
report generat-
ed by the
Report Wizard.

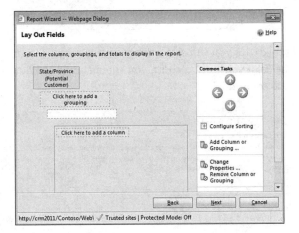

FIGURE 21.13
Selecting group-
ing and specify-
ing columns.

As part of selecting the field to group the records by, you can also select the proper-ties for the grouping. A shown in Figure 21.14, you can specify an ascending sort order and that you want to see a count of records in each group.

Then you need to select the fields to display in the report.

Numeric Field Needed

If you want to create a graph or chart, you need a field that is numeric, and you need to select a summary option for it. Otherwise, the Report Wizard creates only a tabular-format report.

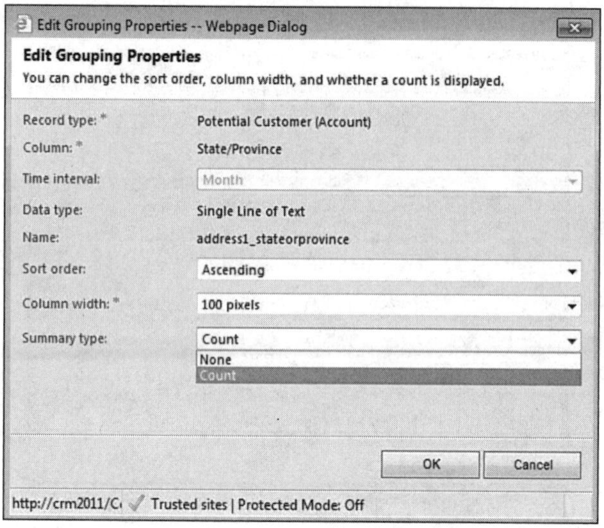

FIGURE 21.14
Defining the
group proper-
ties.

As shown in Figure 21.15, you can select the potential customer name and the estimated revenue fields. If you want a chart, you should group the data in the
Estimated Revenue column.

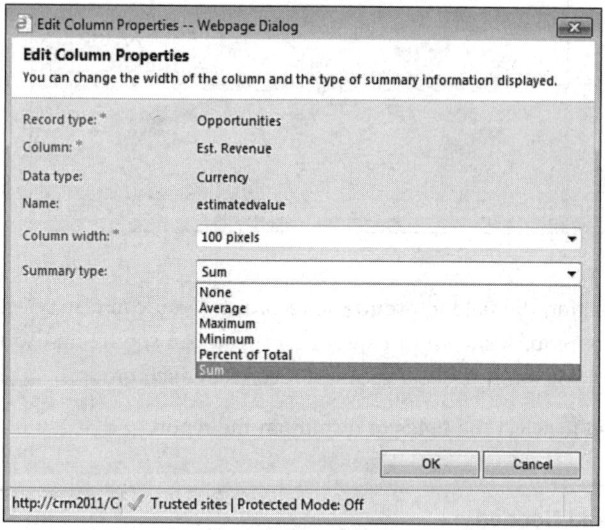

FIGURE 21.15
Defining the
properties for a
column.

Figure 21.16 shows the completed Lay Out Fields page with one level of grouping
and two columns in the report.

After you set the grouping and fields for the report, the remaining wizard choices
are straightforward: defining whether you want a chart in the report, and if so,
defining the text for the axes for the report.

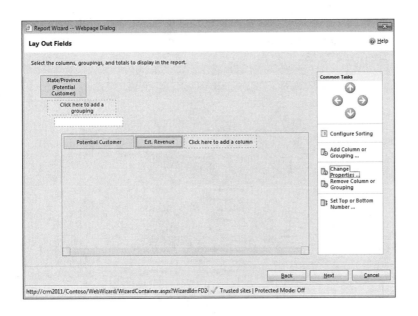

FIGURE 21.16
The completed
specification
for the report
layout.

When you complete the wizard, you can run the report to see the results. If you
selected to create a chart, the chart is on the first page, and the table is on the second page.

Figure 21.17 shows the Opportunities by State report just created.

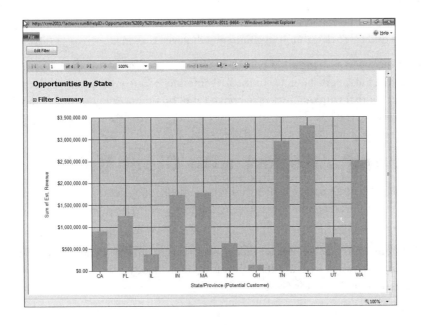

FIGURE 21.17
Page 1 of the
Opportunities
by State report
created with
the Report
Wizard.

Note that charts created with the Report Wizard do not let you drill down to see the table behind the chart. Instead, you must go to the next page of the report to see the details (see Figure 21.18).

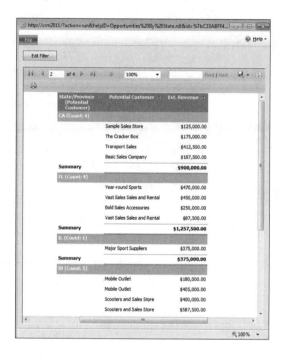

If you don't get a report exactly right on the first try, you can just restart the Report Wizard and go back through it, changing whatever is needed.

When the report is doing what you expect it to do, you can define the properties to make sure the report shows up in the user interface where you need it. If you want, you can share it with other users or convert it to an organization-owned report so that everyone can use it.

Sharing a Report with Other Users

To share with other users a report that you created, you select the Sharing option on the More Actions menu and then specify the teams or users who need to use this report (see Figure 21.19).

When a report is created, it is set up either as an individually owned report or as an organization-owned report. If the report is an individually owned report, it can only be seen and run by that individual or by the people that individual shares it with.

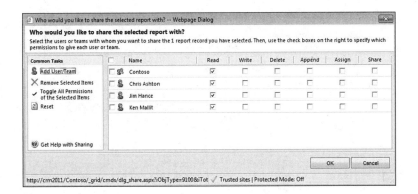

FIGURE 21.19
Sharing a
report.

Adding a File or Web Page as a Report

You can add any type of file as a report and make it available to users through the Microsoft Dynamics CRM user interface. This helps users stay within the Microsoft Dynamics CRM application.

From the Reports area, you click New. In the Report Type box, you click Existing File (see Figure 21.20).

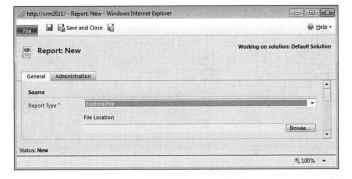

FIGURE 21.20
Adding an
existing file.

For Microsoft Dynamics CRM Online, you can add static files and dynamic Excel files that read data from the Microsoft Dynamics CRM database.

For On-Premises versions, you can add any type of dynamic files that read data directly from the Microsoft Dynamics CRM database, including custom reports.

To add a link to a web page as a report, you click Link to Web page. Notice in Figure 21.21 that the next box changes, giving you a place to specify the URL of the page.

You need to set the rest of the properties to specify where in the user interface this new web page or file should be displayed. For example, suppose you create a dynamic Excel PivotTable to help analyze data related to large accounts. Figure 21.22 shows the Display In options necessary to view this report.

FIGURE 21.21
Linking to a
web page.

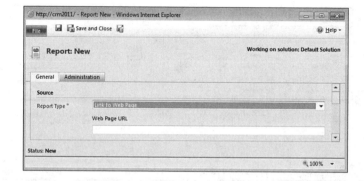

FIGURE 21.22
Specifying
where the new
report will be
visible.

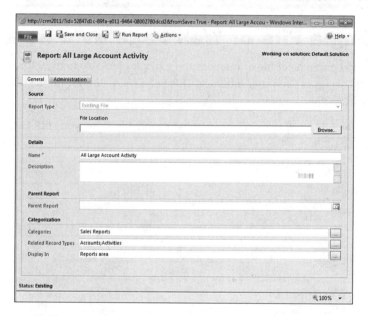

What Reports Do You See?

Each person who opens a report sees data that matches records that she has
permission to view in Microsoft Dynamics CRM. For example, you may be able to
see only data for accounts that are owned by you, but your manager may be able
to see data for accounts owned by everyone in your group.

After you save the new report, the Actions menu will be available (see Figure 21.23).
Depending on your security role, you may see either Sharing or Make Report
Available to Organization—or you might see both—and you can make the web page
or file you added available to those who need it.

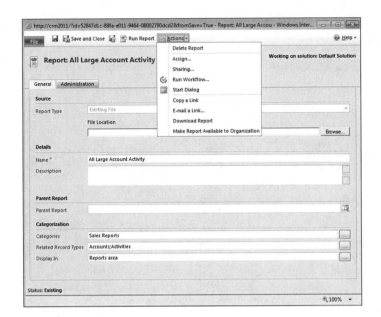

FIGURE 21.23
The Actions menu for a report.

Creating Report Snapshots (On-Premises Only)

Report snapshots let you save the data in a report at a particular moment in time. This is useful for measuring end-of-time-period results. Snapshots can be run on demand or scheduled to run regularly. Figure 21.24 shows the page for scheduling the frequency for creating a snapshot of the Account Distribution report.

The Report Scheduling Wizard shows up on the ribbon of the Report menu, and you can edit its properties to determine where it is available.

Scheduled Reports

Scheduled reports are individually owned by default. If you need them to be visible to other users, be sure to share them or change them to organization owned.

By the Way

Scheduled reports can be set up to be e-mailed to other people. You must set this up in Microsoft SQL Server Reporting Services. For more information on reporting, see the Microsoft Dynamics CRM Team Blog, at http://ow.ly/72H9i.

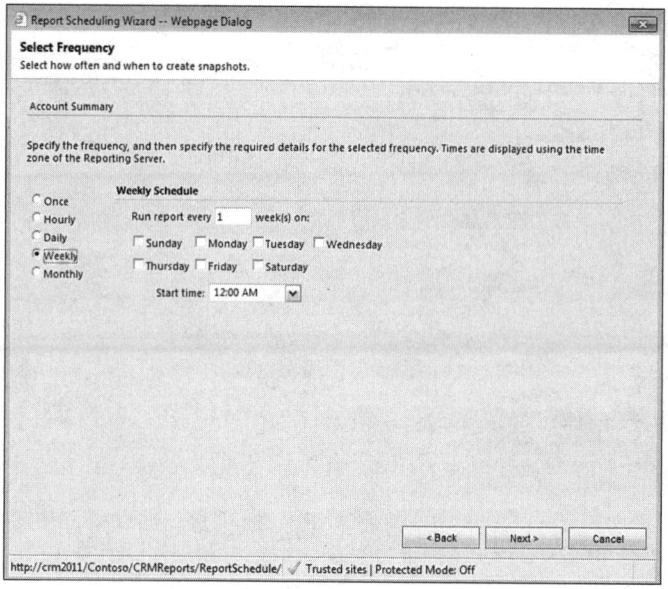

FIGURE 21.24
The Report
Scheduling
Wizard.

FIGURE 21.24
The Report
Scheduling
Wizard.

Tips for Keeping Reports Organized

If your organization does a lot of custom reporting, whether with the Report Wizard or other tools, the list of records in the Reports area can get large. Default views are set up for four categories of reports: Sales, Marketing, Service, and Administration. You can customize these categories for your organization.

Click Settings and then click System Settings. The Report tab provides a place to define and organize the categories (see Figure 21.25).

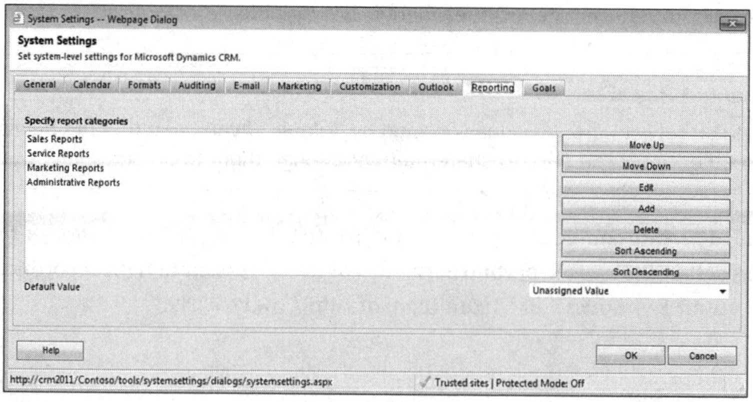

FIGURE 21.25
Defining categories for organizing reports.

After the categories are modified, there are two more steps:

1. For each report, set the values in the Categories field.

2. Customize the views for the Report entity to use the new category names.

Creating Custom Reports Without the Report Wizard

You can create custom reports, such as dashboards, reports with other layouts, or reports with more complex drill-downs into the data reports.

Microsoft Dynamics CRM provides filtered views that make it easy for report writers to use the Microsoft Dynamics security roles. Therefore, even custom reports only show data that a user has permission to see. However, creating custom reports requires a more technical skill set than using the Report Wizard. (Many solution providers specialize in creating custom reports.)

Custom Reports in Microsoft Dynamics CRM On-Premises

For Microsoft Dynamics CRM On-Premises, if you need custom reports beyond what the Report Wizard can create, anyone with the System Customizer or System Administrator security role can modify the default reports or create new reports and upload them to Microsoft Dynamics CRM.

Because the default reports are written using Microsoft SQL Reporting Services, modifying them requires the following report-development environment:

▶ Microsoft Visual Studio or any product that uses the Visual Studio .NET integrated development environment, such as Microsoft Visual Basic .NET

▶ The Microsoft SQL Reporting Services Report Designer

Modifying default reports is usually done by someone who specializes in report design or a programmer, not by a regular user. This is an area where a solution provider can come in handy.

New reports can also be created in any ODBC-compliant application, including Microsoft Access, Microsoft Excel, Microsoft SQL Server Reporting Services, and a wide range of business intelligence tools. These new reports can be added as new reports.

Custom Reports in Microsoft Dynamics CRM Online

For Microsoft Dynamics CRM Online, there are several options for custom reports, each of which requires developer and or report-writing skills:

▶ If you subscribe to Microsoft Dynamics CRM 2011 Online, you can use offline data synchronization to synchronize data locally. Then, you can use any ODBC-compliant tool to write reports against the local data store.

▶ You can use an integration tool to integrate Microsoft Dynamics CRM data with a local database and write reports based on the local data.

▶ You can use the Microsoft Dynamics CRM Software Development Kit (SDK) to develop a custom .NET application. This is usually done by experienced developers or solution providers.

▶ You can use Microsoft Business Intelligence Development Studio (BIDS) and connect to Microsoft Dynamics CRM 2011 Online as it is available to the report-writing tool via the CRM web service. This process is detailed on the Microsoft Developer Network blog at http://ow.ly/72Hhq.

Hours 22, "Integrating Microsoft Dynamics CRM 2011 into Other Applications," and 24, "Microsoft Dynamics CRM as a Development Framework," go into more details about options for extending Microsoft Dynamics CRM.

Workshop

Joyous Fitness is a chain of exercise studios that uses Microsoft Dynamics CRM Online to track members and class attendees. It has made some customizations to Microsoft Dynamics CRM, renaming the Accounts entity to Members and editing the values of all the drop-down lists to match its terminology. It uses the Product entity to track memberships and has created a new entity to track class attendance.

The studio uses the Marketing module of Microsoft Dynamics CRM as is to track mailings to customers and radio advertisements.

Q&A

Q. *We do not use the Service module in Microsoft Dynamics CRM. Can we make it so that those reports are not visible?*

A. Yes. Anyone with the System Administrator or System Customizer security role can modify the properties for those reports and change them so that they are not displayed.

Q. *Can we rename the default reports and change the default filters?*

A. Yes. These changes can be made in both Microsoft Dynamics CRM Online and the On-Premises version.

Q. *Will the default reports work for us, or do we have to create our own?*

A. Because Joyous Fitness is using the Microsoft Dynamics CRM Marketing module without customization, the marketing default reports will work. The sales reports will also work as is, although renaming the reports to use the word Member versus Account would make it easier for employees to identify the proper report.
There are some custom reports that are needed for class attendance. These can be created using the Report Wizard or by exporting data to Microsoft Excel.

Q. *Do we need to hire someone to write these custom reports, or can we do them ourselves?*

A. You can use the Report Wizard or Microsoft Excel to generate the reports, so no special knowledge or expertise is required.

Quiz

1. When I share a report with my manager, why does she see different numbers than I do?

2. What's the best way to save a report that captures data for a specific time period?

3. Are there any best practices I should follow when I create new reports?

4. How many record types can be included in a Report Wizard report?

5. Can I change the layout of a report?

Answers

1. Each person who opens a report sees data that matches records that he or she has permission to view in Microsoft Dynamics CRM. For example, you may only be able to see data for accounts that are owned by you, but your manager may be able to see data for accounts owned by everyone in your group.

2. Run the report and export it to a format, such as PDF, that can be easily archived. In the On-Premises versions, the report can be scheduled to run at the end of a time period and can be stored as a snapshot in Microsoft Dynamics CRM. Because the number of snapshots that can be saved for a report is limited, you'll also want to export the snapshots.

3. Because a report will take longer to run if it includes large numbers of records, default filters are recommended for every report.

4. In an On-Premises version, if you have a report that runs on large data sets, you can use the Report Scheduling Wizard to run it at times when the system is not heavily loaded.

5. When you create a report, you select the two main record types to include in the report. Because data from related record types can be included, you can pull in information from other record types, too.

Regular users cannot change the layout of a report. The layout of reports is fixed. If you are using Microsoft Dynamics CRM On-Premises, a person with a full report development environment and the appropriate security role can change the layout of the default reports.

If you need complete layout flexibility, you can create your report in Excel.

Exercise

To do the basic setup required for Joyous Fitness, complete these steps:

1. Rename all account reports to use the terminology used by the organization.

2. Create a new report using the Report Wizard that shows campaign responses grouped by campaign and sorted by zip code.

3. Modify the properties for the service reports so that they do not show up in the reports list.

Integrating Microsoft Dynamics CRM 2011 into Other Applications

---

What You'll Learn in This Hour:

▶ Bridge software
▶ Points of connect
▶ Integrating Microsoft Dynamics CRM with external web sources
▶ Integrating Microsoft Dynamics CRM into accounting applications
▶ Integration-independent software vendors
▶ Integration risks
▶ Data migration

This lesson looks at options and places to integrate Microsoft Dynamics CRM with other applications and how to best work with third-party independent software vendors (ISVs) and their offerings. This lesson also focuses on integrating with some commonly available tools and using these tools to support data migrations.

Bridge Software

In between any two applications, there might be another application or service that translates information from one database to the next, from one application to the next, from one method to the next, from one service to the next, or from one user interface to the next. As we integrate, extend, and expand Microsoft Dynamics CRM into environments where other software applications already reside and where integration is needed, we are faced with differences between designs and database structure.

How should we approach this situation? There is an option to write custom software to tie multiple applications together, but this can be time-consuming and error-prone, and it can require a long-term investment in updates and upgrades. Luckily, we have another option.

This is where bridge, integration, middleware, or enterprise application integration (EAI) software comes into play. A bridge software application offers a framework to support technology and business rules as data is translated between environments. Software and technologies in this space support the creation of accurate, consistent, and transparent information flows between different systems.

Given that Microsoft Dynamics CRM is built to connect, it is a great application to drop into the technology space of integration and bridge software.

Points of Connect

Microsoft Dynamics CRM has many different places where other applications can connect, but a few common points are as follows:

▶ Importing or synchronizing leads, accounts, or contact details from a web page

▶ Sharing accounting-oriented information, such as quotes, orders, and products, with a back-office accounting application

▶ Synchronizing account-specific financial information, such as invoice history, credit holds, and credit limits, with an accounting application.

▶ Updating internal Microsoft Dynamics CRM data from industry-standard information sources, such as Hoover's, OneSource, Harte Hanks, and others.

▶ Augmenting contact and account information with social media systems such as Facebook, LinkedIn, and Twitter.

Each of these connection points has a number of different solution, design, and architectural approach options.

The following sections cover a couple of these points as they relate to the ISV offerings. For more detailed information about the ISV offerings, set aside an hour to listen in on one or more of the many vendor webinars available and ask questions; it is worth the time investment if connecting Microsoft Dynamics CRM to other applications is a business requirement.

Integrating Microsoft Dynamics CRM with External Web Sources

Extra external software is not necessarily needed to integrate Microsoft Dynamics CRM with an externally facing environment. However, the extra software can offer quick configuration for resolving business rules and regulations. It can also offer a quick ramp-up and a space for a layer of validation.

Take, for instance, a need to filter out leads that have a name of Donald Duck or the need to validate and protect against data changes that impact existing information negatively. You might also have an interest in interacting with users who are not authenticated users of your CRM system prior to offering them access to change anything in your Microsoft Dynamics CRM environment.

Data can be cleansed through website application software or through a piece of middleware software that sits between Microsoft Dynamics CRM and the externally facing website. Search and business rules that look for special characters or for commonly used bogus accounts can be added to this middleware layer, and business validation and external interaction can also be a feature.

Now, shift gears and think about the more trusted audience, perhaps with a customer portal: a website that empowers customers to reduce the need to pick up the phone or to send e-mail when they have a problem or question, a customer portal site that offers a subset of information for validation and updating, or a site that offers the ability to submit and review the status of support cases. Also consider software that takes Microsoft Dynamics CRM data and displays it and that captures data and then turns around and updates Microsoft Dynamics CRM.

There are more reasons to share data with an externally facing website or an internal intranet that might be disconnected from the project, but the key point is that in the past, this was always limited to extensive and expensive custom solutions. This is not the case with Microsoft Dynamics CRM and the supported offerings from the vendor community.

Microsoft offers two free options for getting a website integrated with Microsoft Dynamics CRM to bring leads into CRM. First is the Customer Care Accelerato. This is a free application solution available on the Microsoft CodePlex website (http://pinpoint.microsoft.com/en-us/applications/customer-care-accelerator-for-microsoft-dynamics-crm-2011-12884914795). This application is a customer/partner portal starter kit. In addition, with Microsoft Dynamics CRM Online 2011, you will receive a free CRM web landing page to CRM sales leads.

There is also a specific application that integrates a website into any object in CRM. It is called Web2CRM from CRM Innovation (see http://crminnovation.com/web2crm.asp). This application supports Microsoft Dynamics CRM Online and On-Premises. It lets you build a web form based on the objects in your CRM system quickly and easily. It reads the metadata from Microsoft Dynamics CRM and then builds a form. CRM Innovation hosts the code and lets you carry the HTML to your website. From there, a visitor fills out the form on your website, and his or her applications push the data into your CRM system.

Integrating Microsoft Dynamics CRM into Accounting Applications

Integration of Microsoft Dynamics CRM into accounting applications has technical and business culture contexts.

Business Context

Quite often there is a cultural difference between the needs of the accounting or finance department and the needs of all the other departments in a company. A common request and resistance is to open up access to an accounting application to the entire firm. Opening the accounting data access and the ability to modify this data to the entire firm can seriously compromise auditing and financial controls built into business processes within a company. What is really needed is visibility to a subset of key accounting data for those people who require certain parts of it. This includes the sales team working with prospects and existing clients who need financial history to qualify leads and the service team working with existing customers who can use cutting off service to increase collections for those looking for support.

A salesperson can be empowered to do quotes and take orders, but there are many companies that then cross-reference and check those incoming orders when invoicing occurs.

This is the same for service. Service contracts can be sold, and hours and tickets against those contracts can be used, but generally, the invoicing remains in the finance role.

Technical Context

When setting technical context, it is all about what data needs to be accessed by what department and what people. It is also about what the business processes are around the data and the timing and flow of data between perhaps two or three different applications.

It is not uncommon to have numerous salespeople entering orders and even doing invoicing, but the items often show up in a queue or batch for accounting to manage.

There is always choice, allowing for defining a business process that matches the technology functionality that is offered. In this case, we can setup integration to be either a batch or real time process.

Many companies might decide that real-time data from all the teams is not an issue and the ultimate control will be managed through balancing finances.

A middleware application can handle either real time or batch processing and is an application that translates data coming from Microsoft Dynamics CRM into a format that the accounting software is expecting

Now that we have a general idea of where middleware, integration, or bridge software might fit, the following sections looks at specific options and solutions in this space.

Integration-Independent Software Vendors

There are a number of ISVs in the integration, middleware, data tools, and bridge software space, and there are a number of Microsoft Partners specializing in Microsoft Dynamics CRM who have done numerous custom integration projects. I list a few of the ISVs whose names come up more than once in the Microsoft Dynamics CRM community. Please note that while these ISVs are in business at the time of writing, this may change over time.

The first sets of ISVs offer more options when it comes to integrating many different applications. ISVs that cover a wide variety of different database applications include the following:

- ▶ Scribe (www.scribesoft.com) offers the Scribe Insight product suite. With more than 12,000 customers, this application has become the most widely supported integration platform for Dynamics CRM. It offers integration templates for CRM to GP, AX, NAV, and SL. (See www.scribesoft.com/DynamicsIntegration.asp.)

- ▶ Pervasive Software (www.pervasivesoftware.com) offers the Pervasive Data integrator (www.pervasiveintegration.com/data_connectors/Pages/microsoft_dynamics_integration.aspx).

▶ Microsoft BizTalk (www.microsoft.com/biztalk/en/us/default.aspx) offers the Microsoft BizTalk CRM adapter. This is a highly complex but very robust integration that is very popular in the enterprise space. If considering this solution, one needs to ensure that there is a sufficient plan to manage the ongoing maintenance of the integration as the tool is focused on developers and code-based solutions. (See www.microsoft.com/downloads/details.aspx?familyid=ABD3BB9E-A59A-4EB6-8DE8-FB25B77926D7&displaylang=en.)

▶ Inaplex (www.inaplex.com/Products/Inaport-for-Microsoft-CRM.aspx) is a veteran player in the integration space. It provides connectors for various platforms and allows one to build both migration and integration solutions.

▶ Keelio Software (www.keelio.com/Home/tabid/36/Default.aspx) offers the Dynamics GP SSIS Toolkit and XML SSIS Toolkit (www.keelio.com/Products/tabid/87/Default.aspx).

The following ISVs are vendors with a strong focus on Dynamics GP and who generally have a Dynamics GP background. They focus on application integration with Dynamics GP and have Dynamics CRM–to–Dynamics GP offerings:

▶ eOne (www.eonesolutions.com.au) offers the SmartConnect products (www.eonesolutions.com.au/Content.aspx?page=SmartConnect).

▶ Nolan (www.nolancomputers.co.uk/dynamics/Home.aspx) offers the integration bridge.

There are so many different ways to provide the functionality that you almost need a specialist in the integration space to help translate. If you choose to work with any of these listed vendors and their partners, you will want to get direct information from the involved parties. Here are a few areas and questions that you might want to focus on and areas for deeper consideration:

▶ How have the individual ISVs architected their solutions? Are they talking directly to the various databases? Are they using web services? Do they have a database in the middle that needs to be monitored?

▶ When was the last update released? What did it include? Is the ISV using modern tools or antiquated solutions? Microsoft Dynamics CRM has had numerous releases and design updates over the past six years; has the ISV kept pace?

▶ How are translations handled, such as when data in one database does not map directly to data in the other database? What about when field lengths are different? Is data truncated?

- What are the performance benchmarks for customers using the solution in an environment similar to your own? Performance is unique to each individual environment and is impacted by numerous variables; however, it is worth asking any references about performance concerns they have had.

- How are errors handled? This includes data errors such as one of the databases dropping offline in the middle of processing and business errors, such as a user conflict or a conflict between data entered in two different systems at the same time and the data integration toolkit needing to know which data source takes priority or is an authoritative source.

- How is the solution supported once it is up and running in your organization? Who do you call when you have a problem? If you are working with a partner, is there a backup in case something happens? Is it a solution that another partner or the vendor can support if needed?

We have talked a little bit about your options around ongoing data integration. Now let's look into the world of data migration. Data migration is generally considered an occasional or one-time event.

Integration Risks

When integrating to other systems there is an area that is easy to forget. What happens when the experts you are depending on forget to tell you about functions, rules, business processes, and data within the system you are integrating to?

This is a clear risk area, particularly if your integration is passing data between two systems. Data updated in one system will update the data in the other system and vice versa. The business rules that apply to the system you are integrating to often have to be honored in the new system being built and yet are not always captured as new requirements.

Another area to consider is the quality of data. A task to do some data scrubbing, such as running addresses through a validation process, can significantly reduce the risks that you can face when integrating to other systems.

By the Way

Recommendation

When testing integration, start with a small set of data in a fixed time period before you turn on the flood gates.

Data Migration

Data migration is a world of risk, intrigue, housecleaning, and discovery. You really never know all that you will run into.

Being Realistic About Data Migration
Don't underestimate the time needed or cost of data migrations.

There are also a number of assumptions surrounding data migration. So, if you are a technical person reading this, you should ask a ton of questions and have solid deliverables and a change management process in place. If you are a businessperson reading this, you should understand that data migration can be very complex.

When you are starting with Microsoft Dynamics CRM and considering data migration, you should take a good look at the actual data you want to migrate and convert. You also want to weigh whether it is worth it to migrate the data or if there is perhaps a different option.

CRM Adoption Success
A solid and well-done data migration can make a *huge* difference in how an audience of users feels about the Microsoft Dynamics CRM software moving forward and how they react to the challenge of adoption.

Many firms burden their users with data entry and the task of learning new software. Perhaps they think that users need the excuse to practice with the system and clean their contact details or perhaps there is no other way. In any case, it is difficult to learn a new system and have to do excessive data entry at the same time—all, of course, while keeping up with the tasks of the job! The investment in data migration is worthwhile, even if you save dollars in other ways, such as by migrating only account and contact data or only migrating data from the past six months and leaning on the old system for historical reference. If you have no other choice, the investment in some temporary help can also make a significant difference.

There are different tools available for data migrations that offer different functionality that might not be required when importing a list of contacts or leads.

It is also recommended that you consult with a Microsoft partner who is experienced with data migrations before moving forward, particularly if you are trying to convert from an existing line-of-business application with a database on the back end or from an existing customer relationship management software application that might have data organized differently.

If you do move forward with your own data migration, Microsoft offers a couple different options. Microsoft offers two tools for data import into Microsoft Dynamics CRM: the Import Wizard and the Data Migration Manager (DMM) (in version 4.0 only). Partners have also been known to build their own tools or to use mastery in third-party tools to handle more complex migrations.

The Import Wizard

The Microsoft Dynamics CRM Import Wizard is designed to import a list of fairly structured, flat data. It can be used with a simple list of contacts or a separate list of accounts. It is recommended that if you are going to do a data import, you should separate data into logical groups, such as contacts, accounts, and so on. It is also a good idea to set up a test file of perhaps 10 records and import that until you are comfortable with the data format and your import design.

> **Import Wizard**
>
> The Import Wizard is not designed to do full data migrations with multiple layers of data from different places. For full data migrations, there are other, better-fitting tools to handle some of the complex business rules that apply when moving data from one CRM system to another.

Watch Out!

The DMM

The DMM works on the basis of data maps that define a mapping between the source data schema and the Microsoft Dynamics CRM data schema. This application is now only available in version 4.0, as much of the logic is not incorporated into the Import Wizard function in Microsoft Dynamics CRM 2011. The data map is the core building block of the DMM. In general, a data map is an XML structured file built out of entities used for data mapping during data migration. There are some of the key differences between the DMM and the Import Wizard built into Microsoft Dynamics CRM.

The DMM can do the following:

▶ Import multiple files and work with relational data sets

▶ Maintain the owner of the imported record

▶ Maintain the original creation date, supporting historical context

▶ Import record status and status reasons, such as active and inactive

▶ Create custom entities during the import process (*not recommended*)

▶ Run a batch deletion to delete records that were imported

> **Deleting Imported Records**
> Import can also delete imported records.

The Microsoft DMM is a powerful tool that is worth examining if you currently do not have a solution for data migrations.

The following are a few practical tips to keep in mind about the DMM:

- ▶ It must be run by someone with the System Administrator security role.
- ▶ It must be installed on a separate computer from the CRM Application Server.
- ▶ It includes tools for transforming data as part of the process.
- ▶ It has a wizard interface to guide you through it, although more complex migrations can be done by directly editing the data map.

Microsoft Connector for Microsoft Dynamics

Connector for Microsoft Dynamics is a free integration solution that is targeted specifically at the Microsoft Dynamics product family. Connector provides an out-of-the-box integration between Dynamics CRM and Dynamics ERP solutions. It is an SDK-based model, which in theory allows for extending the integration to other platforms. It is not available to customers directly and must be sourced from ERP partners. This is a new solution that Microsoft introduced in 2010. It was a complete rewrite of the initial BizTalk. Microsoft has made significant investments in making this a supportable and extensible integration across the ERP platforms it develops (see http://blogs.msdn.com/b/dynamicsconnector/).

Workshop

Silver Lining Steel Manufacturing has been using Microsoft Dynamics CRM for two years. It first rolled out the solution to its sales department, with plans to further expand into the solution as it learned more about the product and after it switched the accounting software application. The company has now moved to Microsoft Dynamics NAV and is looking at integrating its Microsoft Dynamics CRM solution to the new Microsoft Dynamics NAV accounting software. It plans to share the details of the client accounts receivable history with the sales team, and it will be empowering the sales team to convert quotes directly into orders, as appropriate, which will then show up as unprocessed orders in Dynamics NAV.

Q&A

Q. *Our small firm is considering doing its own data migration. We hoped to have each salesperson enter his or her own leads, but this lesson indicates that this might not be a good idea. Why is this so?*

A. It makes sense to encourage your salespeople to enter 2 to 10 of their own leads to get the hang of the software, but entering 50 to 200 leads is a poor use of valuable sales energy.

Q. *We want to migrate all our data from Sage ACT!, including e-mail. Are any of these tools a perfect fit for that task?*

A. The best tool for migrating ACT!, including e-mail, is one of the experienced partners with custom solutions for handling ACT! e-mails or an application built for the specific need. ACT! e-mail storage is difficult to migrate.

Q. *We are integrating Microsoft Dynamics CRM with Microsoft Dynamics GP, and our partner recommends Scribe Software. Is there a similar package we can look at for comparison?*

A. You might want to look at eOne Software, http://www.eonesolutions.com/. It specializes in Microsoft Dynamics GP and competes with Scribe.

Quiz

1. What are two common places that people connect Microsoft Dynamics CRM with other applications?

2. Identify two ISVs that offer solutions in the integration and middleware software space.

3. Would using the Data Import Wizard that is built into Microsoft Dynamics CRM be a good choice for a data migration?

Answers

1. Synchronizing leads and sharing accounting information are two common places that people connect Microsoft Dynamics CRM with other applications.

2. Scribe and Microsoft Connection are two ISVs that offer solutions in the integration and middleware software space.

3. No. There are better tools for data migration.

Exercise

1. What are some of the key variables that Silver Lining Steel Manufacturing needs to consider as it looks to integrate its solutions?

2. Given that it is integrating Microsoft Dynamics CRM with Microsoft Dynamics NAV, which three vendors should the company talk with about possible solutions?

3. Does Silver Lining Steel manufacturing need to consider data migration?

HOUR 23

Microsoft Dynamics CRM Tools and Utilities

What You'll Learn in This Hour:

▶ Enhancing contact information
▶ Business intelligence in Microsoft Dynamics CRM
▶ Enabling Microsoft Dynamics CRM for mobile devices
▶ Database tools and utilities
▶ Compliance and auditing tools

In this lesson, we examine specific tools and utilities that increase your productivity with Microsoft Dynamics CRM. Part of the power of Microsoft Dynamics CRM is the number of ways it can be expanded, enhanced, customized, and upgraded. From simple informational tools that retrieve additional contact information online, to tools that help build reports, to database performance enhancements—if there is a tool that you are looking for, chances are it can be found and integrated into your Microsoft Dynamics CRM system.

Enhancing Contact Information

With Microsoft Dynamics CRM's extensible interface, there have been many solutions built to enhance the functionality around accounts, contacts, leads, and opportunities. There are tools such as enhanced e-mail solutions that streamline Microsoft Dynamics CRM processes and bridge the gaps in functionality. In addition, tools can be used to augment the existing information you have in your database, such as connections to online databases of contacts (for example, Hoover's, HarteHanks, InsideView). The current tools are impressive, and the industry is dynamic. A passion for discovering and adopting new trends, new searchable data, new technologies, and changes in traditional business process, such as social marketing and online networks, can extend the business value and adoption rate of your CRM application, and an expansive offering of complementary products can add such value.

Hoovers and LinkedIn Offerings

Take, for instance, Hoover's CRM direct offering, which gives Hoover's customers the ability to instantly update a specific account record with data from more than 65 million companies and 85 million contacts. Another offering for enhancing contact information is the offering from HarteHanks, which offers a data cleansing and address-validation service that cleans data in the Dynamics CRM database.

Online networks extend far and wide, so it is likely that your customers will be registered in one of the many online databases on the market. There are tools out there you can use to connect Microsoft Dynamics CRM to online databases, such as Twitter, Facebook, and LinkedIn, and provide more in-depth knowledge regarding customers that exist in those services. Sales and marketing campaigns can be improved, and targets can be refined when you can add more comprehensive contact information to CRM, including the internal and external connections of your contacts.

Hoover's is a "global database of more than 28 million public and private companies and 36 million executives," according to its website (http://www.hoovers.com/products/100005053-1.html). Hoover's is expected to release its CRM Direct product for CRM 2011 before the end of 2011. Connecting your Microsoft Dynamics CRM deployment to the Hoover's database through their CRM Direct product offering will expand your ability to communicate with your contacts and can potentially fill in missing data that would be invaluable to your users. After you purchase the product, it is a simple matter of installing and connecting to Hoover's so that your current customer information will become a wealth of knowledge about what each customer does, the company he or she works for, and the connections that person has with others. If you start out with just a name and a phone number, the Hoover's database can completely fill in the rest of the information in Microsoft Dynamics CRM for almost any contact and then follow up by providing information about people linked to your original contact who might be of interest to you. In many cases, as many as 50 data points could be available about your prospect. The information that can be gathered allows for targeted campaigns and better prospect qualification, which can lead to better sales pitches and extended growth opportunities.

Another online service that provides similar capabilities is LinkedIn (www.linkedin. com). This online database provides publicly available information about contacts. Currently, no products connect LinkedIn to CRM, but the steps required to customize Microsoft Dynamics CRM and link it to LinkedIn are relatively straightforward. In fact, the Microsoft Dynamics CRM team has provided steps to connect Microsoft Dynamics CRM to LinkedIn on its blog. You can find this information at http://blogs.msdn.com/crm/archive/2008/07/16/linkedin-to-microsoft-dynamics-crm.aspx. Although this article was written for CRM 4.0, the HTML code provided will work when added as a web resource to your CRM customization solution. The LinkedIn content can then be added to a form through an iFrame. This simple connection can increase your knowledge about a contact and enable you to see current records, as updated by the contacts themselves.

Sending HTML E-mails

Microsoft Dynamics CRM provides built-in capabilities to send e-mails to contacts in a number of different ways (e-mail templates, mail merge templates, and marketing campaigns, for example), but these tools don't always meet the complex needs of tracking complex marketing information and more sophisticated HTML e-mails. Complementary tools can help expand Microsoft Dynamics CRM so that it is even easier to send advanced e-mails in a marketing campaign or for any other reason.

One such e-mail enhancement tool is provided by ExactTarget (www.exacttarget. com). Both Microsoft Dynamics CRM 2011 Online and On-Premises support ExactTarget. After you install the e-mail tool provided by ExactTarget, it is a simple matter of selecting a campaign and clicking the custom Send ExactTarget E-mail button. This will allow you to create and send a sophisticated customized advanced e-mail to all those being targeted in the campaign. Beyond initially sending advanced e-mails, there is also an interface that can be used after the e-mails have been sent. This interface enables you to view detailed statistics that have been collected on what happened when the e-mail was received. The marketing analysis of clicks, opens, reads, and forwards is functionality that advanced marketing tool vendors have perfected. For example, you can see the number of e-mails that were not only sent but also opened, and you can see the number of links followed—and all this information allows you to assess the impact of your campaign. The industry of marketing and analytics is a robust and deep niche that is limited only by the imaginations of the creative souls who make it their art to know who is interested in what. Partnering Microsoft Dynamics CRM with an analytics software offering is a match made in heaven.

Business Intelligence in Microsoft Dynamics CRM

Business intelligence (BI) is becoming increasingly important to well-functioning companies, and depending on whom you are talking with about BI, it can vary in its definition. Wikipedia defines BI as follows: "Business intelligence (BI) refers to skills, technologies, applications and practices used to help a business acquire a better understanding of its commercial context. Business intelligence may also refer to the collected information itself."

BI in the following descriptions involves gathering and presenting relevant data on current processes, structure, and organization, including business analysis and planning.

With the right customizations and additions, Microsoft Dynamics CRM can provide a wealth of BI data. It can provide executives with summary reports, sales managers with sales rep statistics, and sales representatives with reports on locales and key performance indicators (KPIs). Microsoft Dynamics CRM is often considered the right tool for the extraction and the presentation of BI data because of how it is structured and because it is easily extensible and customizable.

If you already have Microsoft Dynamics CRM or are planning on deploying it, any savvy user can capitalize on some immediate benefits. The most immediate benefit is being able to run queries and reports that give the current status of a set of sales and marketing campaigns. When retrieving this information inside CRM, a further drill-down on the results can be done quickly by choosing specific cases of interest. Beyond these initial reports, other benefits include being able to get an accurate picture of the sales pipeline with reports on leads and opportunities, being able to see the current rank of sales representatives against specific criteria, and being able to see the history of all those sales representatives. Reports and queries such as these can either be created internally by customizing Microsoft Dynamics CRM with reports developed with SQL Server Reporting Services (SSRS) or purchased from a number of third-party vendors that offer BI packages for CRM.

Basic BI Internal to Microsoft Dynamics CRM

Some basic BI tools can be used right away with any Microsoft Dynamics CRM deployment, including Advanced Find and Reporting, which provide internal tools that can be used immediately to gather data for BI. Furthermore, dashboards and charts built by either power users or developers can provide a visual depiction of key data. Microsoft's investment in these new visualization tools replaces the analytics accelerator from Microsoft Dynamics CRM 4.0. As you learned in Hour 21,

"Reporting and Query Basics," Advanced Find is a tool any Microsoft Dynamics CRM user can use to quickly and easily produce simple BI. Reports are also a great tool that can be used by any user with the time and technical knowledge to produce meaningful results. Both of these approaches have drawbacks, though, because they do not scale for large amounts of data. Furthermore, the time it takes to customize and build these BI tools yourself can be prohibitive.

Microsoft Products That Help with BI

One of the best parts about working with Microsoft Dynamics CRM is the integration points with other Microsoft products. Several Microsoft applications integrate well with Microsoft Dynamics CRM to provide rich BI on top of what can be customized within CRM. Microsoft Excel and Microsoft Dynamics CRM link together through Microsoft Dynamics CRM Excel Connectivity. SQL Server 2008 R2 has built-in support for BI. Microsoft PerformancePoint can be linked directly to CRM, or indirectly through an OLAP cube, to provide structured KPIs or ad hoc analysis. Having these options allows for Microsoft Dynamics CRM customers to evolve from simple BI tools into more sophisticated tools with software and services that are usually already being used within their current organization.

OLAP Cube

Online analytical processing (OLAP) cubes were developed to provide an efficient analysis and presentation of structured data. OLAP cubes are an alternative to standard relational databases, which have limits for analyzing and displaying large amounts of data quickly.

Excel Connectivity

As you learned in Hour 20, "Utilizing the Power of Microsoft Excel with CRM Data," you can connect Excel to the data in Microsoft Dynamics CRM and download that data, based on user selections or customized SQL queries. After the data is in Excel, it can be manipulated and analyzed using all the built-in capabilities of Excel, such as setting up PivotTables and PivotCharts against the data, which works well for a specific individual user. Furthermore, if the option is selected, the data can be reimported into CRM after modifications have been made. For larger corporate analysis, other options are a better fit.

SQL Server 2008 R2

Among the rich set of functionality and features built into SQL Server 2008, several key aspects can be used for BI. The Microsoft SQL Server 2008 Reporting Services are a large part of this and are already used within Microsoft Dynamics CRM itself. The Analysis Services in SQL Server 2008 R2 is another powerful tool that can be leveraged to create OLAP cubes for pivoted fast data analysis. The included Report Builder 3.0 provides a wizard to create SQL reports in a user-friendly fashion. Also part of SQL Server 2008 R2, PowerPivot provides extended the PivotTable functionality found in Microsoft Excel. On top of providing the ability to create OLAP cubes, Analysis Services also provides comprehensive data-mining tools for deep analysis of your existing data.

PerformancePoint

Microsoft Office SharePoint Server's PerformancePoint product is a comprehensive organization and analysis system that can attach directly to Microsoft Dynamics CRM or an OLAP cube. It provides a sophisticated feature set that includes structured reports, multiple data visualization options, reports and notifications for KPIs, and even ad hoc reporting, depending on the setup and configuration of the server. An entire business can be managed from a PerformancePoint server when it is fully integrated into products such as Microsoft Dynamics CRM.

BI Software from Vendors and ISVs

ZAP Technology (www.zaptechnology.com)

ZAP Technology (www.zaptechnology.com) offers a product called Business Analytics, which provides a web-based application that contains a set of prepackaged analytics for sales, marketing, and services. The application provides dashboards, scorecards, KPIs, and reports and drill-down capabilities that link back into Microsoft Dynamics CRM On-Premises for the full view of any record in question. Business Analytics is relatively easy to deploy because it recognizes customizations in Microsoft Dynamics CRM and imports them into a structured cube for fast analysis and reporting. Custom reports and summary reports are quickly and easily created and run, allowing for targeted dashboards and KPIs that can be viewed and updated regularly. Further features include the ability to import user security privileges from Microsoft Dynamics CRM so that Business Analytics only allows access to those records that a user is allowed to view. With such a full-featured product, ZAP Technology has provided an excellent BI product for almost any Microsoft Dynamics CRM system.

Target IT (www.targit.com/en/Products/Fast_integration_tool/ For_MSDynamicsCRM)

The Target IT tools are another offering in the arena of expanding the power of BI with the use and creation of cubes of data. The analytical cubes meet the majority of the requirements of a BI solution, and they are formatted in a way to support both first-time and experienced BI users.

Microsoft BI Offerings (www.microsoft.com/BI/en-us/pages/ home.aspx)

Products from Microsoft that provide functionality within the BI arena include Performance Point and for power users Microsoft Office Excel with PowerPivot and the Microsoft SharePoint Suite. You also have the full power of Microsoft SQL Server and SQL Server Reporting (SRSS).

Enabling Microsoft Dynamics CRM for Mobile Devices

It is increasingly familiar to see sales and marketing staff with mobile devices, such as Windows Phone 7 devices, BlackBerry devices, iPhones, Android devices, and iPads. It is possible to tap into existing resources and allow access to your Microsoft Dynamics CRM data through these devices. Providing access to Microsoft Dynamics CRM through mobile devices becomes a logical and natural extension of the Microsoft Dynamics CRM system that will save time and make your organization more effective.

There are several scenarios where enabling Microsoft Dynamics CRM on mobile devices might help. Quickly browsing Microsoft Dynamics CRM data before a face-to-face sales meeting can make the encounter more productive. It can make a conversation at a conference more personal and focused. Having Microsoft Dynamics CRM data available at an opportune time during a lunch meeting can provide a crucial bit of information necessary to turn a lead into an account. Such scenarios would benefit from mobile access.

If enabling mobile Microsoft Dynamics CRM sounds like something your organization might benefit from, there are several options from which to choose. The Microsoft Dynamics CRM team currently provides the Microsoft Mobile Express solution that can be customized on your system. Companies such as CWR Mobility and TenDigits provide integrated solutions for Windows Mobile and BlackBerry devices that are fully functional and customizable. Choosing a mobile Microsoft Dynamics CRM solution requires more than knowing what device your users will have, though. You need to weigh all the following aspects:

▶ Feature set provided

▶ Customizability

▶ Security

▶ Cost

▶ Supported deployments (in Online versus On-Premises)

▶ Supported devices

Other considerations that might come into play are customer support, documentation, and future development plans. Most solutions provide a website outlining all the information on their products. See Table 23.1 for more information.

TABLE 23.1   Mobile Solutions

Product	Company	Website	Notes
MobileExpress	Microsoft	www.microsoft.com	Supported in CRM Online and On-Premises
CWR Mobile CRM 2011	CWR Mobility	www.cwrmobility.com	Straightforward solution to enable mobile CRM
MobileAccess	TenDigits	http://tendigits.com/mobileaccess.html	Provides both online and offline access to Microsoft Dynamics CRM data

We will look at two of the solutions in depth here and see what options they provide. It's a good idea to research the benefits of all the solutions before selecting one for your custom deployment.

MobileExpress

MobileExpress is a solution included in Microsoft Dynamics CRM 2011. The product is part of the Microsoft Dynamics CRM server and allows for online-only, web-based interaction with Microsoft Dynamics CRM on any mobile device that has a browser and a network connection. Because it uses the browser on the device, no installation or maintenance is necessary on the device itself, but this also means there is no access to records when there is no network connection. MobileExpress is a cost-effective solution that provides administrative configuration on the server, allowing a certain set of entities to be viewed on the device, and it can even be configured down to the field level.

As with the standard Microsoft Dynamics CRM application, in MobileExpress, interface users with different roles can be shown different forms. Any user of the MobileExpress web application will need to have a role that has Go Mobile permission in order to access the application. Then, entities selected for mobile access can be searched, accessed as read-only, and edited, depending on how access was configured on the Microsoft Dynamics CRM server. Additional functionality includes a breadcrumb trail that allows instant access to previously viewed pages and the use of saved queries to filter results retrieved from the server. This solution from Microsoft allows almost any Microsoft Dynamics CRM On-Premises or Online deployment to become mobile quickly and easily, although with limited functionality.

CWR Mobile CRM

CWR Mobile provides both online and offline access to Microsoft Dynamics CRM across a wide range of devices, including the Windows Phone 7 platform from Microsoft. Leveraging background synchronization ensures that users always have access to their data, even when a network connection is not available. By delivering a look and feel very similar to that of Microsoft Dynamics CRM, CWR Mobile enables users to get up and running in no time, no matter which device they prefer.

MobileAccess

MobileAccess is a mobile solution provided by TenDigits that extends Microsoft Dynamics CRM so that it can be accessed on Android, BlackBerry, Apple, and Windows mobile devices. MobileAccess provides standard Microsoft Dynamics CRM functionality, such as searching, creating, editing, deleting, and assigning records from your mobile device. It has been built with automatic synchronization capabilities so that records can be accessed both when connected to the Microsoft Dynamics CRM server and when there is no network connection. Advanced functionality includes notifications and alterations when new records have been created or assigned, integration with mobile capabilities so that initiating a call or e-mail can occur from within CRM, and then tracking of those activities after they have been completed. With all this functionality, MobileAccess is a good choice for mobile integration with Microsoft Dynamics CRM.

Database Tools and Utilities

Supporting and maintaining Microsoft Dynamics CRM is important, but it is also important to do the same for the engine that drives CRM: SQL Server. Microsoft SQL Server is at the heart of CRM, and it provides a stable base to build anything from a moderately sized application to a multi-server, large-scale, high-use system. It is important to keep SQL Server well tuned so that you can fully benefit from the infrastructure it provides. There are tools provided with SQL Server to tune and maintain the databases, and other products can be purchased that help support SQL Server with more specialized tools and user-friendly interfaces.

The original platform that Microsoft Dynamics CRM was built to run on was Microsoft SQL Server 2005. Consumers of Microsoft Dynamics CRM 2011 need Microsoft SQL Server 2008 or higher. SQL Server 2008 vastly improves on the functionality in SQL Server 2005, but the tools included with SQL Server 2008 are not very different from the ones included with SQL Server 2005. The interfaces are similar and provide performance analysis, database backup, and maintenance, but only to those with the technical skill to configure and control SQL Server. An obvious drawback to only having SQL Server 2005 or 2008 is that none of the tools provide automation through the user interface, so they all have to be set up and run either manually through the interface provided or through automation scripts.

After weighing the initial options for supporting the database, you may find yourself looking externally for tools that will be able to tune, manage, and maintain SQL Server. Several options on the market support SQL Server, and two of the most comprehensive ones are the solutions provided by Idera and Red Gate. Idera and Red Gate's applications wrap around Microsoft SQL Server to provide user-friendly interfaces that enable database administrators to easily tune for performance and to maintain and back up their databases. Their products are straightforward to set up and provide automation for most tasks, including backup and defragmentation.

In addition to backup and defragmentation support, Idera's and Red Gate's products can set up notifications so that when tasks are completed, the people who need to track a job's success or failure can be informed. The notifications can also be set up on diagnostic triggers so that if something were to go wrong on the server, such as a sudden sustained spike in CPU usage, the support staff can know about it quickly and deal with the problem in a timely manner. Any complex organization or deployment requires tools such as these to properly manage and maintain their system.

So, what does all this actually mean to your instance of Microsoft Dynamics CRM? The most important things to remember about your deployment are that the data has to be backed up, the database has to be regularly defragmented, and you need plenty of resources (such as disk space) for SQL Server to run properly. Because the data and structure of Microsoft Dynamics CRM are completely contained within the database instances underlying the application, Microsoft Dynamics CRM can be restored from any point both at which the organization database and the configuration databases are backed up. So whether you have nightly, weekly, or monthly backups of your database, make sure you capture both the organization database (or databases, if you are using a multitenant deployment) and the configuration database.

After regular backups, the next most pressing concern to keep SQL Server in peak running order is to defragment the database so that the indexes will do their job and speed up queries instead of slow them down. Indexes on highly used tables—those with the most insertions, updates, and deletions—can become fragmented across a hard drive and slow down queries on those tables. It is important to regularly check and defragment these indexes, if appropriate. Finally, another thing that can cause trouble for a SQL Server is not having enough resources. Whether it is CPU resources, memory, or disk space available, SQL Server generally requires a good deal of it to run at peak performance. That is why it is important to know when one of these resources is running low and take the appropriate action to fix the situation. If all these things are done correctly, SQL Server will continue to support your instance of Microsoft Dynamics CRM the way it was meant to.

Compliance and Auditing Tools

Microsoft Dynamics CRM is used for many different types of applications. Some of those applications have highly sensitive data that requires tracking and analysis. For example it is common to need to know what fields were changed when and also who changed those fields. The simplest form of auditing is automatically enabled in the entity definitions in Microsoft Dynamics CRM. Any entity created as a user-owned entity acquires four attributes that track who created a record (CreatedOn and CreatedBy) and who was the last to change the record (ModifiedOn and ModifiedBy). These fields do not keep a full list of who changed the record and at what time, but they do provide the means to see where the most recent changes came from and who is responsible for creating the given record. This simplistic auditing trail often is not enough.

Microsoft Dynamics CRM also provides auditing capabilities for more complex requirements on a per-entity basis. Auditing must first be enabled in the System Settings window. Then once auditing is enabled on a particular entity, fields on that entity can be selected to track changes. These changes are tracked in a special audit activity.

Global Audit Settings

Figure 23.1 shows the global auditing section of the System Settings window. To get there, do the following:

1. Choose Settings.

2. Choose Auditing under the System subgroup.

3. Chose Global Audit Settings.

4. Click the Start Auditing check box.

5. Click OK to save your changes and exit the form.

FIGURE 23.1
Global auditing
settings.

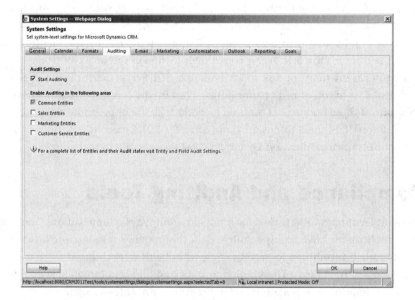

Enabling Auditing on a Specific Entity

Figure 23.2 shows how to enable auditing on the account entity. To get there, do the following:

1. Choose Settings.

2. Choose Customize the System. This will open the default solution.

3. In the left navigation pane, under Components, choose Entities.

4. Choose an entity (for example, Account).

5. On the General tab of the entity, find the Data Services heading. Under it, check the Auditing check box.

6. Click Save and close the form to enable auditing.

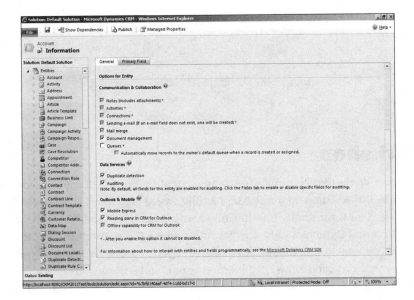

FIGURE 23.2
Entity auditing settings.

Viewing Audit Details for a Specific Record

Figure 23.3 shows audit details on a record in the account entity. To get there, do the following:

1. When auditing is enabled, choose a record to open and update (for example, an account record).

2. Make changes to the record and save it.

3. In the left navigation pane, under Common, choose Audit History.

4. On the window that appears, you see all the recorded changes to the entity. Double-click one of the changes to see the audit details window.

FIGURE 23.3
The audit
details window.

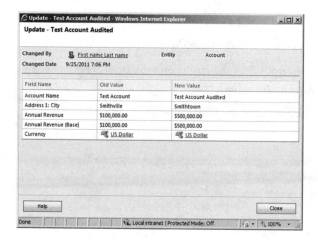

Workshop

Adventure Works Cycle is a midsized company that makes and distributes bicycles across the United States, in a number of locally owned bike shops. It has a small sales force that is constantly traveling and needs to remain connected at all times. It has a Microsoft Dynamics CRM deployment on which it has installed TenDigits's MobileAccess solution so that all of its sales agents can access records anywhere, whether they can get a network connection or not, and retrieve and enter data. Opportunities and sales orders can be tracked immediately by entering information on a mobile device or by gathering orders and entering them at the end of the day from their laptops. Adventure Works Cycle uses Idera's defragment manager to keep the Microsoft SQL Server databases optimized and indexed properly. Sales managers in the head office keep track of how the different agents are doing, through the use of a Business Analytics dashboard from ZAP Technology. Thanks to this product, quarterly and year-end reports are easily generated and presented to keep executives abreast of the current sales, as well as of the sales pipeline that is being developed.

Q&A

Q. We are considering moving into a mobile solution. What things should we consider?

A. One of the first things to consider is whether you need offline capability. Offline adds a significant layer of complexity to any offering.

Q. *For a small company, is it necessary to invest in Microsoft SQL Server management tools?*

A. Not necessarily. Microsoft SQL Server is a robust and powerful database that usually does not need extensive care in a small firm.

Q. *Are there other offerings available? You mentioned so many.*

A. Yes. There are many other offerings available, and a personal apology to all that are not mentioned in this lesson.

Quiz

1. What are two Microsoft products that can be used for gathering business intelligence? What is a non-Microsoft product that can be used for gathering business intelligence?

2. What are the three things that have to be done to ensure that Microsoft SQL Server supports your Microsoft Dynamics CRM deployment properly?

3. What is a useful feature that is new to SQL Server 2008 R2?

4. What are the benefits of using MobileExpress? What are the drawbacks?

Answers

1. Advanced Find and Reporting are two Microsoft products that can be used for gathering business intelligence. ZAP Technology's Business Analytics is a non-Microsoft product that can be used for gathering business intelligence.

2. Three things that have to be done to ensure that Microsoft SQL Server supports your Microsoft Dynamics CRM deployment properly are tune, manage, and maintain Microsoft SQL Server by backing up the database, defragmenting, and indexing.

3. A useful feature that is new to SQL Server 2008 R2 is Report Builder Version 3.0, which provides a user-friendly wizard that allows users to create SQL reports easily.

4. MobileExpress allows for online-only, web-based interaction with Microsoft Dynamics CRM on any mobile device that has a browser and a network connection. This is both an advantage and a disadvantage.

Exercise

Using the blog post provided by the Microsoft Dynamics CRM Online team, http://blogs.msdn.com/dynamicscrmonline/archive/2009/04/07/adding-linkedin-contact-searches.aspx, add a LinkedIn contact search to your Microsoft Dynamics CRM deployment. The post can be followed for both standard and online deployments, so don't worry if you have one or the other. As can be seen from the post, the Name fields can be connected to an action and a button that triggers a search to be performed on all the LinkedIn contacts to see whether a match can be found; if it is, the appropriate information is displayed.

HOUR 24

Microsoft Dynamics CRM as a Development Framework

What You'll Learn in This Hour:

▶ Options: What can be changed?

▶ When Microsoft Dynamics CRM is a good fit

▶ When the core of Microsoft Dynamics CRM 2011 might need additional architecture and design

▶ Skills required: Who can make the changes

Microsoft Dynamics CRM is a product that is as much *xRM* (where *x* can be any relationship-oriented line-of-business application) as it is CRM (where *C* is focused on customer relationship management). Microsoft Dynamics CRM is fully functional and, yet, the expectation in many situations is that it will be expanded, configured, connected, and enhanced. It is also designed to offer control and best practices around extending the platform so that when a new major upgrade is released from Microsoft, it will not break a partner's or customer's development efforts and customizations. In Microsoft Dynamics CRM 2011, both the On-Premises and Online versions support similar extensive customization options.

Options: What Can Be Changed?

Developers who want to fully exploit Microsoft Dynamics CRM need to learn to "think CRM," and they also need to master a number of significantly different development skill sets. Each skill set discussed in this hour is a benefit to the CRM development platform as standalone expertise, but a deep understanding of all technologies can make a significant difference. Developers should remember that the more they can "think CRM," the easier their application will be to support.

Furthermore, when business stakeholders can also "think CRM," new features can be added quickly and effectively. When business users do not "think CRM," it is easy to end up in a conflict-of-interest situation. Users who make demands without considering what they have are asking for delays, frustrations, and long-term road blocks to get what is new and what is next.

Extending the Core Microsoft Dynamics CRM Code

Microsoft Dynamics CRM is a .NET application that can be extended with more .NET code through plug-ins or enhanced with scripts, workflow, and custom ASP.NET Web pages. In addition, Microsoft Dynamics CRM is architected and designed to include a methodology and development framework that wraps the application and any new customizations in such a way to reduce the need to rewrite code with each major release. Microsoft also provides a complete Software Development Kit (SDK). This SDK has tools, samples, documentation, and a methodology for extending the core Microsoft Dynamics CRM code. The following sections look at each area of extension available in Microsoft Dynamics CRM.

Managing Changes Through Solutions

In Microsoft Dynamics CRM 2011, extensions to the core Microsoft Dynamics CRM application are contained in solutions. Like a project in Microsoft Visual Studio, a solution contains everything necessary to build and deploy the extended CRM functionality.

Solutions can contain the following:

▶ Custom entities and forms

▶ Custom fields

▶ Relationships between entities

▶ Plug-in assemblies and steps

▶ Service endpoints

▶ Security roles

▶ Processes

▶ Application ribbon customizations

▶ Dashboards and reports

- ▶ Global option sets (new in 2011!)

- ▶ Field-level security profiles (new in 2011!)

- ▶ Web resources

Web resources include any extra files needed for your CRM customization. They many include custom JavaScript you have written for your forms, custom Silverlight controls, images, or .aspx pages. Solutions can be used to package customizations for sale in the CRM Dynamics marketplace or to separate different development efforts in larger projects. More information about the Dynamics Marketplace is provided later in this chapter.

Solutions can either be *managed* or *unmanaged*. Managed solutions specify what changes can be made to components, whereas unmanaged solutions do not have any restrictions. This is useful for independent solution vendors (ISVs) to restrict how their solutions can be changed or for enterprise architects to enforce standards across an enterprise. If you are unsure of which option to use for your development, choose to use an unmanaged solution. Unmanaged solutions will always win over managed solutions as a choice when you're unsure. When importing solutions if you run into a conflict between data or program files unmanaged solutions offer the option of the last solution applied wins.

Plug-ins

Microsoft Dynamics CRM offers synchronous and asynchronous plug-in models that are based on .NET 4.0. Plug-ins are registered for a single organization, and they are stored in the database (preferred) or on disk. Registering a plug-in in a database enables automatic deployment across a cluster of CRM instances. Plug-ins must be digitally signed when they are compiled in Visual Studio; otherwise, they fail to execute. New in CRM 2011, plug-ins can be "sandboxed" so their access to their host system is limited. In this access level, files cannot be written to the host system, and integration to other databases must be done through Windows Azure services. The benefit of sandboxed plug-ins is that they work in both CRM Online and On-Premises installations. Plug-ins not registered in sandbox mode can still be registered in On-Premises installations but not in CRM Online. In either plug-in model, all work performed in a plug-in can be registered as part of a single transaction. This allows all changes to be rolled back if any part of the plug-in fails. More information about plug-ins can be found in the Microsoft Dynamics CRM 2011 SDK, at www.microsoft.com/download/en/details.aspx?id=24004.

Creating and Adding Workflow Using the Windows Workflow Foundation

Built in to Microsoft Dynamics CRM On-Premises and Online is the Microsoft Windows Workflow Foundation, which is a core component of the development framework. The foundation is also extended with a user-friendly interface to enable end users with limited or no development experience to add workflows. Workflows can create new records, update existing records, send e-mails, reassign records, and change the status of a record. Workflows can be especially helpful for creating tasks for sales personnel base on an opportunity, triggering reminder e-mails to prospects, or seeking manager approval of a new proposal over a certain dollar amount. In CRM 2011, a similar designer is used for both creating new workflows and dialogs. You can access this designer by going to the Settings tab from the CRM homepage and then choosing Processes and clicking the New icon. From the designer, you can create steps for your workflow to perform and conditions to check before performing these actions. For example, you might want to wait seven days after an opportunity is created before sending a reminder e-mail to the customer. Workflows are always related to a specific record type in CRM, such as an account or a contact, and run in the background after an action has been performed. Figure 24.1 shows the workflow designer.

FIGURE 24.1
The workflow designer.

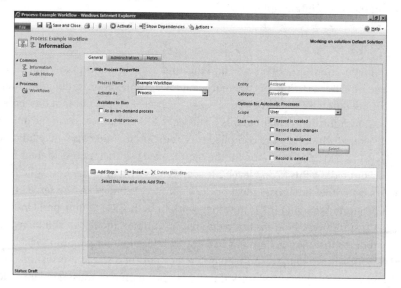

In the designer, the options available to trigger a workflow to run on a record are the following events:

- A new record is created.

- Record status changes.

- A record is assigned to another user.

- Field values in a record are changed.

- A record is deleted.

- A workflow can be run manually by the user.

Dialogs New in CRM 2011

A new feature available in CRM 2011 is the ability to create custom dialogs related to an entity. These custom dialogs can guide users through any defined process so that it is easily repeatable. Dialogs can be helpful for guiding a customer support representative through a support call or enabling a salesperson to complete a sale. Dialogs must be launched manually or from a child dialog and can interact with the end user. Dialogs can be designed to change based on the user's input. In this manner, different actions can be performed, different forms can be displayed, or the dialog may prompt the user to take different actions, based on the initial input.

Extending Forms with Scripts

Forms can be extended by adding code to key areas of the form.

Form OnLoad, OnSave, and Field OnChange

In CRM 2011, entities in Microsoft Dynamics CRM On-Premises and Online can have multiple forms. Each of these forms has an OnLoad event option where JavaScript can be added. JavaScript is client-side code run when the user opens and uses the form. In addition, each field within the form can have an OnChange event where JavaScript can be embedded, offering the ability for events to be performed on specific changes to fields.

Form Behavior

Figure 24.2 shows an example of the form properties OnLoad and OnSave. To get there, do the following:

1. Choose Settings.

2. Choose Customize the System. This will open the default solution.

3. In the left navigation pane, under Components, choose Entities.

4. Choose an entity (for example, Account).

5. In the left navigation pane, select Forms.

6. Choose Form Properties. From here you can attach custom JavaScript files that you have uploaded as Web resources to your form. JavaScript no longer has to be added directly in the form editor.

FIGURE 24.2
Form properties.

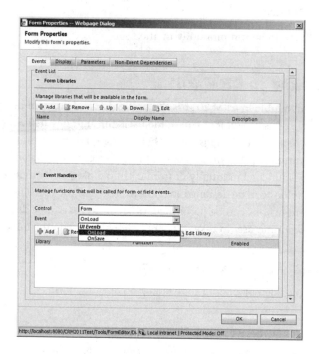

You can also add an OnChange event to a specific field Figure 24.3 shows an example of the area where you would add OnChange event script.

To get to where you would add an OnChange script from the form, complete these steps:

1. Choose a field

2. Choose Change Properties.

3. Choose Events.

4. Choose OnChange.

5. Choose Edit. From here you can attach custom JavaScript files that you have uploaded as Web resources to your form. JavaScript no longer has to be added directly in the form editor.

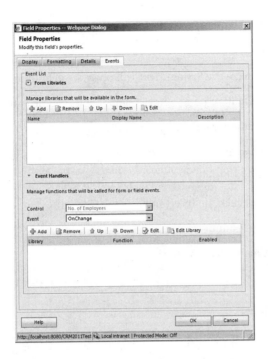

FIGURE 24.3
Field properties.

OnChange Events

A key thing about OnChange events is that they fire only when both of the following conditions occur:

1. The value changed.
2. The user has moved to another field

Alternatively, the OnChange event can be fired using the FireOnChange method. For an example of FireOnChange, see http://msdn.microsoft.com/en-us/library/cc150865.aspx.

By the Way

Adding iFrames to Forms

An iFrame option is available for both Microsoft Dynamics CRM On-Premises and Online and is hosted within the form or on the left navigation pane of a form. Within the world of the iFrame, Microsoft Dynamics CRM will optionally pass the object type code and object ID (GUID) to the provided external URL.

iFrame Interaction

iFrames display web pages within a form and generally do not interact with the data within Microsoft Dynamics CRM.

By the Way

Figure 24.4 shows an example of setting up an iFrame. To get there, do the following:

1. Choose Settings.

2. Choose Customize the System. This will open the default solution.

3. In the left navigation pane, under Components, choose Entities.

4. Choose an entity (for example, Account).

5. In the left navigation pane, select Forms.

6. Choose the main form.

7. On the ribbon, click the Insert tab.

8. Add a new one-column section.

9. Add an iFrame to this new section.

FIGURE 24.4
Adding an
iFrame property.

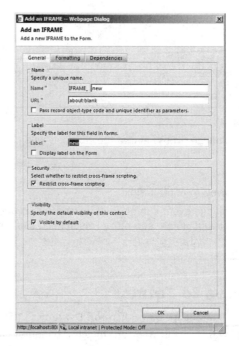

Changing or Adding to the User Interface Menus and Buttons

The drop-down items on the menus and the buttons within the left navigation pane can be changed in Microsoft Dynamics CRM On-Premises. So, you can add new menu items, replace existing menu items, or add or replace buttons (such as the Sales button or Service button). These changes to the user interface menus are made in the Application Ribbon XML file as follows:

1. Select Settings.

2. Choose Solutions.

3. Create a new solution named Application Ribbon. The default publisher and any version number will do.

4. Click Save.

5. Click Add Existing and then choose Application Ribbons.

6. Click Export Solution.

The saved zip file can be extracted, and you can then edit the XML file inside it.

Did you Know?

Ribbon Editor Toolkit

One trick to diving into editing the Office ribbon is available as a free download from CodePlex. Check out Pragma's Toolkit: http://pragmatoolkit.codeplex.com/.

Did you Know?

Ribbon Tips

The ribbon comes from the Microsoft Office team. If you are going to do any type of editing of the ribbon, remember to check for tips by browsing for Office Ribbon Editor.

When your edits are complete, import the modified Application Ribbon file as follows:

1. Choose Settings.

2. Choose Solutions.

3. Choose Import.

4. Upload the modified file.

Enhancing with Silverlight

Silverlight solutions can be added in the web resources section of solutions in CRM. Custom Silverlight pages can provide graphics, animation, and rich media interfaces. These pages can be driven by CRM data or can provide integration with other systems. These custom pages can be displayed in CRM through an iFrame directly on a CRM form or through a custom ISV page. Silverlight is a browser plug-in and is an interesting complement to Microsoft Dynamics CRM extendibility. Silverlight includes items such as skinning and styling, deep zoom, and shadowing, all of which can be used to explode the Microsoft Dynamics user interface into a rich media experience.

Integrating with SharePoint (WSS/MOSS) for Support of Unstructured Data

Many Microsoft Dynamics CRM projects require unstructured data. Unstructured data includes large blocks of text, Word documents, PowerPoint files, and other undefined data that lends itself to organization and enterprise search. Some of this data can be structured into entities (record types) and fields, but other items are much better suited to organization and collaboration software (such as copies of documents). SharePoint meets this need and naturally connects to Microsoft Dynamics CRM. SharePoint can also be highly integrated to Microsoft Dynamics CRM as a dynamic or static component. CRM 2011 provides built in support for integration with SharePoint.

As a dynamic component, SharePoint can bring up and down pages on demand. It can also be setup as a static component, which gives SharePoint a permanent two-way connection to Microsoft Dynamics CRM. Microsoft SharePoint online can now be integrated with Microsoft Dynamics CRM Online. For On-Premises solutions, CRM 2011 can integrate with SharePoint 2007 or 2010. This integration enables the creation of folders in SharePoint for specific records automatically. For example, if SharePoint integration is enabled on the Account entity, a new folder can be created in SharePoint when a new account is won. Once the folder is created, the documents link on this record will provide a portal to this new folder on SharePoint.

You can enable SharePoint integration for a specific entity by taking the following steps:

1. Click the Settings tab.

2. Choose Document Management.

3. Choose Document Management Settings.

4. Click the checkbox for the appropriate entity.

5. Click Next.

6. Choose the folder structure you want and click Next.

7. Click Finish.

Integrating with the World of Finance and ERP, Using a Bridge Application

Just as unstructured data is best managed with technology designed for unstructured data such as SharePoint, financial information for accounting departments is best managed with a well-loved and established accounting software or enterprise resource planning application. Accounting software is focused on tight auditing and control within a smaller audience and has well-vetted software offerings focusing on flexible general ledgers, accounts payable, payroll, and other accounting-specific modules. Microsoft Dynamics CRM never had the intention of being an accounting or general ledger package.

Integrating Microsoft Dynamics CRM with a robust accounting application, however, can be beneficial and can be accomplished seamlessly. Core company accounting data can be pushed to a wide audience of users (such as everyone in the company), while the interactive and delicate finances in an accounting application are controlled and maintained in a company's financial department and financial information audit processes.

External Access: Web Page Integrations

When managing prospect and client information, there is an interest in allowing specific external contacts the ability to interact directly with their contact information and there is also a need to control and retain data quality around that incoming information. The interaction between an external web interface of prospect and client information is part of many Microsoft Dynamics CRM projects.

Some examples of core areas where this applies including capturing leads from a company's website, interacting with possible attendees at hosted events, and working with contacts and companies on support-related issues. Currently, there are several portal accelerators available to integrate CRM with an external customer portal in this way.

Microsoft Dynamics Marketplace

Microsoft Dynamics CRM is so fun to extend that it lends itself to shared and Microsoft-vetted libraries of source code, configurations, and customizations. The Microsoft Dynamics CRM accelerators offer building blocks of source code, configurations, and customizations that empower a Microsoft partner or customer to quickly add features and functionalities. The library of accelerators continues to grow. Some examples include the sales forecasting accelerator, which offers configurations for tracking sales goals, and the analytics accelerator, which offers a set of custom dashboards and reports. Some accelerators work with Microsoft Dynamics CRM

Online, and others require that you have full access and security to the programs in the Microsoft Dynamics CRM On-Premises environment.

A broad selection of accelerators can be found at the Dynamics Marketplace, which is located at http://dynamics.pinpoint.microsoft.com. The Dynamics Marketplace offers solutions from many ISVs that can be installed quickly and easily to extend the functionality of Microsoft Dynamics CRM. Many of the solutions found in the Dynamics Marketplace have been certified by Microsoft as compatible and supported by Microsoft Dynamics CRM. The costs of these solutions vary; some are provided free of charge, and for other solutions it is necessary to contact the vendor to obtain pricing details. When planning to extend CRM, it is important to check the Dynamics Marketplace before writing custom code as the functionality may already be available. In some cases, it might be more cost-effective to purchase from the Dynamics Marketplace than building out the functionality on your own.

Dashboards and Reporting

The creation of dashboards is natively supported in Microsoft Dynamics CRM 2011. Users and developers can create dashboards on the fly, using data in Microsoft Dynamics CRM. Microsoft SQL Server reporting services can also be used with Microsoft Dynamics CRM On-Premises and Online to create more advanced dashboards and various other reports that you can integrate into the reporting menus within Microsoft Dynamics CRM. These reports can be created with the Business Intelligence Development Studio of Visual Studio, using Microsoft Dynamics CRM 2011 BIDS Fetch Extension. This extension uses the query language fetch xml that is native to Microsoft Dynamics CRM.

In addition, you can create reports via the Microsoft Dynamics CRM report wizards and numerous views. If you want to stretch reporting into other areas of presentation, you can also find ISV solutions.

Microsoft Excel Dynamic Spreadsheets and PivotTables

As you learned in earlier hours, the power of Microsoft Excel dynamic spreadsheets is almost beyond imagination. You can tie an Excel spreadsheet to Microsoft Dynamics CRM, and every time this spreadsheet is opened, it will automatically be updated with new CRM data. In addition, a dynamic Excel spreadsheet retains and serves up the correct security so that each person who opens the spreadsheet gets the data that applies to him or her. You can add your own columns and formulas to these spreadsheets, and one way you can share these spreadsheets is by e-mailing them to other Microsoft Dynamics CRM users. Dynamic PivotTables are now supported in the same way as spreadsheets. New in Microsoft Dynamics CRM 2011, both dynamic and static Excel spreadsheets include the option to be formatted in such a way that they can be edited in Excel and have the changes reimported into CRM.

Microsoft Excel Static Spreadsheets

Microsoft Excel static spreadsheets do not get updated with any new Microsoft Dynamics CRM data when opened again and again. Data in static spreadsheets is structured and unchanging and, as such, a static spreadsheet offers a saved version of a data report. In addition, static spreadsheets can be shared with other people who are not Microsoft Dynamics CRM users.

Business Intelligence Analysis

You can pull out slices or cubes of data and do financial analysis, intense statistics, analytics, and more. Adding in third-party business intelligence agents, cubes, and tools allows for functionality not traditionally found in relationship management applications. The third-party tools can come from companies specializing in business intelligence, or you can tap into other products and offerings from Microsoft.

Modifying the Outlook Client for Microsoft Dynamics CRM

Just as the Microsoft Dynamics CRM core application can be modified and extended, so can the Microsoft Dynamics CRM Outlook client. Enhancements to Microsoft Outlook can add usability and allow you to take better advantage of the web-enabled Microsoft Dynamics CRM. For instance, you can set up special folders to access other areas of Microsoft Dynamics CRM, and you can change some of the default folders to favorites. Another way to customize the Microsoft Dynamics CRM client for Outlook is to extend or fine-tune the synchronization functionality between Microsoft Dynamics CRM and Microsoft Outlook e-mail, contacts, tasks, and the calendar.

Mobility

Microsoft Dynamics CRM 2011 has additional support for CRM Mobile Express software. Mobile Express is available as a website address, so there is no application to install, and most mobile devices support it. The mobile form editor allows for custom forms to be created for mobile users so they can access CRM data from their mobile device. In addition, Mobile Express allows for mobile salespeople to enter data while on the go.

Many third-party ISVs also offer mobility solutions, including the following:

▶ CWR Mobility, http://online.cwrmobility.com

▶ softBRIDGE, www.softbridgeinc.com

▶ Softtrends, www.crmmobileplus.com

▶ TenDigits, www.tendigits.com

Now that we have covered a number of areas where Microsoft Dynamics CRM On-Premises and Online can be extended and enhanced, let's look at when using Microsoft Dynamics CRM On-Premises as a development platform makes sense.

When Microsoft Dynamics CRM Is a Good Fit

If you are looking at a development project and you are considering Microsoft Dynamics CRM, you might want to consider the following big-picture questions.

Does Your Project Require You to Track Any Type of Relationships?

If yes, the Microsoft Dynamics CRM framework is definitely something to consider. These relationships can include relationships between two people, relationships between companies, relationships between a person and a company, relationships between things, relationships between parts and a final product, and basically the relationships between any two nouns. Using any other noun than *customer* is called using CRM as an *xRM* framework. The key to a successful xRM project is to find the *x* in your xRM. The *x* in your xRM should be the central hub from which all the data in your system builds.

Does Your Project Require You to Automate or Document a Process?

If yes, the Microsoft Dynamics CRM framework is definitely something to consider. Automated processes can include standardizing the steps that need to happen to get a project done. Such automated processes can include scheduling and completing specific activities, historical reference to the completed activities, association of specific activities to specific people, tracking of specific activities with a specific person or the automation of alerts and notices, using custom dialogues to complete a standardized process, and more.

Does Your Project Require Role-Based Feature and Functional Security and User-Specific or Office-Specific Limited Data Access?

Built in to the Microsoft Dynamics CRM framework is a multilayered configurable security system that helps you to control who can do what and who can access what. Microsoft Dynamics CRM 2011 allows for security on specific custom fields and allows you to display different forms for different users. In addition, the Microsoft Dynamics CRM security is tied to Microsoft Active Directory authentication. (These are features your developers would otherwise have to write and keep updated.)

Does Your Project Require Long-Term Updates, Upgrades, and Support?

The Microsoft Dynamics CRM 2011 release methodology includes rollups and a major upgrade. These upgrades are built to recognize existing customizations and modifications. In order to support this, you should only make customizations to your CRM installation in a way that is supported by Microsoft. Any of the methods mentioned in this book or the CRM SDK are supported. Also provided is the long-term upgrade and update support, the development control and the CRM SDK, and the added features you might not have time to write, such as duplicate checking, user-friendly reporting, integration with Microsoft Office, and layers of data import options.

Does the Project Lend Itself to a Design of Parallel Asynchronous Processes That Could Otherwise Cause Software Bottlenecks and Performance Issues?

If yes, mastery and access to the Microsoft Workflow Foundation in a user-friendly interface within Microsoft Dynamics CRM might make sense.

When the Core of Microsoft Dynamics CRM 2011 Might Need Additional Architecture and Design

Now that we have looked at a few areas where Microsoft Dynamics CRM as a development platform makes sense, let's look at areas where further architecture needs to be added to enhance the core system. If you are looking at a development project and you think that Microsoft Dynamics CRM is not a good option, you might want to consider the following big-picture questions.

Does Your Project Require a Layered Rollback Option?

Microsoft SQL 2005 offered a much more robust and sophisticated option in the world of the core back-end database and for database maintenance. Microsoft SQL 2005 introduced the ability to take part of a Microsoft SQL Server database offline for maintenance, while the rest of the database was still up and running, with a ton of data pouring in. These sophisticated features were not new to the world of huge databases, but they were new to the world of Microsoft SQL Server. Currently, Dynamics CRM databases must be restored through SQL database restoration, and they must be reimported with the Deployment Manager application.

If your project requires a layered rollback option, Microsoft Dynamics CRM 2011 will most likely require additional architecture.

Does Your Project Require Extensive Financial Analysis, Balancing, Data-Driven Statistical Analysis, and Accounting Information?

Microsoft Dynamics CRM is not a statistics-oriented programming language set. If your project depends heavily on financial information, various formulas, or data from mathematical equations that creates data for other mathematical equations that all result in telling the system to do something at a certain time, you most likely will need further architectural design to use Microsoft Dynamics CRM as the base application.

It is not that Microsoft Dynamics CRM can't handle this. Instead, you will find that the core features in this area need additional architecture for you to potentially do all that you want to do.

Does Your Project Require Extensive Interaction with Users Who Are Not Licensed Microsoft Dynamics CRM Users (For Instance, Integration with the Internet for Data Collection)?

Numerous accelerators are available to support your efforts to do event management and extensive marketing; however, your project might need enhanced architecture to do what you want it to do.

Skills Required: Who Can Make the Changes

Now that you have an idea of which projects are a good fit and which projects should be assigned a Microsoft Dynamics CRM architect, let's look at what skills are required to make some of the previously mentioned changes.

Microsoft Dynamics CRM can be modified and extended in different ways, all of which require different skill sets. A user without much training can add data to the system and use the application; a user with a little more training can create personal workflows; and a user with configuration training can change the look and feel of the forms, add new entities, and add new fields. However, even with the easiest features, it is wise to understand the training requirements and the experience that can make such a critical difference to the success of a project.

A number of Microsoft Dynamics CRM exams lead to various certifications that encompass four core skill sets: installation, application, customization, and extending. Each skill set maps to people with a background in four core areas: development/programming, network architecture/infrastructure, CRM consulting/training, and application architecture. These are high-level categories, but they are important to keep in mind. Take, for instance, a senior developer/software programmer. Developers can have many specialties, from the development languages that they are proficient in to their chosen focus for continued training and mastery. Two different developers can be so different that they are more like comparing apples and oranges than apples to apples.

To get a better idea of how Microsoft organizes certification, let's look at some requirements. The core Microsoft Dynamics Certified Technology Specialist exams are as follows:

▶ Extending Microsoft Dynamics CRM 2011

▶ Microsoft Dynamics CRM 2011 Applications

▶ Microsoft Dynamics CRM 2011 Installation and Deployment

▶ Microsoft Dynamics CRM 2011 Customization and Configuration

Each of the certifications requires you to pass a core exam and certain electives. The list of exams and electives can be found within CustomerSource or PartnerSource. In addition, these sites provide excellent study guides and documentation for the Dynamics CRM exams.

Workshop

Radical Rail and Roofing is a company that installs metal roofs and decorative iron porch rails. It has a team of 10 people who work in a local area, replacing old roofs with new, colored roofs and replacing wooden banisters and small fences with decorative iron rails. It also has a sales team, a marketing group, and a number of subcontractors and internal artists it tracks. Radical Rail and Roofing takes pride in its creative, one-of-a-kind railings and the largest selection of colors in the area of metal standing seam roofs. Radical Rail and Roofing is working with a Microsoft Dynamics CRM partner, who is installing Microsoft Dynamics CRM so that Radical Rail and Roofing can keep track of the team schedules and all the choices that its prospects and clients make (from its wide selection of offerings). Radical Rail and Roofing also subcontracts some of its services to local artists who create some of the unique design offerings for its railings, which internal craftsmen then produce.

Radical Rail and Roofing is also extending Microsoft Dynamics CRM to integrate with its Microsoft Dynamics GP accounting software. It will do quotes, orders, and invoicing through Microsoft Dynamics CRM integrated with Microsoft Outlook, and after an invoice has been generated, it will appear in Microsoft Dynamics GP as an unposted invoice for accounting to review and process. In addition, if accounting places a client on credit hold, the sales team, using Microsoft Dynamics CRM, will be notified and will not be able to create a quote or order until the credit hold is resolved.

Q&A

Q. *Are there accounting applications that are a better fit with Microsoft Dynamics CRM, or can we integrate with our existing accounting software?*

A. Some applications are more integration friendly. Just as Microsoft Dynamics CRM is built to be extended and integrated, your accounting application needs to have the necessary hooks to allow outside applications to communicate with it.

Q. *We have internal resources that are going to focus on gaining additional skills in the Microsoft Dynamics CRM area. Where should we focus their efforts?*

A. Depending on their background, you might want to divide and conquer. A developer is a good fit for extending the application using the .NET Framework through plug-ins, customizing form actions through JavaScript, and understanding the Microsoft SQL Server database environment. A network administrator can master all the details of an installation and the long-term maintenance of checking the server logs and dealing with any environment errors. A technical user or manager who understands the business needs can be trained to do many customizations of the user interface, such as revising views, editing drop-down lists, and so on.

Q. *Reporting and business intelligence options are important to us. Is Microsoft Dynamics CRM a good platform for capturing all the data that we might need for sophisticated analysis?*

A. Yes. Microsoft Dynamics CRM is an excellent repository area for layers of data, including data that might be of interest to a specific report, to a custom dashboard or chart, to a Microsoft Excel CRM user, or to some of the more advanced business intelligence tools. With the ability to create dashboards within the CRM user interface on the fly, the data in CRM can be viewed in many different ways.

Quiz

1. Name four areas where a developer can enhance the Microsoft Dynamics CRM software.

2. If you want to control what can be changed in your solution, what type of solution should you use?

3. Name one reason Microsoft Dynamics CRM is a good choice for a new custom development project.

4. What query language can be used to develop reports against the Microsoft Dynamics CRM database?

Answers

1. A developer can enhance the Microsoft Dynamics CRM software with Microsoft Dynamics CRM .NET plug-ins, iFrames, Microsoft Dynamics CRM Workflow, and Form OnSave/OnLoad.

2. If you want to control what can be changed in your solution, you should use a managed solution.

3. The development teams would not have to write code to support security and user authentication. Creation of tables and data entry forms can be done through a simple user interface; the application framework is supported by Microsoft.

4. Reports can be created with the Business Intelligence Development Studio of Visual Studio, using Microsoft Dynamics CRM 2011 BIDS Fetch extension. This extension uses the query language FetchXML that is native to Dynamics CRM.

Exercise

Think about the people who work in your organization and the resources you have access to through a Microsoft partner. As you consider these individuals, who would be a perfect fit to take on the role for your company of Microsoft Dynamics CRM infrastructure expert, Microsoft Dynamics CRM application expert, and Microsoft Dynamics CRM extending and developing expert? What about some of the other categories where you might want to expand, such as an expert on the available third-party or ISV offerings or an expert on reporting and business analysis? List these people and interview them regarding their interests and backgrounds.

Index

asynchronous services, 70

attachments, 262, 321

Audit History, 461

auditing

auditing tools, 459-461

enabling, 460-461

global audit settings, 460

viewing audit details, 461

automating processes, 22-23, 478. See also workflows

asynchronous processes, 324

automating processes with, 332-338

benefits of, 325

book chapter process workflow, 332-338

creating, 325-329

definition of, 323-324

examples of, 324

internal alerts, 329-332

limitations of, 325

availability of staff, defining, 383-384

B

behavior of forms, 469-470

benefits of CRM (Customer Relationship Management), 478-479

for businesses, 7-9

for individuals, 5-7

BI (business intelligence)

built-in BI, 452-453

Excel connectivity, 453

explained, 452

Microsoft BI offerings, 455

OLAP cubes, 453

PerformancePoint, 454

SQL Server 2008 R2, 453

Target IT, 455

ZAP Technology, 454

big business versus small business, 72

Billing Information field (Contacts form), 254

blogs, 23

board of directors (BOD), 13

BOD (board of directors), 13

book chapter process workflow, 332-338

bridge software, 437-438

budgets, creating, 195-196

bulk e-mail, 49, 276-279

business advantages of CRM (Customer Relationship Management), 7-9

business context, 440

business intelligence (BI)

built-in BI, 452-453

Excel connectivity, 453

explained, 452

Microsoft BI offerings, 455

OLAP cubes, 453

PerformancePoint, 454

SQL Server 2008 R2, 453

Target IT, 455

ZAP Technology, 454

business intelligence analysis, 477

business processes

automating, 22-23

capturing, 22-23

documenting, 11-12

explained, 17-20

Business unit access level, 97

business units

explained, 79, 83-84

reorganizing business unit hierarchy, 85

buttons, customizing, 472-473

C

calendars, service calendar, 378-379

CALs (client access licenses), 85-86

Campaign Activities view, 200

Campaign entity, 35

campaigns, 179

activities, 188

creating, 189-190

distributing, 191, 202

creating, 180-181

explained, 35

marketing budgets, creating, 195-196

marketing lists

adding members to, 183-185

creating, 182-183, 186

evaluating members in, 186

M

X

Sams **Teach Yourself**

When you only have time
for the answers™

Whatever your need and whatever your time frame, there's a Sams **Teach Yourself** book for you. With a Sams **Teach Yourself** book as your guide, you can quickly get up to speed on just about any new product or technology—in the absolute shortest period of time possible. Guaranteed.

Learning how to do new things with your computer shouldn't be tedious or time-consuming. Sams **Teach Yourself** makes learning anything quick, easy, and even a little bit fun.

Java in 24 Hours, Sixth Edition

Rogers Cadenhead
ISBN-13: 978-0-672-33575-4

iPad Application Development in 24 Hours, Second Edition

John Ray

ISBN-13: 978-0-672-33439-9

Android Application Development in 24 Hours, Second Edition

Lauren Darcey
Shane Conder

ISBN-13: 978-0-672-33569-3

the Twitter API in 24 Hours

Christopher Peri

ISBN-13: 978-0-672-33110-7

SAP in 24 Hours, Fourth Edition

George W. Anderson

ISBN-13: 978-0-672-33542-6

informIT.com
THE TRUSTED TECHNOLOGY LEARNING SOURCE

Anne Stanton

24 Proven One-hour Lessons

Sams Teach Yourself
Microsoft®
Dynamics
CRM 2011
in 24 Hours

SAMS

FREE Online Edition

Your purchase of **Sams Teach Yourself Microsoft® Dynamics CRM 2011 in 24 Hours** includes access to a free online edition for 45 days through the Safari Books Online subscription service. Nearly every Sams book is available online through Safari Books Online, along with more than 5,000 other technical books and videos from publishers such as Addison-Wesley Professional, Cisco Press, Exam Cram, IBM Press, O'Reilly, Prentice Hall, and Que.

SAFARI BOOKS ONLINE allows you to search for a specific answer, cut and paste code, download chapters, and stay current with emerging technologies.

Activate your FREE Online Edition at
www.informit.com/safarifree

> **STEP 1:** Enter the coupon code: JSWOLCB.

> **STEP 2:** New Safari users, complete the brief registration form.
> Safari subscribers, just log in.

If you have difficulty registering on Safari or accessing the online edition, please e-mail customer-service@safaribooksonline.com